SEREND

in the SEARCH

for JENS, KAREN MARIE, and ANE

SERENDIPITY

in the SEARCH

for JENS, KAREN MARIE, and ANE

A POLYGAMY STORY

ADRIA FULKERSON

SERENDIPITY IN THE SEARCH FOR JENS, KAREN MARIE, AND ANE

Bjorkman Bindery, Hillsboro, OR, 97123

Left cover photo: Front row: Jens and Ane. Back row: Eli, Sophia, Moses.
Right cover photo: Front row: Jens, Elvena, Karen Marie. Back row: Louisa, Jens Peter.

Unless noted otherwise, all images in this book are courtesy the author or Richard Anderson.

Line editing, proofreading, cover design, and interior book design provided by Indigo: Editing, Design, and More:
- Line editor: Susan DeFreitass
- Proofreaders: Ali Shaw and Laura Garwood
- Cover designer: Olivia Croom Hammerman
- Interior book designer and ebook conversion: Vinnie Kinsella
www.indigoediting.com

ISBN: 978-0-578-86009-1
eISBN: 978-0-578-86010-7
LCCN: 2021903194

For my husband and world travel guide Richard, and for my daughter Kjersti and my son Lindsey, and for my grandsons Findlay and Grayson

And for all those who may read this work of my heart: May you find something therein to pique your curiosity or to lift your soul.

CONTENTS

CHAPTER 1

MOTHER TOLD ME STORIES

I am the product of three sets of polygamous ancestors, and in none of them am I descended from the first wife. Like it or not, I owe my existence to the practice of polygamy in the early Mormon Church. Although I should have figured it out earlier, I did not realize until my fifties that both of my grandmothers grew up as daughters of polygamous couples. Neither of them ever spoke of it in my presence, and both died long before I was aware I should have asked them questions. What stories would they have shared if someone had thought to interview them? My mother told me her mother had not liked growing up in a polygamous household, so perhaps she would not have wanted to talk about it. Indeed, my sisters have said they sensed our mother thought it shameful. Whatever anyone might feel about it, it *is* our history.

When I was a young girl, my mother, Flora Bjorkman Fowler, sat with me during summer sunsets on the concrete porch of our white frame house and told tender tales of her maternal grandmother, Ane (Ah-na) Margrethe (Mahr-gretta) Sorensen Hansen. I remember those evenings on the warm porch as we watched darkness infuse the sky, obscure the house across the street, and provide a backdrop for the first star to appear. We shifted our bones on the sunbaked cement and waited for the evening breeze from nearby Ogden Canyon to whiffle through the open windows and cool the house before we ventured inside.

Had I realized then that years later after my mother had died those stories would become vitally interesting to me, I would have listened more intently, asked questions, and taken rudimentary notes in my nine-year-old's scrawl. But I didn't.

One evening Mom said, "My grandmother and I used to sit out on the wooden porch at her home and watch the evening come." Learning the origin of our evenings on the porch touched me. She said they had loved the same amazing cat who could open doors! "I was born in my grandmother's home in a bedroom on the second floor, and we lived with her—Mother and us five kids—while my father went on his mission to Denmark." She paused for a few moments in the darkness. "We had a nice relationship." She often spoke lovingly of this woman with whom she shared a close companionship during her childhood.

I am the last of five children, and the only one to move from Utah and settle elsewhere. Unfortunately, living far from my family prevented my attending most of the blessing and naming of babies, baptisms, graduations, weddings, and funerals.

My four siblings—MauRene, LaMont, LaRelia, and Carla—instituted "genealogy day" after they retired in the mid-1990s. They met every Monday in their homes to work on various genealogy projects, and then went to lunch. Frequently, the day included a field trip to some site connected to our family history. They discovered that taking our aging mother to the places of her childhood and youth triggered her memories, and she told them many stories about her life. Previously, she had refused to talk about her experiences, saying she had had a hard life and no one would want to hear or read about it. I felt sad to miss those genealogy Mondays as well as other family events.

In June of most years, I did travel to Ogden, Utah to spend time with my siblings, and to attend the annual Bjorkman family reunion on my cousin's ranch near Bancroft, Idaho. In 1996, I made an extra trip to Utah in April. My daughter Kjersti and my son Lindsey, who had been eight and six respectively when their father died unexpectedly in 1983, were now grown up and in college, so I was sort of on my own as well. As good fortune would have it, I was in Utah on "genealogy day," and my siblings invited me to choose that week's field trip destination. Although they had been to the town of Newton, Utah, on an earlier occasion to see Great-Grandma Ane's home, my curiosity compelled me to request that as our site for the day, and they agreed.

We started from Carla's yellow brick ranch house in Pleasant View early on the sunny spring morning in the van I had rented so we could all be together to hear Mom's stories. We took I-15 north to exit 385 toward Logan, then followed SR-30 east through farm and scrublands, observing a dramatic rocky notch off to the left like a wedge cut from the gray-purple mountains between us and the town. We turned north on two-lane SR-23, passed through more farmlands and the small town of Cache Junction—formerly a railroad hub—then crossed the bridge over the waters of Bear River/Cutler Reservoir and approached the outskirts of Newton, about sixty miles northwest of Ogden.

Jim, my brother-in-law, sat in the passenger seat. "Turn here," he said, pointing to the right with a twitch of his index finger, his hands resting on his knees.

"Tell her which way to go," Carla, my sister and Jim's wife, said from the back seat. "She doesn't know which way—she wasn't with us when we came before."

"We've got a system down," he said.

"Yeah, we're okay," I said, cranking the wheel to the right, staying on SR-23 as the highway became Main Street through Newton and took us into a quiet residential neighborhood.

"It's this one on the right," MauRene, our eldest sibling, spoke up from the back. I pulled up in front of the light-blue house trimmed in white, the van crunching gravel at the edge of the road. The two-story, late-1800s house and large porch spoke of modest affluence for its time. Decorated with intricate woodwork, the house stood back from the street in a grassy yard encircled by a wire-grid fence of three-inch squares.

"Yes, this is it," our eighty-eight-year-old mother confirmed in her soft voice that had become shaky with age. We sat, the van idling, and looked at the house. A pile of newspapers, each rolled in plastic, lay on the walkway just inside the open gate, and I felt glad no one was home. The vacancy made the house seem less owned somehow; I felt it was a sacrosanct part of our family history that should never have been let go. Ane's husband, Jens Nielsen Hansen, who had died the year before my mother was born, had built this house.

"No one was home when we came here before, either," MauRene commented. "I wonder what the neighbors thought when strangers traipsed onto the property. We took pictures of Mother on the porch. Thought maybe we'd get arrested for trespassing, but no one said anything to us."

"That was a long drive," LaRelia said. "I'm ready to get out and walk around." A chorus of agreement followed. I shut off the engine, the side door rumbled open, and we all exited the van.

I slowly spun around, soaking in the sunshine, the quiet, the fresh air, and the high, jagged gray mountains encircling the basin. A lower range of sawtooth peaks, still capped with snow, ringed the small community that nestled here, far from any large city. The scene was stunningly beautiful, and the ambient silence amazed me, a city girl from Ogden.

"The house has been added onto since I lived here as a child," Mom said. "That part over there, opposite the porch." She walked gingerly from the gravel onto the grass, gesturing left. "And the summer kitchen used to be over there as a lean-to. That's where Grandma used to do the canning so it didn't heat up the house." I mentally created a lean-to and put a woman inside it wearing an ankle-length dark dress and an apron, brushing a wisp of hair out of her eyes as she was enveloped in the steam cloud from a canning pot.

"I was once put out on that porch as a child for misbehaving," Mom said.

"That's impossible, Mom!" I said. "You're too well-behaved." I found her tale hard to believe because she was a paragon of propriety, refinement, and obedience to the tenets of the Mormon Church.

"I must have deserved it, or they wouldn't have punished me." She mused that she and her four siblings "had likely been chasing through the house" when she was sent out. Now she walked with short, halting steps toward the porch, pulling her lavender quilted coat more tightly around her fragile frame. "Back in those days there weren't street lights, and you can't imagine how pitch black it was outside. I huddled as close to the door as I could get." She told her story with humor, yet I wondered why adults would put a young child out on the porch after dark. Eighty-one years earlier in a small town like this, a child probably would have been safer from strangers than in modern metropolitan areas, but what about wild animals?

Mom had sat on this very porch as a little girl with her grandmother, and I felt happy to see it. I wondered whether Great-Grandmother Ane had sat on a porch in Denmark with her own mother or grandmother to watch the evening arrive and the stars appear.

Across the street, where the rock house of Jens's first wife had stood, sat only a vacant lot with yellow weeds and some miscellaneous farm equipment—harrow, rake—sitting idle. The two houses had been the homes of my great-grandfather Jens's two wives during the period of polygamy in the early Church of Jesus Christ of Latter-day Saints..

In order for a Mormon man to have more than one wife in the 1800s, he had to be called to do so by an ecclesiastical leader. He also had to be devotedly living the tenets of the Church, to be financially able to provide for multiple families, and, ideally, to have the permission of the first wife. A minority of Mormon men—an average of about 20 percent, depending on the town—entered into this arrangement, and it wasn't voluntary. Most women at the time did not have the opportunity to pursue an education and work, and because a large percentage of converts to the new religion were women, some people believe that polygamy was intended as a way to provide for them temporally and spiritually, and to give them an opportunity for marriage and children in mortality and for eternity. Other people believe that the principle of plural marriage was given as a revelation from God to a modern-day prophet, Joseph Smith, and that living by this principle, people could build large families in this life that would be together through eternity. Many also believed that subjugating selfishness in this way would earn additional blessings in the next life.

Burdensome emotions were associated with this complex lifestyle, and although most of the people in the practice had the best intentions of overcoming them, being human must have made it immensely trying. People today sometimes find it difficult to imagine that lifestyle. My grandmother, Sophia (sōph-EYE-ya), and her half sister, Louisa (Loo-EYE-za), were born just three days apart in 1880.

"What must that have been like," my mother sometimes mused, "to have another baby fathered by your own husband and born so close in time to your own baby, and living just across the street?"

Mom often said that Jens's two wives, Ane and Karen Marie, had not gotten along well until after his death, but then they became good friends. As a child, my mother had paid visits to the other wife, had admired her lovely flower arbor, and had called her "Auntie." Because Jens died before Mother was born, these visits would have been during the period of reputed friendship between the wives.

Carla and LaRelia each knew several descendants from Great-Grandpa Jens's first family with Karen Marie. When our father died in 1977, two sisters who lived near Carla—LuDean Hawes Carroll and Helen Hawes Stuart—approached her and said they were related to her, that they had seen the obituary of their cousin Flora's husband—our dad—in the newspaper with Carla listed as a daughter. Carla was surprised to learn the two women were descended from our great-grandfather. These sisters subsequently and generously provided us with additional family history.

When my siblings and I were growing up, Mother told us that her Grandpa Hansen had provided potatoes and calicos to our family, and oranges and silks to the other family—a clear indication of his favoritism for his first wife and family. However, when LaRelia told this story in her church foyer to Dale Hawes, another descendant of Jens and Karen Marie, he laughed and said that in their family he had grown up with the story that Great-Grandpa Hansen brought potatoes and calicos to *their* family and oranges and silks to *ours*. Similar to sibling rivalry, the families must have struggled with the desire to feel equal or favored in the relationship.

As we admired the picturesque blue house and milled around the front of the property, Mother said, "I remember someone telling me that one day Grandpa Hansen gave Grandma Hansen the deed to this house. For some reason, the story goes, Grandma didn't trust him, so she gave the deed to her son Eli for safekeeping. Then Grandpa had a change of heart and ransacked the place looking for the deed, but he didn't find it." She laughed softly. "And that made him *mad*." Mom said her mother, Ane's daughter Sophia, had told her that story, "so it must be true."

A bronze sedan drove by, and the hum of its engine and the crunch of its tires intruded upon the silence. The two people in the car watched us as they motored past, and I wondered if someone would soon come to investigate our trespass. Occasionally we heard birdcalls, but few other sounds besides our own voices and footsteps.

"Don't repeat this," Mother said, "but someone told me that at one time Grandma Hansen was so put out with Grandpa that she put *him* out. She set his clothes and belongings out on the porch and told him to go stay with his other family for a while."

"How long did he stay away?" I asked, wondering if the banishment had been permanent.

"I don't know."

I began to wish fervently that my great-grandmother Ane had kept a journal. I would have loved to know her thoughts and feelings about being a plural wife as well as why and for how long she had put Jens out. I longed to know what had influenced her to join the Church of Jesus Christ of Latter-day Saints and how she had the courage to leave her native country and come to America.

Just as she had with the story of Ane putting Jens out, Mother often cautioned us not to repeat things she told us. My sisters and I eventually came to believe that the family had many secrets. This suspicion was substantiated when our mother's younger brother, Uncle Norman Bjorkman, told Carla and LaRelia, "There are things you will *never* know." We've speculated that the secrets might deal with the shame of being poor, or with how hard the children had to work, with even the girls working like men in the fields. Uncle Norman once told me that he and his siblings often had to work in the sugar-beet fields, and that it was horrible work. For a break, they would lie down in the trenches because it was cooler there. Their mother, Sophia, would bring them cool water.

Mother told us her Grandma Hansen had never learned to speak English. As I remember it, Mom said that when she was a child, her parents had their children speak Danish in the home and English outside it. As LaRelia remembers it, the children spoke English only but understood some of the Danish. Whatever the language division, Sophia and Henry wanted their children to be "American." When I was little, Mom taught me several Danish words, such as *glædelig jul* (sounds like *glolla yule* and means "Merry Christmas"), *spise nu* (sounds like *speesa new* and means "eat now"), and *knap dine bukser, Hans* (sounds like *kannup den booksa, Hans*, and means "button your pants or britches"—a handy code we used in public to spare a husband or son embarrassment). LaRelia remembers *alle cklipper har ører* (sounds like *oh croaka hah ern* and means "all crocks have ears," and was used when Grandma or Grandpa thought the children might be listening in on an adult conversation). Mother told of a time when she understood enough Danish to know that her parents were discussing which of their children would drive her father in the horse-drawn sleigh from Central, Idaho to the train station at Alexander, Idaho (approximately seven miles) in the middle of a snowy winter night, and she knew before they told her in English that they had decided it would be her. With a mix of the two languages, my mother and her beloved grandmother communicated well enough to build their special friendship. When Mother was in her nineties, I asked her about these Danish words, but she remembered none of them.

As we stood in front of the blue house, Mom reminisced that when she was about seven, she and her grandma had found their cat dead, likely from squirrel poison, and they wept together. My little-girl mom suggested they cover it with a newspaper, but her grandmother said, "Oh, my dear, I think we'd better bury it." So they did, near the fence of wire squares that yet marked the boundary of the property.

Great-Grandfather Jens, according to Mom, served time in the Utah Territorial Penitentiary for being a polygamist. Carla, LaRelia, and I remember having seen, as young children, a photograph of Jens in a group of men, all in prison stripes. The photo was kept in a round red-and-gold fruitcake tin that was filled with snapshots and topped by a fitted lid. When Mom later had to go into assisted living and asked us to empty and sell her home, we did not find the fruitcake tin, nor did we find the photo in any other container. I said to my sisters, "I want to know what happened to Jens's prison photo."

"Don't we all?" LaRelia responded.

I remember going with Mom and my sisters to visit Uncle Norman and Aunt Gerry, in their home in Soda Springs, Idaho, and hearing him say it must have been difficult for his Grandpa Hansen to be told by the government that he could no longer practice a facet of the religion he believed in, and that he would have to choose between two wives, two families he loved. I had not looked at the situation through Jens's eyes before, and I was moved by Uncle Norman's empathy, though I had not yet learned a whit of the myriad problems Jens and his wives faced because of the plural marriage.

We looked around the property a little longer in the crisp spring air then climbed back into the van and drove to the cemetery to search for family graves, hoping for stories the headstones might tell us, and for more memories that might come to Mom from the stimulus of being there. And I longed to be with the family every Monday.

I was raised in a devout Mormon (Church of Jesus Christ of Latter-day Saints, or LDS) family in Ogden, Utah. We said a blessing at the table over meals, knelt before dinner for family prayer, and knelt again at our bedsides for evening prayers before sleep. We attended church as a family on Sundays. We paid tithing—I remember counting out dimes and nickels from my earnings as a child. We fasted twenty-four hours on the monthly fast Sunday and paid the equivalent of what we would have spent on meals to the Church to provide for the poor. Music filled our home as my father sang in quartets and choirs, and my siblings accompanied him on the piano for special numbers at church. My sisters and I had church callings to teach classes, play organ or piano, direct music, or serve in presidencies of various organizations. The position of Sunday school organist—filled first by MauRene, then LaRelia, then Carla, then me—was thus in our family for twenty-four years. I had wonderful friends through church, from before kindergarten to high school graduation, and many of us are still in touch through email as well as through 20th Ward reunions and high school reunions. I absorbed the religion and culture through my pores.

When I was in my mid-twenties, I worked as a conveyance examiner in Ogden, Utah, using maps, land surveys, rights-of-way, and ownership documents to assemble atlases of land status in the intermountain forests for the US Forest Service. There I met Marshall Fulkerson, a cadastral surveyor who searched for and marked corners for ownership boundaries on the ground in these forests. Our work was connected, so he often came to my office on the fourth floor with questions, and I went to his office on the second floor with questions as well. Eventually we married, and after becoming parents of two sweet children, Marshall—who was raised Protestant and had converted to the Baha'i faith—chose to be baptized into the LDS Church. A year later we were sealed as a family in the Salt Lake Temple. We devoted our lives to our family, our church, and serving others.

Marshall's death, from a recurrence of septicemia on a business trip in 1983, left me feeling gutted out as if by forest fire.

Years later, I met Richard Anderson—a former Lutheran with Buddhist/Taoist leanings—just home from living in Japan, walking in the same neighborhood where I did my daily walks. The year 2000 was pivotal for me as I received my master of arts degree in English, married Richard in my hometown so my mother at age ninety-two could attend the wedding, and found my first postgraduate job at Oregon State University in Corvallis, Oregon, teaching writing in the English Department.

Just before Christmas in 2002, my sister MauRene died suddenly. Six months later Mother died at the age of ninety-five. My mother—the keeper of stories, the wellspring of memories—was gone. I taught one more year, exhausted, grieving silently, making the four-hour round-trip commute to Corvallis twice weekly with Richard, who also taught at the university—courses in world religions, Asian thought, Japanese history and culture, and Chinese history—in the Philosophy Department. Then I took the 2004–2005 academic year off.

During that year, I began to quilt—something I had said I would never do. I also returned to baking bread from scratch, a practice I had abandoned when Marshall died.

Quilting and baking had been creative arts for my mother, and I learned later from a therapist that my espousing them after her death was a way to keep her close to me. The loss of my mother also sparked my passion to know more about the grandmother she had loved and introduced to me. I became more curious about the early family, and I regretted not having pursued more details or recorded what Mom had said. Her stories made me love and want to know my great-grandmother. I ached to ask Mom questions about Ane's unusual life, but it was too late. I would need to find Ane some other way.

A year after Mom died, a small group of my friends gathered at Rose's Tea Room in Gresham, Oregon, and basked in the beauty of a lace-covered table and floral china as we ate finger sandwiches, scones, and dainty desserts. Our conversation turned from the books we were reading to spiritual matters. Each of the women had a different viewpoint from the others, yet everyone agreed there are unseen spirits who sometimes accompany us or touch our lives in some way. We sense or feel when they are near us, and believe they are possibly our departed loved ones. The discussion made me think perhaps my obsession with wanting a nonexistent journal from my great-grandmother might mean she was near me and maybe even wanted me, in some way, to tell her story.

When I spoke that thought aloud, one of the women responded, "Why don't you write her journal for her?" The startling suggestion appealed to me, and I resolved to find whatever I could about Ane.

Back home, I started by digging into a musty-smelling old cardboard box of genealogy records that I had rediscovered in my garage. Marshall had compiled most of these records before his death, and the long-forgotten box had spent twenty-three years in three garages through our moves. Inside it, I found a blue, vinyl-covered metal binder labeled *Book of Remembrance* filled with completed forms labeled *Family Group Record*. These important genealogical forms each listed a couple's names at the top, followed by a grid with each of their children's names on its own boxed line, and these lines were filled in with dates and locations for the listed person's birth, christening, baptism, marriage, death, and burial place, as available. I leafed through the pages until I located the Family Group Record for my great-grandfather, Jens Niels Hansen, and my great-grandmother, Ane Margrethe Sorensen Hansen. The form showed that Ane had borne three children—the first being my grandmother Sophia—all of whom had lived to adulthood.

My initial plan was to focus on Ane and to write her story in a fictional format, but then I looked at the other Family Group Record, the one for Jens and his first wife, Karen Marie Christensen Hansen. When I saw they had had ten children, six of whom had died before reaching the age of eight, I was stunned. Suddenly Karen Marie's life and the tragedies represented by that record became just as interesting and important to me as my own great-grandmother's story. Knowing

Karen Marie's life intertwined closely with Ane's and was a vital part of the story made me realize I had to write with an expanded viewpoint.

I began researching more intently, and the more I learned about the lives Jens, Karen Marie, and Ane had led, and about their tenacity in spite of incredible hardships, the more I came to admire them. I wanted to offer a respectful treatment of whatever it was that led these people to make such devout commitments to an all-encompassing faith. Fiction would not do them justice. At dinner one evening my friend Connie Saylor asked how the book was coming. I told her I was stymied because I had decided I could not write it as fiction. She gave me an imperative: "Then write it as biography. Just get it written, because I'm waiting to read it." Her encouragement motivated me to continue.

Naïvely thinking that all I needed to do to write a book about these ancestors was to list the genealogical data and record the oral stories, I expected to get the task done quickly. These two things, the data and the stories, were all I had at the onset, and I figured it would take thirty pages max—a pamphlet I could hand out at the next family reunion. A trip to the library in Newton, where my ancestors had settled, seemed a good idea, though, to search for a bit more information to add to the story. Newton is a long way from my home in Oregon, so I planned to extend the Utah portion of my next annual family reunion trip in June to allow time to poke around there.

An earlier event had nurtured my tendrils of interest in Ane's story and had given me the first inklings of personal responsibility for recording it. Jane Kirkpatrick, an inspirational writer and speaker, said in her keynote address at a Willamette Writers meeting at the Old Church in Portland, Oregon, in July 2003: "It is not your job to write the great American novel. It is your job to show up and write the story you have been given." Her statement jolted me. I felt that Kirkpatrick had spoken directly to me, that perhaps this family story was being given to me to write, and that "showing up" meant more than merely stirring around in a musty box. I had work to do, and I needed to roll up my sleeves. As my dad, Vernal Fowler, was fond of saying, "If we're not finished, let's get started." I began using Kirkpatrick's empowering statement as a mantra, a mantra that also took the pressure off my previous belief that someday I had to write a great American novel. And writing history would be so much easier than writing fiction. Or so I thought.

CHAPTER 2

OUR SECOND PILGRIMAGE TO NEWTON

Eight years passed before my next trip to Newton, and in that interim we had lost MauRene and Mom. Two guardians of stories had passed their torches to the rest of us. LaMont sometimes quotes an unnamed source, saying, "Each of us is a burning library." Recording and preserving our stories is important, and there is such a narrow—and fragile—window of opportunity for doing so. I could no longer ask my mother questions.

What I knew about Ane from my mother at the beginning of my quest was that she had been born in Denmark to fairly well off parents and had one brother. She had met Mormon missionaries, joined the Church of Jesus Christ of Latter-day Saints, and at the age of thirty-five traveled with a girlfriend and a trunk full of beautiful dresses to the United States, first by ship, and then across the country by train. When the train stopped in Cache Junction, Utah, Ane was selected at random by Jens to become his plural wife. Another man chose Ane's girlfriend and took her to live in St. George, Utah—about as far south in the state as one can go—and the two friends never saw each other again.

Moreover, Ane had known that she would have a husband when she arrived but did not know he would already be married and the father of five children. Mother said Ane was not happy about being a second wife. She lived in a lovely home across the street from the first wife and at some point asked Jens to stay away for a while. She had a feather mattress on her bed, and her little dog, who was unfriendly to everyone but Ane, slept on it with her.

Mother also shared information about Jens, whom she had never met, saying he played the violin in a dance orchestra he had started, wrote a short life sketch, farmed the land, and served time in the state penitentiary for polygamy—all of which affected Ane's life in some way. These skeletal stories intrigued me.

Eager to learn more, I planned another trip to Newton in June 2004, after the family reunion. Since my siblings were more familiar with the area and with our family history than I was (I am the youngest child, seven years younger than the last of the first four), I invited them all to come with me for my first trip to the Newton Town Library. I love being with my family and was happy they accepted. We started off on that sunny, warm Thursday morning from Carla's home in two cars: LaMont and Lorene in one and Carla, LaRelia, and I in the other.

I hoped to find a few more facts to add to what I knew, but I assumed that with nearly one hundred years' passage of time since the Hansen families had lived in Newton, not much evidence would remain. I also hoped that just being in the town and on the soil where our people had lived might help me understand who they were.

Newton is a bucolic town northwest of Logan in Cache Valley, a valley that is surrounded by rugged peaks, intertwined with rivers, and quilted with farmlands. Newton—or New Town—was established in 1869 by some of the Mormons who had previously settled in nearby Clarkston but had found the winter storms and cold temperatures too severe and isolating. A preliminary Newton Townsite survey sketched out blocks and lots, and delineated church and community areas in the center of town surrounded by lots for homes, with farmland acreage outside the town. Families were informally allotted property for homes and farms in this new settlement. Some of the first settlers built their homes out of local rock from a quarry northwest of town, and as of 2020, many of those early rock homes still stand. Other early homes were built of wood from trees harvested near Logan, and others were constructed or reinforced with adobe. The population of one-year-old Newton in 1870 was 195.[1]

Newton at that time had no grocery store or supermarket, but a small family store sold a limited variety of products and fast-food lunch items in the old confectionary building whose warped, weathered wood floors create a gentle roller-coaster effect. No motel dotted the landscape, no gas station existed, no traffic signal blinked, and no whiff of Starbucks infused the air. Only a church, library, town hall, fire station, post office, floral nursery, and a few other businesses provided services to local people and visitors. Newton exudes peace.

The center park block contained the yellow brick courthouse that was originally a schoolhouse, built upon the remains of two earlier schoolhouses. The building then housed the library with its growing local and family history section, the courthouse, and the fire station. The new Church of Jesus Christ of Latter-day Saints meetinghouse built of red bricks in 2002, featured a characteristic steeple, dominated the block, and replaced earlier church buildings: the first built in 1887 and the second in 1931. Across from the library on Center Street once stood the Newton Cooperative Store, the People's Mercantile, and the wooden post office that Great-Grandpa Jens built when he was postmaster in the early 1900s.

On First South, the shell of an old general store leaned, having been struck by lightning and fallen into disrepair. The squared false front rose higher than the angled roof behind it, and the building looked like a stage set for Westerns. Broken windows and empty shelves left it open to nature, though it had long been closed to business. Each time I visited Newton, further deterioration of this relic was evident, and I wondered how much longer it would stand. (I also wondered if this is the store where my mother and her sister traded eggs for candy when they lived with their grandmother Ane as children.)

Newton retained the essence of its inception as a pioneer town. Part of its charm lay in the many ways "progress" had passed the town by, leaving it with a wholesomeness I found attractive. Even though it was a modernized town, entering it felt like stepping into the past. A large percentage of the names in the telephone directory matched those of the early settlers of Newton, and the local people focused on and were proud of their history. The residents were friendly and extremely helpful to me as an outsider, a stranger. The streets were often quiet, and the air was saturated with birdsong.

On internet maps, the streets of Newton then nearly matched those from original maps and surveys. Only an additional street or two expanded the grid in each direction. Main Street runs east and west through the center of town, and Center Street runs north and south, also in the center and adjacent to the park block. These two street names were originally reversed, with Main Street running north and south. The straight streets divide the townsite into large blocks after the pattern set out by Brigham Young: eight blocks to a mile. Nonexistent are dead-end cul-de-sacs like those incorporated into street plans of most cities I have lived in or visited. Newton has new homes, of course, but the plethora of historic homes, the presence of roofs on stilts over haystacks in town, horses by some of the residences, sparse vehicle traffic, the surrounding farmlands and rugged mountains nearby all imbue the town with a special ambience.

Upon our arrival in Newton, we stopped first at the blue house for sentiment's sake, and second at the general store on Main Street where Carla's son, Matt, joined us from Logan. The proprietress told us the location of the library. Upon finding it closed, we noted its hours of operation, then drove to the cemetery, a small, quiet, green rectangle north of town situated among open areas and farmlands.

Single gravel lanes crisscrossed past headstones that varied in style from flat markers to raised headstones and even monuments—everything from old ornate to modern sleek. As our two cars crept slowly along the cemetery lanes, we spotted graves of various distant family members. We parked in the northwest section and wandered on foot through the graves in the hot sun, finding Great-Grandpa Jens Hansen's marker between the headstones of his first wife, Karen M., on his right, and his plural wife, Annie M., on his left. I wondered when Ane had changed the spelling of her name. Or had she? Did someone misspell it on her marker? We found no markers for the six children who had died young. Ane's son who died at age nineteen was buried on her left. A tall monument with the name *HANSEN* stood just a short distance from the graves, but we did not notice some nearby markers that would one day become significant to us.

After lunch in Logan, LaMont and Lorene took their leave. Carla, LaRelia, and Matt sat on benches under a shade tree on Main Street in Logan, while I walked through the blistering heat to the Cache County Recorder's Office for a copy of the Newton Townsite Plat. Inside the cool offices, I also requested—from a young woman behind a desk—a copy of the deed with Jens's name on it for the property where the blue house stands, and I described its location to her. She said the search would take some time, but she would let me know in a few days what she found. I hoped to use the land description in the deed to plot the property on the townsite plat.

At a nearby outfitting store, I purchased the United States Geological Survey quadrangle maps for Newton and the surrounding areas. Having worked for the United States Forest Service with surveys, maps, land titles, and rights-of-way, I eagerly anticipated the story the maps, and eventually the deeds, might reveal about the land my ancestors had inhabited, and about the ancestors themselves. I wanted to learn exactly where on the map and on the ground the properties were located, whose name was on the titles, and what proof of ownership existed.

As we drove back into Newton, we passed the blue house on our right. Just a little farther down the street on the left, we saw a woman pushing a power mower over a huge green lawn surrounding a brick house. "Isn't that Leora's house?" one of my sisters asked. "She died not too long ago. I wonder who's living there now. Is that Vicky mowing the lawn?"

"Who's Leora?" I asked.

"Leora is Eli's daughter," LaRelia said. Eli was Ane's second child, so Leora was Ane's granddaughter and our mom's cousin. Had I come alone on this trip, I would not have known this house and these people were significant. "Shall we go back and see who that is?" LaRelia asked as she made a U-turn, not waiting for an answer.

We stopped at Leora's house and parked on the street. I got out of the car and approached the woman who was then mowing next to the road. She looked up and turned off the loud mower to converse with us. I introduced our group through the open car windows and asked the woman if she knew Leora. "Leora was my mother-in-law," she said and introduced herself as Vicky Jenkins, married to Reed Jenkins, Leora's son. Reed is Eli's grandson, Ane's great-grandson, and our second cousin. We talked with Vicky for a while, asking questions about the blue house down the street and its current owners. Due to this chance meeting, Vicky later provided valuable family information both by phone and through the mail.

Soon Matt departed, and we sisters proceeded to the library in the old schoolhouse. Carla and LaRelia waited on a grassy spot in the shade of a tree near the parked car while I climbed the steps of the yellow building. As I passed through the double glass doors into the darkened entryway, I looked up and was startled to see Great-Grandpa Jens's black-and-white portrait photograph looking down at me from the wall. A few inches to the right appeared another copy of his photo, and each was included among photos of other men. Similar clusters of photos were posted on all the walls of the large entryway, each labeled with the man's name. The clusters progressed around the foyer chronologically from 1900 to current times. I walked across wooden floors that made me nostalgic for the freshly-oiled smell of those in my childhood schoolhouse, and through the open door into the brightly lighted library proper, where I asked the librarian at the desk just inside the door, "Who are those men on the walls, and why are they there?"

The librarian, Carol Milligan, said the men in the photos had been on the Newton Town Board from its inception in 1900 to the present (now known as the Newton Town Council). She provided copies of the Town Board meeting minutes taken during Jens's tenure from 1900 to 1902. I stood at a counter and read the minutes. The frequent references to Jens indicated he had been a busy man in the community at that time, having had a brief assignment as pound keeper (responsible for maintaining an enclosure for loose livestock) as well as having responsibilities for sidewalks and for bringing medical people to the community. His position of responsibility impressed me, and I was surprised it was not included in the family lore. The records also noted that the Board had opened and closed its meetings with prayers, many of them offered by Jens. With the modern focus on separation of church and state, these prayers surprised me. Understanding, though, that Newton was established as a Mormon community and Mormons are encouraged to be a prayerful people, the prayers made sense.

Carol directed my attention to a long aisle running parallel to the library wall on the right side of the doors as one enters, an aisle like an elongated U-shaped cubbyhole that extended several yards to its perpendicular wall. On the left side of the aisle, local and family history materials in bound books and white ring binders lined the shelves. On the right side of the cubbyhole aisle, waist-high cabinets displayed arrangements of documents, and on the walls above the cabinets hung sepia photographs. As my eyes took in the spines and covers of books and binders and I surveyed the historical photographs, I wondered what family treasures I might find.

Carla and LaRelia had previously acquainted me with the existence of a book I now found on these shelves, *A New Town in the Valley: The Centennial History of Newton, Utah 1869–1969*, written by Larry D. Christiansen—a volume that was difficult to find, in fact was considered rare by book dealers. The book is a staple of history in the area and is so well known that it is referred to simply as "Larry's Book." Carla's friends from Jens's first family, LuDean Hawes Carroll and Helen Hawes Stuart, owned a copy and had loaned it to my sisters long enough for them to photocopy the several pages that mentioned Jens by name. The library shelf held the 2nd Edition revised in 1999, but no copies remained for purchase, and I was disappointed to learn that no plans existed to reprint it. Larry's book encompassed the time period during which Ane, Jens, and Karen Marie lived, and I knew I needed to own a copy.

After the librarian duplicated relevant pages from various sources that interested me, I went back out into the heat and reconnected with Carla and LaRelia. As I put my things in the car, a woman of medium build with white hair, wearing slacks and a blouse and a pleasant facial expression, came out of the library and down the concrete stairs. She visited with us for several minutes, and when she introduced herself as Ruby Larsen Woodward, my sisters recognized her as a daughter of Grant Larsen, who had been at the Newton cemetery one cold day when my family was there and our mother was still living. Grant was in his nineties then and had talked with them and with Mother. He remembered Mother's family from the early Newton days, and had known her father, Henry Bjorkman, who had married Ane's daughter, Sophia. Though some in the family thought Henry had overextended his resources and thereby lost his farm, Grant kindly said Henry had been a good farmer who had just gotten down on his luck through bad weather and the Depression. Mom and the family had enjoyed a lengthy visit with Grant in spite of the cold. I later learned that this chance encounter at the cemetery had been written up in their local newspaper. Ruby had heard of this coincidental meeting with her father, and we connected through the shared story.

Ruby had planned to walk to her home, but when we offered her a ride, she accepted. She directed us to a golden brick ranch house on a corner, and I loved her L-shaped driveway that allowed vehicles to enter the property, drive past the house, and exit onto the street without turning around or backing up.

As we drove off waving goodbye, little did I guess that Ruby was one of Newton's historians or that in the near future, she would become a principal contact and an amazing help in my search for my ancestors' stories. I had not been with the family that cold winter day in the Newton cemetery, so had I made this trip alone and met Ruby, I would not have recognized her name as significant to the family.

In retrospect, although this particular trip to Newton seemed like a bit of a lark because I enjoyed the time with my family so much, it proved to be invaluable. I had learned the locations of the recorder's office in Logan and the library in Newton, purchased maps and surveys that still hang on my sewing-room wall, discovered Jens's photos in the library and learned about his role on the Newton Town Board, gathered an assortment of facts from the family history section of the library, and discovered the copy of "Larry's Book." Most importantly—and because of my sisters—I had met Vicky and Ruby, two women who would become vitally important to my search. Larry Christiansen, too, would later play an incredibly rich and significant role in my project. Were those *really* chance encounters? The gossamer web of synchronicity had made its first appearance, and the siren song of Newton was embedded in my heart.

CHAPTER 3

LITTLE GREEN BOOK, TRUE BLUE HOUSE, AND RUMORED THIRD WIFE

I have no formal training as a researcher or as a genealogist. As I moved further into this project, my only plan was to search every place I could think of for information about this early family and the history of the surrounding area. Much to my amazement—especially since I didn't know beforehand what information existed or where to search for it—my scattershot approach yielded surprising discoveries, and some seemed serendipitous.

After I returned to Oregon following that second journey to Newton, the young woman from the Cache County Recorder's office in Logan, Utah, telephoned and said Jens Nielsen Hansen had never owned the lot with the blue house on it. Painfully disappointed, I quizzed her to make sure she understood what I had asked. Confident that her findings were in error, I vowed to get the legal description and to search the county records myself.

A reunion of my father's family drew me again to Utah a month later on 29 July 2004. I stopped at the Newton Town Library en route by car to Ogden and arrived just minutes after the 10:00 a.m. opening. The family history section captivated me, and I spent the day searching for Jens's name in indexes of various books and journals. The librarians allowed me to stay inside during the library's midday closure, and by the time they reopened at 3:00 p.m., I had accumulated a stack of books on the librarian's desk with blue slips of paper indicating the pages I needed to have copied.

When closing time loomed—nine hours after my arrival—my brain shut down. As I waited while the librarian kindly finished the mass of copying I had requested, my eyes wandered over the spines in the family history section one last time and stopped on a book I hadn't noticed before: a thin green volume entitled *Lettie Christensen & Joseph Larsen History*. I slid it from the shelf and skimmed through the index. J. N. Hansen was mentioned five times. As I looked up the references, I discovered one that read, "J. N. Hansen (*Aunt Lizzie's husband*) sent for Carl Jorgensen."[2] A rumor had long persisted in our family that Jens had a third wife, and possibly fourth and fifth wives as well. (Grandma Bjorkman had said her father had five wives.) I wondered, could this be our long-sought proof? Time was too short to have anything more copied before the library closed, so I replaced the book and planned to explore it further when I returned to Utah the following year.

❀

One morning during that same summer as Carla and I lingered over breakfast at her kitchen table, she told me she didn't believe those genealogy trips to the blue house had been to the right place. She said our brother, LaMont, had also expressed some doubts. I felt resistant and questioned, "What makes you think that way?"

Carla showed me an old black-and-white photograph of Ane's house that Mom's sister, Naomi, had given to her. The yard had no landscaping at the time of the photo, but the distinctive "gingerbread" decorations on the house made it lovely. Next she pulled out a photograph of the blue house taken during one of the recent family visits. She put the photos side by side and said, "The door is different." Ane's house had a single-paneled front door and a small, uncovered porch, while the blue house had a double door and a large covered porch.

"Maybe the door was changed when the house was remodeled," I suggested.

"But the double door appears to be original. And my friends from Jens's first family have reunions in Newton, and they told me that the houses of the two wives were located in a different part of town from where Mother took us. In fact, they said Ane's house has been torn down."

My heart sank. I loved the blue house and enjoyed imagining Mother living there with her grandmother, mother, and four siblings, and I loved the stories Mom told while we visited that house.

I remembered, though, that some months earlier, our cousin Ann Bjorkman Ashbaker had told me over lunch that she had gone to Newton once with her dad, Leonard (my mother's eldest brother), and he could not find Ane's house. He was the second-born (1903) child in the Bjorkman family, and my mother was the fourth (1907), so he would have been old enough while living in Ane's home to remember it. Did he just not see the blue house? Or was it truly the wrong house? Or worse, were Carla's friends right and Ane's house had actually been torn down?

❀

The following summer of 2005, I was preparing to leave Carla's house for a research day in Newton, hoping the little green book would still be on the shelves and also hoping to get copies of its pages that referred to J. N. Hansen without violating associated copyright laws. Though I was grateful the librarians would make copies of library materials for me at a minimal cost, there were stringent copyright laws.

As I picked up my purse and notebooks to leave, Carla said, "While you're up there today, could you please find out where Ane's house was actually located?" She must have noticed my hesitation because she continued, "I'm glad Mom had a good time sharing the blue house with us and remembering, but she lived in Newton before she was eight, and she was in her eighties when she identified that house. I'm sure it was similar, but I don't think it was the right one."

Wanting the blue house to be the right one, I said, "That would take me hours in the county recorder's office in Logan, and I *will* do it sometime, but it won't fit into what I have planned for today." In spite of my hope about the blue house, I knew we needed to find the truth.

Upon arriving at the Newton library, I went immediately to the family history shelves where I had found the little green book the previous year. Fearing it might be gone, I searched the titles frantically and was relieved to quickly find the book.

Cleo Griffin—another historian who would become vital to my search—was the librarian that day, and I took the book to her desk just inside the entry and asked, "How much of this book could I have copied?"

"Fourteen percent of anything copyrighted," she said. We started looking together inside the book for the copyright information. "Oh!" she exclaimed. "We just had this book reprinted, and if there are extra copies, you might be able to buy one if you want it."

"I would love that!" I said.

"Ruby might have a copy she could sell. I'll give her a call." Cleo picked up the phone, dialed, spoke a few words I didn't hear, and then handed the phone to me.

The woman's voice on the phone said, "I only bought copies for my children and one extra that I am supposed to take to Logan to put in the Utah State University Special Collections. But I took a bad fall and injured my foot and haven't been able to deliver the book." She said she would call Reed Bartlett, who was responsible for the reprinting, and see if he had any extra copies. (Much later I would have a surprising encounter with Reed Bartlett in Salt Lake City.)

Soon the phone rang. Cleo answered it, spoke briefly, then turned to me and said that Reed had extra copies Ruby could buy, so if I wanted to go to Ruby's house when I finished at the library, she would sell me the copy she had planned to take to the university. Cleo passed the phone to me, and Ruby gave me her address.

As I continued to search the history section, I found a photograph of the early Newton Sunday School staff that included Jens, who had taught Sunday School classes for years. This group photo also included the Elizabeth Christensen who was mentioned as "Aunt Lizzie" in the little green book who we thought might be the possible third wife.

When the library closed at 1:00 p.m., I drove to Ruby's, following the directions she had given me, and arrived in front of a yellow brick ranch house on a corner lot that looked familiar and had an L-shaped driveway in front. This was the home to which my sisters and I had given Grant Larsen's daughter a ride from the library the previous summer, and I realized that the Ruby on the phone was the same woman I had earlier met.

At my ring of the doorbell, a woman's voice called to me through the screen door, "Come in!" Having been raised in a city where people locked their doors and used peepholes, I was taken aback by her trust for a stranger. I opened the screen door, stepped inside the entryway, then walked past the kitchen into the comfortable living room where afghans decorated sofa and chair backs. Ruby sat in a wheelchair with one leg completely encased in a cast and the little green book in her lap. She handed the book to me, and we talked about our having met before as she made change. She made me feel comfortable and welcome.

Ruby said the brother of one of the authors of the green book was working on another book. "Would you like to look at it?" she asked as she handed me a blue folder of pages fastened with brads. "I'm working on a book too," she said, "about all the churches of this area from settlement to the present." She picked up a loose-leaf binder from a coffee table next to her and held it on her lap in the wheelchair.

At her invitation, I sat on the sofa and paged through the blue folder, reading briefly, not knowing what to expect. I flipped past a map that caught my eye and I turned back to it. I was startled to see that someone had drawn, by hand, a diagram of the Newton Townsite dated 1885, with the houses represented by small squares, each with a handwritten number inside. On the opposite page, two handwritten lists—one alphabetical and the other numerical—showed the owner of each numbered house. The map had been signed by J. J. Larsen, one of the authors of the little green book. He was Ruby's grandfather and Grant Larsen's father.

Ruby must have noticed my wide-eyed expression and the page I had open, because she immediately opened her own manuscript to a draftsman's reproduction of the hand-drawn map. Her version had the lists of names and the house numbers typed. I recognized the map even though it was upside down to me, but unfortunately, I found the handwritten lists on my copy difficult to decipher.

As the potential significance of this map began to sink in, I was stunned. "Does this list have J. N. Hansen's name on it?" I asked.

"Yes," she said, looking her lists over. "He had thirty-five and thirty-seven." I skimmed my numerical list until I found numbers 35 and 37, then followed the line over and confirmed that Jens N. Hansen was the name connected to them. Quickly I searched the map to locate those house numbers, and there they were, in the southeast quadrant of the townsite, across the street from each other with number 37 just a little farther south than number 35. But which street? The map didn't have street names on it.

"Can you tell by looking at this map what the streets are?"

"Yes, we are right here on Second East and Main," Ruby said, pointing first out the window in the direction of the street and then at the map. "And the Hansen houses are down this same street—Second East—between First and Second South. Actually one of the houses is gone, and the other one, I think, is one of the old rock houses that has been added onto." This was the second indication that Ane's wood-frame house had been demolished.

Still mentally sorting this new information, and realizing that Ruby was pointing in a different direction than the location of the blue house we had visited, I asked, "Do you know where Reed and Vicky Jenkins live?" (Vicky was the woman who had been mowing her lawn and lived diagonally across the street from the blue house our mother had identified as Ane's.)

"Yes, they are out here on the west side," Ruby said, pointing to a part of the map across town from 35 and 37. There it was. Our answer. But I had to confirm, to erase my last little bit of resistance.

"The house my mother thought was J. N. Hansen's is just across the street from Vicky and Reed Jenkins, so that is the wrong house, isn't it?" I didn't breathe.

"Yes, the Hansen houses were on this side of town."

No doubts, no questions. A confident answer. No trip to the county recorder.

"So if I drive south on this street right outside, I will come to the locations of the two Hansen houses?"

"Yes."

After thanking Ruby heartily, I left her home and drove slowly south on Second East, looking from right to left, left to right, straining and peering, trying to spot anything that looked like Carla's photo of Ane's house or a space where that house might have been torn down, or a rock house modernized. When I reached Second South, I turned around in the quiet intersection and retraced the street going north, searching and searching, until I came back to Main. I could not determine which house along the street was Karen's remodeled old stone house, nor could I find a blank spot where Ane's wooden house might have been. It didn't occur to me at the time that a new house could have been built on its site. Once more I drove down the street and back without figuring out where homes 35 and 37 from Ruby's map were located on the ground.

Although I couldn't spot either house site, I was amazed that without spending hours in the county recorder's office, and without having that specific title search on my to-do list for the day, the facts had literally fallen into my lap.

Just as Carla and LaMont—and later, I learned, also LaRelia—had suspected, the blue house was not the right house. But, like Carla, I felt glad Mom had the joy in her later years of thinking the blue house was the place of her birth and childhood. I am grateful for the memories the house triggered for her. Mom, who had always been reluctant to talk about her life, had bubbled over with stories when we visited the blue house.

The time had come to start back to Ogden, so I noted the general area of the properties shown as Jens's and made a promise to search again in the near future.

❦

Pleased to have obtained a copy of the green book, I thought my next project would be to find out to whom the term "Aunt Lizzie" referred and finally have proof that the rumors of a third wife were true. When Carla and I looked at the recently found Sunday school photograph in which Great-Grandpa Jens and Elizabeth Christensen both appear, we speculated that they had met while serving in Sunday school and then developed a relationship, even though the woman was much younger than Jens. However, toward the end of the little green book, a statement appears saying this woman married later in life to a J. *W.* Hansen, not J. *N.* Hansen. Eventually we found a Family Group Record for her in Salt Lake City showing she had married a Hansen after Jens's death.

I was disappointed that the green book did not confirm a third wife, but because the other information about Jens in the green book was accurate, I wondered whether I had missed something in regard to "Aunt Lizzie." This continued to haunt me, so at my request eight years later, Ruby met with me in her home and went over her family's genealogical information for Elizabeth Christensen. She confirmed that Elizabeth "Lizzie" Christensen had married a James Hansen in 1913. Although Jens had used the name James at some points in his life, he had died in 1906, so clearly had not been Lizzie's husband. Learning that Lizzie had not married Jens did not, however, rule out the rumor of a third wife—and I continued to be curious.

❦

Searching like a detective through old records and discovering information that shed light on the family story excited me, and sometimes gave me euphoria. Sitting in the chair to write the story from my notes, however, required discipline.

And revising required even more discipline! At a Terroir Creative Writing Festival in McMinnville, Oregon, on 24 April 2011, I listened to best-selling author Jean Auel as she delivered the luncheon keynote address. Though I didn't write it on paper, I made a mental note when she said, essentially, that research is like dessert, but writing it up is like sitting down to eat your vegetables.

One of my journal entries reads:

> Writing about Ane is like bashing my head on a wall. I enjoy doing the research, but maybe—as my friend, Natalie Reed, suggested—that is enough. She said if I enjoy the research but don't want to write it, that's okay. But I must remember how the correct location of Ane's house was literally handed to me in a loose-leaf binder on the very day that Carla had asked me to search for it. Something or someone is helping, and I need to trust that and move forward.

How does one explain minor miracles? And how could I refuse to share the story that was taking shape through what was being so generously given?

CHAPTER 4

JENS NIELSEN HANSEN'S LIFE SKETCH: PART I, 1842–1862

Had I been more aware of women's positions in society during the last half of the nineteenth century as I began my search for Ane, I might have predicted that her name would not appear in any index. Karen Marie's name would prove equally elusive. Few women in that time period and location had their names in publications. Most women spent their time taking care of their children, preparing food, doing laundry, cleaning their homes, working in their gardens and orchards, laying food by, and maybe caring for farm animals—not easy tasks before electricity, indoor plumbing, and telephones. So unless a woman became a midwife, teacher, political activist, suffragette, or other public person, she remained hidden from the records.

Jens, however, appeared in the records frequently, so as my research progressed, he became my primary focus. As the parameters of the search expanded, I felt it imperative to include in this work as much of the information I found as possible so no one coming after me would need to spend the time, energy, and money required to rediscover these facts.

As long as I can remember, I have had in my possession copies of the brief life sketch that Jens Nielsen Hansen recorded in his own handwriting on lined notepaper that was 5 ½ by 8 ½ inches with twenty-three preprinted lines on each page. Although Danish was his native language, the sketch is written in nonstandard English, and the record ends just before his 1875 emigration from Denmark. He may have written it after his arrival in the United States. Various transcribers over the years have produced modernized English versions of the sketch and have generously provided photocopies of the transcriptions to all family members. However, the two final pages have always baffled these transcribers.

Although I have always been grateful for Jens's life sketch, I became even more appreciative of it when my husband, Richard, and I traveled to Denmark and Sweden in 2014 to walk in the footsteps of our ancestors. In 2015 we returned to Denmark after a cruise through the Norwegian fjords because we hoped to go inside some of the churches that were connected to the family christenings, confirmations, and marriages but had been locked during our first visit.

When I first read Jens's sketch, the place names meant nothing to me, and they did not show up on any of my maps of Denmark. So I searched for a map on Amazon.com and found the Marco Polo map that reviewers said was appropriate for mounting on a wall but was way too big to unfold inside a car. I knew immediately that was the map for me! When this giant map arrived, I painstakingly pored over it using Jens's sketch, the map's list of towns and villages, and a magnifying glass until I had located almost all of the places Jens had mentioned and had marked them with color-coded sticky arrows. The map was layered with sticky arrows!

Jens's sketch and the gigantic map made it possible for us to find—and stand in—almost all of the towns and farms where Jens had lived and worked. We saw churches, mansions, and barns that had been constructed long before his birth. We were fortunate to meet Danish people who shared information that fleshed out the liminal spaces between Jens's lines. These travels enabled me to experience Denmark's ambience, to more realistically envision Jens's life there, and to fall in love with the country myself.

Except for a brief trip to Jutland for military training as an adult, Jens spent his first thirty-three years of life on the island of Sjælland, or Zealand, a 2,700-square-mile region of green and yellow farms, rolling hills, emerald forests, redbrick buildings, and thatched roofed houses. The old *kirkes*, or churches, were originally Catholic, but upon Denmark's adoption of the Lutheran faith as the state religion in 1536, the buildings were adapted to reflect the change. The churches we visited were built of red brick, though some had been painted white on the exterior. On the inside, some had intricate medieval paintings on the vaulted ceilings illustrating biblical stories, but—much to my sorrow—some church ceiling artwork had been whitewashed. Local people told us the art had been covered to eradicate the Catholic influence. Although we had no hint as to the locations of homes Jens had lived in nor any idea whether they might still be standing, we knew the churches had been erected centuries before he lived and had been important in his life, at least for the ordinances of his Lutheran faith.

The Danish capital city, Copenhagen, lies on the east coast of Sjælland, but the western area of the island, where Jens lived, is dotted with small towns and villages, and also has Trælleborg, a Viking coastal historical site with a meeting hall and a dugout. The island is lapped by the waters of the Øresund on the east, the Baltic Sea on the southeast, the Great Belt on the west, and the Kattegat on the north. Sweden lies just east of the narrow Øresund, and a narrow strip of land along its coast had long been in bitter dispute between the two countries.

The island of Fyn lies just west of Sjælland and separates it from the mainland-connected Jutland further west.

Because Jens is the only one of my maternal ancestors who left a journal, I will introduce him in his own words. His sketch covers the period from his birth in 1842 to his 1875 emigration from Denmark, and I have preserved his spellings and punctuation or lack of it—except for my addition of periods which he *never* used—to retain the flavor of his original document. My clarifying comments appear in brackets throughout.

Jens begins, "i Jens Nielsen was born in Dammark in a little Village Namd Axelholm Holbek Amt [County] on the 16th day of June in the year 1842. My Parents Name Niels Hansen & Hanna Margrethe Andersen." We see patronymics at work here when Jens takes his surname from his father's given name. Only after emigration did Jens adopt the Hansen surname of his father. The kirkes nearest his birthplace were Jyderup to the north and Holmstrup to the south.

※

Richard and I found the Jyderup Kirke during our 2014 visit, and that story will appear later. We returned to Jyderup on 28 July 2015 to visit the priest's office building that stood adjacent to the kirke. The *bing-bong* of the doorbell announced our arrival, and we stood in the entryway as two pastors or priests, Soren Trolddal Nielsen and Henriette Bach Barkholt, came down the hall to assist us. We inquired as to which churches would be open that day, then Priest Barkholt asked where we were going. I said, "To Holmstrup to search for a baptism date and a marriage date for my great-grandfather." She said the church record books had all been sent to the archives, but the information was available on computers. She offered to look it up. We walked down the hall to her office, where she pulled up the christening information and showed us on her screen how difficult the handwriting was to read in some of the records.

Soon Priest Nielsen called to us from his office across the hall saying he had found the same record and had enlarged it, so we went to his office and peered over his shoulder as he painstakingly went through the record of Jens's christening. I asked what else it said below.

"Those are the witnesses."

"Could I have those too, please?" I remembered that when our family researcher, Dr. Gerald M. Haslam, had obtained similar records for other ancestors, he had mentioned how important those witness names were because they often showed family relationships. Priest Nielsen printed the record for me, but it came out so small, I had a hard time reading it. Later, back home, Kaja Voldbæk—a marvelous

Danish researcher who helped us scrutinize many records for this work—also found this record in Danish repositories on the internet. Her additions to the Jyderup information appear in parentheses and mine appear in brackets. Jens's baptism record gives the following information:

> Holbæk Amt [County]
> Parish: Holmstrup, Skippinge District
> Baptism of Jens Nielsen
> 24 July 1842
> Holmstrup
> Parents: (Farmer) Niels Hansen
> Hanne Margrethe Andersen (datter)
> Axelholm
> Witnesses (Sponsors):
> (Maid) Anne Kirstine Andersen (datter)—Svebølle (carried the child)
> (Farmer – Gaardmand) Jens Andersen—Svebølle
> (Farmer – Boelsmand) Hans Larsen—Jerslev (Jordløse)
> (Farmer – Gaardmand) Mads [Anders] Nielsen—Axelholm
> (Farmer – Husmand) Jens Hansen—Holmstrup[3]

Gaardmand means "yard man," *boelsmand* means "farmstead man," and *husmand* means "someone who owns or runs a smallholding."

Our hostess at Kongsgaard Bed and Breakfast in Kalundborg, Denmark, Lisbeth Kristiansen, explained that the first two names in the baptismal or christening record are those of the godparents and that, unlike in some cultures where the godparents were to take over raising the child if something dire happened to the parents, these godparents were responsible for spiritual guidance: they were to help the child learn to love God and to be a good person. She also said that traditionally the first person named was the one who carried the child for the baptism.

Anne Kirstine Andersen (Andersdatter) would likely have been Jens's aunt, a sister to his mother. Hans Larsen is later noted as an uncle for whom Jens worked.

Jens didn't mention it in his sketch, but two brothers had preceded his arrival in the family: Anders Nielsen, born in 1838, and Hans Christian Nielsen, born in 1840. Both Anders and Hans later played key roles in Jens's life.

Between the lines listing his parents' names in his life sketch, Jens inserted, "Shortly after my Birth, my parents moved to a town named Svebolle."

Jens's birthplace of Axelholm, or Akselholm as it appears on current maps, must always have been a small village—indeed, a couple of Danish men told me that it still consists of only a few houses. When Danish people asked me where my great-grandfather was born and I said, "Akselholm," they gave me blank looks or shrugged their shoulders. Not one of them recognized Akselholm.

❧

Immediately after leaving the Jyderup offices, we drove to Holmstrup Kirke. On our trip to Denmark the previous year, we had been told that Holmstrup was the largest village church on Sjælland. It had been locked when we found it, so we had contented ourselves with admiring the exterior architecture from the cemetery garden and observing colorful little snails on the stones. Variegated shades of red and orange bricks formed the outer walls of a long center section that enclosed the chapel inside, and a tower rose at one end, boldly decorated with stair-step crenelations.

This year the door stood open! As we stepped across the threshold, the chapel exuded a stillness and peace that is often found in old churches, a clear divide between the exterior secular life and the interior space for worship and reverence. Paintings and woodcarvings and a Romanesque baptismal font of granite graced the space. We walked the aisles, looking at all the sacred and antique art objects and vaulted white ceilings. As I stood next to the font and put my hand on the cold stone rim of the bowl, I was moved to know I was standing in the spot where Jens's family had gathered to witness his baptism at that same font when he was just a baby, thirty-eight days old.

❧

Jens was two and one-third years old when his first younger sibling was born. His parents, Niels and Hanne Margrethe, had a baby boy on 15 October 1844, named Rasmus Otto Nielsen, their fourth son.

One year later, the Danish census for 1845 in the area lists the following:

Niels Hansen, 30, married, day laborer, born Asnæs, Odsherred;
Hanne AndersDatter, 26, married, his wife, born here in the Parish;
Anders Nielsen, 6, unmarried, born here in the Parish;
Hans Christian Nielsen, 4, unmarried, born Holmstrup, Holbæk
    County;
Jens Nielsen, 3, unmarried, born Holmstrup, Holbæk County;
Rasmus Otto Nielsen, 1, unmarried, born here in the Parish.[4]

This census, then, shows a family with two parents and four young sons, and I like to think they were happy together in spite of their apparently low economic status.

❦

Jens's sketch skips from his 1842 birth to 1848: "When 6 years and 3 month and 10 Dayes my mother Deied." He doesn't say merely that he was six years old—he notes the specific number of days he had lived before this monumental occurrence took place. Originally I thought this indicated the impact of the event, but in August 2013, Richard and I wandered through the windy graveyard on a bluff above the seas at Port Gamble, Washington—an historical mill town—and noted that many of the grave markers of Scandinavian men listed their birth and death dates and then reckoned the lifespan by numbering the years, months, and days of the person's life. I thought perhaps this notation style was a Scandinavian tradition but later learned that it was also used in early Colonial days. Apparently this format makes statistical information easier to calculate.

When my children's father, Frederick Marshall Fulkerson, died in 1983, our daughter, Kjersti, was eight years old and our son, Lindsey, was six—the same age as Jens when his mother died. Later that evening, I found my son in his sister's room crying. When I went to him, he looked up at me with his scrunched-up, teary face and said, "I can't believe he's gone so early in my life." I imagine Jens as a young boy being equally devastated by the loss of his mama.

Various records show that Jens's mother, Hanne Margrethe, died on 26 September 1848, three months short of her thirtieth birthday. The same date is shown for the birth and death of an unnamed son whom the Family Group Record shows as "stillborn."[5] Strangely, that same record lists different locations for the two deaths, with the mother's death shown at Agneas (sic), Svebølle, Holbæk, Denmark, and the son's birth and death in Axelholm, Holmstrup, Svebølle, Denmark.[6] (This listing includes too many towns, but they are all shown on the Family Group Record.) I wondered if this difference might simply be human error in the records, because it seemed unlikely that the mother would have been transported. By horse-drawn conveyance, the trip would have been arduous for a woman who had just given birth and was grieving the baby's death.

When I emailed our researcher, Kaja, about this puzzling record, she sent the following entry:

Entry 149: (no 10) Died 26 September, buried 1 October 1848:
Hanne Margrethe Andersdatter (died during childbirth)

Farmer Niels Hansen's wife in Svebølle, 30 years old.
Entry 139: (no 3) died 26 September, buried 1 October 1848:
a stillborn boy
Farmer Niels Hansen's son in Svebølle, 0 age[7]

Kaja added, "The child is also recorded in the church book Viskinge-Avnsø Parrish, Skippinge District, Holbæk County 1836–1857":

Entry 17 (no 8), died 26 September, buried 1 October 1848: a stillborn boy
Farmer Niels Hansen and wife Hanne Margrethe Andersdatter's son in Svebølle[8]

Kaja explained the absence of Hanne Margrethe's death from this second record in an email message to me on 26 April 2016, saying, "This entry shows parents, but in this church book there are no recorded deaths of women (they probably ran out of pages). The new church book...has both entries for the death of the son and the wife of Niels Hansen." The lesson I learned from this was that just because information is available on the internet in a fancy form does not mean it is correct. Humans make mistakes. However the records list it, the death of this young wife and mother, and the death of the anticipated new baby, must have been a great loss for the family.

Two years later, the Danish census for 1850 lists:

Niels Hansen, 35, widower, day laborer, born Asnæs, Holbæk County;
Jens Nielsen, 8, unmarried, his child, born Holmstrup, Holbæk County.[9]

The stark change from the 1845 census, showing a family with a father and mother and four young sons, to this one in 1850, listing a sorrowing widower and one young motherless son, disturbed me. What painful story can be read between the lines of these two censuses?

What happened to the other three sons? At the time I received these records, I could only guess that possibly the older two sons, Anders and Hans, had already been hired by farmers to work. These boys would have been eleven and nine in 1850, old enough to begin working contracts, as did most young people not of the wealthy class in Denmark. The history of Jens's brother, Hans Christian, states, "His mother died...when Hans Christian was only eight years old...leaving the family without their mother's love to guide them. Hans had to make his way in the world pretty much alone."[10]

The youngest son, Rasmus Otto, would have been six in 1850 and perhaps was being cared for by a relative. Jens includes nothing in his sketch about the circumstances of his brothers, leaving us to wonder. Later records showed that both Hans and Rasmus married, so I knew they had lived past childhood. However, I found no other records for Anders, who seemed to disappear after the 1845 census.

I asked Kaja if she could find anything about Anders, and soon she sent the portion of the 1850 Danish Census that showed Anders Nielsen, eleven years old, and Rasmus Nielsen, five years old, residing with Maren Christensdatter, their widowed grandmother, the mother of their deceased mother. I felt sorry that Hans's life was hard, yet pleased to learn where the other two boys had gone and that they'd had the love of their grandmother as they grieved their shared loss.

Carol May, a therapist, told me during a conversation in 2007 that when a parent dies while a child is young, the child loses *both* parents: one to death and the other to grief. Jens indicated that might have been true of his own circumstances when he wrote that after his mother died:

> my father lived somewhat a rough Life for 5 years. When 10 years and 10 months i was hired out to farmer Hans Larsen [whose name also appears as one of the witnesses to Jens's baptism] in the Villige Jordlose [Jordløse] to hird his Gees and Lamb. i was not Kept very Clean. i Earnt an old suit of Cloose.

This hiring to Hans Larsen was likely in April of 1853, and most contracts at that time were for a one-year period. Many families, including mine, have lore that their ancestral roots include royalty. From this hiring out and his treatment and pay, however, it seems obvious that Jens's line did not come from royalty.

⚜

Denmark had been economically damaged by a series of wars, and Knud J. V. Jespersen, an historian, explains that not only did recovery take a long time but also there were "years of poverty"[11] that affected a large number of Danes. The Hansen family must have been somewhat destitute to send Jens, and probably his brothers, out to work for, to be supported by, and to live with other families where the servants' accommodations were likely "humble quarters in the stables."[12]

Jens's sketch continues: "about September [actually August of 1853] Father Married a girl Named Ane Margrethe Christensen from a little Villge Haunso."

The Family Group Record lists the bride's name as "Ane Christiansdatter" or "Ane Christiansen" without the middle name that Jens ascribed to her. Jens's father, Niels, was thirty-nine and Jens's stepmother, Ane, was just two months away from her twenty-second birthday at the time of the marriage—a significant, eighteen-year age difference. Based on an interview with Jens many years later in Newton, Utah, Assistant LDS Church Historian Andrew Jenson wrote that "in his father's second marriage he was blessed with a good stepmother."[13] Jens records: "sometime in Nov 1853 i return back to my Father and stayed ontil Apr 1854." His stepmother would have been a few months pregnant when Jens left them after about six months. He was nearly twelve years old.

"i then hyred to my Onken a farmer in the same town as my Father leved Named Svebolle. my Onkels Name Jens Andersen [Jens's mother's brother, who also witnessed Jens's baptism and was his godparent]. i hirdet for him 8 month. i Earnt a good suit cloose. i was threated deason." He writes that his uncle "wanted me to stay but as my Father's Wife hade a baby i hade to com home to tend it." Niels and Ane's first child, according to the Family Group Record, was born in Svebølle on 18 October 1854, a girl named Hanne Margrethe Nielsen,[14] her given names similar to those of the deceased first wife, Hanna (sometimes shown as Hanne) Margrethe, mother of Jens and his brothers. I wonder why Jens at age twelve was the one out of the four sons expected to tend the two-month-old baby girl. Where were the other boys? And what were they doing? Later in his life, Jens exhibited traits of compassion and generosity of spirit. Perhaps he tended the baby because these traits were already evident at this young age, or perhaps he developed them because of these experiences.

Accordingly, Jens went home apparently sometime in December of 1854 to tend his half sister and was still there for the Danish census of 1855 that listed:

Niels Hansen, 40, married, joiner or carpenter, born Asnæs, Odsherred;
Ane Christiansdatter, 23, married, his wife, born Asnæs, Odsherred;
Jens Nielsen, 13, unmarried, their child, born Holmstrup;
Hanne Margrethe Nielsdatter, 1, their child, born here in the Parish.[15]

Jens doesn't say how long he stayed at home nor mention any other events for nearly two years. Eventually he addresses his education and mentions a town not previously listed: "on the 4 of Septbr 1856 my Schooling was endet. i was Comfirmed in the town of Viskinde [Viskinge] in the Chapel or Church By Rev: H. C. Rask. a few dayes after [the confirmation, I] pertook of the Sacrament after the manner of the World." Danish formal schooling at that time was finished when the pupil reached the age of fourteen, passed an exam, and took communion, thus signifying that the person was considered capable of making his or her own living and life.

This event made me curious as to why schooling ended at age fourteen and why it was connected to a church function. In his history of Denmark, Jespersen explains:

> The state was involved in setting up a form of compulsory education for all the children of the country in 1736, when the ceremony of confirmation was introduced. For their confirmation at the age of 14, the children had to take a test in elementary evangelical knowledge, and it was compulsory that they were prepared through teaching from the parish priest or his proxy. To some degree this marked the beginning of the general compulsory basic schooling introduced by the Board School Act of 1814—the first of its kind in the world.
>
> Thus, a general educational system, mainly with a religious intention, developed early in Denmark. At least in its ambitions, it was intended for all the children of the country regardless of social status.... The result in Denmark was that widespread illiteracy was eradicated long before most other European countries. Thus, a steadily increasing section of the population learnt the skills of reading and writing which were a prerequisite for becoming good evangelic Christians and useful members of society. This in turn laid the foundations for the farming classes to participate in public life.[16]

Jespersen also states that earlier education in Denmark had been through the Catholic Church, but after the Reformation in 1536, when Christian III "officially proclaimed evangelical Lutheranism as the national religion,"[17] the king wanted the people to be able to read Luther's German Bible for themselves and not just have it interpreted for them by the clergy. For that to happen, the Bible had to be translated into Danish, and the people had to become literate enough to read it.[18] The Danish educational system provided scriptural literacy, and more, for the population.

✄

While at Aarhus (spelled Århus until 2011) at the center of the east coast of Jutland (the peninsula that includes continental Denmark and part of Northern Germany) during 2015, Richard and I visited Den Gamle By, an open-air museum of history and culture, a preserved outdoor village with historical homes and shops representing distinct periods of time from 1700 to the early 1900s. One area of the museum simulated the year 1864, capturing the aura of what life was like when Jens was twenty-two years old. Here I received answers to various questions raised by Jens's comments, as well as additional, surprising information.

One guide, a woman in a costume of the 1864 period—white three-quarter-sleeved blouse with medium-blue plaid jumper, long navy gathered skirt with a pinstriped apron, a blue plaid scarf tied on her head babushka style, and carrying a basket over her right arm—represented the wife of the brew master (*brygmester*) or distiller (*destilleriet*) whom she said played a very important role in the village. People didn't know yet in 1864 why drinking water—sometimes from the well near the horse yards and tasting like dung—made them sick. Boiling the water to make beer killed the pathogens. People didn't know that fact, but *did* know that drinking beer did not make them sick. Everyone drank beer. The first processing at 2 percent to 3 percent alcohol went to the wealthy. The second processing went to the men of the other classes, and the third processing at 1 percent alcohol went to the women and children. Our guide said that beginning in about 1900, beer was made with higher alcohol content and became a social problem. My realization that all of my Danish ancestors probably drank weak beer before water purification became standard intrigued me. Food and drink weave a large part of a person's life and culture, and I had not previously thought about beer in terms of the family's history or survival.

In answer to my questions about young farmworkers, the woman told us that in order for a young person to be hired for work, or even to take training to be hired, he or she had to have a servant's conduct notebook, called a *skudsmaalsbog*, and in order to get this notebook, the person had to have been confirmed in the Lutheran Church. It was common for all young people with a servant's conduct book to work and uncommon for them *not* to work. So Jens had to pass this confirmation milestone in order to obtain his servant's conduct book and to continue working. Confirmation and employment were interdependent. Later we will discuss Jens's servant conduct notebook.

While at Den Gamle By on that sunny day topped with blue skies, Richard and I went for a ride with several other tourists in a black, four-wheeled carriage drawn by one large brown horse through part of the village. As the horse waited for us to board, he shifted his hooves and snorted. The carriage bounced and clattered on the cobblestones. The clippety-clop of the horse's hooves, the rattle of the wheels, and the leather squeak of the shifting carriage created a backdrop of music as we enjoyed the novelty and observed various quaint white structures of the time period. Was this how my family had traveled from their home to the kirke for Jens's first communion?

I wanted to *be* in the church where Jens had been confirmed and had taken communion at age fourteen, but the first summer we visited the kirke in Viskinge, the beautiful red-orange brick building—topped with a red-tile roof, buttressed with crenelated ends, and surrounded by small memorial gardens and a white wall—was closed. Before our return trip the following year, I wrote to the parish priest, Sanne Bojesen Kristensen, and asked if we might be able to see inside the building during our trip that summer. She wrote back with contact information for the person who would be substituting for services while she, herself, was on vacation, and included an invitation to attend services the Sunday we would be in the area. Even though we could contact the priest to go inside any day, we chose to accept her invitation to attend the services.

We arrived early, met the substitute priest, Christina Morsing, in her dark robes outside near the front door, and had a pleasant conversation as we walked into the cool, peaceful space where Jens had experienced his educational milestone. We stood with Priest Morsing under the vaulted center of the church, conversing about various things, including that her sermon in Danish would be about false prophets. We found a place to sit halfway back, just off the left aisle in the chapel. We waited, but no one else came. Although we were the only two people who showed up for the service, the priest started the meeting on time.

The organist played exquisite music—prelude and hymns—on the antique organ, the cantor had a gorgeous baritone voice, and the priest, instead of presenting the prepared longer version of her sermon in Danish, gave a short sermon in English. I appreciated their doing the entire service for only two people—two English-speaking Americans at that! And I was thrilled to be where Jens had been confirmed and taken communion.

At the conclusion the six of us exited the chapel, and the groundskeeper, who had opened the building before services, locked the door behind us. In all fairness to the parishioners who were not there, this was July, a vacation month for Denmark, and many people were away.

Present or absent, the Danes are required by law to pay a church tax. Per Krøyer, our host in July 2015 at Amalie's Apartment Bed and Breakfast in Sorø told us at dinner in his home one evening that everyone who lives in Denmark pays a church tax, no matter what their religious choice. He said he pays his church tax so he can choose not to attend except at Easter and funerals. Then he laughed uproariously, so infectiously that we did too.

After the ceremony that ended Jens's formal schooling, "on the 1ste of Nov 1856 i heired to a Farmer, Hans Jensen, in the town Named Lillefuglede." The orange-roofed, white kirke at Lille Fuglede sits near the water's edge on the northwest shore of Lake Tissø, and is built in a floor plan of the cross. As I took in the scene of the white church, the sparkling blue lake, and the gold-and-green farmlands in the quiet of late afternoon on a sunny day, I wondered if Jens had had time in the midst of his work to appreciate the beauty of the place.

Jens worked for Farmer Jensen "for the Sum of 16 Rigsdaler which is in U.S. Coin $11.50/100 and 4 yard of Flanil 2 rady mad Shirts and one and one half pair Stockins for a Year." Farmer Jensen was the first of Jens's employers to add money to his salary, and cash continued to be included as part of his wages through his subsequent employments. Apparently having finished Denmark's required schooling entitled Jens to the addition of cash to his usual pay of board and room and clothing. He tallies this cash income in rigsdalers, which were replaced in 1873 by the krone, and he also converts the amount to US dollars of the time period, another indication that he may have written his sketch after he arrived in America.

Workers were paid three stockings, Mother told us, because the feet of the stockings wore out first, so the third stocking was unraveled and its yarn was knitted into new stocking feet that were then attached to the ankle sections of the other two stockings. Regarding this custom, Laura Steenhoek, a member of my then-active writing group asked, "Did the men knit their own stockings?"

I shared that question with my sister LaRelia. In answer, she sent a photocopy of a painting of a nineteenth-century shepherd boy attributed to Hans Vermeehren (*sic)* from a Denmark travel guidebook.[19] A pale blue sky with a few puffy, sheep-like clouds arcs above a young boy standing in an open, slightly hilly area painted in greens and rusts. At his feet rests a large black dog. The boy wears a beige, possibly wool, jacket with long holey sleeves, baggy pants with one knee patch, a dark-olive double-breasted vest, and a black cap with a bill. A valise-sized bag snugs up under his left arm, its strap crossing his chest and right shoulder. A straight wooden staff also rests under the boy's left arm. At the left edge of the painting grazes a flock of sheep. The boy holds in his hands three double-pointed knitting needles with a partially knitted stocking divided among them. A small ball of yarn attached to his vest at the front left shoulder feeds the strand of yarn to the stocking. He is obviously in the process of knitting the stocking, so the answer to Laura's question appears to be yes, at least some of the men *did* knit their own stockings or at least replaced the worn-out stocking feet.

Several years before visiting Denmark, I had found on the internet that the painting of the knitting shepherd boy was in a museum in Copenhagen, but in 2015, that information no longer came up when I searched. I wanted to see the painting in person, so at a crowded Copenhagen tourist information office near Tivoli Gardens, I asked a woman behind the counter where to find it. When I told her I had searched the internet with the name of the artist (not knowing yet that it was misspelled in the guidebook) but nothing had come up, she told me to Google a description of the painting: "shepherd boy knitting." Much to my surprise, that search brought up the Statens Museum for Kunst (State Museum of Art), also known as the National Gallery of Denmark. Richard and I went to the museum and found the knitting shepherd boy painting, but it was entitled "A Jutland Shepherd on the Moors." The story is that Vermehren encountered an eighty-two-year-old-shepherd on the moors and this painting resulted from that encounter. The subject apparently is not a young boy at all. Like the *Mona Lisa*, the painting was much smaller than I had imagined it would be, but a delight to see with my own eyes. The correct spelling of the artist's name appears on a wall plaque next to the painting: Frederik Vermehren. He lived from 1823 to 1910[20] and was part of a Danish art movement focusing on the rural and folk life of the mid-1800s. His paintings and those of the other artists of this period helped me to imagine Jens not only knitting his socks as he herded geese or sheep but also going through the tasks of his daily life, both indoors and outdoors, from cooking to threshing.

The same day, we revisited a Røde Cors Butik secondhand shop in Copenhagen, where Richard discovered a three-inch-diameter Royal Copenhagen plate painted in shades of blue and white with the profile view of a hatted, bearded man in loose work clothes. He is holding a staff under his left arm and knitting the foot of a long sock with double-pointed needles, standing in a field of sheep with a dog upright at his feet. The shop's proprietress said the Danish title on the back—*Hosebinder Herning*—loosely means "man who knits socks." We bought the petite plate, and I treasure it.

These artist representations of men knitting socks make me ask again: Did Jens also knit his own stockings? I wish I knew for sure, but I imagine so.

❧

Two weeks after Jens began working for Hans Jensen of Lille Fuglede at the age of fourteen, his father, Niels, and stepmother, Ane, had a son named Soren Peder Nielsen (Hansen) on 16 November 1856. Jens then had a half brother as well as a two-year-old half sister. After noting that he tended the first baby, Jens never again mentions his half siblings in his sketch, and I wonder what part, if any, they played in his life. Did he stay in touch with his father? Did he know he gained more half siblings over the years?

Beginning with this Soren Peder's birth entry and continuing forward, the Family Group Records include the Hansen surname, but that does not mean the family members were actually using it at the time. *Hansen* does not appear on the later emigration lists, indicating that the adoption of this name came sometime after emigration in the mid-1870s, and perhaps was never used by those who did not emigrate.

The next part of the sketch is difficult to decipher because Jens wrote two lines of text instead of his usual one line between the preprinted black lines of the paper. He also drew three curved dividing lines like the second in a set of parentheses in these four lines of text to separate two topics. He has also crossed out some words. He continues, as near as I can tell, "in the beginning of Jan 1858 i took sick of a long fever. My threetment [at Farmer Hans Jensen's in Lille Fuglede] was good althoug Sickness hold out 3 month." Jens mentions illness often enough in his history to raise questions as to what kind of chronic condition he might have had. Asthma runs in my extended family, but it could also have been a number of other things. Next, the phrase "after 18 month" appears to be partially crossed out, and then Jens goes on with "on the 1ste of May 1858, i Left for the reeson i Want to larn Music." He had spent eighteen months working his first job after finishing his required schooling. This entry is the first mention of his desire to play a musical instrument but not the last.

Jens elaborates, "i heired to a little farmer [probably means small farm] Hans Petersen in the town of Svinninge he to Larn me to play Violin and Clarinette and i to Work for him 2 yeare." The Danish census for 1860 confirms Jens working for Hans Pedersen in Svinninge, and that Jens was eighteen years old, born in Holmstrup.[21]

Svinninge lies on the northern edge of the area Jens moved around in during his life in Denmark, and Lille Fuglede is situated on the southwestern edge. The two towns are fourteen or sixteen miles apart depending on which route one takes. Svebølle, where Jens's father lived, sits between the two villages and might have been on Jens's way to Svinninge. Did he have time to visit the family? Did he walk? Did someone he knew take him by wagon? He likely did not make enough money to pay the expenses for a horse of his own.

Jens's father and stepmother had another son, Hans Andreas Nielsen (Hansen), on 23 August 1859, when their other children would have been three and five years old. No story appears about this newborn half brother, but the Family

Group Record shows that he died in Salt Lake City on 23 November 1890 at the age of thirty-one and was buried the very next day.[22] As we shall see later, Jens was in Salt Lake in 1889, and I wonder if he and Hans Andreas were both there and in contact during that time.

❦

The Svinninge Kirke, which was standing when Jens lived, is painted white with a red tile roof. A blue-faced clock with gold numbers adorns the upper part of an outside wall. Unfortunately, the church had been locked in 2014 and was also locked when we arrived in 2015. I was willing to give up getting inside, but Richard said, "We're here." So he looked around at the low yellow-brick buildings near the parking lot for the priest's offices or home and discovered two doors. We agreed that one door looked more promising because through the frosted glass inset, we could see school-age children playing inside.

At our knock, a tall, slim woman came to the door and said the priest was out but she would look in his office and in his coat pockets for the keys to the church. She found the keys, and as we all walked to the church, I told her that my great-grandfather had traded work for violin lessons. She was surprised and said, "There was a violin teacher in Svinninge in 1858?" I was surprised that she had expected to know that part of the history of her town. She unlocked the church and waited inside while we took photographs of the paintings, carved pulpit, hanging red-hulled model ship, ornate art at the front of the chapel, and the baptismal font. She offered to let us keep the keys and bring them back when we finished, but we were ready to leave. I thanked her for giving me the opportunity to sit a few minutes in a pew and think about my great-grandfather as a young man likely having been right here in this church.

❦

Jens continued: "therefore When 2 years had a lapsed i Left for the reason that i hade no clothin to Weare." During this contract, Jens grew from sixteen to eighteen years of age, so he likely had either worn out his clothing or grown out of it or both. His passion to learn music at the sacrifice of a salary says a great deal about this young man, and although he subsequently studied other instruments, the violin would be his primary medium for music.

Ending his music lessons and moving to another farm at age eighteen, Jens explained, "on the 1ste of May 1860 i heired to a farmer J. Petersen in Jordlose for 12 Month for the sum of 20 Rbds: Danish which amount to $14.00 5-⅓ yard of Flanel 2 rady made Shirth, and one and one half pr Stokins. My threatment Was not god." I wish he had been more specific about what had happened that made his treatment not good in Jordløse at the age of eighteen years.

At the 1864 Danish village portion of Den Gamle By, our guide had explained that the master or mistress of the house in the work situations had the right to discipline the workers and could be too harsh with them. She gave an example of the young women workers gathering in an evening circle for song, handwork such as knitting, or prayers, where "The mistress might kick the legs of the young women to wake them up or to keep them awake." She added that sometimes a boy worker would sleep in a room or in the barn with other boys, and those boys could have been hard on him. The thought occurred to me that losing a husband when I was thirty-eight years old had made me compassionate concerning the grief of others. Maybe Jens's loss of his mother at the tender age of six lingered with him as grief or made him more tenderhearted than the other boys—maybe an easy target?

❧

As shown earlier, Jens's first hiring out at age ten in 1852 had been to his uncle Hans Larsen in Jordløse where he was "not kept very clean" and "earnt an old suit of cloose." Again in Jordløse eight years later, he finished working one year (May 1860 to May 1861) for J. Petersen, from whom Jens said his treatment was not good. In spite of two hirings in Jordløse in which his work life was not happy, Jens next returned to the farm where he had been first hired at age ten and listed his second experience on that first farm in this way: "When times up [at Petersen's] i left and heired to Farmer Hans Larsen's same place [Jordløse] for 12 month."

Here my copy of the sketch becomes impossible to read. From an unsigned transcription that was apparently made from a clearer copy, or perhaps even from the original sketch, the transcriber filled in after the "12 month" with: "for 28 Rbds Danish." Then back to the sketch itself: "this is in U.S. Coin $20[,] 5 ½ yard of flannel, 2 ready-made shirts, one pair Stockins. as my treatment was good I sirved 18 month [May 1861 to November 1862]."

What made the difference in the quality of his treatment between these two indenturings to his uncle Hans Larsen? Jens was nineteen years old instead of ten, so perhaps he was better able to look out for himself or was capable of harder work. Or I thought perhaps Hans Larsen had mellowed in some way. However, I later saw Jens's servant conduct notebook and found it had been signed by "Farmer Hans Larsen's Widow, Jordløse." Possibly Widow Larsen, Jens's aunt, was kinder than the farmer himself had been.

CHAPTER 5

JENS NIELSEN HANSEN'S LIFE SKETCH: PART II, 1862–1867

Two farms (Astrup and Kattrup) and one forest (Kongsdal had been in existence for centuries before hiring Jens and were still in operation during our visits to Denmark. Jens had worked at those places well over a century ago, yet the original buildings still stood, and the names of the farms and forest appeared on my enormous map of Denmark. The smaller farms were nameless, and our records gave no clue as to where they could be found. The kirkes in every town predated Jens's birth by half a millennium yet remain as stately edifices. When my feet touched the ground of the farms and forest and churches where Jens had made his living and had observed religious rites, I felt connected.

Before Richard and I traveled to Denmark, the names of Jens's and Ane's and Karen Marie's towns and workplaces were just words. Now those words conjure up memories of lofty churches, elegant estates, rolling farms, wooded forests, blue lakes and seas, thatched roofs, red brick buildings, mustard-yellow houses, musical sounds of the Danish language, generously welcoming people, and a recalled sense of awe at being on that ancestral ground. I wish I could hand it all to others.

Jens's sketch continues: "and the 1ste of Nov. 1862 i hyreit to a big Farmer Grev Bernstoff his Farm named Kattrup." (The translation of *greve* in Danish is "count" or "baron.") This was the first instance of Jens working on an establishment significant enough to have its own name. "i hyrid for 12 month for the Sum of 42 Rbds which is in U.S. Coin $28. but this is to rough life for me." Jens worked at Kattrup from 1 November 1862 until 1 November 1863 (age twenty to twenty-one). What made this life too rough for him? Did his apparently fragile health not support the rigors of hard work? Or did his gentle nature make harsh treatment intolerable? I wish he had explained.

❧

Richard and I stopped at Kattrup in 2014. We passed between two white brick sentry posts and drove into a gray cobbled courtyard facing a street named

Kattrupvej. (*Vej* is pronounced *vie* with a clip to it, and means "way" or "road.") An assemblage of structures surrounded the courtyard and included a white building with three levels of windows, a pointed red-tile roof, and the date of 1852 hanging in black numbers on its face. The building had been ten years old when Jens walked that square. We bumped across the cobbles and parked.

Inside that white, barnlike building, Richard found a young man in the driver's seat of an enormous tractor. He said the boss could better answer our questions, but he was out for about fifteen or twenty minutes, and we could wait if we stayed in front of the white buildings. Other single-story buildings in various colors surrounded the courtyard, and a white mansion with a steep, red-tiled roof and three chimneys graced the far end. In the center of the mansion front, a flight of a dozen stairs with a wrought-iron railing on each side led to a double wooden door flanked by sconces. Rows of tall windows extended along the entire front of the house.

While I obediently paced in the courtyard and waited, Richard disappeared and captured some lovely contraband scenes with his camera, but no one came out to scold. I strolled across the road we had come in on and stood by a short rock wall, as thick as it was tall, and enjoyed a visual feast of a gently undulating valley contoured in a vast stretch of rolling green and yellow fields dotted by leafy green copses that seemed to stretch forever. The scene and the moment fed my soul.

I wondered if the view from Jens's farm in Newton, Utah, on a slight hill north of town had reminded him of Denmark. Sometimes I saw similarities in the geography and geology between Sjælland and Cache Valley. Did Jens find similarities? If so, were they a comfort to him? Or did he long for his homeland?

We waited half an hour but no one showed up, so we left without answers to my questions.

The following summer (2015) after a cruise in the Norwegian fjords, we again stopped at Kattrup—this time in gray rain—giving the place another try and hoping to obtain some information to flesh out Jens's story. I wanted to know what kind of work he had done there, where he had lived, and maybe to discern why it had been a rough life even for someone who was used to working hard.

Richard sat in the car while I got out to reconnoiter. A young man came out of one of the buildings and walked toward me across the cobbles. I told him why we were there as we walked into the same white barn that had housed farm machines the previous year. Another young man sat above us inside an enclosed cab on a large tractor with huge tires and drove it forward slowly. He brought it to a halt and turned off the engine. The young men conversed in Danish while the driver stayed inside the cab. The first young man then told me in English that the owner was home and I could go up to the house and knock.

Back in the car, Richard and I rattled over the cobbles to the end of the court-yard, parked by the huge house (or *castle*, as I later learned those estate homes are called), walked up onto the uncovered porch, and stood in the drizzle. We knocked several times, but no one came to the door as the rain soaked us. We pushed the bell and waited, then pushed it again and waited, looking around at the view from the porch back across the courtyard and road to a strip of those yellow fields and green forests visible in the mists.

Finally, down at ground level on the right-hand side of the house, a young woman opened a door and called to us to come where she was. We went down the stairs, ducked under cover, and entered an expansive sort of mudroom, cluttered with clothes and boots, where she waited for us. In answer to my explanation and questions, she said it was her boyfriend who owned the house—his family had purchased it in 1947—and he was somewhere. She said she would call him but searched in vain for her cell phone. Eventually she put on a hat, neck scarf, and coat and walked in the rain down to the tractor barn we had come from. I watched her as she walked away and became smaller, and I admired her walking style—confident and graceful. Soon she returned and said her boyfriend had disappeared. She took down my telephone number and gave me his. Richard and I told her we might have time to come back on Thursday, and we took our sodden leave.

We did not have time to go back on Thursday. The owner never called me, nor did I call him. We had tried twice in person to learn more about this estate, but no one was interested in helping us, nor did we feel welcome. Almost everywhere else we went in Denmark asking questions, people were kind and friendly. Often the first word they said when they learned we were Americans was "Welcome!" Perhaps negative vibrations have permeated Kattrup for a century and a half. What happened to Jens in this place? We will likely never know why Kattrup gave him a life that was too rough for him. We do know that he did not renew his contract.

❦

Niels and Ane, on 6 November 1862, brought Karen Marie Nielsen (Hansen) into the world. This was the fourth child for Jens's father and stepmother, with the others being eight, six, and three—if still living.

Jens moved on after his rough time at Kattrup and wrote, "after My time was up [1863] i return Back to Hans Larsen Jordlose and hyrid for 12 month [his third contract at this uncle's farm] for 32 Rbds which is in U.S. Coin $23.00 and 5 ½ yard flannel 2 rady made Shirth, one and one half par stockins but after

7 month i took sick [this is his second report of illness] so mots so that i was unable to work and by this reason had to Leave and sestane misel." How did he sustain himself while he was too ill to work?

Jens continues, "and after this i Went home to my Father's house to live [Svebølle] but after one month my meens was eain [eaten? gone?] and When i could not by my own Brade i could not stay home longer." To be ill, unemployed, and homeless must have been a heavy burden. Jens was twenty-two years old at this time, so it is reasonable that he would have been expected to earn his own way. He doesn't say, though, whether his father and stepmother asked him to leave or whether he chose to leave because of his own pride. It troubles me that it appears they were not willing to lend a helping hand temporarily to an ailing adult child, yet they quite possibly had four children under the age of eight for whom to provide. The only one of Jens's four half siblings who had been born by this date and for whom any death date is available is the aforementioned Hans Andreas who lived until age thirty-one.[23] Maybe the other infants didn't live, or the record keepers omitted data, or both.

Jens's record goes on to say, "so i hyred to a beg farmer, Greve Lerke his farm Named Astrup. i hade to hyre by the Day because of sicknes [apparently a continuation of the sickness that had terminated his work and sent him home for a month]. Worked there for 3 month and i was about well."

❧

Richard and I drove south around Lake Skarresø, a small, sparkling blue lake, catching glimpses of the water between buildings and trees, but I wanted to find someplace where we could see the lake as a whole rather than merely in interrupted glances. We drove along the narrow, paved road, and I studied the gigantic map of Sjælland on my lap. As we went under a railroad overpass and the road curved to the right, I happened to look up from the map at the exact split second to spot a huge gray boulder on the left side of the road with *Astrup 1952* etched into it. I shrieked, "Oh my gosh!! Stop the car! Stop! Stop!" Fortunately Richard is a calm person and did not have a heart attack. "Jens worked at this farm!" I continued shrieking. I had not noticed *Astrup* in print on the map so had not been watching for it, but it *was* printed there, and this was the farm that had hired Jens to work by the day as he recovered from his illness.

The boulder and a lamppost, backed by a hedge, stood as sentries. We pulled off the road where a narrow driveway went under an archway constructed through a cream-colored, one-story building, dividing the structure into two sections. We drove through the arch—its length equal to the depth of the building—and found ourselves in a cobbled courtyard surrounded by four long, single-story farm buildings, including the one we had just come through. The buildings each sported a red-tiled roof and nine-paned windows running the structure's length. We bobbled across the stone lot, parked at the far edge, and unfolded ourselves out of the car.

I didn't see where the young man came from, but suddenly he was standing by us, taller than we were. He was probably in his early thirties and had a pleasant expression on his face. I held a sheaf of papers in my hands showing a detailed grid of Jens's history, and I flipped through it quickly to find the information about Astrup. I told the young man that my great-grandfather had been hired by the day there at Astrup in May, June, and July of 1864. He glanced down at my notes and said, "You've done a lot of homework."

"Yes, ten years' worth!" I said, and we laughed. His name was Niels Eriksen. He said it was common at that time—1864—to send children out to work even without a parent dying like in Jens's case, and child-labor laws in Denmark had come after that time. Also, it was common back then at Astrup to hire day workers. The long building we had passed through had previously housed pigs, but those animals at the time of our visit were kept in the hills opposite the complex, on the right side of the road upon which we had come to the farm.

Eriksen said the company had a number of small residences around the area for employees to live in, and Jens likely lived in one of them during his three-month work period at Astrup. I wish we knew what kind of work he did—or was well enough to do—while he was there. Did he help take care of the pigs? Did he work with other animals? Did he help with the spring planting and summer nurturing of crops?

We asked Eriksen if he knew where we could drive to see more of Lake Skarresø, and he said we could walk a path through Astrup's woods directly to the shoreline. We did, and after seeing the lovely lake, we returned past the rear of all the interesting buildings, crossed the cobbled courtyard, and went into Eriksen's office to thank him for his help.

Then we drove back inside the arched tunnel and stopped so I could study the names of previous owners. On one wall of the archway, two mounted plaques listed the names of the *ejere*, or owners, of *Astrup Gods*, or Astrup Estate, beginning with a name that had no date. The next name was followed by the date of 1407. I later learned that the date paired with a name is the date that person *became* the owner and is the same date that ended the ownership of the previously listed person. The third person on the list was followed by 1408, while the next entry had no date and was listed as *Krongods*, which translates as "crown lands," or, in other words, the royal family owned the estate until 1664. Frederik Ferdinand Lerche was Astrup's ejere from 1852 to 1882, so he would have been the benefactor for our ailing Jens whose life sketch lists "Farmer Greve Lerke" as his employer, a phonetic spelling for Lerche. Apparently, Frederik Ferdinand Lerche was not only a farm estate owner but also had a title of count or baron.

Thank goodness I had looked up from the map when I did or we may have entirely missed this historic farm and the perfect spot from which to view the sparkling lake that will have more significance later in the story.

*

During a three-month period at Astrup, then, Jens worked by the day when he felt well enough to do so. He did some kind of farmwork, and he probably stayed in one of the workers' residences. At the end of those three months, he was in better health, and he moved to a new position: "i then hyred to a man hoos Name was Bulmand. he was the hade Bos Looking after a forest." This would have been at a place called Edelsminde. Lisbeth Kristiansen, our hostess at Kongsgaard Bed and Breakfast in Kalundborg, told us Edelsminde likely had been a large farm or forest, but not a village or town. Richard and I were unable to find it on the map or on the ground either year we were on Sjælland.

Jens's story continues:

> about the 1st of Feb: [1864] a Ware brook out Between Denmark and Reusen [Prussia, Austria, Germany] about a cirten peese of Land call Slesvig Holstein [the neck of land that connects Jutland with the European mainland and abuts Germany—a strategically important piece of real estate]. this Ware kept up for a few month and as it was a law in the Country When a Yong man has past 22 years of adge he was compeled to meet at sesion on a cirten plase Where he should be told to be examed if he Was usfuld for a Soldier and as it was a Ware and i hade past 22 years i was call to meet at the City of Kallundborg [located on the west coast of Sjælland and approximately 9 miles west of the area in which Jens had been working] on the 8 day of August 1864 at a sesion to be Examed and as i was found good [in spite of his recurring illnesses] i was to be prepard at anytime When called upon to meet for training to war but in the same days the war stoped about the 30th of September 1864." (Preliminaries of a peace treaty were signed on August 1st with the definitive peace treaty signed October 30, 1864.)

This second Schleswig-Holstein War resulted in a heavy loss of Denmark's dukedoms on the south end of the Jutland Peninsula to Germany. Knud J. V. Jespersen describes it as the "national catastrophe for Denmark in 1864 when the duchies of both Schleswig and Holstein were lost."[24] He elaborates, "Both duchies, including the 200,000 Danish speakers and sympathizers in North Schleswig, were incorporated into Bismarck's New Germany."[25] Had this war continued, Jens presumably would have seen active duty.

Jens returned at that time to his interrupted contract: "i went to my Plase at Bülmand's Where I had hyred for 12 month for 45 Rbds in Danish Which in U.S. Coin is $33, an [it looks like someone wrote a capital *I* over an *it*] I was wery well satysfied there."

While Jens was working at Edelsminde for Bulmand, Niels and Ane had a daughter, Maren Sophie Nielsen (Hansen) on 14 March 1865, their fifth child. Niels was fifty-one years old; Ane was thirty-four; Jens was twenty-three. This half sister of Jens's lived until 12 April 1886, when she was twenty-one years of age.[26]

Although Jens was "wery well satysfied" at Edelsminde, he suffered a significant disappointment: "but as i was to be rady at anytime for the millitary Sirvis he [Bülmand] tock one in my plase on the first of Mai 1865." It seemed sad that Jens's boss did not allow him to renew his contract because of the military requirements attached to him.

Jens did not waste any time finding another appointment. One month later, "about the 1st of June 1865 i hyred [to] Hans Jensen in Svebolle the plase where my Father lives, about of July i tock Sick of a Long fever Which held me for over Weeks. i Was out of my head for about 2 Dayes. got Well after about 3 weeks." This is the third major illness recounted in Jens's sketch. I wish he had recorded what kind of health challenges he faced.

Two months after Jens's contract with *this* Hans Jensen started, he began a year of military training. He says, "on the 8 Day of August [1865] i had to present meselv in the big City of Kjobenhavn to be traind for milletairy Work. i was there 12 month and one day. dooring that time i was traind a little in music for millitary use and in the latter time i Lirned for my own use. on the 9th Day of August 1866 i Was release from the milletary Sirvis and i hyred a Room of my Brother H.C. [Hans Christian] Nielsen on Vaiebro Fellevei Noll for one month and undertook to Lirn more music on Brass instrument and payd 1 [unclear—looks like *f*] for each hour. it is in U.S. Coin 11 Cent an hour." Jens must have enjoyed these opportunities to feed his craving to learn music, as he again exhibited his desire and determination to do so. Perhaps he received military pay for his one year in Copenhagen that made it possible for him to afford a room and music lessons.

I wanted to see the place where Jens had lived for a month in Copenhagen, to walk where he had walked, and to imagine another portion of his life. I searched in vain for *Vaiebro Fellevei Noll* on maps, in atlases, and online. Then I consulted the life history of Hans Christian, Jens's brother, which says he had lived in Copenhagen at Folledvei #4 with a roommate.[27] In 2014, Richard and I stayed in Værløse in the northern outskirts of Copenhagen at a bed and breakfast farm. In the guest dining room at breakfast, Eva, our hostess, sat at the end of our table and studied both my map of Copenhagen and my notes. With those notes upside down to me on the table, I realized that *Noll* could possibly be read as *No. 4* or *No. 11*. A closer study of Jens's handwriting showed the left side of the *V* in *Vaibro* actually had a thin upstroke, thus rendering it as an *N* for *Naibro* and indicating that possibly it referred to Copenhagen's Nørrebro neighborhood that encompassed a Fælledvej street—probably Jens's Fellevie and Hans's Folledvie—that we located on the map.

Later in the day as we walked the busy sidewalks of downtown Copenhagen, we stopped to study the city map. Pedestrians parted around us and traffic whizzed past while we tried to puzzle out how to get to Nørrebro. A young woman pushing a bicycle stopped and asked if she could help us. When we pointed on the map to Nørrebro, she said it wasn't far and that if she were going there, she could walk that distance in thirty minutes. When she said the old buildings were still standing and the neighborhood was still in central Copenhagen, I was delighted. She also explained the train and bus routes and stations in that area. After she went on her way, we decided not only that we likely couldn't match her thirty-minute pace but also it was getting too late in the day to start such a round-trip walk. A better idea seemed to be that the next morning when we took the train from the farm into the city, we would get off at the nearby Nørreport Station she had pointed out to us.

In the morning after Eva served us a wonderful Danish breakfast—cold cuts, cheese, rolls, soft-cooked eggs in Danish egg cups, yogurt with fruit and nuts, sliced peppers and tomatoes and cucumbers, juice, tea, coffee, and a foil-wrapped oblong of chocolate—we rode the train into Copenhagen and got off at Nørreport Station. We walked west along Frederiksborggade, crossed the Dronning (Queen) Louises Bro (Bridge) between canal segments of Peblinge Lake and Sortedams Lake, where graceful swans swam on the blue waters in the sunny morning, and then we continued on Nørrebrogade. (All three named sections comprise one continuous street.) Finally we turned right onto Fælledvej, a short avenue lined on both sides by brick buildings of various colors and widths, exhibiting heights of three to five stories, with one church located at the south end and two churches at the north end. Our No. 4 sat on the corner to our right as we turned onto the street. It was three stories high, constructed of a rose/rust/adobe-color brick, with a black wrought-iron gated entrance to a courtyard behind the building. It was formerly an apartment building, but at the time of our visit was a Røde Cors Butik—a Red Cross secondhand shop.

A plaque on the front wall in Danish caught our attention, and we asked a passerby to translate for us. He said the plaque memorializes the Swedish soldiers who died in a storm and were buried there in 1659. I assumed it was a respectful tribute to foreigners in freak weather but later learned that *storm* was also a word used for one of the Sweden-Denmark battles from 1658 to 1660. In fact, Copenhagen was assaulted by Sweden on 11 February 1659, the date on the plaque, and Knud J. V. Jespersen says, "the Swedish troops laid siege to [Copenhagen]…and attempted to storm it."[28] The Danes and Swedes battled regularly for centuries, and those commemorated on this plaque were not hapless sailors lost in a storm at sea but marauding Swedish invaders lost in a storm attack who had died at Copenhagen's North Rampart in the Assault on Copenhagen.[29] The plaque translated reads: *In memory of the Copenhagen Siege. Under this property rests the remains of the Swedish Soldiers who were killed during the storm on Nørre Wall* [or Gate] *of 11 February 1659.* The plaque predated Jens, and he probably saw it as he lived and walked on this street, humming the music he was learning to play on his brass instruments.

We told the women on staff in the secondhand shop at No. 4 Fælledvej why we were there, and they made us most welcome. They took us out the side door into the courtyard so we could see the back and sides and windows of the building. Inside, they let us go up the curved, ornately banistered staircase to the second level, where the former apartments had been. Although the rooms were filled with merchandise, it was fun to try to decipher the layout of the rooms and to imagine where Jens might have "taken a room" of his brother Hans.

After Richard and I returned to Oregon, I pondered the difference between the "No. 11" in Jens's sketch, and the "No. 4" in Hans's history. Was Hans's room in building No. 4 and Jens's room down the street on the opposite side in building No. 11? LaRelia said Hans had a reputation as a meticulous record keeper, so wouldn't his written No. 4 be the most reliable? Or could Hans's historian have misread a No. 11 as a No. 4? The number Jens wrote in his sketch is clearly an "11" (eleven), but a notation following that one states that "11" (eleven) cents was the price he paid for music lessons. Could he have accidentally written the identical number for each statement while his mind was pondering something else? I wanted to go back to Denmark to check it out, but I never dreamed we would.

After our cruise the following year, however, Richard and I again went to Copenhagen, returned to Fælledvej, and paid attention this time to building No. 11 across the street and north a few buildings from No. 4. The five-story, rosy-peach building had a small café at street level and was topped with three dormer windows. My guess for the street level in 1866 would be a glossy lobby with a wall of mailboxes and an ornate staircase.

Which building did Jens live in? I am unable to say with any certainty. I can say, though, that the neighborhood must have had some gentility about it at the time. Jens might have strolled among the modest buildings lining this street, visited the old churches that bookended the neighborhood, and watched swans on the nearby canal. He must have enjoyed being near his brother, being finished with his unit of military training, and best of all, taking more music lessons.

❦

His month came to an end, though, and Jens says, "after that i left Kjöbenhavn for home and Went unto a town Named Bregninge to my Onkel for 2 Weeks." I wonder what Jens considered "home" as he left Copenhagen? I don't know who his uncle in Bregninge might have been, but the village has a beautiful red brick kirke that was standing while he spent time with this part of his family.

Jens continues his journal with "after Which i concloodit to Lirning Clooh making." One transcriber took this word to be "cloak" but also put "(clog?)" immediately after it. Later in the sketch, Jens uses the term *clog making*, so my best guess is that *clooh* means "clog." Working between the two languages of Danish and English is complicated because a specific letter in English will have one pronunciation, while the same letter in Danish might have a completely different sound. For example, the town name of Jyderup seemed fairly straightforward as Jie-der-up, but Danish people corrected me. The word sounds like Yeerderuoop, rolled around deep in the back of the throat before escaping through the teeth and lips. Even when I tried to say it correctly, the Danes didn't recognize what I was saying until after I had spelled it, which I did in a small tour group at the five-spired Church of Our Lady in Kalundborg. Then the group exclaimed en masse, "Ah! Yeerderuoop!" I emailed two Danish women (Aase Beaulieu and Kaja Voldbæk) about the puzzling word *clooh*, and though both tried diligently to interpret it, neither felt she could do so confidently. Jens was writing in his adopted language of English and possibly blended his native Danish in this case. So for our purposes, *clog* it is.

To learn this skill of clog making, Jens says, "i then made rancement With Ole Petersen, Holmstrup to lirn in two month"—probably November and December 1866.

❧

What did *clog making* mean? Richard and I met with Karen Margrethe Nielsen, the secretary to the Jyderup Kirke priest, at her office on Tuesday, 8 July 2014, where she graciously spent nearly an hour answering my questions as she sat at her desk using her computer to find answers and maps. I told her that Jens had learned clog making from an Ole Petersen in nearby Holmstrup, and I asked if anyone in the area could explain how clogs were made back in 1866.

She cocked her head and looked off into the distance and thought for quite some time—long enough that I was sure the answer would be no. Instead she eventually said, "There's a craft store in Buerup which isn't too far from here. Local people create things and put them in the store to sell. There used to be a man there who made clogs. I think his name is Gert." She didn't think he made them anymore, but he might be there to talk with. She found a map online and printed it off for us.

Signs advertising the craft shop appeared along the road at the outskirts of the small town of Buerup. We parked across the road from the shop and went inside. A woman who spoke a little English greeted us immediately. The shop opened into a large L-shaped room and also had a back room and an upper level. Display tables filled the rooms, loaded with a rainbow of color from glittery doll clothes, carved wooden bowls and birdhouses, glass objects, paintings of scenery and people and religious icons, crocheted toy animals and purses, baby clothes, earrings, necklaces, woven baskets, candles in all colors, honey, hats, slippers, decorative pillows, platters, and trays.

Two or three other women also tended the shop, and a gray-haired man wearing dark-rimmed glasses stood at the back of the main room. We asked the woman who had greeted us if there were a Mr. Gert with whom we could speak, and the man came forward, smiling. He spoke only a little English, and unfortunately we spoke no Danish, but the woman stayed close and interpreted for us.

I explained that the secretary at the Jyderup Kirke had sent us, that my great-grandfather had studied clog making in Holmstrup in 1866, and that I wanted to know what clogs were like then and how they had been made.

The woman said that four years earlier, Mr. Gert and the shop had gotten rid of all the clogs and the tools used in making them due to the rise in preference for, and machine production of, modern plastic clogs. No one wanted the traditional clogs anymore. She explained that the handmade clogs were constructed of real leather and wood, that alder was preferred because it is very light, but maple was sometimes used.

Disappointed, I wandered into the back room full of art and crafts and discovered a television on the wall playing a video of Mr. Gert teaching a class on modern clog making in Danish. Mr. Gert and the woman followed and watched with me, explaining mostly in Danish what was happening in the film. Richard came over, got my attention, and motioned for me to follow him. I didn't want to rudely walk away, so I signaled "just a minute" and watched a moment longer.

When an appropriate break occurred, I went in search of Richard who then led me through the back displays and up a few stairs into a room where racks of hangers held handmade clothing in luxurious fabrics. In the middle of the room, on a wooden stand supporting an alder log about a yard long, perched a pair of golden-hued wooden clogs, handmade in the old style, each wedged into a cutout space in the log for display. The log was the exact circumference for creating a pair of clogs like Jens made entirely by hand. I was delighted! As well as grateful that Richard is insatiably curious.

A metal tool—a long-handled *t* (like a lower-case letter t) with a spoon-like scoop at the bottom and cross-handles near the top—projected from the opening of one clog. The woman caught up with us then and showed us how the tool was used to scoop the wood out from inside the clog. She explained that the blunt end of the tool would be braced against the stomach on a shield of leather while a shoemaker was holding and working with the adjacent handles. Later I saw a photograph of a worker who had a sheet of leather about ten inches square, with a cord attached at two adjacent corners and slipped over his head, to rest around his neck and hold the shield in place. Then Mr. Gert arrived, picked up the tool, and began to pantomime the scooping. He and the woman seemed surprised to have forgotten these historic clogs were there! Or maybe they were surprised to realize what I had been asking. I took a video with my phone as he proceeded to demonstrate how the tool worked by scooping from the center of the clog, scooping from the right, and scooping from the left, accompanied by his own lovely stream of musical Danish. He finished with that tool and put it away next to similar scoops of differing sizes.

Next he picked up a hatchet, removed a clog from its display, braced the heel of the clog against the log, and supporting the clog by one hand holding the toe, he started to mime with the hatchet how the outside of the clog was shaped. He made striking motions on the sides of the clog, then on the sole, the toe, the heel, and the arch. He indicated that the scooping was done after the outside shaping. He replaced the hatchet near others of varying sizes and wedged the clog back into the log with a triangular piece of wood. He seemed excited to be talking about traditional clog making.

Mr. Gert told us through the interpreter that evidence of clogs, including those on the feet of saints in paintings, goes back to 1150, the earliest renderings found so far. People wore wooden clogs over their expensive leather shoes, and the half-moon strip of leather across the forward edge of the opening protected those shoes as they were inserted into the clogs. In the old times, walkways and streets were muddy, and clogs allowed for better movement in the mud and in the fields while protecting leather shoes.

When I asked Mr. Gert if he had made the clogs he was wearing, he lifted the cuff of his pants leg and showed us his clogs were plastic and that he was not wearing shoes inside them. Then he made a joke about times changing and his changing with them. We had found him just in time.

As we started to leave the charming craft store, the women and Mr. Gert followed us out the door with smiles and farewells, and it was sweet. After we got into the car and were waving goodbye, Richard commented that they would be talking about us at dinner that night. Only then did I realize how hard it must have been for Mr. Gert to give up making the traditional clogs because no one cared anymore. For him to give up a craft he loved, and then to have Americans show up in a French car wanting to know how it was done, must have, as Richard said, "made his day." It made my day too, and I so appreciated having knowledge in place of my questions about what Jens had made and how. Thanks to Mr. Gert—this delightful artisan—I have a deeper understanding of how hard my ancestor Jens worked. Making clogs was no easy task.

Jens completed his clog-making lessons and continued: "after Which i i [*sic*] Went to Board at Jens Christensens in Axelholm [the small village of his birth] Whose Daughter Karen Marie i hade formed an aquintency With and on the 20th Day of Apr 1867 i maried Karen Marie Christensen, Datter of Jens Christensen." Marriage is such an important event, yet Jens does not say where or by whom the ceremony was conducted, whether it was in church or civil, how they traveled, whether anyone accompanied them, or if they had a celebration of some sort afterward. He says so much yet leaves so much unsaid with his modest understatement.

Wondering whether Jens and Karen Marie had been married in the Jyderup Kirke near Akselholm, I asked the priests there in 2015 if they had a record of Jens and Karen Marie's marriage. Priest Henriette Bach Barkholt looked up the date on her computer and showed me that no marriages at all had taken place in the Jyderup Kirke or in the Holmstrup Kirke during April of 1867. She suggested checking the records at the church in the birthplace of the bride—Starreklinte—because it was traditional to marry in the presence of the bride's family. But that family no longer lived at Starreklinte at the time of the marriage. Kaja later found the following record:

Marriage: Jyderup 20 April 1867
Bachelor Jens Nielsen, 25 years old, Axelholm, and
Karen Marie Jensen, 22 years old, Jyderup
Sponsors/Witnesses/Guarantors:
Jens Hansen, Svebølle, and
Jens Christensen, Axelholm
Married in the church 20 April 1867[30]

I loved finding out where they were married and that Karen Marie had her father as a witness. But I wondered about the Jens Hansen as witness. I emailed Kaja and asked if the record showed relationships, and whether this man could be a relative I didn't know about. She responded that the record does show, in error, Jens Hansen. However, she had found a different record that shows:

Bachelor Jens Nielsen, 25 Years old, in Axelholm and
Karen Marie Jensdatter, 22 years old, in Jyderup
Sponsors/Witnesses/Guarantors:
Niels Hansen, Svebølle, and
Jens Christensen, Axelholm[31]

This makes more sense that Jens also had his father as witness. It is easy to see how a recorder could have made a simple error if copying from a record into a book—jotting down the groom's given name or the bride's father's name instead of the name of the groom's father. Or, in a handwritten record, the names of Jens and Niels could each have been easily misread for the other. I have seen some of the handwriting! Perhaps the priests in Jyderup were looking in a wrong place for that marriage date. Kaja saved me fruitless searches in Viskinge and Starreklinte, and I appreciate not only her finding the information but also her searching further to clarify the witness.

Little is known about Karen Marie Jensdatter/Christensen prior to her marriage to Jens and their life together. Family records show that she was born in Starreklinte, Vallekilde, Holbæk, Denmark on 19 April 1845, to Jens Christensen and Kirsten Hansen. Starreklinte is near the sea and offers lovely glimpses of the blue waters as one drives through the golden farms of the area.

Interestingly, a christening record shows an earlier birth date for her:

Karen Marie Jensdatter, born 18 April 1845 [one day's difference—why?]
Parents: Jens Christensen and Kirsten Hansdatter
Ane Cathrine Rasmusdatter carried the child

> Sponsors: Farmer (Husmand) [crofter] Jens Pedersen and wife (Jens
> Pedersen's wife is Karen Hansdatter, a sister to Kirsten)
> Farmer Jens Pedersen
> Tenant Mads Christensen, Bjergene [possibly an uncle]

A christening date for Karen Marie is shown on a Family Group Record as 8 June 1845 in Vallekilde, Holbæk, Denmark.[32]

Karen Marie likely completed the compulsory curriculum, passed her exams, and took communion when she was fourteen years old. She would have received a servant's conduct book and been eligible to work in various indoor and outdoor jobs on farms or in homes in the surrounding area. Perhaps the "aquintency" Jens had made with her came about when they were working on neighboring farms or even on the same farm.

I had thought Karen Marie was a farmer's daughter and probably knew how to do various kinds of chores on the family farm and in the home. I thought her family must have been above poverty to have their own farm and to hire Jens to work and board there. However, Jens did not say he worked for Jens Christensen but only that he *boarded* there. Indeed the 1850 census for Vallekilde shows Jens Christensen, Kirsten Hansdatter, and their children: Hans Jensen, ten; Lars Peter Jensen, eight; and Karen Marie Jensdatter, five; at the *teglværket*, or brick factory. Jens Christensen's occupation is listed as *inderste, arbejdsmand ved værket* and loosely translates as "innermost worker by the piece."[33]

Just three years later, the records show that tenant Jens Christensen and his wife, Kirsten Hansdatter, left Vallekilde 7 August 1853 for Axelholm.[34] Another record shows that they moved for the purpose of working at the brick factory at Delhoved, a forest between Jyderup and Holmstrup, near Lake Skarresø.[35] Karen Marie would have been around eight years old when they moved. She was not, then, a farmer's daughter but a brick worker's daughter.

※

My sisters, Carla and LaRelia, in the Ogden, Utah, area, knew approximately six descendants, or spouses of deceased descendants, of Jens and Karen Marie when I started this project: sisters LuDean Hawes Carroll and Helen Hawes Stuart; Dale Hawes and his wife, Joyce Hawes; and Iris Peterson, who had been married to Verlo Peterson, and Iris's son, Val Peterson—all descendants through Louisa Hansen Peterson. These people generously shared various historical materials with us, but when we requested more information about Karen Marie, they responded that they had none. Some of her descendants believe that her not having learned

English was a contributing factor in her neither telling them stories nor leaving a journal. Some have also mentioned the expense and scarcity of paper and ink during her lifetime.

❦

I noticed that a number of marriages in the family history—including Jens and Karen Marie's marriage—were followed by a possibly early birth of the first baby. So I asked Lisbeth, our hostess in Kalundborg, over breakfast in her guest dining room in July 2015, if being pregnant before marriage carried a stigma in those days. She explained that in the old days, a couple would become engaged for a period of six months, during which time they would "try each other out," and if the bride was pregnant at the marriage ceremony, it was cause for celebration. She added that later, public opinion changed and pregnancy before marriage became severely looked down upon. "And now, today," she said with a flip of her hand, "anything goes and nobody cares!" So if Jens and Karen Marie were already expecting their first baby when they got married, they had reason for joy.

At this point in their lives, newly married and expecting a baby, Jens and Karen Marie became interested in the Church of Jesus Christ of Latter-day Saints, colloquially—and sometimes epithetically—referred to as the Mormon Church. This American church had come into existence in 1830, twelve years before Jens was born and thirty-seven years before he and Karen Marie married. Karen Marie's father and mother had already joined this church, but for reasons unknown to me, their children had chosen to wait.

What was this new religion? And how would it dramatically change the trajectory of their lives?

❦

Prior to Jens's birth, events had taken place in the United States that would affect religious choices he would make when he encountered the Church of Jesus Christ of Latter-day Saints later as an adult. As the Nielsen family adjusted to baby Jens's arrival in 1842, they probably had no knowledge of this church because its missionaries had not yet arrived in Denmark.

Joseph Smith was born in 1805 in Sharon, Vermont, and his family settled in Manchester, New York, when he was fourteen. Smith wrote that a year after their arrival in Manchester, or around 1820, a religious revival started and the ministers of the various sects competed for converts. Several in his family joined the Presbyterian Church, while he leaned toward the Methodists. He wrote, "In the midst of this war of words and tumult of opinions, I often said to myself: What is to be done? Who of all these parties are right; or, are they all wrong together? If any one of them be right, which is it, and how shall I know it?"[36]

Young Joseph read in James, "If any of you lack wisdom, let him ask of God, that giveth to all men liberally, and upbraideth not; and it shall be given him."[37] So he sequestered himself in a grove of trees near his family's farm and prayed earnestly to know which church was right. His own writings describe a vision in which he saw:

> a pillar of light…above the brightness of the sun…. When the light rested upon me, I saw two personages, whose brightness and glory defy all description, standing above me in the air. One of them [spoke] unto me, calling me by name and said—pointing to the other—"This is My Beloved Son. Hear Him!"[38]

In answer to his question about which church was right, he was told to join none of them. He was also told many things he did not write, and apparently he knew then that he had been called to a particular work.

As word of his vision of God and Christ spread, Smith became the target of much persecution, but he said, "I was led to say in my heart: Why persecute me for telling the truth? I have actually seen a vision; and who am I that I can withstand God, or why does the world think to make me deny what I have actually seen? For I had seen a vision; I knew it, and I knew that God knew it, and I could not deny it, neither dared I do it; at least I knew that by so doing I would offend God, and come under condemnation."[39]

Smith recounted that when he was eighteen years old, an angel named Moroni visited him and told him of gold plates, covered with inscriptions containing the fullness of the gospel of Jesus Christ, buried in nearby Hill Cumorah. After several years of annual tutoring visits from Moroni, Smith was given access to the gold plates, the inscriptions on which he translated as *The Book of Mormon*, named for the man who scribed the history of his own time and abridged other records that are preserved and included. Following the publication of this book, Smith organized The Church of Jesus Christ on 6 April 1830, and in 1838, the words "of Latter-day Saints" were added to the name. Its members believed the new religion restored the organization and ordinances of the church that Jesus Christ had established during his life on earth and that had been lost after the deaths of his apostles and the disappearance of the priesthood of God from the earth.

After this congregation of church members had moved and settled in Ohio, Smith described a visitation in the Kirtland temple from the prophet Elijah, who appeared in fulfillment of Malachi: "Behold, I will send you Elijah the prophet before the coming of the great and dreadful day of the Lord: And he shall turn the heart of the fathers to the children, and the heart of the children to their fathers."[40] Elijah conveyed to Smith the sealing powers of the priesthood that had been lost, and which, among other things, would allow couples to be married not just "until death do you part" but "for time and eternity." This concept was of great importance, as it provided the assurance that after death, couples and families could be reunited forever. Their belief in this sealing power for time without end played an important role in decisions some members, including Jens, would make during later historical developments.

Smith wrote a series of thirteen statements known as "The Articles of Faith of The Church of Jesus Christ of Latter-day Saints" to explain what this new church believed and taught. The articles include the basic beliefs of faith in God, Jesus Christ, and the Holy Spirit as well as baptism by immersion, revelation, freedom of worship for all humans, and obedience to the laws of the land. The set ends with Article 13: "We believe in being honest, true, chaste, benevolent, virtuous, and in doing good to all men.... If there is anything virtuous, lovely, or of good report or praiseworthy, we seek after these things."[41] The basic teachings of this new church focused on striving to follow the example of Christ, serving others, and being good people.

One of the more difficult concepts Smith later introduced, one that tried the faith of even some of the most devoted members, was the order of plural marriage: a man's taking of an additional wife or wives after marrying his first wife, as practiced in the Old Testament by Abraham, Jacob, Elkanah, Rehoboam, Abijah, David, and Solomon.[42] He said he had received a revelation regarding the reestablishment or restoration of this order on 12 July 1843, when baby Jens was one year old, and Smith shared this information with a small, select group of devout people who apparently began to practice the principle privately while denying it publicly. One of those devout members of the Church with whom the revelation was shared was Brigham Young, who later expressed his feelings about it this way:

> Some of these my brethren know what my feelings were at the time Joseph revealed the doctrine; I was not desirous of shrinking from any duty, nor of failing in the least to do as I was commanded, but it was the first time in my life that I had desired the grave, and I could hardly get over it for a long time. And when I saw a funeral, I felt to envy the corpse its situation, and to regret that I was not in the coffin.[43]

In spite of his initial repugnance, Young did eventually capitulate and married a number of additional wives.

The members of the new Church gradually migrated again, some arriving in Missouri as early as 1833. Here the dramatic increase in Church membership—much of it from immigration—along with its perceived intention to become politically independent, its antislavery stand while situated in a slave state, and the likely local awareness of its practice of plural marriage, all resulted in hostile feelings toward the Mormon Church. Following a skirmish—the Battle of Crooked River—on 25 October 1838 between armed Mormons and the state militia known as the Missouri Guard, Missouri governor Lilburn Williams Boggs issued the Extermination Order dated 27 October 1838, to his military officers:

> Your orders are therefore to hasten your operation with all possible speed. The Mormons must be treated as enemies, and must be exterminated or driven from the state if necessary for the public peace—their outrages are beyond all description.[44]

The day after the Extermination Order was given, violent outrages were hammered upon the Saints:

> A company of so-called militia…fell upon the unsuspecting Saints of the Haun's Mill settlement. Seventeen were massacred outright. Twelve escaped into the woods severely wounded. The houses were looted and women insulted.[45]

Eventually the Missourians forcefully—sometimes burning the Mormons' homes and crops—drove them from their settlements in that state. Boggs's Extermination Order was not rescinded until *138 years later*, as part of the commemoration of the 200th birthday of the United States.

Lorenzo Dow Young, brother of Brigham Young and father of Franklin Wheeler Young (who will later figure in Jens's story), had an experience that illustrates the Missouri conflict. Young lived in the Mormon settlement of Far West, Missouri, with home, animals, and crops growing well in 1838. One day he was out working in his fields when a man from town came galloping up on a horse that was sweating profusely from its arduous exertion. The rider told Young that twenty men in the nearby town of Gallatin were planning to come in a few hours to lock him and his family inside their house and then to burn his house down. Young thanked him, and then the rider raced away, taking a different route back, having risked his own life to give this warning. Young got his wife and four children—and what bedding, clothing, food, and utensils they could grab—loaded up the wagon, and fled. They were never permitted to return to their home and crops, nor were they remunerated in any way for the value of the property. This left the family, and others robbed in the same way, destitute. The US Army also stole two of Lorenzo's oxen and used them for beef, never making good on their promise to pay for them.[46]

The body of the Mormon Church fled from Missouri to Illinois, where they established the city of Nauvoo on the banks of the Mississippi River and prospered for a time. However, again anti-Mormon sentiment arose. A history of my paternal ancestor who lived in Nauvoo at the time states:

> During the winter of 1843–44, mob activity and persecutions increased. A police force was organized and a watch kept around the city night and day to protect the Saints from their enemies. There was dissension within the church as well as persecutions from outside.[47]

The dissatisfaction among a number of members resulted in their apostatizing. Even some important leaders fell away.

Jens had just turned two years old in Denmark in June 1844, when in America, Joseph Smith was charged with inciting a riot that allegedly destroyed a printing press at the *Nauvoo Expositor* after it published information about polygamy and slandered him. He gave himself up and was put in an upstairs cell at Carthage Jail in the county seat, accompanied by his brother, Hyrum Smith, as well as his friends, John Taylor and Willard Richards. While the Smith brothers awaited trial, a mob of about 150 men—some with blackened faces to prevent recognition—stormed the jail. Some of the mob climbed the stairs and fired guns through the door, while others shot from the ground outside through the upstairs window. Joseph had a six-shooter that was quickly emptied with some misfiring in his ineffectual defense against the mob. The shots from the mob killed Hyrum and wounded John Taylor, though not fatally. Willard Richards survived, and in his account of the incident said:

> Joseph attempted as the last resort, to leap the…window…when two balls pierced him from the door, and one entered the right breast from without, and he fell outward, exclaiming, "O Lord, my God!" As his feet went out of the window, my head went in, the balls whistling all around. He fell on his left side, a dead man.[48]

Someone called out, "The Mormons are coming!" and though it wasn't true, the mob dispersed.

That time in Nauvoo is described in a brief history of my Great-great-grandmother Charlotte Amelia Van Orden West Peck, in my paternal family history:

> Charlotte and her family were present and mourned with the saints in Nauvoo when Joseph Smith and his brother Hyrum were martyred on June 27, 1844....
>
> The news soon spread through the city. Mourning was depicted on every countenance; that day was truly a day of mourning with the Saints. About three o'clock in the afternoon the procession was formed in the east of the city to receive the bodies of our martyred Prophet and Patriarch as carriages were sent to convey them to Nauvoo. We did not wait long before we saw them mournfully winding their way across the prairies. Their bodies were received with tears by the Saints and conveyed to the Mansion [Joseph and Emma's home] amidst the cries and lamentations of the people.[49]

Fearing theft and degradation of the bodies of their slain leaders, the people placed guards around them until the funeral. One guard, my ancestor William Van Orden, died two weeks later from an illness (bloody flux) believed to have been contracted while guarding the Smith brothers. His three-year-old son died one month later from the same cause.[50]

The enemies of the Mormon Church rejoiced that Joseph Smith was slain and assumed the Church would falter and die without his leadership. However, that did not happen. The members of The Church of Jesus Christ of Latter-day Saints continued their commitment to their faith, and the anti-Mormons in Nauvoo continued to persecute them.

After Joseph Smith's death, Brigham Young, who had been the President of the Quorum of the Twelve Apostles when Joseph Smith died, became President and Prophet of the LDS Church. He would eventually lead the Saints from their lovely city of Nauvoo, where, in a repeat of earlier Missouri history, non-Mormons were driving the Mormons out from their homes and property and burning their new temple.

My paternal history continues:

> Persecutions were worsening, and the exodus from Nauvoo began in February of 1846. The Saints were encouraged to sell their property and prepare to gather in the Rocky Mountains of the west. [The Nauvoo

properties sold at a fraction of their value.] The...families, along with other Saints, were forced to flee their beautiful Nauvoo, suffering the trials and hardships of the winter of 1846–7 at Winter Quarters.

The first pioneer company, led by Brigham Young, left Winter Quarters, Nebraska, on April 14, 1847 and arrived in the Salt Lake Valley on July 24, 1847.[51]

Several people from this family group, including young children, died during their time in Nauvoo and in Winter Quarters.

These Mormons who lived in Illinois, a state since 1818, were denied their rights as United States citizens and were literally driven from their homes, their temple, and their country. They traveled across the plains of the Midwest by wagons into Mexican territory, now the Salt Lake Valley, in waves following the first companies of 1847.

Of the arrival of the first party to the valley, Wilford Woodruff wrote:

> On the twenty-fourth I drove my carriage, with President Young [who was ill] lying on a bed in it, into the open valley, the rest of the company following. When we came out of the canyon [Emigration Canyon], into full view of the valley, I turned the side of my carriage around, open to the west, and President Young arose from his bed and took a survey of the country. While gazing on the scene before us, he was enwrapped in vision for several minutes. He had seen the valley before in vision, and upon the occasion he saw the future glory of Zion and Israel, as they would be, planted in the valleys of the mountains. When the vision had passed, he said, "...This is the right place. Drive on."[52]

This was the place Young had been shown in vision where his people could live, free from their tormentors, and build a new Zion, a holy city, dedicated to God. Those who had entered the order of plural marriage also hoped, no doubt, that since they were now in Mexican territory, they could practice their religion (particularly the tenet of plural marriage) peacefully, without harassment. Although the practice of polygamy was illegal in Mexico, Mexican authorities did not enforce the law.

The Mexican-American War from 1846 to 1848 resulted in the Treaty of Guadalupe Hidalgo that ceded a vast expanse of Mexican lands, including those areas upon which the Mormons had found refuge, to the Federal Government of the United States. The Salt Lake Valley became part of the Territory of Utah upon its creation in 1850. I find it painfully ironic that these people who had had their civil rights violated in Missouri and Illinois and who had been driven from their own country into a foreign country seeking peace, now found themselves once again—without having moved—subject to the same government from which they had briefly escaped. Instead of peace, further persecutions were coming.

At the time six-year-old Jens lost his mother in Denmark in 1848, members of the new Church of Jesus Christ of Latter-day Saints in America were eager to share the knowledge of this church they had joined. Missionaries began to travel within America and overseas to spread their message of hope. Erastus Snow, an apostle in the Mormon Church, along with Peter Olsen Hansen and two other men, were called by the Church presidency to serve as missionaries in Scandinavia.

> Hansen arrived first in Copenhagen on May 12, 1850, and immediately visited a Baptist congregation. The first Danish Mormon converts later came from that group. Elder[s] Snow, Forsgren, and Dykes arrived on June 13, 1850.... On August 12, eight men and seven women were baptized...near Copenhagen. The first Danish branch [ecclesiastical group] of about fifty members was organized in Copenhagen a month later.[53]

The church of state in Denmark was Lutheran, and the success of this conversion among the Baptists was in part because they were already outside the parameters of the state church.

The Mormon successes in proselytizing were possible partially because "on June 5, 1849, only months before the first LDS missionaries came to Denmark, King Frederik VII signed the new Danish Constitution, which guaranteed the people freedom of speech, press, and religion."[54] Even so, many Danes objected to the missionaries, and in some villages disrupted their meetings, drove them out, or jailed them. In spite of such persecution, the missionary work moved forward, and "when Elder Snow left Denmark for his return to Salt Lake City, at the end of twenty-two months, the Danish Church numbered 600 members. The Book of Mormon...had been translated and published in the Danish language."[55] The missionaries of the Church of Jesus Christ of Latter-day Saints had established roots that would later put forth tendrils into Jens's life.

※

At a large LDS General Conference in Salt Lake City in April 1852, the principle of plural marriage—previously known only to a few—was publicly announced to Church membership at large. As one would expect when something of this nature was introduced into a culturally monogamous society, reactions were mixed, varying from devout acceptance to incredulity expressed by both men and women who had somehow not previously been aware that a small number of people within the Church were practicing the principle—often in secret.

My own family gives proof that plural marriage was practiced by leaders in the Church prior to its announcement to the general membership in 1852. Among those who made the trek from Nauvoo across the plains in the second year of exodus was my paternal great-great-grandfather, Martin Horton Peck, who as a blacksmith had been asked to stay behind during the first year of the Mormon migration west so he could help prepare the wagon wheels of subsequent travelers. Peck had become a polygamist in Nauvoo before the westward movement. A list compiled by George D. Smith of 146 men of Nauvoo who had plural wives includes Martin Horton Peck.[56]

At the time plural marriage was announced in Salt Lake in 1852, Jens was ten years old in Denmark and had been without his mother for four years. He was beginning his first annual contract with a farmer.

✿

Back in the United States, where Mexican land had become US territory and the valley the Mormons inhabited had become the Utah Territory, President Abraham Lincoln signed the Morrill Anti-Bigamy Act into law on 8 July 1862. Sponsored by Justin Smith Morrill of Vermont, the act "prohibited plural marriage in the territories, disincorporated the Church, and restricted the Church's ownership of property to $50,000. Although Lincoln signed the bill, the nation was in the midst of the Civil War and he reportedly said, 'You tell Brigham Young if he will leave me alone, I'll leave him alone.'"[57] The Mormons had had only fifteen years of peace between their arrival in the Salt Lake Valley and the signing of this bill.

Though the Morrill Act was not strictly enforced, it did lay the groundwork for later persecution of those who participated in plural marriage as well as for passage of subsequent laws that clamped down ever more tightly on the Mormon Church and its members, even those who did not practice polygamy. Some say, "But they were breaking the law." However, the devout members who lived the principle of polygamy believed they were obeying the law of God and that their eternal position with him in the next life was more important than a rule of man that conflicted with God's higher requirements. Such conviction must have been part of what empowered these people to endure countless incredible harassments.

Jens was twenty years old, working on a farm in Jordløse, Denmark, at the time Lincoln signed the 1862 Morrill Act, and he likely had no knowledge of this law or of the Church of Jesus Christ of Latter-day Saints, and he certainly had no idea that groundwork was being laid and creating ripples that would eventually impact his life.

CHAPTER 6

JENS NIELSEN HANSEN'S LIFE SKETCH: PART III, 1867–1874

The substantial early growth of the Church of Jesus Christ of Latter-day Saints worldwide seems surprising when one considers the intense opposition usually exerted against it. What would cause a person to choose contrary to the opinion of family, friends, priest, and government in regard to a religious matter? In spite of external opposition, many people describe a significant experience that touched their hearts and served as a catalyst for their conversion to this new religion.

One example of such a life-altering experience is that of my paternal great-great-grandfather, Martin Horton Peck, recorded by my sister, MauRene Wiggins. She wrote that at the age of twenty-three in 1829, Peck was living with his wife in Danville, Vermont:

> when he heard of the Prophet Joseph Smith and the religion he espoused. He was not favorably impressed. At his house raising, Martin was critical of the Prophet and convinced his neighbors who were helping with the house raising to go with him after their day's work to break up a meeting the Prophet was planning to hold in the nearby woods that evening.[58]

Cherry Wolf, my neighbor since 1982 in Oregon who is also descended from Martin Horton Peck, shared from her family stories in 2008 that this group had taken tomatoes with them to pelt at Smith and his associates. MauRene continued:

> As the group approached the meeting place, the Prophet was speaking. The would-be troublemakers stopped at a distance to listen. Later, Martin bore testimony that he hadn't heard more than a few minutes of Joseph Smith's message before the Spirit bore witness to him that what the Prophet was saying was indeed true.[59]

Vernice Rosenvall comments on Peck's story in this way:

> Intending to cause a disturbance, he found himself converted instead.
>   Many times after[,] he was heard to testify that before the Prophet
> had spoken five minutes, [Peck] had received a thorough assurance
> of the Divinity of his mission, which testimony remained with him
> all his life.[60]

Shortly after this incident, Peck was baptized into the Church of Jesus Christ
of Latter-day Saints, and in spite of persecution and hardship, he spent the remainder of his life in unshakable commitment and devoted service to its tenets
and teachings.

I assumed Jens had met Mormon missionaries, and I wondered when and
how that had happened, but a note from Larry Christiansen suggested a different
story. Karen Marie's father had been baptized in 1856, followed by her mother
a year later in 1857, having chosen to wait until she was sure the decision was
right for her. When our Jens began boarding at Jens Christensen's early in 1867,
he was then living with an LDS couple. Perhaps that was his first contact with
the Church.

After Jens and Karen Marie were married in April, they apparently continued
to live with her parents in Axelholm. Jens must have worked throughout that
summer and into the labor of autumn because when harvest was finished, he
had free time to check out a Mormon meeting nearby. Perhaps he went to this
meeting because he was inspired by his parents-in-law to seek more knowledge
of their religion.

Mormon missionaries had been proselytizing in Denmark for seventeen years
when Jens became interested in the Church. He says in his life sketch that "after
Harvest i vent to the first Mormon Meething in a Settlement named Bakkerup.
Elder Gundersen Presided an i tok delight in the hymn: the Kindom of God is
again Restord to the Earth: and sins that i begine to lesten to the Gosbel a little."
At this meeting, he would likely have come in contact with missionaries—called
elders—if not before.

❦

While in Denmark in 2014, I wanted to see this town of Bakkerup, even though
I knew that much would have changed from the time Jens had been there nearly
150 years earlier. Richard and I turned off a main road onto Bakkerupvej, hoping
to find remnants of something that might have existed when Jens went to this

town for his first Mormon meeting. After driving a short distance—residential in nature and maybe a few blocks long—we had already passed through the town and crossed a railroad track. We turned around and drove back to see if we had missed a turn onto a main street, but we had not. An aerial photograph shows this small town surrounded by other villages and towns, with a church a short distance away. Probably Jens's meeting was held in someone's home, but we had no way of learning where it might have been or if it was still standing. I was contented, though, to briefly be in Bakkerup, a place of significance to Jens's story.

❧

Jens's sketch continues, "at the Evening of Dcbr 27th [1867] at elevn o clock our first son Where boren [Akselholm, Holmstrup, Holbaek, Denmark] and named Jens Peter Nielsen." The record shows Jens Peder Nielsen was born 28 December 1867 to Tenant Jens Nielsen and wife Karen Marie Jensen from Axelholm.[61] So eight months after Jens and Karen Marie married, their first child was born in Akselholm—the same birthplace as the baby's father. (The record shows this son's name as Jens *Peder*, yet Jens's sketch shows it as Jens *Peter*. Jens's life sketch was apparently written after his immigration to Utah, and that might explain why he used the Anglicized form of the name. The son also occasionally went by James. In this record, I will use whichever version of the name appears in the document or documents being cited.)

Jens's sketch says, "and about 6: Weeks after [the birth,] he Was in the Church of Jyderup to be Babtised after the fasion of the World." The record shows the baby's Lutheran baptism actually took place more like nine and one-half weeks after the birth, and was indeed in the Jyderup Kirke:

Jens Peder Nielsen
Baptized in Jyderup Church 8 March 1868
Parents: Jens Nielsen and wife Karen Marie Jensen in Axelholm
Sponsors: Forester Anders Andersen's widow from Delhoved
Farmer Mads Nielsen
Blacksmith Hans Jensen in Axelholm
Farmer Hans Jensen in Thorslunde [likely Karen Marie's brother]

After the baptism "it Became such a turreble Snow and Wend Storm and after that time [i] listened more to the Gosbel and rade more the Scribture." One can imagine a storm so intense it functioned as an omen encouraging deeper spirituality.

❦

On our first trip to Denmark, Richard and I found the Jyderup Kirke after aimlessly driving around. No one we had asked at the busy pizza place or on the street in town knew where the church was located! As we parked in the lot and walked onto the grounds, we saw that the tallest section of the church was constructed of variegated red brick, with several other sections built of what appeared to be the same brick but painted white, and all were roofed with red-orange tiles. The grounds held a patchwork of miniature family plots delineated by low hedges and gravel walkways, and each parcel displayed small headstones and various vibrant plants.

Much to our surprise, the building was open! We walked around inside the chapel, enjoying the quiet, the art, and the sense of sacred space. A book on a table in the entryway said the artwork in the church was from the 1400s, and the font was Romanesque. Given our American tear-it-down culture, this longevity of buildings stunned me. A plaque in the chapel listed the names of the priests through the years and the dates of the end of their tenure. The priest Lindhardt, who had been Jens's contemporary and had signed off on one of Jens's travels in his employment record, appeared on the plaque, along with his first name, Bendt, which was not in the record I had—a delightful discovery.

Seeing the font and knowing Jens and Karen Marie had been in the same place with little Jens Peter for his baptism created a tender moment. To stand in their footsteps and put my hand on the granite font made me feel a profound connection to them and to the long-distant past. Though the stone was cold to the touch, I was warmed by the knowledge that Jens had been in this exact place.

As we were leaving, an older man arrived outside, a workman planning to meet another man to repair a brick pathway. He knew more English than we knew Danish and was charming to visit with. He could not believe we were from the "oooo esss aaay" because we were driving a French car with French license plates. Soon a younger man arrived. In our snatches of broken conversation, we said we planned to come back tomorrow—Monday—to find a priest who could answer questions, but they told us Monday was a bad day to visit churches because it is the priest's day off after working all day Sunday. I enjoyed listening to the men speak Danish in between their addressing us in English, and I appreciated the local knowledge that enabled us to plan more effectively.

Nielen Hicks and Verba Petersen Haws, descendants of Jens and Karen Marie, compiled a history based on Jens's sketch with additions apparently based on their family records and stories. Verba's daughters, LuDean Hawes Carroll and Helen Hawes Stuart, generously shared a copy of their history with our family. In regard to baby Jens Peter's baptism in the Lutheran Church, the Hicks history says:

> This infant baptism rather puzzled [Jens and Karen Marie], and they began to investigate Mormonism more earnestly, becoming convinced that the Latter-day Saint belief compared more correctly with the teachings of the Bible than their church did.[62]

The history doesn't say whether Jens and Karen Marie questioned the necessity of baptism of innocent infants, or questioned the manner of the baptism being by sprinkling or pouring as in the Lutheran Church versus immersion as in the LDS Church, but their questioning interested me, and I wish Jens had provided more details in his sketch. The practice in the Church of Jesus Christ of Latter-day Saints is baptism by immersion at or after the age of eight, when children are considered old enough to understand the difference between right and wrong choices.

Whatever the catalyst for their conversions, less than two months after having their baby boy baptized in the Lutheran Church, Jens and Karen Marie were baptized into the LDS Church 22 April 1868—two different baptism methods just 7 ½ weeks apart. The juxtaposition of the two events and their methods intrigued me.

Each individual who joined the new American church had a uniquely personal reason for doing so. That reason may have varied from something dramatic, like a vision, to something so subtle as a quiet feeling. Thomas Tyler, an LDS ecclesiastical leader said in an Institute class in 1980 at the LDS Stake Center in Coeur d'Alene, Idaho: "We all want choirs of angels in our bedrooms, but what we get is a fifteen-watt light bulb." Sometimes day-to-day spiritual guidance comes softly, so one has to pay attention.

Although I have always been aware that my chain of grandparents and great-grandparents is composed of Mormon couples, only in my adult years did I realize that these converted individuals must have left another faith to become members of the LDS Church. Sometimes I say with a smile that my ancestors were religious rebels, but I truly respect their courage in leaving behind the familiar in order to demonstrate faith for a new church, frequently in spite of trying circumstances.

My father, Vernal William Fowler, came from the Peck Mormon pioneer family. Technically, pioneers were those who made the trip to Utah by wagon or handcart before train travel became possible. My mother, Flora Bjorkman Fowler, came from the Hansen and Bjorkman families who later arrived in Utah by train.

With this Mormon heritage, I didn't have to search—the religion was handed to me. Even so, for a time after I became a widow, my faith was deeply shaken.

My violin teacher, Tara Burke, in a lesson September 2012, commented that her mother has always said, "If you want to experience miracles in your life, do genealogy." After I started working on this family history project, many "coincidences" or synchronicities manifested themselves. Those serendipitous surprises, coupled with the incredible stories of devout and courageous people in the early history of the LDS Church and in my own family, lured me to an appreciation of this heritage and to a pondering of modern "minor miracles," or as my sisters say, "tender mercies." Due to these stories of faith and courage, and my fortuitous experiences in discovering information for this work, my fractured faith healed.

Jens didn't write of a specific experience or reason why he and Karen Marie chose to join the Mormon Church or why they were willing to forego any previous religious affiliations to do so, but something clearly brought about their decision to be baptized. Whether it was centered on their reasoning about infant baptism, or influenced by a storm they interpreted as an omen, or the message from a hymn, or just a persistent feeling, the sketch says, "on Apr 22—1868 one Year an 2 Days after We Was marreit[,] on the Evening at 11 o clock We Were Boght Babtised i the Lake Skareso' belo Chr. Petersens House of Eld[er] Gunderson and two Days after We Were Confirmed of Eld[er] Gundersen & N. P. Petersen now [at the time Jens wrote this] in Brigham and We lived at my wifes Parents House ontil the Month of June [1868]." (The Newton Ward Record says they were confirmed 23 April 1868, Jens by Niels Peter Petersen and Karen Marie by Elder Gundersen.) When Jens and Karen Marie joined the LDS Church, he was nearly twenty-six years old, she was nearly twenty-three, and their baby, Jens Peter, was four months old. This profound action would alter their life course significantly because subsequent major decisions would be driven by this one.

❧

Richard and I drove on a road that circled Lake Skarresø, the shimmering blue lake in which Jens and Karen Marie had been baptized into the Church of Jesus Christ of Latter-day Saints a century and a half earlier. We caught glimpses of the lake between buildings and greenery and searched for a spot where we could get a complete picture. As mentioned earlier, we stopped at Astrup farm and asked Niels Eriksen if he knew where we could drive to get a good view of the lake. He told us we could walk a path through the woods of Astrup, which began just at the end of the long building we were facing. He took us into his office in the low building and showed us a wall map that depicted the estate and its layout of buildings, company residences, trails, and the lake, so we had a mental image of the property, where we were, and where we would go.

We walked on a soft path through red-trunked woods under a green canopy in immense quiet. After a half mile or so, the path opened out at the grassy edge of the lake and gave us a wide-angle view. A dome of blue sky rose above a ring of white clouds around the lake, with low green hills on the other side. I gazed for a long time at the sparkling gray-blue lake, the water so clear I could see the rocks and pebbles on the bottom. I did not know where "below Chr. Petersen's house" had been on the lake for Jens's and Karen Marie's baptisms in 1868, but I imagined Jens and the officiating elder dressed in white and walking out into the water, the sacred words being said with Elder Gundersen's right hand raised heavenward as he spoke the baptismal ordinance words with his priesthood authority, then immersed Jens in the cold lake waters and brought him up out of the water a new person, a person whose whole life would be changed from that moment on.

Jens and Karen Marie each made a commitment in those scenic waters, a commitment requiring total dedication, a commitment that would alter their lives and eventually lead them to Utah. Even though there might have been additional motivations for leaving their country—such as persecution and poverty—their devotion stayed strong through their difficulties. Did they know yet that polygamy was being practiced in Utah? A number of missionaries who served in Denmark were polygamist Danes sent from Utah, so it is possible they knew, but Jens's taking a second wife ten years later likely had not entered their minds.

Both baptismal sites—the small Jyderup font where baby Jens Peter was sprinkled for baptism as a Lutheran and Lake Skarresø where Jens and Karen Marie's LDS immersion took place—held deep significance.

Jens's life sketch states, "on the Evening at 11 oclock we were boght Babtised." I had read and reread this sketch over the years, but not until I was checking the information in the sketch to include it in this story did I realize that 11 o'clock in the evening was *not* a metaphor. I called my sister LaRelia and asked if I was correct in my assumption that the baptisms were performed at night in order to avoid persecution. She said that in a letter from our grandfather Henry Albert Bjorkman, to our brother, LaMont, Henry had written that his own baptism in the icy seas off Copenhagen, on 10 February 1892, had been done at night, and our family's assumption had always been that this was to avoid persecution for participating in that ordinance.

Although Denmark allowed Mormon missionaries into the country to proselytize, there were frequent reports of harassment by ministers of other religions and also from some of the people.

A Scandinavian mission president wrote to Brigham Young in 1865:

> In Denmark we are enjoying all the liberty we can expect, the clergy, of course, doing their best to prejudice their parishioners against us, using all the circulating stories, lies and apostate letters they may pick up; but in spite of all this trash, the gospel of the kingdom is spreading to every nook and corner.... The Danes are not naturally a religious people, and do not read the Bible much; therefore, when in combat with the Elders, in the absence of Scriptural proofs, they sometime use striking arguments—namely fists, rocks and sticks, and occasionally disturb our meetings by rough and boisterous behavior; but, after all, the people are honest and upright as a general thing, and embrace the truth when they have had sufficient time to be enlightened.[63]

In spite of the oppression and persecution, many good things came from the work of the missionaries.

Erastus Snow, one of the first three LDS missionaries to Denmark, wrote in his journal:

> We did not advertise our meetings, but still our hall soon became filled, especially in the evenings, and we had confirmation nearly every Sunday: the baptizing we did in a quiet way, mostly week evenings, to avoid excitement.[64]

Andrew Jenson also acknowledged disturbances of various kinds as tormentors tried to break up the Mormon meetings:

> The brethren also appealed to the mayor and chief of police for protection, but the police looked through their fingers at these proceedings of the mob and neglected to do their duty [and] apparently encouraged the mob in their acts of violence.[65]

Richard and I had visited Lake Skarresø on a sunny July day, but Jens and Karen Marie were baptized in its waters during the night hours in April. Sunset would have taken place around 8:30 p.m., so the area must have been pitch black. Did they have candles or lanterns to light the way? Did the mentioned Chr. Petersen have a way of lighting his section of lakeshore? The average temperature for nearby Copenhagen on that day of the year is a low of 36 degrees Fahrenheit and a high of 50 degrees Fahrenheit, so it might have been chilly, but the lake not frozen.

❧

As Richard and I walked away from the sun-sparkled lake and meandered along the soft trail back through the magical forest toward the farm buildings, we passed a small pickup truck with the Astrup farm logo on it, parked on the right and just off the trail. Soon a heavy-set man jumped into the truck and drove after us. As he pulled up alongside us on my right, I said to him through his open window, "I'll bet you're here to see what we're up to." We were, after all, on private property. He laughed and said yes. When I told him my great-grandfather had worked at Astrup in 1864, and that Niels Eriksen had told us we could look around, the driver smiled, waved, and sped off.

The perimeter patrol by truck impressed upon me that this private property was not generally open to the public, and that it had been a generous gift of the owner through Niels Eriksen to allow us to take this walk. What a treat to have been at that perfect spot from which to view the sparkling lake of Jens's and Karen Marie's baptisms!

❧

Just three weeks after Jens and Karen Marie were baptized, Jens's father and stepmother had their sixth child, Carl Christian Nielsen, born on 10 May 1868.

In his sketch, Jens says he again had military duty: "on the 12 day of the Month [likely June 1868] i had to apere at the army in Kjobenhavn and there i was sent together With the rest to Jydland [Jutland] to a plase they call Hal one mile Danish from the city of Veeborg [Viborg] We remaind there about 35 Dayes and then sent back to the city of Kjobenhavn the whole time incloodit 45 Dayes." Karen Marie and little Jens Peter probably continued to stay with her parents during Jens's military obligation. He wrote, "i came back first in August. i then mad our livelihood by makin Clogs and by Music," indicating that he was not farming at this time. Another line was inserted in a different hand, floating below the line in which he mentioned "Jydland," that says, "also choir leader in Denmark." Jens had worked hard to learn music and then used his musical knowledge and talents in both paid and volunteer service to others.

Jens's sketch says that "on the 1 of May 1869 My Wife hired to a big Farmer Hansen in a place call Kongsdall and 8 Dayes after[,] i hired to the same place and We sirved there until the 1st of May 1870." Jens and Karen Marie worked on the Kongsdal farm for a period of one year, and it seems probable they also had their toddler son, Jens Peter, with them. Jens doesn't say what their respective responsibilities were, but perhaps he worked on the farm itself while Karen Marie worked inside the house. Who looked after the little one while they worked? Jens didn't mention their pay as he had in regard to his own earlier employments, but likely the farmer paid them and provided room and board. When they finished this contract in 1870, Jens was one month away from his twenty-eighth birthday and Karen Marie had just turned twenty-five.

❧

As Richard and I prepared for our first visit to Denmark in July 2014, I was startled to discover on my oversized map of Sjælland or Zealand the name *Kongsdal* with a small green triangular tree next to it. Could that possibly be the same place Jens had mentioned in his sketch? But he said it was a farm, and the map showed it as a forest. Full of questions, I put it on my list of places to find.

The skies were blue in Denmark that summer, with yellow daylight from 3:30 a.m. until 10:30 p.m. and unseasonably high temperatures. Sjælland (alternate spelling: *Zealand*) is a low, rolling island with checkerboards of farm crops in golds and greens, and slender deciduous trees with fluttery canopies, and red brick buildings everywhere, interspersed with homes painted "Danish yellow" (a cross between lemons and French's mustard). And the Danes were incredibly helpful everywhere we asked questions.

On a Sunday in July, we programed the GPS of our rented Renault for the village of Undløse, located at the end of Road 231, the road shown bisecting the Kongsdal area on the map. As we drove, we passed what looked like an old monastery with a house nearby. We stopped at the house and knocked. A woman, too far away to hear us, was putting a few horses through routines near a large pond. We continued driving as the road laced its way into a lovely forest of slender, medium-tall trees, where the sunshine on the canopy turned it a lovely yellow-green that glowed.

Soon we came to two houses sitting side by side near the left edge of the road. We stopped and knocked at each one, but no one came. We continued driving south but saw no signs or administrative buildings to identify the woods as Kongsdal. Unsure how far the trees would continue or whether Kongsdal was still ahead, I kept waiting to take photographs. Soon the trees gave way to farmlands, and we arrived at the village of Undløse, obviously past Kongsdal. We stopped at the side of the road and asked two women who were walking on the sidewalk—one pushing a baby carriage—whether the forest we had passed through was Kongsdal, and they said yes. I wanted to go back for a photo, but it was dinnertime, and both Richard and I were tired and hungry, so we continued on to find a place to eat and to return to our bed and breakfast for the night.

Checking my notes later, I learned that the village of Undløse was also spelled Ondløse and was the village that Jens had been required to sign into and out of with the priest at the beginning and end of his Kongsdal contract. We had missed not only a photograph of the forest but also a visit to the kirke in Undløse that had played a role in Jens's and Karen Marie's lives. I desired intensely to return for both, but didn't know how we could fit that into our remaining tight time schedule.

After a visit to Sweden, we returned to Sjælland. On our last day there, I wanted to visit the remaining villages pertaining to family history *and* to return to Kongsdal for a photograph. We drove through golden farmlands, enjoyed intermittent views of the sea, and stopped in two villages, finding only one kirke open. I had three more villages on my list that pertained mostly to Jens's wives. I wanted to see them, but I began to feel a sense of urgency for a photograph of the Kongsdal forest. So I abandoned plans to stop in the remaining villages and programmed the GPS—this time with the word *Kongsdal*—and off we went.

The GPS took us back on the same road and through the same scenic woods, past the monastery-like structure, past the two houses, and then indicated a fishhook right turn and ended. I was disbelieving because I knew there was no road there. But suddenly the hint of a dirt road snaked into thick woods, so I gave the wheel a sharp right crank, and we abruptly found ourselves past the trees and inside a huge open estate with an imposing brick house, farm buildings of various types and sizes, and a cobbled drive that bobbled us along as we continued forward. None of this had been visible from the road due to the forest.

I parked in the shade of a small tree, a bit away from the huge house with its subtle signs discouraging trespass. We walked toward a two-story building—constructed of large rocks on the lower level and of painted red bricks on the upper one—with two cars car parked by it and an open door, leading us to think we might find someone to talk with. We scared up a flurry of about fifty ducks from a pond, their wings motoring away. When we approached the building, a duet of loud barking started, and two golden labs—one huge and the other only a little smaller—came out of the open door into a wire enclosure attached to the building at the doorway. They barked their heads off, but I breathed a sigh of relief when they stopped at the end of, and inside of, their enclosure. But next they *jumped over* the fence and came toward us, continuing the earsplitting cacophony of barking. Alarmed, I started talking to them sweetly in a low voice, avoiding eye contact, and they swirled around our feet. We heard fast-paced, heavy footfalls from inside approaching us on a hardwood floor, and then a man appeared in the doorway. With a word from him, both dogs stopped barking, milled about a little, then leaped gracefully back into their kennel. The man wore a blue-gray T-shirt and khaki shorts and appeared to be in his forties, with close-cropped dark-with-a-touch-of-gray hair.

"Thank you!" I breathed, gratefully. "Is this Kongsdal?"

"Yes."

"My great-grandfather worked here in 1869."

"Welcome!" he boomed.

We spent a chunk of time standing there in the bright sun conversing. Ulrich Hansen, farm manager, was most gracious about answering questions and giving us information. He said the trees back in Jens's time were harvested for heating and that Jens could have been a forest worker or could have worked in the fields. Later I learned that Jens had been listed at Kongsdal as "Farmhand Jens Nielsen." Kongsdal at the time of our visit had 500 hectares in forest and 500 hectares of farm (500 hectares equals 1,235.53 acres). Kongsdal grew rape for rapeseed oil, winter barley and spring barley (some of the barley was used to make beer), and grass seed for lawns and golf courses, as well as wheat and rye. At the time of our visit, the forest was still used for heating but less so than during Jens's time. Fewer workers were hired—they had only three when we visited—because they used machines, but likely in Jens's time the dorms were full. Kongsdal had cows when Jens and Karen Marie worked there, but Hansen said no one raises cows anymore, and the former cow fields are green areas. The estate at the time we were there had pigs but had not had them in Jens's time.

The hired workers back then stayed in the very building Hansen had come out of, in dorm rooms upstairs. He said my ancestor would have lived in that building, and I was touched to think of it, yet later wondered if, since Jens was married, the two of them might have stayed elsewhere on the estate. And was their toddler son, Jens Peter, with them? Or did the child stay with Karen Marie's parents nearby while they worked?

When I asked Hansen what Jens's wife might have done as an employee in 1869, he said she probably worked in the castle—not the *house* but the *castle*—preparing food, cleaning, or gardening. Or she might have tended fish in the three ponds, each pond containing a different type and size of fish kept for eating.

I later learned that while at Kongsdal, Jens worked for a farm bailiff named Hansen. Was our informant Ulrich Hansen a descendant of the person Jens had worked for? The Estrup family had owned Kongsdal for six generations, beginning in 1835, and I wondered if the position of farm manager had also stayed in one family. Hansen said the owner, Hans Iakob Estrup, was in Copenhagen for the day. He assured us the owner was friendly, and he gave me Estrup's phone number in case I had any further questions.

Our conversation wandered to other things—grasses grown and beers produced in Denmark and Oregon, pharmaceuticals produced in Denmark, and other things not related to family history. We enjoyed this jovial man so much that we invited him to contact us if he ever came to Oregon.

Hansen gave me a detailed map of the estate, told us to feel free to wander and take pictures, and added that if anyone talked to us, to tell them Ulrich had given us permission. Then he said he was glad we had come at the moment we did because he had been away all day with harvesting on another part of the estate and he soon had to leave again. We had shown up during the only window of time in which we would have found him. Where had my sense of urgency to get back to Kongsdal come from?

As we left Hansen at the dorms, Richard and I started walking around the grounds to take photos, and I was grateful we had returned at the right time to discover this estate that had been hidden the first time we drove down that road. Taking a photo of the forest would have satisfied me in my ignorance of better things, but the GPS had reached beyond our human vision and taken us to a treasure of expanded understanding.

We were a ways from the dorm building when we looked back and saw a tiny Hansen—reduced in apparent size because of the distance between us—come out of the now-small dorm building, get into his tiny car, and drive away. Had we gone to those remaining villages first, we truly would have missed him completely.

Hansen had told us construction on the castle had started in 1567 but took some time to finish. As we walked around, we saw *1598* on the house along with *GNKFG OMTI* way up high in black bricks. We have not found anyone who knows what those letters mean. When the castle was started in 1567, Kongsdal was under control of the *kronen*, or crown, and when it was finished thirty-one years later in 1598, its owner was Peder Reedtz. Perhaps the letters were some secret message known to his family.

We discovered that the separate ponds for fish were not located randomly but actually form a moat around the castle. One of the rock bridges on the property exhibited the date *1847* on one side and *1864* on the other—perhaps the beginning and ending dates of construction? It predates the era when Jens and Karen Marie worked there, so they likely walked across it, perhaps holding hands after a day's work.

Kongsdal had first been a farmhouse, which was given to Sorø Abbey in 1180 and later passed through other hands—including, briefly, two Danish kings—and then had become private property. The wings of the incredible castle were constructed over time, and the completed structure was extant when Jens and Karen Marie worked on the establishment.[66] Some of the outbuildings were not yet constructed when they were there, but it gratified me to know that I was walking on grounds where my great-grandfather had walked.

※

After roaming Kongsdal's grounds, we continued south on the same road toward Undløse. When we arrived at the town, we found the kirke, stunning white with a red roof, a long body with a tower at one end, and crenelations. We parked in the lot, and then noticed signs announcing the kirke was closed for renovation. Thinking Jens may have attended church services here while working at Kongsdal, we decided to explore the exterior of the white building. A gardener who was working in the plants and flowers offered to see if the conservator would let us come in, since we were American tourists. How he deduced what we were in five seconds is beyond me. He disappeared inside, then returned and said she would see us.

Inside the church, we climbed a tall jury-rigged set of wacky stairs and ladders—enclosed in a canvas drape—all the way up to a wooden platform just under the painted, arched ceiling of the church. The apparatus felt insecure and the climb was scary. But I had never before seen marvelous medieval paintings within inches of my nose, and the colors against the white were hypnotic. There we met Isabel Dwyer who was born in Chicago, which explained her interest in speaking with us Americans. She had two master's degrees and was an expert in restoring medieval fresco paintings. Unfortunately, the United States has *none* of those, so she had lived in Denmark for twenty-eight years to ply her art. Talking with her was fascinating. She described some of the well-meaning but bumbling earlier attempts made by others to preserve the paintings, and the tedious task of freeing them from the old and destructive chemicals in order to preserve the artwork using new techniques. Comparing the art she had restored to the faded illustrations yet to be worked upon made me deeply appreciative of the movement for preservation as well as the excellence of her work.

As we drove away to find a place to eat, Richard commented that the pattern of the six-month or one-year contracts for the Danish workers, providing board and room, some clothing and—after confirmation at age fourteen—also some cash, barely allowed them to subsist, to eke out an existence. Jens's life after his mother died had been an extremely difficult one. He was twenty-seven years old when he and Karen Marie worked at Kongsdal, and he had spent thirteen years officially working, plus those years from age ten to his confirmation during which he had worked before cash payments were added. He reported that some work situations had been unsatisfactory, from one when as a child he was not kept clean, to another at which the life was too rough for him, with at least one other that he had commented upon as being difficult. In addition, one employer had not kept Jens's position for him because of his military obligations. Jens benefited in the long term, however, in one employment position where he was paid in music lessons in lieu of cash and new clothing.

Although people at most of the places connected to Jens's history treated us well and answered our questions, those at the place where he had said life was too rough for him, Jordløse, did not. Clearly in this social construction, the power had been stacked in favor of the employer and not the employees. Did these farms and forests keep records of their employees? Would the records have shown mistreatment at Jordløse? Were the people there just too busy to be bothered with Americans seeking their roots? Or were they hiding something?

I cherish Jens's life sketch and simultaneously long for more information. I wish he had included the causes of his feelings when he sometimes wrote that the work life was too rough for him.

❧

Continuing with Jens's sketch, he wrote: "we then went home again to the old place." The Hicks history says, "On 12 September 1869 Jens was ordained to the office of a Teacher in the Church."[67] (Teacher is the second level in the Aaronic, or lower level, priesthood of the Church.) This would have taken place during his contract at Kongsdal.

But then Jens writes: "in Septbr 1869 i Was Call again to the Cirvise of Melitare to Kjobenhavn for 30 dayes [their contracts would have been completed in May 1870]. after May 1870 we stayed at my Wifes Parents Place in Axelholm." During this period of staying with her parents, Karen Marie would have been expecting their second child.

Jens then wrote: "on the 17 of March 1871 our Second Son Where Born [Akselholm, Holmstrup, Holbaek Denmark] and We call him Soren P. Nielsen. on the ___ of ___ [no dates given] i Was Ordin Preest [Priest is the third level in the Aaronic Priesthood] in the Chirch of Jesus Christ of Later Day Saints and sat apart to help the [almost illegible—looks like *finance director*] and lobored in this capasaty for years." Again from the Hicks history: "In April of 1872, he was ordained an Elder." However, the Newton Ward Record shows that Jens was ordained an Elder in the LDS Church on 31 August 1872. (Elder is the first level in the Melchizedek, or higher Priesthood.) The Hicks history adds that Jens "was chosen to preside over the Skarso [Skarresø] Branch on the Island of Schotland [Sjælland]. He held this position until 1875, when he left for America."[68]

Jens's saying he was "sat apart" refers to receiving a special blessing. The Church of Jesus Christ of Latter-day Saints has a lay clergy, and all members who are willing to serve in some capacity have the opportunity to do so. When one is called—by a bishop or other person with authority to issue a calling—to serve in a specific position with specific responsibilities, the person is "set apart" with a special blessing by the laying on of hands by priesthood holders, one of whom offers a prayer asking or promising guidance and help for the individual in carrying out those responsibilities.

Jens's half brother, Jorgen Frederick Nielsen, was born 3 April 1871, in Svebølle, to Niels and Ane, the seventh of their eight children. Depending on the route one takes, the villages of Svebølle and Akselholm are six to eight miles apart, but Jens did not write of interactions with his father's second family. Perhaps there were few contacts, though I've never heard criticism of his father or stepmother.

"on the 1ste May 1872 i With famely [wife; son, four and a half; and son, fourteen months] moved to Adlessborg Brig makkerfactory to make our Livelihud." The Hicks history says that Karen Marie and Jens worked together in this brickyard for three years to earn enough money for their passage to America.[69] Having joined the LDS Church and decided to immigrate to Utah, the family members were working to amass the needed financial resources to meet their goal.

❧

In July 2014, the priest's informative secretary at Jyderup, Karen Margrethe Nielsen, didn't know of an Adlessborg Brick Factory but did know of an old, inactive brick factory nearby called Knabstrup. Our search for it was a struggle, but we finally found the remains of this factory, which had ceased the production of bricks a century earlier. Then it produced ceramics before being purchased by a benefactor for a commune of artists. Even so, the skeletons of the large buildings and the tall smokestack and the ancient outdoor ovens that had been dug into the grassy hillside made me sigh at the likely hot and intense working conditions for Jens and Karen Marie. Jens's journal says they *moved to* the factory. Richard saw some small homes around this factory that might have been workers' residences, but none of them looked old.

Later, back at Amalie's Apartment, our bed and breakfast in Sorø, I asked our host, Per Krøyer, if it had always been Knabstrup Brick Factory. He said that a hundred years ago there were hundreds of brick factories in Denmark, but they are gone now. So even though Knabstrup is in the area Jens signed into and out of, Per thought it unlikely that this was *the* brick factory of Jens and Karen Marie's employ.

In fact, Kaja—who did so much research for this project—sent information in May 2016 about Georg Adeler who had built the Adelersborg Brick Factory, located near Starreklinte, where Karen Marie had been born. This may have been the same factory where the census shows the entire Christensen family living when Karen Marie was five years old. The actual brick factory where Jens and Karen Marie worked, then, was a distance north and slightly west of the ruin we had visited to gain an understanding of that facet of their lives.

❧

On 12 November 1873, Jens and Karen Marie's daughter Hanne Margaret was born (Starreklinte, Vallekilde, Holbæk, Denmark), the last of their children to be born in Denmark. During the job at the brickyard, Karen Marie would have worked through at least part of this pregnancy.

In June 1874, the Christensen-Nielsen (Hansen) family began its exodus from Denmark as Karen Marie's parents, Jens and Kirsten Christensen, took young Jens Peter with them and traveled, along with Jens's brother Hans Christian and his family, to settle in Utah. This left Jens and Karen Marie in Denmark with their two younger children.

The Hicks history says Jens and Karen Marie spent three years at the brickyard, moved from Starreklinte on 11 October 1874, and arrived at Holmstrup 23 October 1874. Since the brickyard at Starreklinte was geographically a distance from Holmstrup, I imagine they did not continue working there after this move. Their time at the brickyard then would have been closer to two and one-half years rather than the three years as stated in the Hicks history.

❧

The physical appearance of the last two pages of Jens's sketch seems important. On the penultimate page, the words "sat apart to help" are the final words of a full page of handwriting. On the next and apparently last page, the conclusion of his sketch consists of four lines at the top of the page that end with "to make our livelihud" at the brick factory. Below those four lines, the remainder of that page is blank.

In addition, two more pages in Jens's hand appear behind that apparent ending, but they are quite different in content and tone from the body of the sketch itself. One of my copies of the handwritten sketch does not include those back two pages, and I wonder who chose to leave them off. One unnamed transcriber of the sketch wrote: "*Note*: That is the end of the handwritten notes that have to do with Mr. Hansen's life history. The last two pages appear to be journal entries, so I am typing them separate from the above." Another transcriber, my sister LaRelia, wrote: "*Note*: That is the end of Mr. Hansen's handwritten account of his life. The next two pages of the record appear to be journal entries. However, they are cryptic, undated, and have no apparent relevance to the foregoing and, therefore, have not been included in this transcription."

When I first read the final two pages myself, I thought perhaps Jens had written them during an incoherent phase of a final illness or while on medication for such an illness. My note to myself regarding these mysterious pages read: "A few other insightful entries, but not sure of the year. Making mats, using his knife, etc. Put in someplace later. Sounds like entries after coming to Utah because he mentions [the towns of] Logan and Portage." Later in Jens's story, the significance of these final two confusing pages will become startlingly clear.

And so we come to the end of Jens's words in his brief life sketch. I shudder to think how little we would know of his life if he had not written this account. My heart ached with sorrow not only upon the death of his mother when he was six years old but also at how he moved from contract to contract, from farm to farm, throughout his life from age ten onward. His father lost his wife and fifth baby in childbirth and was left with four sons ages ten, eight, six, and four, whom he seemed ill equipped to provide for or to keep together. Jens said his father lived a rough life for a while—his grief must have been enormous and his responsibilities overwhelming. Young Jens was hardworking and poor, and though the record says he had a good stepmother, he didn't seem to spend much time with her and his father. Jens's father, Niels, and his second wife had eight children, but I don't know whether they lived to adulthood, or if Jens had any relationships with his half siblings. Perhaps they were also farmed out. Not only was that customary in poverty-ridden Denmark, but also it would have provided for this second family of children.

I am grateful for Jens's sketch because it not only hints as to why he and Karen Marie came to be baptized into the LDS faith but also chronicles the places and dates he worked. His sketch, coupled with my gigantic map, enabled us to find most of the farms and forests where Jens had lived and worked as we traveled in Denmark and walked in his footsteps. Standing in places where he and Karen Marie and Ane had lived and breathed in their home country was a sacred, never-to-be-forgotten experience for me. Without his sketch, little of that would have been possible.

I grieve, though, that his written record ends before his family's emigration from Denmark, and I wish we had a similar record for the remainder of his life. However, clues from other sources continued to surface in surprising places and from amazingly helpful people, situating more pieces into the jigsaw puzzle of Jens's life with Karen Marie and Ane. Sometimes a clue not only answered a nagging question but also raised a dozen new questions, some of which eluded answers, thus creating a tantalizing sense of mystery.

CHAPTER 7

SKUDSMAALSBOG

On 28 June 2011, a bright sunny morning in Salt Lake City, with clear blue sky and a perfect temperature that would become almost unbearably hot by midafternoon, I made my way on foot to the LDS Family History Library located just across the street from the west wall of Temple Square. The gray spires of the temple stood out against the azure sky, and the purple mountains to the east rose to spectacular heights. The gray pioneer assembly hall, with its pointed white spires visible over the gray wall surrounding Temple Square, exhibited stunning architecture, and I wondered why I had not realized, when I lived in Utah, how beautiful these buildings and this city were. Salt Lake City has an extraordinary history. Everywhere I looked, I saw reminders of the spiritual values inherent in the culture. I also saw many local people who genuinely tried to include God in their daily lives and I found it refreshing.

Amidst a small crowd, I entered the multistoried white-brick and glass library carrying my ten-ton tote bag loaded for the day and wearing a lost expression. I planned to meet my nephew, Lyle Wiggins—a library employee and the eldest son of my deceased sister, MauRene—at 10:00 a.m., after his employees meeting. I had contacted him a few weeks earlier and asked if he would meet with me while I was in Salt Lake and show me some of the genealogical treasures he had found in his mother's things after she died. He readily agreed to do so. It was 8:20 a.m. when I arrived. The lobby contained open space and numerous information desks staffed by volunteers who were busy answering people's questions. A small theater in one area had a sign over the door that read *Orientation*, and because this was my first visit, I walked into the darkened auditorium. A helpful female volunteer asked if I would like to see the nine-minute movie, and I said yes. It presented an overview of the library's resources, organization, and staggering accumulation of records. One goal of the Church is to preserve all possible genealogical records, as well as to rescue for preservation those records endangered or damaged by natural disasters or war. The movie showed the Church vaults of records deep in the mountains east of Salt Lake, kept there for protection. Also featured were vignettes of several men and women who told touching stories of finding facts in the library that connected them to their ancestors.

When the movie ended, the volunteer asked if I would like help getting started in an expansive adjacent library room filled with desks, computers, file cabinets, and a hive of people busily working. I wanted to find information about Ane Sophie Christensen, a woman whom my niece, Shauna Fowler Payne, had found in the records as a possible additional wife of Jens Hansen. As the hostess and I stood in the doorway of the theater, she gestured to a female volunteer standing near the center of the library, who came over to us and asked how she might help me. We moved to a computer where we sat together while she demonstrated incredible skill at searching for Ane Sophie in places I neither knew existed nor how to access. We made copies of a census record and an emigration list that appeared to hold some promise but found nothing conclusive. As we sat puzzling by the computer, she said, "I should call my husband over here because he knows a lot about Newton. He lived there when he was young and is related to J. J. Larsen."

"I have J. J.'s little green book!" I exclaimed. "My family knew Grant Larsen! Ruby Larsen Woodward is my main contact in Newton—she helps me with so many things."

The volunteer looked at me quizzically and asked, "Are you from Portland?"

Caught off-balance by her surprising question, I could only manage a hesitant "Yeeesss?"

"Ruby's our cousin!" she said. "We were at her place in Newton last Saturday, and she told us all about you! But I never dreamed I'd get to meet you." I was astonished to learn I had been the topic of a conversation many miles away and that a stranger was happy to meet me.

She pointed out her husband just across the room and motioned to him to join us. Then we talked of Newton. I told him about my family bumping into his relative Grant Larsen at the Newton cemetery several years earlier (November 1995). He said he remembered seeing that chance visit written up in the newspaper and that he couldn't get over it. I assume he meant he couldn't get over the coincidence of Grant Larsen, as cemetery sexton, being present in the cemetery on a cold winter day when my mother (who was eighty-seven) and my siblings had gone there to look for family graves. As they conversed, Grant and my family discovered that he had known Mother's dad, Henry Bjorkman, and her older siblings. They had a long and satisfying conversation.

The volunteer couple introduced themselves as Reed and Afton Bartlett, and I realized he was the man responsible for the reprinting of J. J. Larsen's little green book that I had been so excited to acquire. Of all the dozens of volunteers in the library, what were the chances that these two with connections to Newton, Grant, Ruby, and the little green book would be the ones to help me?

When ten o'clock arrived, I thanked them effusively for their help, then stepped out to the lobby and telephoned Lyle, who said he would be right down. He arrived quickly, and we rode the elevator to the third floor, passed through another lobby and lots of library stacks, then arrived at his spacious office that he described as "controlled chaos"—a term that also fits my study.

We sat at a round table that was nestled between the open door and one end of Lyle's expansive L-shaped desk. Several envelopes and various other items lay stacked in the center of the table for our perusal. Still excited about meeting Afton and Reed downstairs, I gushed out the story of the amazing coincidence. Lyle nodded knowingly, and said, "I hear those kinds of stories here *all* the time."

Lyle set a couple of manila folders off the stack onto the area directly in front of us, and the first thing he pulled out was a small, thin notebook in a hard cover of brown and green floral print, with two narrow brown ribbons hanging about an inch out the bottom. He said the notebook had belonged to Jens Niels Hansen, who was my great-grandfather and Lyle's great-great-grandfather.

I took the notebook in both hands and held it reverently. To think I was holding something that Jens had actually touched gave me a feeling of awe. I leafed gently through the pages filled with handwriting in Danish, noticing the dates, the strokes of fading brown ink, the maroon wax seal on the inside back cover, and the aura of history the pages exuded. Interspersed in the handwriting appeared dates in chronological order, each date accompanied by a notation.

Lyle said the notebook had never been translated, and neither of us had any idea what it was. He told me a woman in his office with some knowledge of Danish had said the entries appeared to refer to Lutheran feast days, which made sense with that being Denmark's state church, and with Jens's connection to that faith until his conversion to Mormonism. Yet I felt like we needed more substantiated information.

A double ribbon, ingeniously attached to the lower left side of the cover, ran from the front inside cover through the book via a small hole in each page just above the bottom edge and near the spine, and the ribbons led to a wax seal on the inside back cover. Lyle commented that apparently Jens had placed the wax seal and while it was soft, had put the ribbon ends in it as a means of sealing the book so he would know if anyone had opened it. I wondered whether the seal might have had some traditional or cultural origin as well. It seemed to indicate some need for secrecy or a level of distrust. Because the ribbon was attached to the front and ran through to the back, it could easily have served to seal the book by being attached to the wax. But after one use, how could the wax be reactivated for additional sealings?

I pointed out to Lyle that there were initials in the wax, and he said he hadn't noticed them before. The indentation was very shallow and easy to miss, but three gorgeous cursive letters were embedded. Lyle got out a rectangular black velvet bag about the size of a 4" x 6" index card—similar to the dimensions of Jens's notebook—and removed from it a magnifying glass, swiveled the folded handle into place, and examined the mysterious initials. We talked of several possible ways to make them out. I thought of using a CSI dusting powder, though I feared that might damage the book. Lyle thought of making a photocopy upon which to connect the lines of the letters by pencil where they are obscured by the ribbons' depression.

Another thing that gave rise to no end of curiosity in both Lyle and me, and probably to others over the years, is the fact that one page had been neatly sliced out of this book, close to the spine.

I asked if I might take a photo of the notebook, and, saying yes, Lyle got out a portable photo background kit, set it on the table, thumbed through the various colored squares of cloth seamed together at one edge, selected the blue one, and flipped it out onto the table. He placed the notebook on the blue cloth, and I took several pictures. He kindly made photocopies of the notebook pages, the cover, and the seal for me.

Lyle showed me more items of interest, including a swatch of fabric that is directly connected to Ane through a story told by my mother that will appear later in this work. He shared other family records over the next several hours. Then we walked in the hot sun and gusty desert wind along Salt Lake's business district streets to a nearby Blue Iguana for lunch, where we continued to share family stories. Over the years since, both of us have commented what a memorable and enjoyable day that was.

❦

When I returned home to Oregon clutching my copy of Jens's notebook, I searched the internet for translation services in the Portland area, to no avail. LaRelia gave a copy of the notebook to a cousin of her husband, Bob, who knew someone who might be able to translate it, and I turned my attention to other things while waiting to hear the outcome of that search.

Later that summer, Richard read a newspaper article in the *Oregonian* about a Swedish man in Portland, Sir Ross Fogelquist (knighted by the King of Sweden), who had asked for and received permission to build a Swedish-style decoration for the bus stop across the street from his home.[70] Richard emailed the reporter who, upon Richard's request, provided Fogelquist's email address. Richard then emailed Mr. Fogelquist telling him that we were planning a trip to Scandinavia sometime in the next few years and asking if he could recommend some "must-see" sites in Sweden. Fogelquist generously responded, "Come to my house, and we'll talk."

We made an appointment for 10:00 a.m. Friday, 9 September 2011, and took homemade chocolate chip cookies for him as a thank-you. As Mr. Fogelquist showed us through his distinctively decorated Scandinavian home, one of his antiques that surprised and fascinated me was an immigrant trunk from Denmark. The wooden trunk and lid were painted in black enamel, covered with a motif of blue flowers, with *1880* painted in pale yellow. The trunk was smaller than I had imagined them to be in that era. As I stood staring, it dawned on me that the trunk Ane brought with her in 1878, which is often mentioned in family lore, may have looked very much like this one, and given its size, she probably needed to travel with more than one.

After the tour of Mr. Fogelquist's home, he made tea while we sat at the kitchen table surrounded by his unique kitchenware, red Swedish horses of various sizes, and Scandinavian antiques. I felt like we were in another country and loved it. He served the cookies I had brought and the tea, and then spread out a huge, colorful map of Sweden that took up the whole table. We studied the map as he pointed out the areas that would yield wonderful experiences of his home country, which he obviously loved, and he told delightful stories about why we would find them highly interesting to visit.

As we talked, a question started rising up from the mists of my brain, swirled into shape, and became concrete: "Do you know of anyone in the Portland area who could do Danish-to-English translation? I've searched on the internet but haven't found anyone, and I have a copy of a notebook that belonged to my great-grandfather that I'd like translated."

Without needing a fraction of a second to think about it, he said, "When we finish here, go next door to the Scandinavian Heritage Foundation [later called Nordic Northwest] and ask for Aase [pronounced Oh-suh]." Later we walked next door to a small white house and stepped inside an office where the young woman behind the desk told us that Aase Beaulieu was out. She gave us Aase's contact information, and we left a note for her as well. Aase and I corresponded through email, and we decided since I was leaving town on vacation, the best way to get a copy of Jens's notebook to her was by mail. I sent a copy on 14 September 2011 with the following letter:

Dear Aase:

Enclosed is the copy of my great-grandfather's notebook for your perusal. I look forward to learning what you think can be done for translating it.

Also, the mechanism with the ribbons is very interesting to me. The big splotch on the inside back cover is red wax with initials in it. Is that a traditional Danish way of securing privacy in a notebook or journal?

Also of notice to my nephew (who provided me the copy) and me is that one page has been neatly sliced out.

Thank you so much for your help.

A few days later on 19 September 2011, Aase responded through email:

I received your package today, with the copy of your great-grandfather's *Skudsmaalsbog* (employment record, or servants' conduct book).

The first part, printed in old script, spells out the laws surrounding the book: including fines for many things, for instance tearing out pages!!! (Maybe your great-grandfather didn't like his employer's comments on that particular page! Which page number was sliced out—it must have been 18–19, perhaps?)

The second part, all the hand-written notes, are from employers and outline the length of employment, sometimes what Jens did for them, and some comments about his performance. The period covered is from 1856 through 1874.

Both parts are somewhat difficult to read, some of the hand-written notes downright impossible to decipher (for me at least). My guess is the red wax with initials stamped in it is a feeble security measure.

I will take the copy with me on Wednesday, to a meeting of the Northwest Danish American Association Oregon Committee, and ask whether anyone would tackle the translation—assuming you still want it? If anyone wants to do it, I'll ask them to quote a price as well for your consideration.

Quite a historic book! The practice of *Skudsmaalsboger* was discontinued in 1921.

Best Regards,
Aase

A follow-up email 23 September 2011 from Aase said:

> I did find someone, and she is looking at the book over the weekend!
> I'll let you know what she thinks next week.

The woman she referred to was Kaja Voldbæk, who, with her husband, Erik, did accept the translation project. I inquired of Aase what the cost of the translation would be, concerned after the fact that I had given the go-ahead without knowing the fee. On 4 October 2011 another email came from Aase, saying,

> The translator said she doesn't want any money—instead, she says she
> will be happy if instead you become a member of the Scandinavian
> Heritage Foundation at the family level or higher—is that acceptable
> to you?

Of course it was.

When the translation was finished, Aase made arrangements to deliver it to me at the home of my daughter, Kjersti, and son-in-law, Greg, where I was tending my then three-year-old grandson, who was napping when she arrived. She carried the letter-size manila envelope in which I had sent the document, and on the back of it was handwritten in pencil the word *skudsmaalsbog* with an underline. When she sat down, she said, "Now before I give this to you, let me say that there is nothing negative in it. Your ancestor must have been a real sweetheart because everyone said good things about him." That pleased me. I served chocolate chip cookies, and we spent a pleasant hour visiting about a variety of things.

As near as I understand and can duplicate it, *skudsmaalsbog* is pronounced *skoos-muls-bow-en*. Aase commented upon the sliced-out page, saying that perhaps Jens was parsimonious and had cut the page out of the skudsmaalsbog after it was no longer being used as a work record because he needed paper for some reason and paper was scarce. She also said the record is a significant artifact, especially since its last entry was in 1874, just before Jens emigrated. The first entry was made when he was fourteen years old, when he was confirmed and took communion after finishing his education. I later learned at Den Gamle By that only young people who had been confirmed were eligible to receive a skudsmaalsbog or to have the right to work or to be trained for work. At this point in his life, however, Jens had already worked several years before receiving this formal document.

Jens's skudsmaalsbog and additional data provided by Kaja contain information that had not appeared in other sources, including the fact that Jens's father, Niels Hansen, was a cabinetmaker. Perhaps this explains why later in Newton, both Jens and his brother Hans were fine homebuilders. The skudsmaalsbog shows that Jens was baptized 24 July 1842, as an infant of thirty-nine days, and was vaccinated 29 July 1843, when he was one year, one month, and thirteen days old. The skudsmaalsbog and Jens's sketch show a slight discrepancy: Jens says in his sketch that his schooling was ended on 4 September 1856, a Thursday, and that he was confirmed a few days after—probably on Sunday, 7 September 1856. However, the skudsmaalsbog says that Jens was confirmed the Sunday after Mikkelsdag 1856, and the translator says that Mikkelsdag is Saint Michaels Day, always 29 September, a fixed holiday.[71] The calendar for 1856 shows 29 September on a Monday, and the following Sunday was 5 October 1856. For some reason, the two listed dates of confirmation are a month apart and it is difficult to say which, if either, is correct. In a nice tribute to Jens, the skudsmaalsbog says regarding his confirmation: "His notes (remarks in the church book)" are "good knowledge and abilities, and good behavior."[72]

The first section of the notebook expounds the law concerning the skudsmaalsbog and says:

> Every servant should have a Servant's Conduct Book. Before such a book can be used, it must be sealed by the Police Authority in Copenhagen and other cities. In the country, it must be sealed by the parish priest. The seal should be placed above the string going through the book.[73]

This explains the ribbon through the book and the wax seal at the end. The unit was designed as a temporary seal to show that the book had been examined by the proper authority and was ready to be used as a record for the servant.

The book was given to each person who needed it upon finishing his or her compulsory education, or it could be obtained by showing a proof of baptism or other documents to the authorities before the book was sealed. Before a servant left any job, his or her employer for that job had to write the dates when the servant started and was leaving the job and what their responsibilities had been. Writing an evaluation of the employee's work was the option of the employer.[74] The law further states:

> An employer who gives an employee a good recommendation in spite of poor performance, and it gives the next employer a wrong impression of the servant, shall, according to the ordinary rules of law, be responsible for the losses of the next employer, and can be fined up to 20 Rigsdalers depending on the circumstance.

If the employer gives the servant a poor recommendation in the Servant's Conduct Book, which can result in difficulties for the servant in getting another job, and the employer cannot present any information which gives acceptable proofs that he has sufficient reason to be given the bad review, then he shall pay the servant for his losses hereby caused and the employer shall be punished according to the law regarding Offending Accusations in Words or a fine up to 20 Rigsdalers.[75]

A servant who came to:

a parish in the country where he or she has not lived before, shall report …to the parish priest in order to have the Servant's Conduct Book certified. In such cases the employer who has hired the servant should also report such employment to the authorities. The report shall be filed within…four days after the arrival of the servant in the country.[76]

In the cities, the servant was required to report to the police within twenty-four hours of arrival.[77]

A person:

who tears pages out of his/hers Servant's Conduct Book or who purposely makes some of the text illegible should be fined between 5 and 10 Rigsdalers, or be punished with simple jail up to eight days or jail on water and bread up to three days.[78]

This brings us back to the question: Why is there a page missing from Jens's skudsmaalsbog? Was it removed after he stopped being a servant? Or did he pay a penalty for slicing a page out of this restrictive document? It would have to have been a final page, because everything that appears in the record is in chronological order.

The translators, Kaja and Erik, generously included notes that explain the practice of these hirings and their records:

There is no good English word for *tyende*. The Danish word for *tyende* comes from the Old Norse word *phy*, which means female slave. I have selected to translate it to *servant*.

Tyende in the Danish law: "*Tyendeloven*" covered the group of citizens that was hired for a fixed time of a year—usually for the summer months—May 1st to November 1st—and/or the winter months—November 1st to May 1st. The enumeration included room and board together with a certain amount of cash payment payable at the end of the period.

In general, the members in the group were from the age of fourteen—when most children left school—and up.

The boys would work on a farm as farm helpers, and the girls as maids on farms, and in city households as helpers.

Tyendeloven was issued by Christian VII in 1800 and continued in force until 1921 when it was replaced by a new law called *Medhjaelperloven.*

Skudsmaalsbogen was a part of *Tyendeloven. Tyendeloven* gave the man of the house the same power over the servants as he had over other members of his family. He could punish the servants if he found it to be necessary and it was not unusual that he would strike the younger ones if they misbehaved.[79]

Could this be why Jens sometimes rated his treatment as not good? The translators' notes continue:

The employer could also withhold any cash payment until the servant had ended his or her agreed upon term, so if a servant left before the end of the period, he or she would not be paid, and it would also show up on the Servant Conduct Book, which could make it difficult for them to get another job.

It also gave certain rights to the servants. For example, a servant could not be discharged because of sickness.[80]

This would explain why Jens was able to stay on in certain positions in spite of his recurring illnesses.

I was surprised to learn that the skudsmaalsbog contains, between entries and evaluations by the hiring farmers, trip data including the date that Jens departed one town and the date he arrived at the next. These departures and arrivals connecting contracts were attested to in the record by a third party. The way these records were kept makes it seem like the person was not free to decide where to travel or whether to continue working. Jens was tracked at all times. In between the tracking travel notes are the sections denoting the place and time period of the contract, sometimes the amount and type of wages, and sometimes words of evaluation of Jens's performance on the job. Few of the later entries had any evaluative words, which were optional according to the law, but listed only the work dates and a signature.

The evaluators chose complimentary words to describe Jens and his performance over the years. Hans Jensen of Lille Fuglede, upon Jens's departure, stated "Farmhand Jens Nielsen has worked for me from 1 November 1856 to 1 May 1858, and in that time [has] shown loyalty and diligence in all respects."[81]

Hans Pedersen of Svinninge said of Jens that he had "been faithful, willing, and decent. I do not omit informing this truthful report as he now after resignation leaves his job here, Svinninge, 1 May 1860."[82] This was where Jens worked for music lessons.

Farmer Jens Pedersen of Jordløse said Jens "has conducted himself as faithful and good-natured, which I hereby testify."[83] Those same words were used by Farmer Hans Larsen's widow (Jordløse)[84]; and by Schou, a Farm Bailiff at Kattrup[85]; and again by Farmer Hans Larsen's widow in a later entry (Jordløse).[86]

Bülmann of Edelsminde, 1 August 1865, said Jens had shown "hard work and faithfulness to my satisfaction and leaves his job because of military service."

I wonder if the reason Jens was able to be so specific about his workplaces, dates, bosses, and military service in writing his life sketch later was because he had this notebook in his possession and used it as a guide. I am not sure when he wrote the sketch, but it was after he had learned English and was duplicating the sounds of the new language in his writing. I am puzzled as to why he ended the sketch before his emigration. Perhaps because that is where the skudsmaalsbog ends? Or did he write more but pages are missing?

We are not sure how MauRene came to have this small notebook in her things, or even how we, as Jens's second family, came to possess it at all, but we are excited to have the translation as one more intimate connection to our ancestor.

The newspaper article and Richard's interest in it were fortuitous in leading us to Ross Fogelquist, Aase Beaulieu, and Kaja and Erik Voldbæk. When Richard and I planned to visit Ross Fogelquist in his home, it did not occur to me that we would learn anything beyond the travel information he could provide. Instead, we also found answers to some of the family puzzle through the generous spirit of total strangers who appeared at just the right time and shared their knowledge. I felt that something serendipitous was at work on behalf of this history. What else would appear in amazing ways?

CHAPTER 8

EMIGRATION, FIRST WAVE: 1874

*J*ens apparently wrote his life sketch years after all of the events noted in it had taken place and ended his narrative at 1872, except for two pages depicting events in 1889. (Perhaps he wrote his entire sketch in 1889.) The Danish skudsmaalsbog documenting his work history ended in October 1874, with the attested record of Jens's travel from Starreklinte to Holmstrup with his wife and the younger two of his three children. When that notation was made, his oldest son, his wife's parents, and the family of his brother Hans had already traveled to America. Where did Jens and Karen Marie live after arriving back in Holmstrup in October 1874? Did they continue to work as they made their own plans to soon depart Denmark for America? If so, where? What motivated this entire family to pull up stakes and move across the world?

❧

Brigham Young, along with the first party of Mormons fleeing Nauvoo, arrived in the Salt Lake Valley in 1847. They were followed over the next years by companies of pioneers in oxen-pulled, covered wagons loaded with all their goods. Other pioneers walked, pushing or pulling heavily laden handcarts. Upon arrival, they began to settle this desert area. Shelters, homes, churches, schools, and barns had to be built; farms laid out and crops planted; irrigation implemented; and a temple and tabernacle constructed. *Industry* was the watchword, and the busy beehive became the territorial symbol of the cooperative work required of the Mormon people to achieve these goals.

Young was a man of great organizational gifts as well as spiritual insights, and he began bringing to fruition his vision of turning this remote, arid desert into a new Zion, a self-sufficient and protected center where the Mormons could be left alone to live their religious beliefs and practices in peace. He continued the policy of sending missionaries out into the world as well as sending scouts to find locations in the Great Basin amenable to habitation. He then called groups of families to move into those areas and create settlements. Young also issued a call to new converts in foreign countries to immigrate to this new center of the Church to help establish Zion.

The Church of Jesus Christ of Latter-day Saints is a worldwide church that since the early 1900s has encouraged new converts to stay in place and build up the kingdom of God by serving where they live. In the early era, however, due to successful proselytizing by missionaries, large numbers of converts to the LDS Church in England, Scandinavia, and other parts of the world heeded the call to leave their lifelong homes, friends, other family members, and everything familiar in order to move where the Church was centered. Why were people willing to do this? In protracted conversations at church in 2018 with Donovan Davisson, a gentleman who was well-read in the early history of the Church, I learned that in addition to having testimonies and a desire to follow their prophet, these people were promised that they would have safety in their journey, that those loved ones they left behind would be all right, and that they would prosper and thrive. Additional promises included that they would have the opportunity to be sealed as families for eternity in the Endowment House and temples, that they would live in a covenant society where all espoused the same beliefs, and that the poor would be taken care of. The resulting large-scale period of immigration across an ocean and a continent to the new settlements continued for several decades.

Knowing that many converts were too poor to make the journey, Young established the Perpetual Emigration Fund in 1849 with donations from members. The emigrants could borrow some or all of their passage from this fund, and then, after arrival in Utah Territory, would repay what each was able so that others might continue to benefit from this ongoing treasury.

Perhaps additional reasons contributed to the dramatic influx of immigrants from Scandinavia. John Langeland wrote:

> Many Scandinavian members…emigrated [sic] to the United States. Particularly in the nineteenth century, poverty, starvation, persecution, and hopelessness motivated people to seek a better life and, for Latter-day Saints, the spirit of gathering to the "Promised Land" in Utah was strong.[87]

Whatever the complex motivation, thousands chose to embark on the rigorous journey and settle in various locations radiating out from Salt Lake Valley.

Among those who eventually answered the call to emigrate and gather were members of Jens's and Karen Marie's families as well as Jens and Karen Marie themselves. Larry Christiansen wrote that Karen Marie's father, Jens

Christensen—the man in Axelholm with whom Jens had boarded—was the first in that family to join the Church of Jesus Christ of Latter-day Saints, and he was baptized on 9 November 1856, eleven years before our Jens arrived at the Christensen home. His wife, Kirsten, was baptized seven months later on 13 June 1857. At the time of her father's baptism, Karen Marie was eleven years old, and her siblings were Hans, sixteen; Lars Peter, fourteen; and Christian, six. None of these children were baptized until later, and the family waited seventeen years to emigrate.[88]

Christiansen continued, saying, "There appeared to be an arrangement made" wherein the family would emigrate in two groups from Denmark to join with the body of the Church in Utah Territory.[89] The first group included Karen Marie's parents. They traveled with and assumed responsibility for little Jens Peter, the six-year-old son of Jens and Karen Marie.

> [They] sold their possessions and readied to move, possibly thinking they could handle young Jens also, and possibly assist their daughter, Karen, and her husband, Jens…ready themselves to come the following year. This could involve economic considerations as well as physical care.[90]

Jens's brother Hans Christian Nielsen (Hansen) and his family are also listed among those who traveled on the same date as Karen Marie's parents. At first I assumed they had all traveled as a unit but later could find no evidence as to why I had drawn that conclusion—except that it seemed logical, since all were connected with or related to Jens Nielsen, that they would have formed a family group and perhaps the little cousins would have enjoyed playing together. None of the histories, however, state that the Christensens and Nielsens actually traveled together within the larger group of emigrants.

Watkins Ward's history of Hans, who was two years older almost to the day than his brother Jens, says:

> The gospel of the Church of Jesus Christ of Latter-day Saints was brought to Hans Christian by his brother in 1868, and he readily accepted it and was baptized 15 June 1868.[91]

Because Jens had been baptized two months earlier on 22 April 1868, and because the two brothers' lives would later be intertwined in a number of ways, I speculated that the brother who was instrumental in Hans's conversion had been Jens. Later discoveries, though, would yield speculation regarding other brothers' possible roles as that catalyst. Hans's wife, Karen Marie Pedersdatter, joined the Church one year after Hans did. (In order to avoid confusion with Jens's wife, also named Karen Marie, I will hereafter refer to Hans's wife as Karen M.) Hans and Karen M. had five children born in Denmark, one of whom—the third born, Christine—had died in 1867 at eleven months of age.[92] Cause of death is not listed.

The second group would stay in Denmark "working...to earn enough money to emigrate...the following year."[93] The group waiting to travel in 1875 included our Jens Nielsen, his wife Karen Marie Christensen Nielsen, and their second and third children: Soren Peter Nielsen, three, and Hanne Margaret Nielsen, seven months. Also waiting were Karen Marie's brother, Lars Peter Christensen (baptized in 1873), his wife Christine K. Sorensen Christensen (baptized just before the June 1875 travels), and their two children: Caroline, seven (who as an adult would become grandmother to Larry Christiansen), and Jens P., one.

I don't know how the decision was made as to who went in the first group and who worked and waited, but I am curious as to why Jens and Karen Marie's eldest son went in the first group with his grandparents instead of waiting a year to travel with his parents. The cost of travel may have figured into the decision. As a mother, I would find it painfully difficult to send a young child on a long voyage that meant, in addition to the dangers involved, a one-year separation. But Jens and Karen Marie, working at the brickyard, maybe found that having two children to care for instead of three made it economically possible to achieve their goal of being ready to emigrate by 1875. When our first grandson was five years old, he was at ease enough with Richard and me that I can envision little Jens Peter being comfortable traveling with his grandparents, eager for adventure and still naïve about danger.

Surely speaking the thoughts of many, one emigrant wrote:

> I believed in the principal of the gathering and felt it my duty to go although it was a severe trial to me, in my feelings to leave my native land and the pleasing associations that I had formed here; but my heart was fixed. I knew in whom I had trusted and with the fire of Israel's God burning in my bosom, I forsook my home.[94]

My mother would say in one sentence that her father or her grandmother or her grandfather had come to America from Denmark. Also in a single sentence, she would relate that her father had returned to Denmark to serve a mission for the Mormon Church—leaving his wife and five children to do so—and had then traveled back to America. Encapsulating these overseas journeys in one sentence always made the travel sound easy. As more details about those journeys surfaced, however, a realization of the enormity and risks of such an undertaking obliterated my naïveté. The simple sentence was just a loosely tied bow on a complex package.

Reading between the lines of that simple sentence, I learned that our families of Mormon Danish emigrants traveled from their homes overland with their trunks by some kind of horse-drawn vehicle to the train station nearest their village of residence in Holbæk County. That may have been Ringsted, but more likely it would have been Roskilde, at a distance of about thirty miles, requiring maybe eight to ten hours of travel. Then the train carried them from Ringsted or Roskilde to the port of Copenhagen, with perhaps one or two days required for this leg of travel. The sea route from Copenhagen to the next stop at Hull, England, involved passage on a ship through the Øresund, which is a narrow channel between Sweden and Sjælland, then north into Kattegat Bay, and then onto the waters of Skagerrak, a strait that leads to the North Sea. This waterway links the Baltic Sea and the North Sea and can be subject to severe storms. Next the ship would cross the North Sea to England, traverse the Humber Estuary, and then glide up the Hull River to dock at the town of Hull, located almost at the midpoint of the eastern coast of England. This voyage from Copenhagen to Hull might take two days.[95]

At Hull, the emigrants boarded another train and traveled west across the waist-band of England dotted by Sheffield, Leeds, and Manchester to Liverpool, where the River Mersey pours into Liverpool Bay just north of the northeastern corner of Wales on the western side of England. If the ship arrived at Hull early enough in the day, the train trip from there to Liverpool could be managed the same day.

At Liverpool, the emigrants boarded a larger steamship, crossed the Irish Sea, passed through Saint George's Channel, and moved over the Celtic Sea to dock at Queenstown (now Cobh), Ireland, to take Irish emigrants aboard. The ship once again crossed a portion of the Celtic Sea to glide onto the Atlantic Ocean, and then plied across that vast expanse to New York in America. This voyage averaged twelve days.

After arriving at New York and checking in at Castle Garden (now Castle Clinton National Monument), the immigrants took a river steamer to Jersey City and boarded still another train to travel west across the North American continent to Salt Lake City in Utah Territory. This last part of the journey by train took approximately nine days. So the entire trip might have taken twenty-five days. That's *all* travel, and arduous travel at that.

I entertained one fleeting thought that in order to complete my research, I needed to fly to Copenhagen, travel by ship to Hull, train to Liverpool, ship to

New York, train to Salt Lake, and then by train to the stop nearest Newton—but the task seemed inordinately daunting to me even with today's improved travel conditions, and I gave up the idea. Due to that moment of mental engagement with an imaginary journey, however, I was struck with a much deeper appreciation of what these family members—and thousands of other Mormon immigrants—were willing to endure in order to follow their religious faith and their hopes and dreams of economic improvement to the center of the Church's geographical settlement. Even when I later was transported to Scandinavia by jet airplane and then traveled its roads by car, it was a long journey.

The LDS Church Copenhagen Conference Emigration List for the SS *Idaho* (the ship that would take our group from Copenhagen to Hull, England) on 19 June 1874 shows the first family group just as listed previously in this text:

> No. 420 Jens Christensen (59)
> No. 421 Kirsten Christensen (59)
> No. 413 Jens P. Nielsen (4)

Jens Peter was actually approximately six and one-half years old, and I wonder if stating a lower age resulted in some kind of savings in the fare, for which the record says Jens had paid twenty-five dollars. Also on this Emigration List appears the following:

> No. 295 Hans C. Nielsen (33) [Jens Nielsen's brother]
> No. 296 Karen M. Nielsen (34) [Hans's wife]

The children with Hans and Karen M. were listed as follows:

> No. 297 Lars C. (11)
> No. 298 Hanne M. (10)
> No. 299 Niels P.J. (8)
> No. 300 Fransine M. (4)
> No. 301 Jacob D. (¾)

Karen M. was pregnant during the voyage. Our first family group of immigrants, then, consisted of four adults and six children from age eleven down to a twenty-two-month-old toddler. (I'm not sure why Jacob D.'s age is on the Emigration List as nine months old when his actual age was one year and ten months.)

The eleven-year-old boy, Lars (not to be confused with Karen Marie's brother Lars, who waited with the second family group until 1875), who is shown on the

Emigration List as Hans's child, does not appear on their Family Group Record or in the history of Hans written by his great-granddaughter, thus giving rise to questions of whether he was someone else's son merely traveling with Hans and Karen M. or whether there is an error on the records. Their oldest child listed in the Family Group Record, Hanne Margrethe, was younger than Lars and had been born seven months after Hans and Karen M.'s marriage date. If Lars was their child, either by birth or by adoption, he should have been shown on the Family Group Record, but errors appear in even the most meticulously kept records. However, some of these questions are put to rest by a statement from the Hans Christian Nielsen (Hansen) history that says, "Five of the children were born in Denmark, with the first child, Hanne Margrethe being born 14 July 1864."[96] Hanne, not Lars, is declared as the eldest child. Lars is not listed at all in Hans's history as one of the children of this marriage. Who was he? And why was he traveling with Hans's family?

Perhaps the numbers on the Emigration List give a clue as to whether the two families were traveling together within the group of travelers. One hundred twenty-five people are on the list between Hans Christian Nielsen as number 295 and Jens Christensen as number 420. And Larry Christiansen (who is descended from Karen Marie's brother, Lars) was surprised when I told him Hans had been on the same ship as Jens and Kirsten.

What must it have been like for these ten people, representing three generations, to prepare for their journey and leave part of the family behind? It's difficult to imagine the emotions they felt as they sold their possessions, packed their trunks, and bade goodbye to their families and friends to embark on a serious journey, with communication possible only through ship-carried letters, and eventually a transatlantic telegraph cable. Would they ever see some of these beloved people again? These Mormon immigrants also left behind their native country—which they must have loved in spite of its economic difficulties—and gave up being surrounded by those who shared their language, their cultural customs, and the foods they were used to. They must have had high hopes and imaginations full of dreams for a wonderful new life. Surely they also felt a degree of apprehension, knowing there would be difficulties, hardships, and dangers, as most travel brings with it a mix of anticipation and anxiety about the unknowns. Yet they proceeded to sacrifice and risk with profound faith.

In the early days of emigration, prior to the advent of steamships and trains, travel conditions for the Mormons coming from Europe were not only difficult but also took nearly six months to complete. But by the time our first family traveled, sailing ships and ox-pulled wagons had faded into the past. Church leaders in Salt Lake had created a system in which emigrants had escorts for their travel in large groups, and had also made an agreement with the Guion shipping line to offer the emigrants more comfortable passage and better accommodations at a reduced rate. Conway B. Sonne observed, "Mormon emigrants could pay as much as one third less than regular steerage passengers."[97] Unfortunately, some "gentiles" or non-Mormon "relatives and friends" began coming aboard pretending to be Mormons in order to take unfair advantage of the improved conditions and lower travel fees to which they were not entitled.[98] This program facilitating emigrant journeys for large groups of Mormons was already in place when the Christensen and Hansen families voyaged, so whether the two families associated aboard or not, they were no doubt among other people they knew from the Copenhagen Conference—the LDS Church district in their area.

The passengers on these voyages included not only Mormon and "gentile" emigrants but also men who had just completed missions for the Church of Jesus Christ of Latter-day Saints in Europe. One of these returning missionaries would be placed in general leadership over the LDS group on board, while the ship's captain still had final authority not only over the Mormons but also over the other passengers, the crew, and the ship itself. Captain Forsyth directed the 24 June 1874 sailing, and Peter Cornelius Carstensen was the missionary presiding over the Mormon entourage aboard, including our family.

Carstensen and our group of emigrants traveled across the Atlantic on the SS *Idaho*. Conway B. Sonne relates a wry note about one of the *Idaho*'s sailings from Liverpool and gives some facts about this ship:

> In the summer of 1874 the British steamship *Idaho* carrying 806 Mormons to New York encountered a frightening Atlantic storm. During the severest turbulence the vessel's captain commented "that there were too many 'Mormons' on board for the ship to be harmed; he had carried companies for 18 years and had never heard of a ship carrying 'Mormons' being lost." This 3,132-ton Guion liner, from September 7, 1870, to the fall of 1877, transported six emigrant companies totaling 3,057 Saints from Liverpool to America.
>
> The *Idaho* [was one of] the first two Guion straight-stem steamers. The *Idaho* was a single-screw, iron-hull steamship with two masts, one funnel, and inverted engines. Her rated speed was 11 knots, and the average time of the six crossings was 12.8 days.[99]

The Sonne statement above regarding the ship that carried 806 Mormons does not give a specific sailing date, and I wondered whether the group of passengers needing assurance of safety during a storm at sea included the little band of the Christensen and Nielsen (Hansen) families. To check it out, I looked in Andrew Jenson's *Church Chronology* and found a notation for 24 June 1874, the date we know this family group sailed from Liverpool:

> The steamship *Idaho* sailed from Liverpool, England, with 806 Saints (about 700 Scandinavian and 110 British), in charge of P. C. Carstensen. The company arrived at New York July 6th, and at Salt Lake City July 15th.[100]

Both Sonne and Jenson list 806 passengers, and no other voyage during the summer of 1874, for which I found record, listed that same total. Also, the mention of Carstensen in each source further supports my conclusion that Sonne was speaking of the group with whom our principals sailed. They experienced the turbulent storm he described, and they stayed safe, just as the captain had predicted.

A history of Jens's brother, Hans Christian Nielsen (Hansen), who was on that sailing, does not mention the storm on the Atlantic but does tell of a storm on the initial sailing from Copenhagen to Hull:

> On the 19th of June 1874, they set sail from Copenhagen for Hull, England, by Skagen Rau (the northern tip of Denmark). A terrible storm arose and the lives of those aboard were in great danger. The brethern [*sic*] of Utah were sick, and President Christensen gave orders that those who were not sick should join in prayer in behalf of the sick, that the Lord would spare their lives and calm the tempest. It fell to Hans Christian to pray as he was not sick. They held him while he prayed to God to protect their lives from the storm. The ocean almost at once became calm and the waves ceased to rise. They arrived in Hull, England, the following morning.[101]

I was puzzled by this part of Hans's history because it places the storm at sea during the journey across the smaller seas between Copenhagen and Hull instead of *after* their departure from Liverpool and while on the Atlantic Ocean as recounted by Sonne. Could the historians have been confused about the location? Hans has a reputation of having been a meticulous record keeper, so his historians would likely have had access to his accurate journal from which to construct their records. So were there two storms that impacted our family group? An online posting entitled "A Compilation of General Voyage Notes" says:

A company of Scandinavian emigrants bound for Zion, numbering 703 souls, sailed from Copenhagen, June 18, 1874, together with five returning elders, namely, Peter C. Carstensen, Christian F. Schade, Peter C. Christensen, Mathias B. Nilsson, and Jens Hansen.[not our Jens Hansen]. The first company of 517 souls left by the steamer "Milo" and arrived safely in Hull, England, Monday, June 22nd in the forenoon and the same day were taken by rail to Liverpool. Another company of 186 souls, in charge of Elder Christian F. Schade, left on the steamer "Humber" and had a hard voyage across the North Sea on account of rough weather, for which reason the captain ordered a lot of cattle to be thrown overboard; but the ship arrived nevertheless safely at Hull on the 22nd in the evening, and on the following day the emigrants arrived by train in Liverpool, where all the Scandinavian Saints, together with a number of other emigrants, went on board the steamer "Idaho," which sailed from Liverpool on Wednesday afternoon June 24th.[102]

Because the records for the following year of 1875 show that the passengers in two ships from Copenhagen were divided by Conference or District, I am concluding that a portion of the Copenhagen Conference in 1874 that included both of our family groups was among the passengers on this second vessel to leave Copenhagen. The Compilation of General Voyage Notes corroborates Hans's history, so we see that our family groups *did* encounter not one, but two notable storms: first, on the smaller *Humber* en route from Copenhagen to Hull, and second, aboard the larger SS *Idaho* on the Atlantic between Liverpool and New York. Several well-traveled friends have told me that even today storms on the Atlantic can be treacherous.

The day after setting sail from Liverpool, Carstensen—leader of the Mormon emigrants—sent the first of three reports to Joseph F. Smith, then President of the European Mission 1874–75. (Joseph F. Smith was the son of Hyrum Smith, the elder brother of the Mormon prophet and founder, Joseph Smith. Hyrum was also murdered at Carthage Jail when this little son, Joseph F. Smith, was nearly six years old.) As mission president years later, Joseph F. Smith was responsible for arranging transportation for emigrant converts.[103]

Carstensen's letters narrate some events and practices that took place on board the ship and likely affected our families as part of the group. His letters are among the few records I have found specific to this voyage and therefore seem of significant value. Carstensen begins:

CORRESPONDENCE AT SEA
S. S. *Idaho*, off Queenstown [Ireland] June 25, 1874
Prest. Jos. F. Smith

Dear Brother,

Soon after bidding "good bye" to you and the brethren and sisters who accompanied us on board, we completed our berthing arrangements and organized the company into ten wards [organizational units], appointing four chaplains (three Scandinavian and one English,) and the requisite number of guard captains for night service.

After singing and prayer, in the different compartments, all retired last night, feeling well, the water being very smooth.

This morning there is a little more motion to the vessel, of which a few of the people seem to be fully conscious, for the casting up of accounts has commenced, while some others begin to experience that indescribable something which never fails to impart very peculiar feelings.

Most of the Saints are well and, as a matter of course, the songs of Zion are heard reverberating through the air.

The total number of passengers on board is 1,117. [My note: I don't know why Carstensen's total differs from the other computations, unless it includes non-Mormon travelers.]

We trust that, through the blessing of the Lord, our company will arrive in health and safety.

Kindly remember us in your prayers, and accept our united love and best wishes.

We are, your brethren,
P. C. CARSTENSEN,
GEO. F. GIBBS,
JOHN CLARK.[104]

What stands out to me in this letter is that the LDS people aboard were organized into wards just like they are on land, and that chaplains (or bishops) supervised the wards. Three Scandinavian chaplains and one English chaplain were appointed, a possible indication of the ratio of the people from those two geographical areas and the proportional language differences. I wonder whether the Christensens and their little grandson were placed in the same ward as Hans and his family. I love that there was much singing on board, and probably much of the music consisted of hymns or folksongs many of the people would have known by heart. Hans was known for his fine voice and musical talent, and perhaps he had responsibility for some of the singing. Carstensen's subdued account of what Sonne described as a terrifying Atlantic storm makes me wonder what other details he chose to put a positive spin upon. Even with his subtlety, though, his description of the event takes up a large portion of the letter, indicating that the storm veiled by his obscuring language was a significant one.

Another passenger aboard the ship during that storm, but *not* connected to our family, was Emma Palmer Manfull, who was eight years old at the time of the voyage and probably English. She later wrote her observations about the voyage and the captain in her journal:

> Every morning we held meetings on the boat.... I remember being quite seasick for a few days. When we reached what was called Devil's Pass we encountered a storm. This Devil's Pass is a place where if a boat gets too near will whirl it about and very few ever get out of it again. In this storm the boat drifted over into Devil's Pass and about two in the afternoon the sailors began to holler "down deck, down deck" meaning for everyone to go down to the lower deck. It was terrible and water was coming in through the portholes and everything was slipping and sliding all over the deck. Mother put us children up in a top bunk with a lot of Danish children.... Mother sat by the bed until about four o'clock in the morning so as to watch and care for us children. After the storm was all over and we were out of the Devil's Pass the captain said if it hadn't been for the Saints on board nothing could have saved us. There had never been a ship go down that had any Saints on it.[105]

Her story not only provides vivid details but also further confirms that the famous statement made by the captain referred to the June 1874 voyage that included both families of our group. However, the captain may have made this statement on other voyages as well.

A further description of the storm appears in "A Compilation of General Voyage Notes":

> With the exception of one stormy day, the weather was favorable all the way. On that day the waves rolled like mountains, and a mighty

wave rushed over the deck, and (the hatchway happening to be open) a great volume of water went down below, so that mess boxes, baskets and the like were seen floating about, while the passengers were forced into the bunks till the water was pumped out. A remarkable calm was observed among the Saints on that occasion, while the opposite was the case with the other passengers, who were badly frightened. Captain Forsyth, relating the occurrence on the following morning at the breakfast table, said that he went down to the people in the forepart [non-Mormons] to allay their fears, as they were crying aloud, "Lost, we are lost!" But after he had assured them that there was no danger, because there were too many "Mormons" aboard for the ship to be harmed, order and quiet was restored. A Catholic priest, who was present, took exception to this statement, but the captain said that he had now for 18 years conveyed the "Mormons" safely across the Atlantic, and he had never heard of the loss of any ship carrying "Mormons."[106]

Two notable storms, then, took place during the voyages of our first group of emigrants. Although they arrived safely in New York after thirteen days on the SS *Idaho*, those storms must have been of deep concern in spite of the calm description and the captain's faith in his ship's being protected from collapse because Mormons were on it. I wonder how Hans's wife, Karen M., felt during the storms with the additional vigil of her pregnancy, and how the children re-acted to the unpredictable elements. Were they among the Danish children who shared an upper bunk with the young Emma Palmer Manfull?

Carstensen wrote again to Joseph F. Smith almost two weeks after his first letter, this one upon the ending of the sea voyage and the safe arrival of the *Idaho* in New York:

CORRESPONDENCE
AMERICA
New York, July 7, 1874
Prest. Jos. F. Smith

Dear Brother,
We are very much pleased and thankful to inform you that our com-pany reached New York yesterday morning early, in good health.
　　The passage was all that could be desired, with the exception of one night's "fresh gale." Which caused a little consternation among

some. The weather was cool and breezy all the way, which was most fortunate for the good health and comfort of many. Capt. Forsyth and the doctor said that they had never seen so healthy a lot of passengers brought to New York; neither had they seen so clean a lot.

The Captain paid us much courtesy and attention, and indeed all the officers did likewise.

The passengers are now on the river steamer [to cross the Hudson River to the railroad depot in Jersey City] wending their way to the railroad cars, all counted and ticketed.

Please excuse these very few lines, for we have had no time to do anything but look after the passengers, and now the railroad officials say we must be off. We shall write to you on our arrival home.

With united love and best wishes to yourself and the brethren, we remain yours in the Gospel,
P. C. CARSTENSEN,
JOHN CLARK,
GEO. F. GIBBS.[107]

After safe arrival at New York, our party checked in through Castle Garden and saw their luggage transferred from the ship to a steamer. They had been personally counted, received their tickets, and were en route on a river steamer to the "cars," or train, for the journey overland.

True to his word, Carstensen followed up with his final letter sixteen days later with a more complete report after the travelers had arrived in Ogden:

CORRESPONDENCE
AMERICA
Ogden, U.T. [Utah Territory] July 23, 1874
Prest. Jos. F. Smith

Dear Brother,
I am very thankful to be able to write to you favorable intelligence concerning the progress of our company, which left Liverpool, per steamship *Idaho*, on the 24th of June last.

As we have already informed you, our passage to New York was a pleasant and healthy one—no trouble of any kind, no sickness, no death. It was made in eleven and half days. Brother W. C. Staines, who awaited our arrival, came on board with the Custom House

Officers, and made every arrangement possible for the speedy transfer of our emigrants. Our people and their luggage were landed first, and it took all day to do it, while the "gentile" portion of our fellow-passengers—both steerage and intermediate—waited rather impatiently until this unshipping process was through. We were told several times by our good Captain Forsyth that our troubles would commence after we left his ship. We were reminded of his words, when in Castle Garden, as bedtime approached.[108]

Castle Garden was the original immigration center at the Battery in Lower Manhattan. A circular building near the water between the Hudson and East Rivers of New York, it had been first a fort and then a theater that seated eight thousand people. It was transformed in 1855 into the entry point for the "emigrants from Europe" upon their arrival.[109] I'm not sure what Captain Forsyth was warning Carstensen about, nor why Carstensen referred to Castle Garden as fulfillment of that warning, but Sonne explains that Castle Garden:

> was prepared for the benefit of the emigrants. Castle Garden was intended to be a source of helpful information and assistance to the new arrivals....
>
> Although swindlers and confidence men were naturally forbidden to enter the premises, in practice Castle Garden became an ideal place for all kinds of cheats and crooks with their clever schemes to victimize the new-comers. The predators stalked the unwary emigrants, trying to separate them from their money.... It was often difficult for a stranger, particularly one with a limited knowledge of English, to determine who legitimately represented the rail, coach, and steamboat transit systems. Mormon leaders early recognized the problem of the exposure of their converts to the unscrupulous element and established their own agents at all major ports of embarkation and debarkation. Profiting from years of experience and an effective organization, these church representatives smoothly arranged transportation from Castle Garden and protected and sheltered their people from dishonest operators.[110]

The rest of Carstensen's final letter to President Joseph F. Smith continues with his report of the overland portion of the remaining travel for his group of charges:

> On Tuesday, the 7th inst., [instant: the present or current month] our company, which occupied seventeen cars, left New York. Our train

being a long one, many a bystander watched us speed by.... [Carstensen next reports the deaths of two children.] While I am sorry to record the death of any, we all very readily acknowledge the preserving hand of the Lord in bringing us through so happily and well.

At Laramie City, two extra cars were attached to our train for the accommodation of some non-"Mormon" emigrants.... [He describes a serious injury and a passenger's misconnection with the train.] This intelligence was perhaps invaluable to our people, for many of them, up to that time, had been very careless, contrary to our advice and instructions. It would be well for our brethren and sisters who may come after us, to be very cautious, for they know not what trouble they might suffer by being careless.

We were all very glad to reach Ogden on Wednesday, the 15th inst., about 6 o'clock p.m. Brother Erastus Snow [who had opened the first LDS mission in Denmark in 1850] and son met us and cordially gave us their welcome home. At about 8 o'clock the company went down to Salt Lake City. On Thursday, the 16th, the emigrants got their luggage, with a few exceptional cases where their luggage had not arrived.

A meeting was held in the Tithing yard, in the afternoon, when brother Snow gave many good counsels and instructions to the newly arrived Saints, and spoke in the Danish language. After meeting was closed the company separated, the Saints going with their relations and friends to their homes.

I remain your brother in the New and Everlasting Covenant,
P. C. CARSTENSEN.[111]

Carstensen's letters relate unexpected events of which our family members may or may not have been aware. As to the meeting in the tithing yard, Mormons are asked to tithe, or give 10 percent of their net increase to the Church. In the early days, tithes were customarily paid in grain, produce, and animals. The tithing yard where the people delivered these commodities was located at that time upon the ground later occupied by the Joseph Smith Memorial Building, formerly the opulent Hotel Utah, across the street from the Salt Lake Temple.

After retrieving their luggage from the train at Salt Lake, Karen Marie's parents and their little grandson would have attended these welcoming meetings, then made their way to Brigham City, Utah, a growing community located about sixty miles north of Salt Lake. Perhaps Karen Marie's parents chose to settle in

Brigham because they knew someone who lived there, possibly a family of one of the several missionaries who were instrumental in their conversions.

Brigham in 1874 was a relatively new town, having been originally established in 1851 by a few settlers on Box Elder Creek who built a fort with farmlands around it. Log cabins and adobe houses were built outside the fort. The railroads had lines in operation through the area in the early 1870s.[112] Small businesses such as a mercantile and a tannery came into existence, and most of the skilled artisans were Danish converts.[113]

In Brigham and other new settlements, people who had wagons often lived in them until they could build more permanent and comfortable shelter. Others lived in dugouts. No family lore tells whether our group lived with a missionary's family, built a house, found existing housing, or built a dugout upon their arrival, but Jens and Kirsten Christensen and their little grandson settled in Brigham City.

The Hans Christian Nielsen (Hansen) family also went originally to Brigham City. Perhaps they *were* traveling with Karen Marie's parents, and they settled near them briefly. Hans's history says of their arrival and settlement:

> The [Hans C.] Hansen family arrived in Ogden, Utah, (the railroad center for Utah) on 17 July 1874. [However, Andrew Jenson's *Church Chronology* lists the arrival as Salt Lake on 15 July]. They went at once to Brigham City, Utah, and stayed there for a couple of weeks; and then they decided to locate in Newton, Cache County, Utah and make their home there.[114]

Hans had been confirmed a member of the Church of Jesus Christ of Latter-day Saints by Christian Daniel Fjeldsted in Denmark on 20 June 1868.[115] Fjeldsted was originally from Denmark but in 1868 was a missionary from Utah serving in Copenhagen. He returned to Utah in 1870, settled in Logan, and was living in Cache Valley in 1874 when Hans and his family arrived from their home country.[116] Because these two men had known each other in Denmark, and because "in Newton on 18 August 1875, Brother C.D. Fjeldsted and Chris Larsen from Logan, Utah, came and set Hans Christian apart as President of the Scandinavian people,"[117] it may have been Fjeldsted who influenced Hans and his family to move north from Brigham into the budding townsite of Newton in gorgeous Cache Valley.

Newton was likely a bit more rustic than Brigham City, having been established only five years before the family's arrival from Denmark. Into this untamed and austere site in a wide, gently rolling valley surrounded by majestic mountains,

Hans and his family traveled from Brigham, perhaps by wagon, to Newton. Or they may have journeyed by train to Logan or Mendon, where Fjeldsted may have met them and taken them to Newton in his own conveyance.

As a first order of business upon arrival in Newton, Hans either acquired or built a dugout for shelter, and his family moved into it: Hans, Karen M., and four—possibly five—children. I don't know whether Lars, the mysterious child, stayed with them or met with other family and left the group. Living in this primitive-sounding structure in a new and struggling town, Hans's family began the work of settling in and building—perhaps even just surviving—while they looked forward to the other half of the family arriving in a year's time.

Building a dugout was in itself a demanding bit of work. A description appears in *Box Elder Lore*:

> The dugout was generally one small room about 12–14 feet. Settlers would dig a hole in the hillside about four feet deep. The rooms had a rock wall or a pole lining…to keep the dirt from caving in…. Poles for the roof were laid lengthwise resting on the rocks or poles at each end. Small logs were hued [*sic*—hewed]…with an axe so they fit close together for the roof…. Bulrush, hay or native wheat grass…was placed on the logs, and next came dirt on top of the hay. Rocks were placed together inside the dugout to make a fireplace, and a round hole was placed above it in the roof for the smoke to escape…. Dirt was banked up against the wall around the dugout to the bottom of the roof. Native wheat grass hay was placed on the ground floor for a carpet, and this made it both clean and warm…. They could make the door and window with a small frame, then stretch pelts, hides, sacks, or anything they had over the frame and hold it there with pegs or homemade strings…. Can you imagine a modern mother enduring children's antics closed in such small areas in the dead of winter?[118]

The settlers in the fledgling town of Newton faced the same challenges the people in Salt Lake had grappled with upon their 1847 and later arrivals: shelter, homes, kitchens, outhouses, crops, food, a church, a school, streets, medicine, irrigation, a well system, and everything else humans need for comfort, health, and safety. Food was scarce. The dugout may have seemed crowded and it was probably difficult to keep as tidy or sanitary as they would have liked. Winter would be coming soon, and some winters in Newton were harsh. Perhaps the winters in Denmark were similar enough that the people were acclimated to the weather, but staying warm and fed would not be an easy task.

During the year of new beginnings and settlement after their arrival, Hans C. and Karen M. suffered two great losses. Karen M., who was pregnant during the emigration, gave birth on 27 October 1874 "to a stillborn girl"[119] whom they named Hedvig. Were the privations of the journey and the work of settlement partially responsible for this stillbirth?

Just a few weeks before the remaining family group from Denmark was expected to arrive in Utah, Hans C. and Karen M.'s son, Jacob Daniel, died on 2 June 1875, of diphtheria just short of his third birthday. Jacob Daniel had traveled from Denmark to Utah as a two-year-old. Diphtheria kept reappearing in this era as epidemics undulated through the communities of Cache Valley. Losing these two children in one year in a new country—after having lost a child before leaving Denmark—must have been difficult for this family to abide. Things must have seemed bleak to them at this point. Did they have regrets? Did they rail and ask why? Or did they stoically soldier on?

Or both?

※

Back home in Denmark, Jens and Karen Marie had been working at the Adelersborg Brick Factory near Starreklinte to earn money for their journey. Many established businesses had residences or dorms for their employees, and apparently Jens, Karen Marie, and their two children who were still with them lived at the brick factory while they worked there.

Jens's skudsmaalsbog shows that on 27 April 1872, he departed Jyderup for Vallekilde as witnessed by the priest Bendt Lindhardt of Jyderup Kirke, and two weeks later on 10 May 1872 he arrived at Starreklinte as witnessed by F. G. Hoffmann. This would put his actual arrival later than his stated contract start date of 1 May 1872.

Interestingly enough, the family histories and lore say that Jens and Karen Marie worked at the brick factory until their departure to America. But the skudsmaalsbog says that on 11 October 1874, Jens departed from Starreklinte Vallekilde Parish to travel to Holmstrup, as attested by Binzer, Parish Minister. No comments were written in the servant conduct book about the quality of his/their work at the brick factory. Nearly two weeks later, on 23 October 1874, he arrived at Holmstrup as again witnessed by Priest Lindhardt. This is the last entry in the skudsmaalsbog, so for the eight months from October 1874 until Jens and his family's emigration in June 1875, we have no indication of where they stayed or what they did.

The Newton Ward Records, however, show that they continued interacting with the Church in the area, because on 19 April 1875, Jens N. Hansen both baptized and confirmed a Karen Kirstine Petersen Hansen as a member of the Church of Jesus Christ of Latter-day Saints. No location is given, but the time was prior to Jens's emigration, so the baptism obviously took place in Denmark. Since they were apparently living at Holmstrup at the time, the baptism could have been in the same lake in which Jens and Karen Marie had been baptized—Lake Skarresø.

Who was this woman? She will show up again later in the story with more clues, yet she will remain a mystery.

Perhaps Jens and his family boarded with someone during those final months in Holmstrup—a family member, maybe? They must have continued to work in some capacity so they would have enough funds for their travels. We do know that on Wednesday, 25 June 1875, the second family group set sail from Copenhagen.

⁂

In researching this part of the family history, I developed an intense admiration for these individuals who worked to make a living, heard the message of a new religion, chose to be baptized in spite of local persecution, and made a commitment to a new lifestyle. I marveled at their tenacity in traveling over multiple bodies of water and wide stretches of land—probably suffering seasickness and homesickness—to arrive at a strange place where they could be near the center of their religious faith and live the tenets of that faith in peace. What strength they demonstrated to endure hardship, and to sacrifice so much to make a new start in a beautiful but sometimes inhospitable valley. I asked myself: Could I have done that? I have trouble just parting with clutter, let alone ripping myself away from all that I hold dear. I struggle to navigate through foreign language phrases for a few weeks' vacation, so I can only imagine what it would be like to move to a land I had never seen, where I knew nothing of the language. Still, I like to think some aspects of their journey were a novel adventure, or were at least enjoyable, or maybe even exciting. I hope so.

CHAPTER 9

EMIGRATION, SECOND WAVE: 1875

While the young son of Karen Marie and Jens settled with her parents in Brigham City, and Jens's brother Hans and his family made a new start in a dugout in Newton, Jens and Karen Marie and their other two children made plans to join them. Also emigrating in this second wave were Karen Marie's brother Lars, his wife, Christine, and their children. They all had worked to earn money, sold their possessions, packed for travel, and left their homes and other family members and friends. They traveled by carriage and by train to arrive in Copenhagen by land at about the same time as Peter Christian Geertsen and his company arrived by sea. These seven men had been serving as Mormon missionaries in Scandinavia, and would travel to Utah Territory as supervisors for the group of emigrants on this ship. In addition, Peter Christian Geertsen kept a meticulous journal. In every detail he recorded, I imagine Jens, Karen Marie, Lars, Christine, and all of their children among the passengers, and I ponder how the events Geertsen observed may have affected our families. Geertsen was nearly forty-eight years old when he wrote on 30 May 1875:

> I received a letter from President Larsen stating that I would be re-
> leased [as a missionary] to go home with the first emigration this
> year. I was happy for that privilege and was glad that I could now
> soon enjoy the society of my own dear family. I was also informed
> that [unreadable number] Rigsdalers would be at my disposal for the
> purpose of emigrating poor.[120]

Geertsen makes various entries about the details of preparing lists of emigrants and handling money for the voyage. He served in the Aarhus Conference (or district), and after he received Larsen's letter, he wrote on 22 June 1875:

I left Aarhus [on the coast of Jutland] with a company of saints feeling glad for the signs of love and good will from the saints that was left behind. We arrived in Copenhagen at 9 p.m. without having any sickness. The weather being very fine & sea calm.... All feeling well.[121]

Two smaller ships, this time the SS *Cato* and the SS *Pacific*, carried emigrants from Copenhagen to Hull, where the passengers transferred to rail cars for the journey across England and then boarded the larger ship for the transatlantic voyage to New York. Geertsen writes on Thursday, 24 June 1875, that he has exchanged money and had some notes signed, and further:

In the afternoon about 6 p.m. we went onboard "The Cato", Captain J. King.... I was appointed captain for the emigrants to England on this steamer, Elder A. Jenson from Aalborg Conference being with me. The Saints was from Aarhus, Aalborg, Stockholm & Goteborg Conferences, while the saints from Copenhagen, Christiania & Malmo Conferences went on "The Pacific", Captain Soulsby. President C.G. Larsen, Elders J. Frantzen, L.S. Andersen, N. Andersen was with that company.[122]

From this entry, we learn that the emigrants from the Copenhagen Conference—including our people—traveled from Copenhagen to Hull, England, on the SS *Pacific*, an iron-screw steamer built in Hull in 1860, 204 feet long, 27 feet wide, with a 16-foot draft.[123] We are indebted to Geertsen for providing details—especially those not found in any other sources—about this journey for the emigrants. This group also found the route from Copenhagen to Hull over the North Sea held its challenges.

Geertsen writes:

Friday June 25: At 2 a.m. we went onboard [the *Cato*] and soon we started off, "The Pacific" being about 20 minutes ahead of us. The weather fine and not a wave to be seen. We soon passed the other steamer [the *Pacific* with our people on it] and salute was seen from one vessel to the other. At 7 p.m., we passed The Skaw [Skagen, the northernmost tip of Denmark] and turned towards the west. We had very fine [weather] all day and no sickness was seen among us. I had guards put out in the night to watch, and appointed chaplains.

Saturday June 26: In the morning The Pacific was lost out of sight. Weather fine. All feeling well until towards night when the wind commenced to blow a little harder. Several was sick.

Sunday June 27: The ship was rolling some, causing some seasickness among us. I was sick too, but soon got better and went all round looking after the saints. We had no meeting, the sickness preventing us.[124]

We know the waterway from Copenhagen to Hull is subject to storms. Although Geertsen described the rolling seas and the seasickness aboard his own vessel, the *Cato*, we can surmise that the passengers aboard the SS *Pacific* experienced similar seas and sickness. The *Pacific* departed Copenhagen first but arrived at Hull sometime after the *Cato*.

Geertsen continues his journal details:

Monday June 28: About 1 a.m. we passed Grimsby [a town in England] going up the river Humber and arrived at Hull at 3 a.m. The Captain and crew has been very kind to us, and treated us with respect.

We now laid at anchor about 8 a.m. "The Pacific" came in and we was taken to shore about 11 a.m. and started 3 p.m. to Liverpool per railroad. Distance from Copenhagen to Hull is 300 Miles [by sea] and from Hull to Liverpool 175 miles [by land] traveled in 4 days. I felt to thank God for his mercy in bringing the saints so quick on their way. We arrived in Liverpool a little after 9.[125]

With one sea voyage and one train trip behind them, our group embarked on the sailing voyage across the Atlantic aboard the SS *Idaho*, the same ship the first family group had sailed aboard the previous year.

The Copenhagen Conference Emigration List for SS *Idaho* on 25 June 1875 shows:

No. 400 Jens Nielsen (33)
No. 401 Karen Marie Nielsen (30)
No. 402 Soren Peter Nielsen (4) [their son]
No. 403 Hanne M. Nielsen (2 ½) [their daughter]
No. 406 Lars P. Christensen (34) [Karen Marie's brother]
No. 407 Christine K. Christensen (32) [Lars's wife]
No. 408 Jens P. Christensen (1) [their son]
No. 409 Caroline Christensen (7) [their daughter][126]

The emigration list confirms that Jens had not yet adopted the Hansen surname of his father. This second group consisted of four adults and four children from age seven to one year, and—like Hans's wife the year before—Karen Marie was pregnant.

Another passenger, John Anderson, an emigrant from Sweden who had come on the *Cato* with many who were sick, wrote: "The 29th we went on board the ship *Idaho*, which was to take us over the Atlantic to America. Went out to — [dash appears in journal and apparently indicates an omission of the location name] and loaded coal…until the 1 July."[127]

Evidently quite a load of coal was required for the long voyage across the Atlantic. Geertsen notes the preparations for the coming voyage after arrival at Liverpool:

> The saints was taken down to dock on board the "S.S. Idaho", Captain Beddoes. Some of the brethren was taken along with the goods to look out that nothing was lost. It took us most of the night to get into order and some did not find berths till next day.

> Tuesday June 29: The elders was very busy to get the emigrants into berths…. L. S. Andersen and I went up to the office and returned tickets.[128]

At first this returning of tickets puzzled me, but then I remembered that when Richard and I took the night train from Paris to Florence some years ago, all the passengers had to turn their passports over to the conductor when he made rounds after the train pulled out of the station in the late afternoon. This policy made me very nervous; I didn't like surrendering possession of my travel document. But first thing in the morning, our passports were returned to us. I'm guessing what Geertsen refers to as "returned tickets" was a similar process. He writes:

> Wednesday June 30: Tickets was examined and all [passengers] passed the Government Doctor. Everything found right. We was laying in the river a few hours after going out of dock. President J[oseph] F. Smith appointed C.G. Larsen as President, the others as counselors to him. And about 6 p.m. the anchor was hoisted and we started for America [with] weather fair and very calm.

Even though this large group of emigrants had traveled to Copenhagen, to Hull, and to Liverpool, Geertsen notes that as the anchor was hoisted and the ship began to move out of the River Mersey, *then* they "started for America"! The preliminary journeys were behind them, and this enormous voyage to their destination in America had commenced in earnest. What thoughts did these people have as they watched Liverpool recede and the vast expanse of ocean waves become the only thing they could see? They would have had sunrise near 5:00 in the morning , and daylight until about 9:30 in the evening, so lots of light for the days of the voyage.

The LDS Millennial Star carried the following notice 5 July 1875:

> EMIGRATION.—On Wednesday last, June 30th, at 6 p. m., the third company of Saints, this year, sailed from this port for New York on board Guion & Co.'s United States Mail Steamer *Idaho*, Capt. Beddoes. There were 765 passengers—consisting of 666 Scandinavians, namely, 447 adults; 188 children; 25 infants, and 6 returning missionaries:—English, 56 adults; 38 children; 4 infants, and 1 returning missionary.
>
> The company were all feeling well—being in the enjoyment of good health and spirits. We anticipate for them a safe and pleasant journey to their mountain home. They have the services of seven very able men in the Elders returning to Zion. God bless them! May He control the elements in their favor![129]

Geertsen tells us that he and the other missionaries responsible for the Mormon emigrants immediately began to get the people organized and settled. There was much to be done aboard the ship.

> Thursday July 1: President Larsen called a council and Elder A. Jenson [later well-known as Andrew Jenson, the historian] was appointed captain of the guard. The saints was divided into wards and a president of each appointed, while the Elders should have a special oversight over the different Districts. The weather continued fair except a little fog. Having now got organized, we commenced to feel a little more at ease. We found it a rest to us after several days' hard labor and care. The organization was now as follows:

C.G. Larsen.	President
J. Frantzen.	Clerk
L.S. Andersen	Presidents on the different decks.
N. Andersen	
P.C. Geertsen	

Miles Williams
A. Jenson   Captain of Guard
and 762 [*sic*] Saints in all. Elders included.
We arrived at Queenstown [Ireland] at 7 p.m.[130]

C. G. Larsen, the missionary appointed as president over the emigrating Mormons, wrote his first letter to the mission president, Joseph F. Smith, just before this arrival at Queenstown, Ireland:

CORRESPONDENCE AT SEA
On board the *S. S. Idaho*
Off Queenstown, July 1st, 1875
Prest. Jos. F. Smith

Dear Brother,
Having so favorable an opportunity we write you a few lines to mail at Queenstown, where we expect to arrive about six o'clock this evening. We have had a very pleasant voyage so far, the sea still and everything fine and agreeable. This morning was a little rainy and foggy, for which reason we will not reach Queenstown so soon as we otherwise would have done; but now the weather is clear and fine, most all the passengers are on deck and they seem to enjoy themselves first rate.

We have organized the company into six wards, with a President and two assistants for each ward, who also may call on others to help them if it should be necessary. Also a captain of the guard with his helpers to assist him. Elder Frantzen will continue to be our Secretary.

The Captain and officers on board, so far as we yet know, are gentlemen, and we feel assured they will do everything to make it comfortable and agreeable for our people.

We feel under many obligations to you, bro. Smith, for your kindness to us while in Liverpool, and the good and valuable instructions we received just before starting, which we shall endeavor to carry out to the best of our ability.

We also appreciate your labors and exertions in arranging everything so comfortably for so large a company, consisting of 765 souls of our people, two stewards and seven returning Elders included.

With kind love to yourself, Elders Young and Hanham, and the brethren associated with you, praying God to bless you in all your administrations we remain

Your brethren in the Gospel,
C. G. LARSEN,
M. L. WILLIAMS,
John FRANTZEN,
L. S. ANDERSEN,
N. ANDERSON,
P. C. GEERTSON,
Andrew JENSON.[131]

Perhaps these reports were meant to cover only the portion of the travels from Liverpool to New York. Otherwise the rolling seas and sickness aboard the smaller ship from Copenhagen to Hull would merit mention.

Jens and Lars and their families were included in these groups that were organized into six wards, so they would have participated in prayers and singing during the voyage, and would thus have built a community for the trip.

Geertsen faithfully continues in his journal: "Friday July 2: We had head wind and rolling sea which caused much sickness all over. I was in bed most of the time till toward night."[132] John Anderson, who helped with the coal, also comments on this storm: "On the 2nd, it blew so that the water threw up over the front of the boat."[133]

Geertsen keeps writing a little bit each day, snippets that say a great deal:

Saturday July 3: Head wind continued but not so much sea [rough waters] and less sickness. I went all round and tended to those feeling ill. Fairer weather toward night. Run 236 miles.

Sunday July 4: The sea calm and smooth. Religious service in the saloon. We held meeting on deck where all the elders spoke and most all felt well. I tended [perhaps he means attended] prayer with the English saints and spoke to them and also to those of the Scandinavians put in my charge. The run was 244 ½ miles.[134]

John Anderson wrote, "On the 4th we held a service; we had a good song choir along from Norway, and they gave us song many times during the voyage."[135] Jens and Lars and their families would have participated in these Sabbath services and probably had their hearts encouraged and lightened by the music and the warm association with other people who were traveling and singing with them. Jens had a good voice and loved to sing. Did he help with the music aboard ship? He must have brought his violin. Did he play it?

More entries penned by Geertsen convey details about the conditions of travel:

Monday July 5: The wind was on the raise but favored us a little. Distance made 264. We was now about ⅓ of the Distance to New York.

Tuesday July 6: I had a bad headache. Made 234 ½ miles. Sea calm and nice. We stopped 2 hours to clean some pipes.

Wednesday July 7: A sister from Sweden was moved to hospital being very sick. Several others was bad. We went 227 miles—half the distance was now made to New York.

Thursday July 8: We had fair weather but head wind. Made 240 miles. An old sister died from Sweden 70 years old by the name of Kjersti Swensen on the 7th at 5 p.m. and was buried in the sea at 10 p.m. Service was done by Captain Beddoes.

Friday July 9: Made 255 miles. I wrote some notes for money borrowed. Fair weather. Rain at night.

Saturday July 10: We made only 225 ½ miles. Several was sick and had been for some time but was getting a little better. I used my time to assist the sick and tried to get something to strengthen them.

Sunday July 11: We sailed 263 ½ miles; had strong winds against us but sea stream was favorable. We could not hold meeting on deck. Several became seasick.[136]

Did Jens and his family retreat to their bunks to wait out the storm? Was Karen Marie affected more by seasickness because she was pregnant? Apparently not all became seasick, but most were probably counting the days until the port of New York would appear on the horizon.

Monday July 12: Weather fine but head wind continued. Sailed 235 miles. Got pilot on board. [Perhaps at Newfoundland or Canada? A knowledgeable pilot would give guidance to the captain regarding dangers to avoid as they approached land.] We gathered a little money for the stewards.

Meeting on deck at 2 p.m.

Tuesday July 13: We sailed 268 miles. Weather very fine and sea smooth. I wrote a letter home and one to Aarhus to President A.R. Andersen.

In the afternoon we came within 6 miles of New York and cast anchor waiting to be passed by doctor in the morning.

Many cried for joy.[137]

Geertsen's report that "many cried for joy" moves me. Perhaps some also cried with relief from the seasickness and maybe even cried from homesickness. But their arrival at New York brought them closer to their dreams and hopes. What did Jens and Karen Marie feel as they waited just off New York for the final formalities of the sailing journey? Were their two children excited about being this much closer to their reunion with their older brother?

Earlier that day and just prior to arrival, President Larsen had written a letter of report:

CORRESPONDENCE AT SEA
On board the S. S. *Idaho*, July 13, 1875, Off New York.
Prest. Jos. F. Smith

Dear Brother,

We are now within 50 miles of New York, fine weather and all well on board—expect to get into the harbor sometime this afternoon. We can truly say that we have had a very pleasant and agreeable voyage, still and smooth waters a great portion of the way, and in fact we have had no heavy seas at all. Nevertheless, a little sea-sickness has been prevalent once in a while, as many of our people have, as it were, never been on the water before, but as land and even the sight of land is an excellent cure for such a disease, we find almost everybody on deck this morning, and we trust, notwithstanding there are two or three of our Scandinavian Saints who are quite weak yet, having been confined to their berths for several days, that they will be able to proceed on their journey with the rest of the company when we leave New York.

One death has occurred since we left Queenstown—an aged lady from Sweden by the name of Kjersti Swenson, 73 years old. She was sick before she left and died on the 7th instant [the present or current month].

All the Saints have been called together for prayers in the different wards every morning, at 7 o'clock, and in the evening at 8. Two public meetings have been held, one yesterday, and one on Sunday, 4th instant, when general instructions have been given for the benefit of the whole company necessary under their present circumstances.

We wish to express our entire satisfaction with our treatment on board. Captain Beddoes is a fine gentleman and has done everything for our people that we have asked for, and the sick have never been neglected. The same we can say of all the officers, stewards, and all we have had to do with. Good provisions and plenty of them, has been given to all, and none have any cause to complain, and I believe everybody feels satisfied.

All the returning Elders feel well and have labored diligently among the people and assisted them all they could. The English Saints are all well, and brother Williams has confined his labors mostly among them. When we get into Castle Garden, we shall write a little more.

New York, July 14.

We came in to dock 9 o'clock this morning all well, with the exception of one or two, who are quite feeble, and we do not know yet whether they will be able to go along on the cars [train] or not. Elder Staines met us on board and bade us all welcome, feeling well both in body and spirit. By one o'clock, p.m., all our people and their luggage were safely lodged in Castle Garden, where we will remain till to-morrow morning, the 15th, when we expect to leave by train at 10 o'clock....

We feel truly thankful for the blessings of God, and His preserving care which has been extended unto us on our journey so far, and hope we may all reach our place of destination in safety.

With kind love to yourself and the brethren in the office, in which all join, praying God to bless you in all your administrations.

Your brethren in the Gospel,

C. G. LARSEN,
M. L. WILLIAMS,
JOHN FRANTZEN,
L. S. ANDERSEN,
N. ANDERSON,
P. C. GEERTSEN,
ANDREW JENSON.[138]

C. G. Larsen paints a rosy picture of the storms by saying "no heavy seas at all." Other accounts depict a different scene, but he gets points for his positive attitude. I loved knowing that Jens and Karen Marie and the other family members had been assigned to wards, had prayer with their specific group of passengers every morning and evening, sang hymns, nurtured their children, saw amazing sights, and were about to set their feet for the first time on American soil and to begin the final overland leg of their toilsome travels.

The faithful Geertsen records:

> Wednesday July 14: Doctor came by sun rise and passed us; and soon anchor was hoisted and we was taken to dock No. 15 New York, from which place we was taken on a tender to "Castle Garden" where we arrived about 1 p.m. We could get provision and every thing in this place in that line. Money exchange was also here. After our names was booked and the people settled, some of us went out in town and bought a few articles. I bought a hat & revolver.[139]

What kind of hat did Geertsen purchase? What thoughts led him to buy a gun? He evidently knew about the kinds of rascals that might attempt to board the train to commit theft. As Richard and I prepared for sleep on that previously mentioned Paris-to-Florence night train rumbling and clacking in the dark, we folded the three seats on each side of the compartment into upper, middle, and lower berths to sleep six. We and our four random compartment mates—three male Paris university students and a female American artist—all made it a point to settle our small backpacks and especially our valuables under our heads and shoulders as pillows before going to sleep, and we locked our compartment door from the inside because we had been warned of vagrants boarding at the various stops through the night with intent to rob sleeping passengers. Indeed, we heard a ruckus in the hallway during the night and someone rattled the handle of our door, but we lost nothing except a little sleep.

Next Geertsen describes the process of getting the luggage and taking the steamer across the Hudson River to the train station in Jersey City:

> Thursday July 15: At 6 a.m. our luggage was checked and put on a boat which took several hours hard labour. We left the Garden at 11 a.m. and went to dock 1 from where we was taken to railroad depot in Jersey City. We got good and comfortable cars and at 3 p.m. we started off on the Pennsylvania Railroad.... We rode through New Jersey and arrived at Philadelphia, 90 Miles from New Jersey & New York cities about

sundown. We went now through the state of Pennsylvania, and went up the Susquehanna River near which place Joseph Smith finished the translation of the Book of Mormon. Heavy rain in the night. We came to Altoona [Pennsylvania] in the morning.[140]

At the time that Jens's emigrating family was clearing Castle Gardens in New York, making their way to the trains in Jersey City by steamer, and starting their train journey, his father, Niels (sixty-one), and stepmother, Ane (forty-four), back in Svebølle, Denmark, had their eighth and final child, Frederick Ferdinand Nielsen. Some of Jens's eight half siblings were peers in age to his own children though they were the aunts and uncles. An example: my first nephew, Lyle Wiggins, was born when I was five years old. As he appears in this work several times, you may observe that he is more like a brother to me.

Geertsen's record continues:

Friday July 16: In Altoona the train was divided in two as it was considerable uphill. We made good time and arrived at Pittsburgh at 12 a.m. We was now taken in the Pittsburgh Cincinnati St. Louis Railroad into Ohio. This is a good State with rich land. At 1 a.m. we arrived at Columbus City, which is the seat of Government. We had now traveled 637 miles on railroad from New York. Heavy rain.

Saturday July 17: We went on pretty slow most all day. At 12 a.m., we came to Union City on the line of state between Ohio & Indiana and 741 miles from New York. The distance we traveled in Ohio was 253 miles from east to west.

We came now into the state of Indiana and at 6 p.m., we arrived at a place called Logansport. We here crossed two rivers called Wabash & Eel River. The last river empties into the first, and that falls into Mississippi River. We got a new Conductor and fresh supply of water. Being nearly dark before we left, we went through the rest of Indiana in the night and passed into Illinois.

Sunday July 18: We arrived at a place called Peoria 1,074 miles from New York at 20 minutes past 5 a.m. Stopped a few minutes and continued our travel to Burlington [Illinois] where we came to at 12 a.m. We came within a few miles of Nauvoo from which the Mormon people was expelled in 1846. We crossed on a fine bridge over the Mississippi River. Burlington has about 30,000 Inhabitants. We had to change cars here. After which we continued our journey through "Iowa" being short of bread and on Sunday we had to telegraph ahead and got supply at a City called Ottumwa…(10,000 inhabitants)…. We crossed the Des Moines River where the water a while back had been very high and dangerous to travel, but all was good and safe now.

Monday July 19: At 7 a.m. we arrived at Council Bluffs [Iowa]. Luggage was changed and unchecked and put into other cars of which Elder J. Frantzen and myself was put to oversee, while the other elders went with the emigrants to Omaha [Nebraska]. This took us till 11 a.m. when we (J. Frantzen, myself & some other brethren left to assist us) was taken over to Omaha. The bridge over the river is about 1 mile long and is resting on 20 iron pillars. After our arrival I was appointed to take charge of one company of emigrants as we was divided and would go on two trains from here to Utah. [Our people probably traveled on the other train as the Copenhagen Conference.]

About 3 p.m. the first train left on which I was with Elders N. Andersen & Andrew Jenson to assist me on the way. After getting started I went through the cars with the conductor & counted the passengers which came off very well. The Conductor was a fine man.

Tuesday July 20: About 6 p.m. we arrived at Sidney [Nebraska] 414 miles from Omaha. Stopped about 45 minutes and [was] overtaken by the other train [with our family on it]. We was glad to learn that all had went well thus far. We started on ahead again.

Wednesday July 21: At 7 a.m. we arrived at Laramie City [Wyoming], 573 miles from Omaha. We went pretty lively from here. At 4 p.m. we arrived at Rawlins [Wyoming], 709 miles from Omaha. I had hard work to keep the emigrants on the train and not be exposed to danger. And I laboured unceasingly with them. And we also had to keep a guard all night on every platform. As the road was full of what is called deadheads or loafers who goes along to steal what they can get their hands on.[141]

Perhaps Geertsen's revolver offered some security in these circumstances. He must never have slept a peaceful wink with his responsibilities being so vital to the safety of the group in his charge.

Thursday July 22: About 12 a.m., we arrived at Echo City [Utah] where we was met by Bishop W.W. Cluff and other saints. After a short stop, we continued our travel and arrived in Ogden City about 6 p.m. Here I was met by my wifes Mariane & Mary Anne and my son Peter Christian. He had grown considerable during my 2 years absents. I learned that all the emigrants had to go to Salt Lake City to get their luggage. I had much to tend to and could not get much time to speak to my family. And being oblige to go to Salt Lake City, I had to leave them in Ogden.

Friday July 23: At 1 a.m. we arrived in Salt Lake City and stopped in the cars till morning. At 7 the emigrants was taken to the Tithing Office where they was provided for with provision.

I called at President Young's Office and saw Elder Albert Carrington (One of the twelve [apostles])[.] I also went to [the] Historian's Office and reported my return. At 1 p.m. our luggage came and I went to get it separated and returned to Ogden with those going north. [This would have included our family]. We arrived very late and could not get it and off the cars till next morning. I also found that some of the emigrants had been without bread all day.

One of the brethren went to the Bishop and got some provision.

I stopped all night at Mary Farr's.

Saturday July 24: After some bother we got our luggage, and I also got passage secured on the Utah Northern for those who was out of money. And with a hearty farewell to my brethren and sisters, I went on my way home with Brother N.B. Mortensen's team [horses] and arrived in my home in Huntsville, Utah, in the afternoon about 3 p.m.[142]

This ends the part of Geertsen's journal that pertains to our family units' travel to America. Huntsville is in a beautiful valley arrived at by a drive through craggy, geologically stunning Ogden Canyon.

Several people told me Geertsen's journal is difficult to read, but as I take the time to study his writings closely, I can imagine myself there on the ship with my great-grandfather and his family. The journal makes it possible to visualize Jens's experience in ways that its absence does not, and I am grateful to this man for his detailed record.

Andrew Jenson, renowned for his *Church Chronology* and other publications, says in summary under Wednesday, 30 June 1875: "The steamship *Idaho* sailed from Liverpool, England, with 765 Saints, under the direction of a returning missionary named Christen G. Larsen. The company arrived at New York July 14th, and at Ogden July 22nd."[143]

And he would know, because he traveled with this group and served as captain of the guard on the ship as he returned from his mission in the Aalborg Conference.

Jens and Karen Marie with their young children, Soren Peter and Hanne, along with Lars and Christine with their little Jens P. and Caroline, were probably fatigued from the rigors of ocean travel and the overland train. They would likely have checked with someone to make sure their luggage was on the train going north rather than being on a train continuing south. They may have stopped in Ogden and then continued on, or they may have changed trains in Ogden for the travel to Brigham.

Karen Marie's parents might have brought little Jens Peter to the station to be reunited with his parents and siblings. He must have matured in many ways over a year's absence from his parents, having gained knowledge from traveling and living in a new environment as well as having grown physically. Perhaps Hans made the trip from Newton to Brigham to greet his brother's train if he could leave his fieldwork. The arrival must have been joyous for reunions with loved ones but tinged with sorrow for the absence of Hans and Christine's three children who had died. This second group of family members had arrived successfully—no small achievement, physically and financially—but in spite of their determination and delight, hard times lay ahead.

CHAPTER 10

SETTLING IN CACHE VALLEY: 1875–1878

After the family members from the 1874 and 1875 immigration waves were reunited, Jens and Karen Marie and their children stayed for a couple of weeks in Brigham City with Karen Marie's parents. They must have been relieved and happy to be together again after the rigors of separation and travel. The Hicks history written by Karen Marie's descendants gives additional insights about the second family group's travel and arrival:

> They came to Brigham City, Utah, arriving at the home of Karren [variant spelling indicating correct Danish pronunciation] Marie's parents, who had come to Brigham about a year before and brought Jens' and Karren Marie's oldest son Jens with them. Jens Hansen had a brother, Hans [Christian] Hansen, who had previously [settled] in Newton, Cache, Utah. Newton was then a new settlement of about five years....
>
> Hans persuaded Jens and his family to come [to Newton] and try to make a home, and homestead some land there.... Their family moved to Newton on 05 July 1875. [My note: This move date is not possible because Jens and Karen Marie were still en route from Denmark.] They moved in with Jens' brother Hans and his family into a dugout in the ground. There wasn't enough food to go around and they had to ration it out among themselves to keep from starving to death.[144]

Whatever the actual move date, the two families lived for a time in Hans's dugout in Newton. Hans and Karen M. still had three living children. Jens and Karen Marie had three children, including Jens Peter, from whom they had been separated for a year. Their fourth child was due in just a few months. So imagine all of these people—four adults and six children—living together in a dugout in a small town that is struggling to become established in a somewhat arid valley, with not enough to eat and a cold winter only several months away.

Prior to the arrivals of the family, Bishop William F. Rigby had been instructed on March 9, 1869, in regard to Newton's establishment:

> to lay out a town site to consist of sixteen 10-acre blocks, each to contain eight lots of 1 ¼ acres in each lot. The following Monday, James H. Martineau commenced surveying. In the course of three weeks, he surveyed the townsite and a number of 5-acre lots on the north and another field of 10-acre lots south of the town. The meadowland on the Bear River was surveyed in 5-acre lots. A number of families settled on the newly surveyed townsite.... The houses were built of logs with dirt roofs and floors.[145]

These properties were distributed by the bishop and settled by people who had moved from Clarkston as well as immigrants like those in our family group.

Cleo Griffin, a Newton historian, said during one of our conversations at the Newton Town Library in June 2013 that those early days in Newton were difficult for everyone but more difficult for some. Not only did many people live in dugouts at the time with little to eat, but they were also faced with the extremely challenging work of establishing homes and a new community. In addition, the English people who had moved to Newton considered themselves above the Scandinavians and had difficulty understanding them, so a class system was in place that was in part signified by language differences.

Jens learned English, but Karen Marie did not. Were they among those whose speech was difficult for the English to understand? It makes me sad to think that good-natured, hardworking Jens might have been marginalized in any way by his origin, thought less of because he spoke with an accent, or disadvantaged because he had less money than others. Yet it appears, through various school and tax records, that money was a struggle for him and his family.

Superimposed over these social challenges was the nonexistence of conveniences people in modern times often take for granted: electricity, telephones, running water, and indoor plumbing. My mother spoke of coal oil lamps from her childhood in the early 1900s, and of taking the horse-drawn wagon to the river to fill barrels with water for the family's weekly use. Mom had an old round metal washtub in our basement that she would fill with warm, sudsy water so her little grandchildren could take an old-fashioned style of bath. She said that was how they had bathed in those old days. Her family had used candles on their Christmas trees because they had no electric lights. The outhouse was a short walk from the house.

An unattributed family history says, "The two families lived together in a dugout on the corner of the lot now owned by Arthur Crookston."[146] When I first read this, I didn't know which property had been Arthur Crookston's nor the date the history was written, nor any legal description, so I could not determine where the dugout had been located nor its role in the subsequent property involvements. However, Vicky Jenkins (the woman who had been mowing her lawn on our previous visit) had become a valuable contact. She was the wife of Reed Jenkins, who was the son of LeOra Jenkins, who was the daughter of Eli Hansen, who was the son of Ane and Jens Niels Hansen. When I mentioned to her on the phone in November 2010 that I planned to go to the Cache County Recorder's Office next time I could get to Logan because I needed to find the location of Arthur Crookston's property, she exclaimed, "I know where Arthur Crookston lived! It was just north of where Norris Cooley's house is now."[147] So the dugout had been in Newton on the north half of Lots 7 and 8, Block 11, Plat A on the southwest corner of the intersection of Second East and First South that later made up part of the property on which Ane's house was eventually built.

At the Cache County Recorder's Office in Logan, Utah, I later located a warranty deed verifying that ownership:

> C.A. Quigley and Effie G. Quigley[,] his wife[,] grantors of Salt Lake, County of Salt Lake[,] State of Utah, hereby Convey and Warrant to Arthur Crookston[,] grantee of Newton[,] Cache County[,] for the sum of Three hundred & 00/100 Dollars, the following described tract of land in Cache County, State of Utah:
>
> All of the North half of Lot seven (7) and eight (8) in Block Eleven Plat "A" of Newton Townsite Survey. Situated in township thirteen (13) north of range one (1) West of Salt Lake Meridian.[148]

The instrument was executed 14 December 1915 and filed for record 24 March 1917 and shows that Hans's dugout had been situated on property that became—after the period of our family history in which it played a key role—Arthur Crookston's.

Once again, property ownership information had come to me verbally through Newton residents rather than through hours in the Cache County Recorder's Office. What a gratifying feeling came from being able to visualize exactly where that often-referred-to dugout had been located and where family events had transpired.

No doubt, there was much to learn and do in this new location, where a combination of English and Scandinavian converts came together to settle. Historian and librarian Carol Milligan told me in a conversation July 2011 that many people who came to Newton were from the Danish island of Bornholm where they built round churches and spoke a unique dialect of Danish.[149] Cultural customs in early Newton must have been a curious mix. The central focus the people had in common, and whose purposes bound them together, was their membership in the Church of Jesus Christ of Latter-day Saints. Even with this commonality, though, for a long period of time there were two church meetings held each week—one in English and one in a Scandinavian language. In spite of language and cultural differences, here as in other settlements populated by members of this then-forty-five-year-old Church, people helped each other, attempted co-op living for a time, and worked toward the goal of being self-sufficient. The Church at that time played not only an ecclesiastical role but also a civic one.

Those first months after arrival in Newton must have been a busy time for Jens and Karen Marie, living in the dugout, perhaps planting for a late harvest, putting by supplies for the winter, and determining where they might construct a better shelter. The Hicks history states: "Jens immediately went to work to make himself a new home. His experience in the brickyard proved to be of good use to him. He made some adobes and built a two-room house and moved his family into it."[150]

Our family lore, however, had always claimed that Karen Marie had a rock house. Local rock, quarried northwesterly on the outskirts of Newton, was often used in building houses and could have been used for her home. As I remember it, Lyle Cooley, a local resident, had told Ruby on 24 June 2009 when I was present that a rock house had stood across from Ane's home and had been torn down earlier than he could remember. He said he had used some of the stone from that property and hauled the rest away. A low rock wall runs along the driveway of a home on or near the earlier location of Karen Marie's house, but I don't know whether the wall was built from rock already on the property, or from a previous house—maybe Karen Marie's—or from rock hauled in for that purpose.

Larry Christiansen wrote:

> Rock from the Newton Rock Quarry was the prime building material after logs.... The only mention of adobe that I have ever run across in Newton concerns my Grandfather Niels Christiansen. He...came to reside in the northwestern part of [Newton], and a block east of his home there was water running in a small slough by an adjacent clay bank. My grandfather made adobes here in molds, sun dried them, and they were used inside the outer walls of frame homes for insulation. The houses he built were first log and then frame (with adobes in the

outside walls of the latter). By going up into the attic [of the old Beck home in Newton] you could see the adobe blocks in the outside walls....

After existing in a dugout, possibly almost anything could be better, so maybe J.N. tried one of adobe and found they were not the best, but temporarily better than a dugout until something better could be built. Maybe a few adobe houses were tried and found not very good, due to clay availability or weather conditions, etc.[151]

Karen Marie's house no longer stands, so it is difficult to ascertain the material from which it was built. I have found no one who can say for certain whether her house was adobe or rock.

Hicks further states that Karen Marie's "home consisted of two rooms downstairs and one in the attic that was used for a bedroom."[152] The house stood across Second Street and south a short distance from Hans's dugout and was situated on Lots 3 and 8, Block 2, Plat B of the Newton Townsite Survey.

In a telephone call to Ruby Woodward during late June 2011, I asked (at Richard's suggestion) whether she knew someone in Newton who might let me see inside their rock home to get an idea of what the living space of our early family had been like. Ruby said, "You asked at the perfect time. Newton is having a tour of several rock homes in just a few weeks."

I flew back to Utah, and LaRelia, Carla, and I visited Newton while the town was celebrating Mormon Pioneer Day, commemorating the arrival of the first pioneer party from Nauvoo into the Salt Lake Valley. Normally this day is observed on July 24th, but it fell on Sunday that year so was observed on Saturday, 23 July 2011.

On this day, numerous present-day owners of the original rock houses built by early Mormon settlers allowed visitors to tour inside them. One rock house that we visited had been added onto, but the owner had preserved the original rock walls inside the additions, so we were able to see how Karen Marie's downstairs area could have been divided into a kitchen and a living area. This home had a space-saving, steep stairway leading up to the attic, though that owner did not open the upstairs to the tour. In a different home on the tour, we did go upstairs into a large attic where we could stand tall and move about, and the charming young hostess in period costume told us that originally the attic had been one open room filled with beds for the children. At one home on the rock-home tour, I observed that adobe was used between its inner and outer walls as insulation.

Those generous people who opened their homes and history made it possible for us to imagine what Karen Marie's home might have been like, and I was grateful.

�֍

Amid all the sunshine and festivities of this 24th of July celebration, I visited the town library, where Larry Christiansen's book appeared on the shelves of the local history section, along with a white binder of his notes. I stood in the area by the front desk and remembered how often, when I had looked up a Cache Valley town or an historical incident or local census on the internet, what came up would invariably be Larry's work. Having been overwhelmed with gratitude to him for some time for all the help his historical research and records were giving me, I asked the librarian, Cheri Ballard, "Is Larry Christiansen still living? And if so, is there a way I could get his current address so I can send him a thank-you note?"

"I don't know," she said, "but his nephew is our mayor, so I'll make a few calls and find out."

I busied myself among the records in the family history section, and several minutes later, she reappeared with a smile and a Post-it Note that had Larry's and his wife's names on it, and an address in North Carolina. I was delighted.

Back home in Oregon, while Richard and I were preparing to go on vacation to the San Juan Islands, my gremlin voices started saying, "Who do you think you *are* to write to someone so famous?" But reminding myself how frequently aspects of my online research had brought up work by Larry Christiansen, that his thick book about Newton had laid the foundation for most of my understanding of the past in that town, and that I truly felt deep gratitude that had to be expressed, I wrote the note of thanks including a bit about my project and how his work had helped. When LaRelia learned that I hadn't mailed it, she reminded me that that a thank-you note is a one-way communication, so I mailed it and we left on our trip.

When we returned from vacation, Richard went to the post office to pick up the mail that had been held in our absence. He brought back a large white plastic basket full of mail, magazines, and flyers. As I stirred through it, I found a small envelope with Larry Christiansen's return address on it. "Oh my gosh!" I whispered to myself. Normally I use my thumb to rip envelopes open, but I went in search of a knife or letter opener to slice this one open crisply and respectfully.

I unfolded the single sheet from inside and found it nearly filled with small typewritten font. He thanked me for my letter and said, "I am pleased that possibly my efforts have been of some value. To add to that I have a connection and interest in Jens Nielsen Hansen," and he explained that his great-grandfather, Lars, was Karen Marie's brother, and that Lars's daughter, Caroline, was Larry's grandmother. He then gave a history that supported some facts I knew, and introduced much new information that I found fascinating and helpful. He asked which child in Jens's second family I am descended from. The last paragraph said, "I will close for now and perhaps if you want further contact, we can do it via email."[153] And he included his email address.

Of course I emailed him! In return, he sent an eleven-page attachment that included newspaper articles about my great-grandfather Jens that I had not known existed, including a write-up of Jens's funeral that I had searched for and not found. Larry and I emailed almost daily for a month, and frequently thereafter, exchanging questions and information for a number of years. I sent him a copy of some family histories, a copy of the probate file, and other discoveries of interest. He answered countless questions, gave me obscure website addresses where I found fascinating information about my ancestors, and sent me important documents. We are still in occasional email contact as of 2020, and we always exchange holiday greetings. He has been of enormous help in genealogical and historical research—a marvelous informant and guide—and though we have never met, I feel like he is a friend.

I had been searching for information about Karen Marie's brother Lars, whose family came on the ship with her and Jens. In my draft I had left myself a note: "If anything is found on Lars Christensen, insert it here." When I learned that Lars was Larry's great-grandfather, I asked some questions about him that Larry answered, and he even included a story about Lars and his family in Newton when the water rose quickly:

> My Grandmother Caroline (between age of 9 and 10) recalled that at Newton they first lived in a dugout and the ensuing spring water came into the dugout in such manner that Lars Peter had to get his wife and children out through a window.[154]

In a subsequent email, Larry further explained:

> The window in the dugout had me wondering if the dugout was positioned on the ground sloping toward the creek, since dugouts were most easily constructed on sloping ground. I have worked this over in my mind many different ways, and at this point believe the sudden rush of water could only come from an area near the creek that flooded by a

heavy runoff. I can think of no scenario where it could have happened up on the more level ground where the houses were built along the eastern most street in town.[155]

I had a raft of questions that made their way to Larry over the years, and he always gave deeply informative answers. Sending a simple thank-you note turned out to bring a rich blessing into my life. I am so glad I did not chicken out, and I am intensely indebted to Larry, who has been so kind and generous with his incredible knowledge.

❦

Karen Marie gave birth in Newton on 9 December 1875 to her and Jens's fourth child, a daughter named Elsie Jensine, their first child born in America. I have found no date specified as to when Jens and Karen Marie moved their family out of the dugout and into the two-room rock or adobe house, but the Hicks history recounts the move, and the next sentence says, "A new baby was soon born."[156] Then this record moves abruptly into events that occurred three years later, and provides no further detail as to which child was born or when the move occurred.

The happy event of baby Elsie Jensine's birth was overshadowed four days later by the death of Karen Marie's father, Jens Christensen, on 13 December 1875, in Brigham City. He was sixty-two years old. The Hicks history says: "After Grandfather Christensen died in Brigham, Grandmother [Kirsten] Christensen, Jens, Karren Marie, and their family moved to Newton on 05 July 1875."[157]

Here again, the date is problematic, showing the widow's move as six months prior to her husband's death. Jens and Karen Marie had already settled in Newton in the summer, several months before her father's death. Though the dates are contradictory (and impossible), the record makes it clear that Karen Marie's mother moved to Newton upon the death of her husband. The Hicks history indicates that her mother lived with them in the dugout for a time, and later Jens built her a home of her own.[158] "They built Grandmother Christensen a small log house that she lived in the rest of her life, except for a short time before she died [when she] couldn't take care of herself."[159] Family lore and family histories sequence things differently, yet the important facts are there.

Little information is available on Karen Marie's brother Lars and his family, but because he was her sibling and they made the journey from Denmark together, the direction he took after immigrating seems important to Jens and Karen Marie's story. Apparently he too went to Newton with the others for a time, though I do not know his family's living situation after the dugout Larry Christiansen mentioned. Larry also wrote:

> Lars Peter Christensen left Newton late in 1877 and moved to Logan where he worked for the railroad apparently in one of the shops there. He later moved to the Preston area [southeastern Idaho] taking up a homestead for the first time just east of the community. He lived on his farm and when a son took over the farm, Lars moved into Preston where he died and is buried.[160]

An online International Genealogical Index record shows that Lars died 18 June 1927 and was buried 21 June 1927, in Preston, Franklin County, Idaho.[161]

Apparently, Hans Christian, Jens's brother, also stayed in Newton for only a short time. Various sources say Hans's family moved to Clarkston, and later to Logan. Eventually, Hans acquired a quarter section of land (160 acres) in the area of Preston, Idaho (where Lars also settled). Hans fulfilled a mission to Denmark from 1886 to 1888, departing from the Preston Ward after being set apart by C. D. Fjeldsted,[162] the man who had confirmed him in Denmark when he joined the Church of Jesus Christ of Latter-day Saints. Hans's history states:

> [Hans] lived in Salt Lake upon his return. He engaged in polygamy by marrying several wives, and struggled to support his large family. He was a fine carpenter and a kind man. He later settled in Riverton, Utah, about 1890, and in Abraham, Utah, about 1899. His family and loved ones affectionately called him "Red Beard."[163]

After Hans and his family left the area, Jens was able to acquire the dugout property as part of the land to which he later claimed title.

Although their brothers left Newton shortly after arriving, Jens and Karen Marie stayed in the community. Karen Marie was again pregnant during the winter of 1877, and on 5 March 1878, gave birth to Niels Peter Nephi Hansen, their fifth child. At the time of Nephi's birth, his brother Jens Peter was ten years old, Soren Peter was seven, Hanne Margaret was nearly four and a half, and Elsie Jensine was two and one-quarter years old. Nearly three years had passed since the family arrived in Utah. Likely baby Nephi was born at home, perhaps with a midwife in attendance.

The early Scandinavian emigrants made decisions that had far-reaching effects summarized fittingly in a novel by Vilhelm Moberg, in which he wrote:

The couple agreed: they would look for passage [from Sweden to North America] in the spring of next year.

So the decision had been reached, a decision which determined the course of life for both of them, which determined the fate of their children, the result of which would stretch through time to come to unborn generations—the decision which was to determine the birthplace of their grandchildren, and their grandchildren's children.[164]

Jens and Karen Marie chose to immigrate to Utah. As time went on, not only did Jens stay in Newton, but he also became instrumental in bringing additional people, including Ane, from Denmark to Newton. Because of the choices these people made, I was born in Ogden, Utah, instead of Axelholm, Denmark. My primary language is English rather than Danish; indeed, I made my living teaching writing in the English language at colleges and universities. Having visited Denmark twice, I love what I learned about the country and the people, and I want to espouse more of my Danish heritage even though my primary cultural identity as an American may make that a challenge. My very existence, as well as the places I have lived, I owe to decisions made by others more than a lifetime before I was born. Moberg was right.

My ancestors not only chose to emigrate from their countries of origin but also chose to join the Church of Jesus Christ of Latter-day Saints, and their decisions in this regard also affected my life, as the Church was central to my upbringing. The frequent serendipitous events in the research for this project caused me to appreciate more about my heritage, both secular and religious.

Jens and Karen Marie and their extended families made major decisions that resulted in an epic journey. They settled near the heart of their new Church, struggled to sculpt a new life in a foreign country, and forged improved circumstances. Babies were born, children died, homes were built, family members moved around, and also settled in. Things seemed to be at a stasis of sorts in spite of the ongoing hard work of survival, but the coming year would bring the beginning of trials they had not even imagined as the twin specters of diphtheria and polygamy entered their lives.

CHAPTER 11

ANE ARRIVES: 1878

Twenty-three years before Jens and Karen Marie emigrated, the principle of polygamy had been announced to the members of the Church of Jesus Christ of Latter-day Saints Church at large, but it was not incumbent upon every man and woman to enter into the practice, and the majority did not.

Polygamy in Newton is evident in the 1880 census transcribed by Larry Christiansen showing the population of Newton in 1880 as 304.[165] The census shows forty-four men and ten women as heads of households. Twelve men are shown with more than one wife: eleven men had two wives, and one man had four wives.[166] Some of the men later would take additional wives. (Some households included adult male brothers, fathers, in-laws, and servants, but these men were not considered in my calculations.) Twelve polygamist men in a town of forty-four male heads of households adds up to 27 percent of the men in Newton in 1880 having plural wives.

In his book detailing the history of polygamy, Richard S. Van Wagoner comments that the percentage of polygamous households varied from community to community, and that a study of forty Mormon towns in 1880 found that about 40 percent of households in St. George were polygamous, 11 percent in Harrisburg/Leeds, 10 percent in Rockville, 67 percent in Orderville, 5 percent in South Weber, nearly 30 percent in Bountiful, 15 percent in Springville, and 63 percent in the Mexican colonies.[167]

According to a worker in the LDS Church History Library, a call to take a plural wife usually came through one's bishop, so Bishop William Rigby probably called Jens Niels Hansen sometime in 1878 to do so. Given Jens's apparent devotion, he likely took this calling very seriously, even if he and Karen Marie were uncomfortable with the concept. He may have followed the recommended courtesy of asking the first wife's permission before taking an additional wife. Often the first wife would say yes yet discover it was more difficult and sorrowful than she had imagined. Some records attest of wives who said no but whose husband married another wife anyway. Many women in polygamy gave public support to the practice and believed it was a revelation from God while writing in their private journals of their heartbreak and loneliness.[168] The Hicks history says: "This second marriage was very much against Karren's wishes."[169]

How did Jens decide whom to marry after being asked by his bishop to choose a second wife? Our family lore claims that he selected her at random from the arrivals on a train at Cache Junction, but I questioned that.

Who was this woman Jens would take as his plural wife and thus enter an emotionally turbulent triangle? Who was this woman with whom Karen Marie would share her husband after eleven exclusive years with him? Who was this woman who would leave not only her homeland but also her family to be in the heart of her new Church's Zion, to have a husband, and perhaps to have children? Who was this woman my mother had loved so deeply in her childhood?

During those summer evenings on the porch, my mother's stories of her beloved grandmother painted a portrait of a gentle woman, a loving woman, a woman who perhaps was reserved but also courageous. As an adult, these remembered stories made me yearn for more information about my maternal great-grandmother, Ane Margrethe Sorensen. Most of the information I found in public records, though, referred to Jens Niels Hansen. Fortunately, descendants from Jens's first family, with Karen Marie, shared their written histories that added details to my mother's precious stories. Two genealogical researchers, Dr. Gerald M. Haslam and Kaja Voldbæk, found information about Ane in Danish records, but her early life remains shrouded in mystery. Ane wrote no life sketch or journal, and information about her life prior to her 1878 immigration to the United States at the age of thirty-five is sparse.

We do know that Ane was the first baby born to her parents, and her birth took place on 24 February 1843 in Kyringe, Store Tåstrup, Holbæk, Denmark, a small village. She was christened or baptized on 17 April 1843, in Store Tåstrup, Holbæk, Denmark, when she was nearly two months old. She was the daughter of lodger Hans Sorensen and wife Karen Jensdatter of Kyringe. (A lodger was someone who resided in another person's house and worked for the owner of the property.) Baby Ane's christening was witnessed by "farmer Soren Hansen and daughter Ane Sorensen, evidently the paternal grandfather and paternal aunt, ... [and by] cottager [farmer] Peder Hansen [Sorensen] (evidently paternal uncle of the child), all of them of Kyringe, etc."[170]

Laura Steenhoek raised a question in our writing group in August 2010 about the Sorensen name needing to be added to those family members for whom it had been omitted in Ane's christening record. LaRelia addressed that question to Dr. Haslam, who responded 17 June 2010 that the surname shown as Hansen in his letter and in the researcher's personal notes in LaRelia's possession is apparently an oversight by the priest or the recorder because the Family Group Record shows all children of that marriage using the surname of Sorensen and following the patronymic pattern."[171]

Kaja Voldbæk also found christening records, in which an additional name appears at the end of the list of Ane's sponsors, that of Forester Hans Ludvigsen of Allingemagle.[172] I don't know who he was or why he is absent from the first report. Early records also show that Ane was vaccinated against smallpox by Dr. Weis on 26 July 1843 when she was five months old.[173]

One might assume from the christening record that since Ane's father, paternal grandfather, aunt, and uncle participated, her father's family were likely observant Lutherans. Although Lutheranism had earlier been established as the state religion in Denmark, for many Danes it was not a religious faith requiring a devout practice and active attendance but was more a tradition that included observance of ceremonies. I am curious why no one from Ane's mother's family was listed for the christening. Perhaps her mother's family was present but not required as witnesses or sponsors.

The Family Group Record shows that Ane's parents later had a son, Niels Hansen Sorensen, born 21 December 1844, in Kyringe.[174] He was twenty-two months younger than Ane, and was her only sibling.

The 1845 Danish Census record for Kyringe shows the following:

Hans Sørensen, 31, Tenant, Thresher, Laborer, born in the parish
Karen Jensdatter, 30, his wife, born in the parish
Ane Margrethe Hansdatter, 2, their daughter, born in the parish
Niels Hansen, 1, their son, born in the parish.[175]

The 1850 Danish Census locates the family still in Kyringe.[176]
Dr. Haslam further reports:

According to the probate…for the grandfather Soren Hansen in 1858, his son Hans Sorensen [Ane's father]…was at that time residing in Munke Bjergby, and indeed the confirmations there the prior year, 1857 on the first Sunday after Easter, show Ane Margrethe Hansdatter of Munke Bjergby, dau[ghter] of cottager Hans Sorensen and Karen Jensdatter of Kyringe, born 24 Feb 1843; and record that she received "very good" marks for deportment and for understanding of the catechism.[177]

An online calendar for 1857 and a list of dates for Easter show that particular Easter Sunday fell on 12 April 1857, so Ane's confirmation would have taken place on 19 April 1857, when she was fourteen years and two months old.

Comparing the 1850 census in Kyringe with the 1857 probate in Munke Bjergby, we discover that Ane's family had moved sometime between those dates from their home in Kyringe, Store Tåstrup, Holbæk, across the county line to Munke Bjergby, Sorø, and her father's descriptive title had changed from *lodger* to *cottager*. Dr. Haslam writes:

> A cottager leased a cottage and the surrounding acre or less of ground from a landowner, often the lord of the local manor. There was just enough land to make a subsistence living raising essential crops, and he also had to work a day or two each week on the landowner's estate as part of his leasehold agreement.[178]

A later email from Dr. Haslam clarifies that "[the] change from lodger to cottager would mean a slight improvement in living circumstances for Ane Margrethe's father."[179]

The distance between Ane's birthplace, Kyringe, and the new location, Munke Bjergby, is approximately eight miles, depending on the route taken. Was the family happy about the relocation? Were they more comfortable socially and economically in the new town?

Though those questions may never be answered, after years of my wondering *when* they had moved, Kaja found this:

> Departure from Kyringe, Store Tåstrup Parish, to Munke Bjergby in Sorø County, 18 July 1852, Entry 170:
> Hans Sørensen, 38
> Karen Jensen, 37
> Ane Margrethe Hansen, 9 ½
> Niels Hansen, 7 ½ [180]

So Ane and her brother were school-age children when the family moved. A distance of eight miles seems short with modern transportation, but moving a family that far with horse and wagon would have required a good reason for doing so.

The Danish census for 1855 in Munkebjergby By [town] lists:

> Hans Sørensen, 41, Gift [married], Husmand [crofter], Træskomager [clog maker], born in Taastrup Sogn [parish], Holbæk Amt [county]

Karen Jensdatter, 40, Gift, hans Kone [his wife], born in Taastrup
Sogn, Holbæk Amt

Ane Margrethe Hansen, 12, Ugift [unmarried], deres Børn [their
child], born in Taastrup Sogn, Holbæk Amt

Niels Hansen, 11, Ugift, deres Børn [their child], born in Tåstrup
Sogn, Holbæk Amt[181]

Two years later in 1857, at age fourteen, Ane passed confirmation and communion, receiving "very good" marks for deportment and understanding of the
catechism. She was well mannered, and either smart or studious or both. By
passing confirmation and taking communion at fourteen years of age, she had
completed Denmark's compulsory education.

Knud J.V. Jespersen's comments on confirmation appear in Chapter 4 in
connection with Jens. Here I would like to add that multiple sources say confirmation was an important occasion for the parents as well as for the young
person. The young people studied with the minister for about six months.
For the ceremony of confirmation that followed this study, the young people
dressed in their finest clothing. If they didn't have fine clothing, they would
borrow what they could. After demonstrating that they knew the teachings of
the Lutheran Church, they took communion and were expected to continue
taking communion at least annually throughout their lives. This significant
ceremony marked the young person's passage into adulthood, and they were
expected to begin working the customary annual contracts. Each young person
who passed the testing received a skudsmaalsbog or servant conduct book to
keep a record of their work history and their employers' comments at the end
of each contract.

After confirmation, Ane would have been eligible for work and may have
been given a skudsmaalsbog to keep track of her employment, supervisors'
comments, and travel. Indeed, the Danish census for Munke Bjergby in
1860 shows:

Hans Sørensen, 47, Farmer, born in Tåstrup
Karen Jensdatter, 46, his wife, born in Tåstrup
Niels Hansen, 16, born in Tåstrup[182]

Ane is absent from this record of her family. Where was she?

LaRelia asked Dr. Haslam what Ane might have done between her confirmation and her emigration, or more specifically, "what kind of occupations women
had during that era."[183] He responded:

From the time of her confirmation, Ane probably did what most young women at the time did—worked as a servant at a farm, either in her home parish or in the vicinity. Her chores would probably have been milking cows, feeding hens and chickens, and assisting with the harvest at that time of year.[184]

Ane's life, then, might have been similar to Jens's, with contracts for work at various farms.

Ane's absence from her family in the Munke Bjergby 1860 census, is explained by her appearance on a different census for the same year in the same community:

Munke Bjergby, Munke Bjergby sogn, [parish] Munkebjergby, en Gaard [farm]...

Jacob Rasmussen, 56, Gift [married], Gaardmand [yard man], Husfader [Goodman], Bjergby

Kirsten Jensdatter, 52, Gift, hans Kone [his wife], Bjergby

Jens Jacobsen, 10, Ugift, deres Søn [their son], Bjergby

Ane Margrethe Hansdatter, 17, Ugift, deres Tjenestefolk [servant] Stenmagle, Sorø Amt [county] [emphasis mine]

Peder Jensen, 19, Ugift, deres Tjenestefolk, Bjergby

Hans Christoffersen, 15, Ugift, deres Tjenestefolk, Bjergby

Karen Sophie Pedersen, 12, Ugift, deres Tjenestefolk, Bjergby[185]

The name and age match our Ane, but this record shows her born in Stenmagle. Kaja checked the church book from Stenmagle, but no Ane Margrethe Hansdatter was born there between 1842 and 1846, and she said, "so it may be a mistake in the census records."[186]

Ane appears again at the age of nineteen in an arrival record that shows her departure from the Rasmussen family in Munke Bjergby—lending credence to the above census as referring to our Ane—and her arrival at nearby Sorø: "Ane Margrethe Hansen, 19, moving from Jacob Rasmussen to Sorø."[187] This record is from 1 May 1862, so Ane would have worked for Rasmussen at least from the census of 1860, and perhaps earlier, maybe even from the time of her 1857 confirmation. Perhaps this record of Ane's arrival at Sorø was for her to work a contract as a maid at Kammergave, which was a farm in the old days.

Our next found record of Ane is from seven years later, an arrival record that also shows her departure: Ane Margrethe Hansen, twenty-five, maid at Kammergave in Sorø, arriving in Munke Bjergby 1 May 1869.[188] Maybe Ane had worked as a maid the entire time between her 1862 arrival in Sorø and her

1869 departure to Munke Bjergby. Or she may have worked other contracts in Sorø before Kammergave that have not yet been found in the records.

Why did she return to Munke Bjergby? Apparently when she came home from her contract in Sorø, she stayed for a while. She was still in Munke Bjergby at age twenty-six for the 1870 census the year after her return:

> Hans Sørensen, 55, Wooden Shoemaker, Born in Kyringe, Holbæk County
> Karen Jensen, 54, his wife, born in Kyringe, Holbæk County
> Niels Hansen, 25, Wooden Shoemaker, born in Kyringe
> Ane Margrethe, 26, born in Kyringe[189]

Was Ane taking care of an ailing mother?

Kaja commented:

> Unfortunately the departure and arrival records only go as far as 1874; some parishes even less. I do not see Ane Margrethe Hansen leave again from Munke Bjergby in that time period to 1874, and census records jump from 1870 to 1880, so they are no help either.[190]

We know from these few records that Ane worked and lived at various places to support herself. This, in conjunction with what we've learned of Jens's life in Denmark, clearly debunks the family lore that they—and we—were near to royalty.

The history of my mother's sister, Eleda Bjorkman Smith, includes information that would have come from Ane's mouth as she interacted with this young granddaughter decades later, or from the words of Eleda's mother, Sophia Hansen Bjorkman. Eleda wrote:

> Ane's mother, Sophia Karen Jensen . . . . died while my grandmother [Ane] was a young girl. Great Grandmother was 54 years old when she passed away. My grandma, Ane Margrethe, stayed at home and took care of her father.[191]

According to a Family Group Record in my files, Ane's mother, Karen (my great-great-grandmother), was born 11 November 1815. (Eleda's history lists Ane's mother's name as Sophia Karen. LaRelia and I have tried to find information to support the first name as Sophia, but have found her listed only as Karen.) Kaja searched the Danish records and found that Karen Jensdatter died 22 March

1873 and was buried 29 March 1873. The record gives Karen's age as fifty-seven,[192] so Ane would have been thirty years old when her mother died—not exactly a young girl—and it is feasible that she took care of her father to some degree from that time until her departure from Denmark five years later in 1878. Maybe taking responsibility for her father was one reason why she was still single at age thirty-five. If it is true that Ane was involved in his care, then he likely had reasons beyond her membership in the new Church for adamantly objecting to her leaving Denmark. Eleda's history continues:

> They owned a cow, a horse, a chicken or two, and a small plot of ground where they planted their garden.
>
> Grandma had a brother, Soren [however, the records show him as Niels] of whom she spoke occasionally. He was married and had a family. When we asked what he did, Grandma would say, "He went to sea."[193] [Yet the 1870 census listed above shows Niels and his father as wooden shoemakers.]

Moving from Eleda's history back to other records, we find that when Ane was thirty-two, she joined the Church of Jesus Christ of Latter-day Saints. We have no story of how she encountered the missionaries, but they would have taught her about the restoration and the doctrines. She must have studied and prayed about her decision before she accepted the new religion and entered the waters of baptism. A Family Group Record shows the date of Ane's baptism and confirmation as 2 July 1874, but the Newton Ward Records of 1870–1941 show the date for both as 10 March 1875.[194] Assuming that Ane herself gave the information that appears in the ward records, that is the date I will use. She was baptized and confirmed by Elder Jepsen,[195] a man who had been ordained in the priesthood and who immersed her completely then lifted her up out of the water as a symbolic death of her old life and birth of her new one. He then laid his hands upon her head and confirmed her a member of the Church of Jesus Christ of Latter-day Saints and promised her the companionship of the Holy Spirit as she lived a worthy life.

What did this decision mean for Ane? Baptism not only signifies joining the Church as a member but also includes a covenant:

> To be called [God's] people, and [be] willing to bear one another's burdens, that they may be light…and [be] willing to mourn with those that mourn…and comfort those that stand in need of comfort, and to stand as witnesses of God at all times and in all things, and in all

places that ye may be in, even until death, that ye may be redeemed of God, and be numbered with those of the first resurrection, that ye may have eternal life...if this be the desire of your hearts, what have you against being baptized in the name of the Lord, as a witness before him that ye have entered into a covenant with him, that ye will serve him and keep his commandments, that he may pour out his Spirit more abundantly upon you?"[196]

Accepting the invitation to baptism and a converted life requires serious thought and commitment, and Ane probably would not have entered into it lightly.

No location is given for Ane's baptism, but it could have been a nearby lake or river. Though the baptism records differ, we know that Ane was in her early thirties when she joined the Mormon Church. Did the Mormon belief in eternal families appeal to Ane, who must have been missing her mother? Her baptism was almost two years to the day after her mother's death.

Our lore says Ane's family was very much against her decision and that her father disowned her. My mother's words were, "She lost her inheritance." What emotions must Ane have felt as she walked the line between her independent devotion to her new faith and her respect for and duty to her father?

What did being disowned mean for a Danish woman in her early thirties in that time period? We know Ane worked contracts instead of being dependent upon her father, so perhaps the lore of disownment is not completely accurate. Contracts for work were common for Danish young people. Was her father able to work? Did he just need someone to cook, clean, and do laundry? Or did he need financial support as well? Did Ane save money for her emigration? Did she realize at that time that she would be emigrating?

The next thing we know for sure about Ane is that in 1878—three years after her baptism—she left Denmark. My mother said that Ane knew she was to be married to someone in Utah, but she didn't know she was to be a second or plural wife rather than a first and only wife, and she wasn't happy about being second when she realized it. What did she know? And when did she know it? Mother further explained that Ane had agreed with sponsors to marry when she got to Utah. Who sponsored her? Was the prospect of a husband for an unmarried, thirty-five-year-old woman a significant part of her motivation for the arduous journey? Or was she motivated solely by the call from the Church to come to Zion? Was she partially motivated to escape caring for her father, who disapproved of her decisions? Did she hope to better herself financially?

Of interest is the 1880 census for Munke Bjergby two years after Ane's departure to America, showing her brother as head of household:

Niels Hansen, 25, Parcelist [small farmer], born in Kyringe

Dorthe Kirstine Poulsen, [no age listed], his wife, born in Munkebjergby

Karen Mathilde Hansen, 1, their daughter

Hans Sørensen, 65, pensioner, and widower, born in Kyringe [emphasis
    mine]

Kjersten Rasmussen, 11, a maid, born in Bromme[197]

With his daughter, Ane, gone, Hans Sørensen was living with his son and daughter-in-law.

One of my nagging questions is whether Jens had met Ane before he and Karen Marie emigrated. If Ane's March 1875 baptism date is correct, there is a three-month overlap between her baptism and Jens and Karen Marie's June 1875 departure from Denmark, during which they could have met through church involvement. Jens had a leadership position as president of the Skarresø Branch that would have made him known to the church people in his area, which may or may not have included Ane. Moreover, Vicky Jenkins (whom we met as she was mowing her lawn in Newton) suggested in a telephone conversation with me on 29 September 2010 that Ane and Jens might both have worked for the same farmer at some point, or may at least have met on someone's farm. Munke Bjergby is about six miles from several of the places Jens lived and worked. Traveling that distance in those days was difficult but not impossible, yet the secretary at Jyderup Kirke said the distance was too far for Church connections.

In conversations during our stays in both 2014 and 2015, Lisbeth Kristiansen, our hostess in Kalundborg, Denmark, told us her Kongsgaard Bed and Breakfast business was located in her family's old manor house on a long-established farm that had servants in its early days. She said that in the old days, they had held dances on Saturday nights for all the servants near and far. One of her relatives from a distant island had even come to the local dances. Both the milkman who delivered to the houses and the mailman from whom people picked up their mail (no deliveries in those days) spread word to all the farms, and the young people met at the event for music and dancing and a respite from the workweek. Might Jens and Ane have met at one of these dances? If they did meet—before or after he was married—it wouldn't have needed to foster a romantic interest, but merely might have created in each an awareness of the other person's existence.

My biggest question was this: After Jens settled in Newton and received a calling, likely from Bishop William Rigby, to practice the principle of plural marriage by taking a second wife, did he send for Ane? Did she come to America to marry Jens specifically? Or did they meet for the first time when she arrived, as the family lore claimed?

Whatever Ane's motivation, she made preparations to leave her home for America, and traveled in September 1878, at the age of thirty-five. She would have journeyed from her home in Munke Bjergby by horse-drawn carriage to the nearest railroad station, then taken the train to Copenhagen to board a ship to Hull, England.

❦

As Richard and I drove from Sorø toward Roskilde in July 2014, I discovered in the guidebook that Roskilde's train station was built in 1847—so that meant a place Ane had stood was still extant, and it instantly went on my list of things to see. The first railway line in Denmark had been built in 1847, connecting Roskilde and Copenhagen.[198]

In Roskilde, we found a tourist information center, acquired a map, and planned our walking route to the train station. A knowledgeable man at the information counter told us that when plans were made for refurbishing the weathered train station, they had not known what colors it was originally painted. Then they discovered an old painting of the train station so were able to duplicate the bright, original colors—peach, burnt sienna, and deep blue—around the tall arched windows.

We walked in the burning heat to the train station, which turned out to be farther away than it looked on the map. The cobblestone streets were packed with tourists, and the various shops displayed merchandise out in front—dresses, shoes, scarves, jewelry, books—and it seemed that everyone passing by in the crowd was eating a vanilla soft serve ice cream cone. When we finally arrived at what was then a 168-year-old station, the vivid colors and the gold brick entranced me. Most of the building looked original, although parts of it had been modernized. We wandered all through the building and then outside in back where the tracks that had brought Ane's train to this place shimmered in the sunlight. Everywhere I looked, I imagined Ane in her long dress, tired from the journey so far yet excited and maybe apprehensive about the new life that awaited her.

As I soaked it all up, I realized that not only Ane but also all of the other Nielsen/Hansen/Christensen members of the two families traveling in 1874 and 1875 had been at this train station. I felt surrounded by an invisible crowd from the pages of my history, and I created a miniature movie in my head of these family members of all ages being here in the station—dressed in period clothing, moving about, waiting in anticipation and exhaustion, keeping track of their possessions and each other.

Later, as Richard and I walked away from the building and back toward the shops, I kept turning around for just one more glimpse of the vibrantly colorful train station as it became smaller and smaller in the distance.

We returned to the information center in the heart of Roskilde and found that the knowledgeable man, Ebbe, had just returned from lunch. On a piece of paper, I wrote *Munke Bjergby to Copenhagen—1878*, and I asked him how my ancestor would have traveled between those cities in that year. Ebbe spent considerable time on his computer, then told me there were some small private trains at the time of Ane's travel. She would have taken a carriage from Munke Bjergby to Ringsted and traveled from Ringsted to Roskilde by train (I assume this was one of the private trains) and then from Roskilde to Copenhagen on the main train line.

✻

After Ane reached Copenhagen, she boarded a ship for Hull, England. I am indebted to those souls emigrating in the same company with Ane who took it upon themselves to make notes about their travels. One record says, "A company of 218 emigrating Saints [including] eight returning missionaries sailed from Copenhagen on the steamer 'Bravo,' Sept. 7, 1878, under the leadership of Elder August W. Carlson."[199]

The *Bravo* was a smaller ship than the one Ane would soon board in Liverpool for her voyage to America. The vessel was a 1,076 gross ton ship measuring 240 feet in length with a beam of 29 feet and depth of 16.1 feet. She was built in 1866 and ran the Baltic and North Seas to Hull until 1904.[200] The record next notes that three days later:

> On Tuesday, Sept. 10th, the company arrived in Hull, England, and the following day continued to journey to Liverpool by rail. Here the Scandinavian Saints, together with 321 British and 57 Swiss and German Saints, embarked on the steamer "Wyoming" and sailed from Liverpool Sept. 14th.[201]

Although we have no journal from Ane, one traveler who *did* make a record of his journey from Denmark to Utah was my great-uncle Oscar Cornelius Bjorkman. Oscar apparently dictated or wrote his recollections after his 1890 emigration from Denmark as a Mormon convert, and though he traveled twelve years after Ane did, perhaps some of his experiences were similar to hers and will offer insights into her journey as well.

When Richard and I visited the Liverpool docks in 2017 to see where our ancestors had sailed from, we also went into the Maritime Archives and Library at the Merseyside Maritime Museum, where we asked some questions of one of the librarians. As we conversed, I mentioned Oscar's journal, and she said, "Every family hopes to discover such a treasure."

Both Ane and Oscar sailed across the Atlantic aboard the SS *Wyoming*, and Oscar's sailing was the ship's final voyage. Of most importance is the fact that his record expresses the thoughts and feelings of a passenger. I am including some lengthy excerpts from this journal to foster speculation about what Ane's travels might have been like, and because his words charm me. He records:

> I purchased my ticket (third class), which entitled me to steerage passage on the boat. I would not go that way again; I would rather wait six months longer. It was an awful mess. Not more than a year later, the church authorities put a stop to it. My two brothers, Walt and Henry, for whose emigration I sent the money, came second-class.[202]

Did Ane also feel that her travel in third class experience was "an awful mess"? Or was she so full of excitement that she overlooked any inconveniences?

> Next I packed my belongings in a trunk and a suitcase and, having my ticket, I was all set to leave home on September 13, 1890. My dad hauled my few belongings to the dock [at Copenhagen] on a handcart he had either borrowed or hired. When we arrived there, my things were there but he was not, so the last I saw of him was when we left for the dock. I can't remember now how many came to see me off, but I know that my mother and my sister were there, my uncle, my mother's brother Peter, my cousins whom I have mentioned, my brother Victor, and his girl friend Anna Petersen who is now his wife. They all seemed to be down in the dumps, as the saying is. Walt and Henry [Oscar's brothers] were working. I was as calm and contented, feeling as though I was going to Sweden for a visit.[203]

Oscar lived in Copenhagen, so it was easier for his people to see him off than for Ane, whose home village was approximately fifty-four miles southwest of Copenhagen. Did anyone go to the dock to see Ane off? More likely they would have said goodbye at her village as she left by carriage. Or maybe they took her as far as Ringsted, then said goodbye.

Oscar's reminiscence continues:

Third class passengers were required to furnish their own bedding and dishes, and they had to go to the kitchen and obtain what was cooked, while second class sat up to tables and had their meals brought to them. Third classers also had to have five dollars, American money, when they entered the U.S. I had that and a few more, but not many. Don't know what was required of seconders or firsts, but I suppose they were supposed to have the required dough or they would be thirders like I happened to be.

The ship was scheduled to leave at three o'clock in the afternoon, but for some reason it didn't leave till five-thirty and it was getting dark. All the folks accompanied me on board…When the bell sounded, which meant ten minutes before leaving of the ship, I bid them all good-bye. Natalie was not there. I knew the reason for it, but I was brave. The last two I saw were Victor and Anna, who waved at me till I could see them no more, and so I left my beloved country "DENMARK" and I said to myself, "America here I come. What have you to offer?" I'll admit I felt a little peculiar when I was alone, and I became just a little nauseated when I smelled the oil and steam mixture from the engines, but I slept well all night, due I think, to the fact that I was tired.

The next morning was beautiful, clear skies and a calm ocean. I had deep thoughts as to my future. The ship was heading for Hull, England, which she expected to reach in three days, according to schedule. Nothing of interest to me happened on this short part of the journey. I was wondering what will I do next, having left my homeland, my folks, friends, and a fairly good position for a boy, you might say, but I had all the future before me, like we all have. Some of us strike it just right, while others have a hard time to make it. Can you tell me why it is so? If you can, I shall be happy to hear from you, although it is a little late to be of benefit to me.[204]

What did Ane think and feel as she watched Copenhagen shrink in the distance as the ship got underway? Did she feel queasy from the smell of the oil and steam from the engines? Did she experience the same mix of emotions Oscar expressed as she sailed toward new places? What did she hope to find in her new life across the sea?

Oscar's journal says:

We reached Hull on the third morning after our leaving Copenhagen. The tide was out, so we had to wait till it came in before we could land. At Hull we got on the train, which took us across England in a northwesterly direction to Liverpool, where we stayed a couple of days. The trip from Hull to Liverpool was very nice. We saw lots of nice towns and there was a lot of manufacturing going on.

Then we got on a much larger ship, the name of which was *Wyoming* and that brought us across the Atlantic to New York. We...made a short stop at Queenstown, Ireland, to take on passengers, light freight and mail. Nothing of any consequence happened crossing the Atlantic Ocean. We had some fine weather and some quite bad, but I enjoyed it. Something went wrong with the machinery on mid-ocean so we drifted back quite a bit. It was a calm day or it might have been bad for us.

Ane's name appears on the emigration list for the SS *Wyoming* on 7 September 1878. She is number 16 on the list for the Copenhagen Conference as "Sorensen, Ane Margrethe, age 35, destination Ogden, savings fund $50.00, cash paid $240.00," with the remarks column blank.[205]

Ane's sailing time from Liverpool is more specifically noted: "DEPARTURE (3rd Company).—The S.S. Wyoming left the [River] Mersey at 11:30 a.m., on Saturday the 14th instant."[206] The Compilation Notes tell us "Henry W. Naisbitt who, during the absence of President Joseph F. Smith, had presided over the European Mission, was appointed leader of this company of emigrants, with Daniel D. McArthur and Alfred Hanson as his assistants."[207] Naisbitt appears as a leader in a number of historical documents and must have been a most capable and inspirational person in many respects. Did his leadership give Ane comfort?

How did Ane feel as she boarded this larger ship to cross the Atlantic? Was she impressed by its size? Had she made friends in the group? Did she already know people from church among the passengers? Was she traveling with a girl-friend, as my mother said? Was she keeping an eye on her Scandinavian emigrant trunks and her precious things?

The ship's list for the SS *Wyoming*, arriving 24 September 1878 in New York, shows "#568 Ane M. Sorenson, 35, female, spinster" traveling in steerage. Her line shows her home country as Sweden, but the next line and those that follow show Denmark. Someone made an error in her country of origin. Several other "spinsters" are listed, but they were either much older or much younger than Ane. She likely would have had more in common with someone her own age for travel, but that may not have been the situation. The ages of other spinsters from Denmark were 51, 22, 26, 59, 14, and 17. The two names preceding Ane's on the list were spinsters from Sweden (unless those lines also had the country in error) who were ages 53 and 54.[208] They may have been from Denmark, but neither seems likely to have been Ane's mystery friend.

The SS *Wyoming* is discussed in Sonne's *Saints on the Seas*:

> No ship carried as many Mormons to America under either sail or steam as the Guion liner *Wyoming*. Over nearly twenty years this British flag steamer made 38 voyages carrying a total of 10,473 Latter-day Saints from Liverpool to New York, in companies ranging from 10 to 775 emigrants....
>
> The 3,283-ton *Wyoming* was similar to other Guion liners of her day; sporting an iron hull, single screw, two masts, one funnel, three decks and a speed of 11 ½ knots. She was. . . . one of the earliest steamers with compound engines. [209]

After Ane boarded and the *Wyoming* got underway, no mention is made of the ship docking in Queensland, Ireland, to take on additional passengers and goods, as most other ships from Liverpool did, but it may have done so.

Oscar tells of a passenger picked up in Queenstown when the *Wyoming* stopped there to pick up emigrants on his later voyage:

> A...big Norwegian, who boarded the ship at Queenstown, said, "I know I am going to be seasick," so he crawled into his bunk. He was a third classer, and he stayed there till we reached New York. A friend of his carried food to him from the kitchen. What he did for a restroom I don't know, but I know that I didn't see him up for two weeks, but of course he was resting. I spent most of my time on the upper deck. I looked at his bunk when we reached New York and he got up. It was a sight. It contained soup bones, ox joints and pieces of ox tails, bones from pig's feet, eggshells, pieces of salt herring, and a lot of other items. It would seem from this that he had not been too sick to eat, but that he had been enjoying himself.[210]

Did Ane's fresh foods on her voyage include soups, oxtails, eggs, and salt herring? Did she have favorite foods to which she would have been partial? Were there people aboard who entertained her along the way?

❦

The Mormon passengers would have been divided into wards, or congregations, and each ward assigned to a returning missionary. The wards would likely have been formed along national lines and therefore also by language. Ane would have met in her group every morning and evening for prayers and the singing of hymns. She would have mingled with those whose language she understood but is unlikely to have done so with the English, Swiss, or German passengers.

The Compilation Notes report, "During the voyage the emigrants encountered three days of stormy weather, which caused much seasickness among the passengers."[211] How did Ane react to the storms? Did she get seasick? None of my family does, so perhaps she was impervious.

❧

Ane's grandchildren later said she always slept on a feather ticking (a mattress covered with tightly woven fabric to keep feathers from escaping) that she had brought with her from Denmark. If so, she would have slept on it during these travels. Did she wear her dresses that my mother and Eleda's history said were lovely? Or did she wear more functional travel clothes? Was she happy? Scared? Hopeful? Did she miss her father and brother? Grieve her mother? Was she excited about the prospect of marriage at her age?

They crossed the Atlantic safely, and Naisbitt wrote his end-of-voyage report aboard the SS *Wyoming* on 24 September 1878, one day before arrival in New York, to the President of the European Mission. He describes the context of Ane's voyage:

> President William Budge
>
> Dear Brother,
>
> As we are now reaching the borders of Zion, I feel it a pleasure to drop you a line, by way of reporting progress, regretting only that in my hurry I forgot paper, and that ink is a very rare thing among the Saints; and I am using my bunk for a writing place. To be sure the sea is smooth, scarce a ripple breaks its surface, and Long Island reaches away in the distance, prophesying the harbor not far off. But we have had stormy times; head winds and much rain, early on the way. It caught us just out of port, and continued until the Saints were exhausted, and many thought, "There's no place like home." However, now there are light hearts and pleasant voices, and the prospect of release is inspiring everyone....
>
> In a moral sense we have been healthy; one "lewd fellow of the baser sort," made suggestions to a sister which made me declare myself

in our first public meeting, and since then it has been understood that we have no compromise with "either knave or fool."

I hear of some of the Welsh Saints who have not a sixpence with which to purchase provision on the way from here to Utah. They are going out by the Fund [Perpetual Emigration Fund].

The officers have given us good attention, but I have been on hand for inspection every time, and have really run early and late seeing to the Saints.

Your blessing has been upon us, and God has been with us by his spirit. We have after all, had a good time; that is, a time of peace. And I hope this spirit may continue, not only in the trip, but after we reach our home in the mountains. It is now near six. We shall anchor about midnight; and bright and early we hope to have everything packed ready for a move.

When you receive this we shall be enjoying home and friends, and you, along with Brothers Nibley and Nicholson, will be prosecuting the labors of your mission....

We have not a case of sickness aboard at present.

May God bless you in your labors, endow you with wisdom continually, and so lead all like faithful men to "that rest which remaineth for the people of God."

The 25th; Arrived today all well. God bless you all, and give you peace and wisdom and success in all your labors.

Yours truly,
H. W. Naisbitt[212]

The next day, the ship arrived in New York. The passengers were processed through Castle Garden, then sailed aboard a steamer to the railroad depot across the river in New Jersey, where they boarded the train for Utah.

Oscar describes his arrival in America:

After having been two weeks on the Atlantic, we reached New York entering "Castle Gardens" for inspection and questioning. Such questions as "Have you any relatives in America?" "Has anyone sent you the money for your immigration?" "Has anyone promised you work in this country?" "How much money do you have?" and of course they had to be shown. Other questions were asked, but I don't remember them. There were a few girl immigrants. They were asked the same questions. There were some Priests [denominations not stated] hanging around there, advising them not to go to Utah, but if they were determined to go, when they got there and if they didn't like it, for them to write to them and they would see to it that tickets were sent for their return to the country they came from.[213] (This practice was apparently evidence of prejudice against the Mormon populace.)

What questions were asked of Ane twelve years prior to Oscar's trip? Did she feel harassed when she went through the process of entering this country? Was she happy to have the first voyage over and a train excursion about to begin? Or was she tired and wishing the train trip was over too?

Oscar's observations continue, "The last day at sea, the third classers were required to throw their mattresses into the Ocean, so out they went.... As I now remember it, we the immigrants, stayed in New York a couple of days."[214] Did Ane toss her mattress? If so, the one her grandchildren remembered would have been a new one she acquired after her arrival.

At this point Oscar's route differs from Ane's in that his group went next by ship to Norfolk, Virginia, where they boarded a train to cross the country, whereas Ane went by steamer to Jersey City to board her train to cross the continent. Oscar says that on the overnight voyage to Norfolk, the straw mattress from this ship gave him the itch.[215] Then he continues:

> But later on, on the journey, I had something equally bad, namely sleeping on wooden benches on the train from Norfolk to where, I don't remember now, but I guess it was not far from Denver, Colorado, and that is a long way from Norfolk. The train was an old timer; besides having old-time seats, it was supplied with old-time cast iron stoves for heating. Coal and wood were supplied at various stations en route. The women did a little cooking on the stoves, but not very much....
>
> Nothing of any consequence happened on the train ride. Since most of us could not speak English, we would make out a list of what we needed, pay them the cash for it, and they would make the purchases. I ate quite a bit of canned salmon, which I had not tasted before. I liked it then. Now I don't care for it except once in awhile.[216]

Speaking no English, Ane must have communicated her food preferences or other purchases with a list or through someone who spoke both Danish and English.

Oscar describes colorful side stories and some risks of train travel:

> Here is one incident that happened going through one of the southern
> states. It was about midnight; the train stopped at a station. Most of
> the passengers were asleep. The door opens, in comes a fellow, grabs
> the overcoat from a sleeping immigrant just opposite from where I
> was sitting with my coat around me, and out he runs and shuts the
> door. I jumped up trying to catch him, but it was done so quickly that
> it was of no use trying. The coat was gone and I suppose mine would
> have been gone, too, had I not had it on.[217]

This was one of the very hazards the travelers had been warned about. Did
Ane witness anything untoward on her journey? Was she victimized by anyone?
She and her fellow Mormon travelers likely looked out for each other.

Oscar continues:

> We [reached]...Denver, Colorado, and were informed that it would
> be awhile before our train would be leaving for the west. How long
> a delay I don't remember, but we had sufficient time to take a walk
> uptown. One of the passengers failed to come back on time, although
> the train left ten minutes after schedule. What happened to him I
> don't know, but I know that the conductor had his necessary papers
> to travel [still held his passport].
>
> Denver is a very nice city. There for the first time I saw a real
> Indian with his squaw and a papoose. We [left]...Denver and on
> a much nicer train. Don't remember if the coaches were heated by
> steam or by stoves, but the seats were quite nice and comfortable;
> they naturally would be since we would soon be at the journey's end.
> I don't recall very much of the trip from Denver to Ogden, but I
> remember it was beginning to turn cold at night...it was the early
> part of October and I was glad I had my overcoat and felt sorry for
> the fellow who lost his en route. You understand we thirders traveled
> in ordinary coaches all the way from Norfolk, Virginia, to Denver,
> Colorado. Quite a distance....
>
> [We] reached Ogden, Utah. How long we stayed there, I do not
> recall, but I remember we reached Logan the following day at noon,
> October 10, 1890. The track from Ogden to Logan was the narrow
> gauge and the first settlement we struck was Mendon. From there
> we crossed the [Cache] Valley to Logan. Soon after this the narrow

track was abandoned, the Union Pacific having completed their new line to Collinston and along Bear River to Cache Junction and on up through Idaho and into Montana.[218]

Oscar's information about the trains confirms that Ane, who had traveled twelve years earlier, could *not* have disembarked from the train at Cache Junction as our family lore claimed because that station was not yet in service.

Although the emigration list shows Ane's destination as Ogden, one record says: "After a somewhat tiresome journey by rail from Jersey City, the company arrived in Salt Lake City, Oct. 3, 1878."[219] I don't know whether Ane went all the way to Salt Lake and then back to Ogden or got off the train upon its first arrival in Ogden, then boarded another train bound northward, most likely for Brigham, but possibly for Logan.

Oscar comments on his arrival:

> It was raining on our arrival in Logan, the roads were muddy and no pavements anywhere till at least twenty years later. Main Street and Center Street had boardwalks, and when it was raining hard a person would have to have a boat to cross the streets, but we must bear in mind that Logan had been settled only about thirty-one years by this time. How strange it all seems to me, and as I thought of the happenings during the past thirty days, prior to which time I had been manager of what was considered an up-to-date store in Copenhagen and I was not yet nineteen years of age, I wondered what it was all about.[220]

The muddy streets of Logan make me wonder what Ane found the streets of Brigham and Newton to be like on her arrival in 1878. Much work probably still needed to be done to create the amenities the settlers visualized.

Oscar apparently hadn't known exactly what he would be doing once he arrived in Utah, for he goes on to say:

> A Mrs. Winkler, an acquaintance of my mother, and one of the immigrants was told before she left Copenhagen by a missionary by the name of Chas. Thorstensen, to go to his place and stay until she could locate her children, two boys and two girls all grown, and as I had no place to go she said, "You had better come along with me and see what you can do for a place to stay." We got into one of the hacks hauling passengers and landed at the above-named place. Mrs. T. gave us a real nice welcome, giving us a nice lunch. Some of the

neighbors came in to see what we looked like, I suppose. Someone, I don't remember who it was, helped me find a place to stay. It was at Mrs. C.D. Fjeldsted's.[221]

Earlier, C. D. Fjeldsted had confirmed Jens's brother, Hans, in Denmark, and later in Utah, Fjeldsted called Hans to serve as a leader among the Scandinavians. He also set Hans apart as a missionary in 1886, so there was a Hansen family connection. Now, years later, Oscar Bjorkman was also connected to the Fjeldsted family.

Oscar writes:

> The next thing now and most important to me was to find work and since I could not speak English, I could not go out and look for it myself and it was very hard to get work in those days. In about thirty days after my arrival in Logan, with the help of a returned missionary whom I had met in Copenhagen, I obtained work as chore boy, taking care of a couple of fancy horses and a couple of cows to milk and doing various jobs in and around the house.... [As the man] was an American[,] we had to do our talking by motions. He paid me fifteen dollars a month and board and room. My room was the whole barn so I could choose the spot.[222]

Dr. Haslam, our Danish researcher, had described the accommodations for young Danish workers like Jens as often being a room in the barn, so Oscar's American situation was reminiscent of the Danish tradition.

Even though Ane traveled in the company of fellow Mormons and maybe a girlfriend, she had undertaken an enormous risk. What made her bold enough to choose a different life for herself, in a radical departure from anything she had previously experienced? Maybe she entertained hopeful and excited visions of a new life that enticed her. Or maybe she saw it solely as obedience to the call of gathering issued by the leaders of her new religion, and she was willing to sacrifice all for what she believed was the will of God. What were her thoughts and feelings upon arrival in Utah?

During the early days of the Church, it was customary, as recommended by Brigham Young, for members of the LDS Church to be rebaptized to rededicate themselves to the principles of the religion or to prepare for temple ordinances.

The longing for home and the duress of other challenges sometimes distracted people from spiritual observances as they grappled with the physical tasks of eking out a living and establishing new communities. Consequently, Young asked immigrants to recommit themselves to a spiritual focus in life by the renewing their covenants through the ordinance of rebaptism. Oscar notes in his journal that after his arrival in Logan:

> Several persons had told me that I was not a member of the church till I had been rebaptized, so to be sure I went to my Bishop.... I told him what I had been informed and he said, "Yes, my boy, that is the ruling of the church authorities. So if you want to become a full fledged member of the church, you had better have it done." I told him that was what I wanted to be and that I came to America for that purpose.[223]

In saying he had come to America for that purpose, Oscar makes his motivation clear. We do not have to wonder why he immigrated. Like many others, he came to be near the Church and to be a committed member of it.

> He set the day, the first week in December and the place, the mill race [the water channel that drives the mill wheel] across from Langton's where I was working. On the appointed day and time (8:20 A.M.) I was there and so was the man who was to perform the ceremony. It was quite chilly and snowing.... The following Sunday I was confirmed a member of the church and I was happy about that. The requirement by the church of immigrant's rebaptism was abandoned soon after.[224]

Oscar's recollections have a charm of their own and provide insights as to how Ane's odyssey may have been. We get an inkling of what her experiences and feelings during the bustle of the long journey and the early days of settling in may have been like.

Interestingly and in contrast to my mother's lore that Ane had traveled with a girlfriend, Aunt Eleda's journal says Ane "came with a family by the name of Hansen."[225] This is a completely different version from my mother's story, and it becomes significant later.

Ane arrived in New York on 25 September 1878.[226] Ogden, her destination on the emigration list, was a railroad hub not far from Promontory Summit, where the Union Pacific Railroad tracks came from the east and the Central Pacific Railroad tracks came from the west and were joined together as the Transcontinental Railroad with a golden spike in 1869.

From Ogden, she may have taken another train north to Brigham or Logan, depending on where she planned to live. The family lore of Jens meeting Ane's train at Cache Junction in 1878 is historically incorrect, as that station wasn't constructed until around 1890. He would most likely have met her at Ogden or Brigham or maybe even Logan, and taken her to her lodgings in Brigham.

One story that lingered in the lore for some reason was that after Ane's arrival in Utah in 1878, she lived with Karen Marie's parents in Brigham City until her marriage to Jens took place two months later. But Karen Marie's father was dead and her mother had moved to Newton, so they were no longer in Brigham when Ane arrived. However, Karen Marie's history states: "Jens married Ane Margrethe Sorensen *of Brigham City* [emphasis mine], his plural wife."[227] Many early Church members stayed with the family of the missionary who converted them until they could find their own place. Perhaps Elder Jepsen, the missionary who baptized Ane, had family in Brigham with whom Ane stayed.

In a telephone conversation in August 2010 with my nephew Lyle Wiggins, a professional genealogist, I commented that as organized and particular as the LDS Church is, I found it difficult to believe that Jens and Ane's meeting at the train station was random. How could Ane come so far without having chosen her destination for a specific reason? Oscar emigrated on hope, and perhaps Ane did as well, but she had to have a reason for choosing Newton, Utah, as her destination. And why would Jens travel to the train station to select a stranger for another wife? Lyle agreed, saying the Church authorities called specific men to enter into the covenant of the order of plural marriage. In addition to the first wife being consulted for her permission, she sometimes was involved in helping to choose the plural wife or wives. Indeed, the involvement of the first wife and her family was encouraged.

Did Ane and Jens know in the beginning that the principle of plural marriage—as evidenced by many stories of sorrow—would not be easy to live by? Did they trust in other, more hopeful stories recounted of vows of determination to rise above the petty jealousies and frictions natural to being human? Did they expect that they could tame the frictions created by polygamy itself? Did they believe, like many men and women, that to eschew the call to enter a plural marriage was to be guaranteed the loss of eternal blessings, even to merit the disapproval of God himself and the removal of earthly blessings? Did they feel happiness at the prospect, or dread? Or both?

Joseph Stuart, a researcher I encountered at a table in a research room of the LDS Church History Library on 26 June 2012 told me that many people think polygamy was about sex, but it really was about establishing multiple eternal family units—though to support and maintain multiple families was extremely difficult. Those who entered a plural marriage needed to be selfless, dedicated people who believed polygamy was a commandment revealed from God, and who felt that accepting the challenges and developing Christ-like attitudes, in spite of the hardships of such a lifestyle, would put their feet on a path to eternal blessings through subjugation of selfishness.

The practice of rebaptism that Oscar mentioned in his journal prevailed for a time in the early Church. In the Jens Peter Benson history by Carol Milligan, a former Newton librarian, it says, "In accordance with the custom of that day when a couple was married in the temple, they were re-baptized (before endowment and sealing)."[228] Dr. Haslam's letter shows that Ane was rebaptized by Jas Allen Berry on 13 October 1878. The ward records agree and further show that she was reconfirmed on the same date by Christian Andersen. Dr. Haslam doesn't give the location, but this was after she had arrived in Utah and before she married Jens.[229] Jens had been rebaptized 1 August 1875 by John Griffin and reconfirmed 1 August 1875 by Amos Clarke. Karen Marie had been rebaptized and reconfirmed on the same date and by the same people as Jens had been, after their immigration to Utah. These dates are also confirmed in the Newton Ward Records.

❦

Mother's story was that Jens met Ane at the train station that marked the end of her rail journey. Unlike Oscar, who depended on the kindness of strangers when he arrived, she was not alone in the new country. But that doesn't mean she wasn't lonely. Was she? What emotions did she feel as she ended her long journey from her home country and began a life in America? Did she miss her father and brother in spite of the frictions over her joining the Mormon Church? Were there friends she had left behind? Was she glad to be in a community of fellow Mormons? Was she scared of anything? Was she genuinely upset when she learned she was to be a plural wife? Did she wish to escape but had nowhere to go and no one else to depend upon? Or had no money? Did she fall in love with the beauty of Cache Valley, surrounded by mountains and threaded by streams and rivers? How did she feel about Karen Marie? Did she learn to love the five children of Jens and Karen Marie?

One amazing journey for Ane ended with her arrival at the train station where she met Jens—maybe not for the first time—and another amazing journey began.

CHAPTER 12

DOUBLE DAZZLING SURPRISES

T he story that Jens selected Ane at random out of the crowd at the train station kept nagging at me, and then we heard a different version of the story from Jens's other family.

❧

Carla telephoned me on 12 August 2013 and said that LuDean Hawes Carroll—one of the two sisters descended from Jens and Karen Marie who lived near her in Pleasant View, Utah—had called and said she had too much produce in her garden, and she asked if Carla would like some. LuDean was in her eighties at the time and enjoyed planting a large garden. When Carla arrived at the house just a block away, LuDean gave her cucumbers, tomatoes, zucchini, and other colorful homegrown vegetables. Carla and her son, Matt, used some of the cucumbers to make bread-and-butter pickles.

A few days later, LuDean called offering more vegetables from her garden. Carla gladly went over again, taking a jar of the pickles to give her as a thank-you. This time as Carla prepared to leave with the fresh produce, LuDean said, "Come in here," gesturing toward her living room. "I want to show you something." She led Carla across the room to a china cabinet and pointed out a crystal butter dish, creamer, and sugar bowl, all with wide rose edging. "Your great-grandmother brought this set from Denmark to America as a gift for the first wife."

We were astonished! I adore this story even though it conflicts with our own family lore, or maybe *because* this conflict gives us new possibilities for the truth of the past. If this story is true, then Ane must have known before she came to America that she was going to be a plural wife. But Richard suggested a different scenario: perhaps she brought the crystal set for her own trousseau but, upon learning there was a first wife, decided to give the exquisite set to her as a gift, maybe even as a peace offering.

Two families. Two different stories that offer contrasting versions of this very important beginning. The crystal seems to call into question the lore of random selection. Carla and I have speculated that our mother—and apparently others in her family—seemed to think polygamy was a shameful thing. Perhaps their depicting Ane as an innocent, unaware of the polygamous arrangements ahead of time, mitigated their discomfort and made this facet of the family history more tolerable to them.

The beautiful crystal set was passed down through Karen Marie's eldest and only living daughter at the time of her death, Louisa (who had been born three days before my grandmother Sophia). From Louisa, it went to her daughter, Verba, who then passed it to her daughter, LuDean. Clearly the crystal was considered by LuDean's family to be a treasure, in spite of the difficulties its original owners might have had with living life in the principle of polygamy. Carla texted me photographs, and I could see why the family cherished the gorgeous set.

❄

While I was in Utah in June 2014, LuDean and I sat next to each other in Relief Society, the women's meeting, at church in Carla's ward. I asked if she would allow me to come to her home to see the crystal, and without hesitation, she said yes. On the arranged morning, Carla and I drove through her neighborhood of brick ranch houses with green, well-tended lawns and flowers, to LuDean's home where she welcomed us warmly into her lovely living room. Carla sat on a sofa, and I walked directly to the china cabinet where the crystal trio with deep pink edges on a center shelf immediately drew my eyes. It was exquisite, and I said so.

"Don't you want to take it out and hold it?" LuDean asked. "Don't you want to take some photographs?" Yes, of course, I did, but I also had a fear of breaking something!

She opened the glass door, and I reverently placed both hands under and around the sugar bowl and carried it to her coffee table in front of the sofa, and then I repeated the action with the covered butter dish, and then the creamer. Each piece nestled in and filled my doubled hands. They were larger than any sugar bowls or creamers or butter dishes I had seen and were extra heavy for their size. Richard's skepticism made me ask myself, did my great-grandmother Ane touch this crystal? Did she bring it all the way here from Denmark? I believed so, and I enjoyed the feeling of awe it gave me to hold it. I gently arranged the pieces on the table and began to photograph with my phone.

"Don't you want a backdrop of some kind to make it look nicer for your pictures?" LuDean asked. "When Carla came over to photograph, she brought a throw the same color as the rose on the crystal, and it was perfect."

Carla said I could find the throw on the back of a chair just inside the door from her garage into the kitchen, so I drove fast to her house, let myself in, found the throw, closed up the house, jumped in the car, and raced back to LuDean's. When I got to the front door, I stood on the porch and hesitated, asking myself, "Do I just walk in? Do I ring the bell?" We were relatives but were in some ways still strangers. What was the proper thing to do? Wanting to err on the side of being polite instead of presumptuous, I rang the bell.

LuDean opened the door, stood aside to let me in, and said, "What's the matter with you? Can't you lift the door latch?" My nervousness evaporated in laughter, and I loved both the dry humor of her comment and that she felt comfortable enough to tease me. I wondered if the sense of humor in both our families has its roots in Jens somehow.

I gently placed the soft throw under the individual pieces of crystal, arranged some graceful folds, and took several photos. Even in photographs, the set is stunning.

"How did Ane manage to bring this set here from Denmark?" I asked.

"On the ships, they packed delicate things in barrels with sawdust," LuDean answered. "And they had to be watchful against theft."

LuDean said she had twisted her mother's arm to pass the set on to her—otherwise her sister would have gotten it. She bemoaned the fact that she had accidently broken the lid to the sugar bowl. I remembered things of my own mother's that I had broken and still grieved. We talked a bit more, then I put the crystal—piece by piece—back in the display cabinet, but I did not get it arranged so the glass door could close properly. As LuDean came to my rescue and shifted the pieces just a bit so the door closed, it occurred to me that I needed to ask some questions.

"Our family lore says that Jens picked Ane out from the crowd at the train station. Does your family have other information?"

As LuDean shut the cabinet door with a click, she looked directly at me with her clear blue eyes and said, slowly enunciating every word: "He—sent—for—her." That news stunned me, and I wanted to know more.

LuDean went on to say that someone in Newton—she couldn't remember whether it was a friend or a family member—knew Ane from Denmark and wanted her to come over, so Jens had agreed to sponsor her and marry her. This intrigued me. Maybe Jens and Ane *hadn't* met before she arrived at the train station. I can accept the story that Jens agreed to bring her because someone else wanted her to be in Utah, and to marry her because his bishop had likely called him to enter a plural marriage. And Jens later sponsored others to come to America—so why not Ane?

I looked at LuDean and asked, "How did Karen Marie feel about that?"

"How would you feel if your husband wanted to take another wife?"

"I'd kill them both," I said, and all three of us laughed.

We sat then on LuDean's comfortable chairs and sofa and talked of many things in the peace of her living room, spending a happy time there. I loved the new details of their family story, and I wanted to know more. Who was the person, or persons, in Newton who knew Ane and wanted her to come from Denmark? In my heart of hearts, I still entertained the possibility that Ane and Jens *might* have met in Denmark. Was his willingness to bring her based partially on his already knowing who she was? Or did they actually agree to marry sight unseen?

I prefer the other family's story to ours. But Richard points out that either one of them could be true, or versions of the truth, or partial truths, or even both false.

❧

I was curious as to where Ane might have obtained this beautiful crystal set, so while in Denmark in July 2014, I showed photographs of the crystal pieces to various antique dealers in shops and at flea markets at Sorø, Roskilde, and Copenhagen. Answers to my question, "Where was this made?" included: "Not in Denmark." "It isn't Danish." "Maybe England." "Maybe Eastern Europe." "Maybe Germany—Denmark had a lot of trade over the years with Germany."

Finally, in Copenhagen on 12 July 2014, I asked my question of a well-dressed and knowledgeable woman, Margit Lillelund, in the Røde Kors Butik (the thrift store that was formerly an apartment building where Jens possibly stayed a month with his brother Hans at Fælledvej 4), and she decisively stated it had been made in old Czechoslovakia. She showed me a variety of crystal pieces with similar rose edgings displayed on a table nearby. I asked if the set in my photos might have been made as early as 1875, and she said yes. To get a totally reliable evaluation of the crystal, one would need to take the actual pieces of crystal to an expert to see with their own eyes, rather than just photographs, but it isn't mine for doing so.

I don't know where Ane purchased the crystal or how she got money to buy something so luxurious, or whether it came from someplace other than old Czechoslovakia, but I appreciate that LuDean shared her lovely treasure and her family's story with us. I am especially grateful to have been given the gift of their story at that moment in time, for LuDean passed away on 6 February 2016, at the age of eighty-eight, and I miss her. It is too late to ask her more questions, and I don't know what became of the crystal.

*

A second surprise came as we learned more about Jens's eldest brother, Anders, who was born 13 October 1838.[230] This baby was baptized at home 17 October (perhaps he was off to a rough start?) and then was baptized again in the church two months later on 21 December 1838:

> Parents: Niels Hansen, Tenant (Insider, person who rents and lives in the home of a farmer) and Betrothed Hanne Margrethe Andersdatter in
> Svebølle
> Ane Kirstine Andersdatter, Svebølle, carried the child
> Sponsors: Peder Pedersen, County Manager, Steenrandgaard [Stone Rim Farm]
> Christen Andersen, Svebølle
> Bachelor Jens Andersen, Svebølle[231]

The 1845 census shows Jens's parents and their four sons, with Anders, the firstborn, being 6 years old.[232] After that point Anders disappeared from the records we had, and none of the records or oral histories indicated whether he had survived childhood.

I asked Kaja if she would try to find information about Anders after his mother died in 1848. (The 1850 census shows Jens at age 8 living with his father, noted as a widower and day laborer—just the two of them.[233]) Soon she responded that the 1850 census shows Anders, 11, and the youngest brother, Rasmus Otto, 5, living with their maternal grandmother, Maren Christensdatter, a widow,[234] who was 66 at the time. She was my great-great-great-grandmother, and I wondered how she must have felt, having lost her husband twenty-four years earlier[235] and then losing a daughter and her baby. Did she cherish the two grandsons and the gift of time with them? Or was caring for them alone at her age a heavy responsibility?

Maren probably did not have responsibility for the boys very long, because they began working contracts at young ages, as was customary in Denmark at that time. Rasmus Otto is shown in an 1855 census at age 11 with Soren Hansen, 62, and Ane Kirstine Anders(datter?), 39. (perhaps she was the one who carried Anders at his baptism?). The record lists him "in the place of the son." The couple also had two servants, ages 14 and 19.[236]

Anders was confirmed following completion of his mandatory education in 1853 in the Avnsø Kirke.[237] He would have started contracts after confirmation, and he is shown in 1855 as a hired hand in Ugerløse, and in 1857 in Avnsøgaard.[238] Anders arrived from Avnsø at Stårup in November 1861 and likely continued with other contracts in other locations until 30 April 1866 when, at age twenty-seven and a half, he traveled from Hønsinge to Højby to work at Annebjerg, a forested area just east of Højby right at the Isefjord.[239]

A young woman named Maren Sørensen arrived at Trundholm, just south of Højby, from Hønsinge in November 1861.[240] Somehow the two of them met, and the record shows this:

> Bachelor Anders Nielsen, hired hand at Anneberg, born in Svebølle 13 October 1838, And Maid Maren Sørensen, maid at Anneberg, born in Hørve 15 December 1837, were married 1 November 1867.
> Witnesses: P.F. Rasmussen, Manager at Annebjerg, and Peter Sørensen, Farmer in Eskildstrup.[241]

So Anders and Maren were married seven months after Jens and Karen Marie had been. In 1870 they had a son they named Soren Peter. Jens and Karen Marie had a son in 1871 they named Soren Peter. Four years later, Anders and Maren had a daughter named Hanne Margrethe. Jens already had a daughter named Hanne Margaret. Were they competing? Honoring ancestors? Trying to confuse their descendants?

The 1870 Danish census shows Anders, 31, Maren, 32, and Soren Peter, who had been born in August.[242] The notation of Hanne Margrethe's birth in November 1874 in Vallekilde shows her parents as "Laborer Anders Nielsen and wife Maren Sørensen, Starreklinte Brick Factory. The parents are of Mormon Faith."[243] Kaja noted this possibly might have been the Adelersborg Brick Factory, the same place Jens and Karen Marie later worked. Kaja also wrote that later Anders and Maren emigrated in 1878—the same year as Ane!

Several immigrant ships sailed from Liverpool to New York in 1878, and I wanted to find which one Anders and Maren had traveled on. I planned to search the emigration lists and ship passenger lists in Salt Lake on my next trip. However, I had a copy of one page of an emigration list of the SS *Wyoming* that set sail on 7 September 1878 with our Ane aboard. The chance of Anders and Maren being on the same ship as Ane, and of appearing on that single page of the emigration list with Ane, were less than minuscule, but I could at least start by checking that.

As I carefully perused that single sheet, I couldn't believe what I saw! Above Ane's name two strangers' names appeared on the list, separating her name from those of Anders, Maren, and Hanne M., 3. (Anders and Maren's son, Soren Peter, does not appear on this emigration sheet, or on the complete emigration list. Kaja checked other emigration lists of the time and did not find Soren Peter on any of them. However, he is listed in Newton's 1880 census and is buried in the Newton cemetery, so he did immigrate to Utah prior to 1880.)[244] Ane and the brother of Jens—her sponsor—were not only on the same ship but were also listed almost adjacently, drawing me to conclude that Ane was not traveling alone at random to Newton, Utah. I believe that her future husband's brother and his wife escorted Ane on this significant voyage. This brings us back to Aunt Eleda's note saying that Ane had traveled "with a family by the name of Hansen." At the time of emigration, however, they still used the patronymic Nielsen, and only later adopted their father's surname of Hansen. Even so, Aunt Eleda seems to have remembered the story more accurately than other relatives.

This new scoop negates my family lore that Ane was ignorant and innocent of the polygamous arrangement and chose her destination at random. Or does it? Perhaps she was specifically chosen to wed Jens upon her arrival but not informed of his existing marriage to Karen Marie. And what role did the crystal play?

If Ane worked as a maid, and perhaps then was caregiver for her mother, followed by being caregiver for her father, how and where would she have acquired this lovely crystal? Would she have had enough money to purchase it for herself? Might it have been an inheritance from a relative? Was it a family treasure passed down from her mother?

Maybe Richard is right that, even with all this new information, we cannot be sure of the veracity of either story. I prefer the stories that say Ane brought the crystal for the first wife and that she was escorted by her future brother-in-law, over my family story that she traveled at random and was chosen at random. The solution to this puzzle seems to have evaporated in the swirling mists of time. We will likely never know for sure.

CHAPTER 13

JENS, KAREN MARIE, AND ANE: 1878–1880

The emigration list shows the final destination of both Ane and Anders's family as Ogden—a railroad hub—and the train probably stopped there before going on to Salt Lake City. They all likely then boarded another train going north to Mendon or Logan. The family records do not say that Jens also met his brother, sister-in-law, and niece at the same train station and time, nor do they say whether anyone accompanied him. He probably traveled in a horse-drawn buggy and may have transported Ane to someone's home in Brigham, where she resided until their marriage two months later. Perhaps Jens took Anders and his family to stay with someone in Newton, because Anders, Maren, Hannah, Soren Peter, and Mary all appear in dwelling #10 in the 1880 Newton census.

Whether Ane and Jens had met in Denmark through Church or work contracts or servant dances or some other means, or had not met at all, they probably spent time during those two months between her arrival and their marriage in becoming acquainted, or better acquainted. In some potential polygamy relationships, the man actually courted the woman even though he already had a wife or wives. We have no lore about this time period for Jens and Ane, but perhaps they courted in some way.

Could Ane truly not have been informed of the marital status of the man who was sponsoring and planning to marry her? Taking a husband with whom one envisions an exclusive relationship is an entirely different thing from entering into the challenges of a plural relationship, a relationship that forever prevents exclusivity for the new wife and erases it for the first wife. In fact, Jens and Karen Marie had been married eleven years and had five children, and possibly also had some responsibility for Karen Marie's mother—a complicated situation for a new bride to become part of.

Sharing a husband sounds like an extremely painful thing to do, but it was also viewed as a stepping-stone to more blessings in the next life. Marriages in the Endowment House or temple were celestial marriages "for time and all eternity," not "till death do you part." Polygamy was seen as a pathway to aid the faithful in preparing for the next life, creating eternal families, and rejoicing in the presence of God.

I hope Jens had a tender consideration for Karen Marie's feelings and asked her permission. Perhaps she gave lip service permission for Jens to marry Ane even if in her heart she had reservations as mentioned in the Hicks history: "This second marriage was very much against Karren's wishes."[245] Some stories indicate that though a woman may have had difficulty accepting the idea of allowing her husband to bring another wife into the equation, she likely was conflicted due to concern that refusing would put her at odds with God's will.

And how did Ane feel, knowing she was going to marry a man who had a family of long duration? How did their relationship take shape during those two months? Apparently neither found cause to break the engagement, because on 15 November 1878, Jens Nielsen Hansen and Ane Margrethe Sorensen made the trip, possibly by buggy or carriage—or perhaps by train, having arranged transportation to and from the train stops at both ends of the trip—from Newton and Brigham to Salt Lake City, where they were married in the Endowment House for time and eternity. And thus they entered the order of plural marriage.

The journey of ninety-seven miles between Newton and Salt Lake City by horse-drawn conveyance or by train to reach the Endowment House, have the ordinance performed, and return home may have required a couple of days. Did they go alone? Did other family members go with them? What did they talk about? What did they eat? Did they stay in an inn or in the conveyance? What were Karen Marie's thoughts and feelings while they were gone? Or did she go with them? How did they explain to the children—ages eleven, seven, five, three, and eight months—what was taking place? What did the children think about having a new woman marry their father and become "Auntie" to them?

One can only wonder what the feelings were of the two women involved in this extraordinary change and adjustment in their lives. No doubt every woman whose life was touched in some way by *the principle* [emphasis mine], as plural marriage was called, had a unique perspective on the practice. Although we have no journals from Ane or Karen Marie, perhaps by considering records of other women who lived in polygamy, we can get a glimpse of some of the feelings Jens's two wives might have had.

One example is from the life of Miles Romney, who married his first wife, Hannah, in 1862. Later he took a second wife, who, after bearing two children, divorced him and left the area.[246] Later, another young woman, Catharine Cottam, was charmed by Romney, and the feelings were mutual. They traveled from St. George, Utah, to Salt Lake City—a distance of 303 miles—and were married in the Endowment House. Maybe words from the first wife's heart speak for legions of women in polygamy:

> Hannah remained in St. George and worked on fixing up the house. She carried warp and rags for a new carpet to the weavers and hauled the finished product home after dark to tack down in Catharine's room. "I had a room finished for Catherine [*sic*] with new carpet and furniture all ready for her," Hannah wrote. "I cannot explain how I suffered in my feelings while I was doing all this hard work, but I felt I would do my duty if my heart did ache. I had such a hard time with his [second] wife that I feared I would have the same kind of trial again, but when I came to live with Sister Catherine [*sic*] it was quite different. She was very considerate of my feelings and good to the children. She helped in the house and did not expect all of *my* [emphasis mine] husband's attention. When he came home he appreciated what I had done. He admired the home arrangements and was surprised that I had accomplished so much in such a short time. His appreciation of my work partly took away the heart ache."[247]

Another example of the misgivings of a first wife whose husband is taking a second bride is found in the writings of Fanny Stenhouse, who later became critical of the Mormon Church, defected from it, and was excommunicated. She attained some notoriety as a circuit lecturer:

> The time at length arrived for us to go to the "Endowment House," and there at the altar the first wife is expected to give proof of her faith in her religion by placing the hand of the new wife in that of her husband. She is asked the question… "Are you willing to give this woman to your husband, to be his lawful and wedded wife, for time and for all eternity? If you are, you will manifest it by placing her right hand within the right hand of your husband." I did so. But what words can describe my feelings?… When it was done, I felt that I had laid every thing upon the altar, and that there was no more to sacrifice. I had given away my husband. What more could the Lord require of me that I could not do? Nothing! [Meaning any other sacrifice would be small and easy by comparison with this one.]
>
> I was bewildered and almost beside myself, and yet I had to hide my feelings; for to whom should I turn for sympathy among those

who were around me? My husband was there, it is true; but he was now the husband of another woman, and a newly-made bridegroom. I felt that I stood alone, our union was severed. I had given away my husband, and he no longer belonged only to me!... From that day, I began to hide all my sorrow from my husband....

I remember well that when I returned home—that "home" which was now to become hateful to me, for his young wife was to live there—my husband said to me, "You have been very brave; but it is not so hard to do, after all, is it?" He had seen me bear it so well, that he even supposed I was indifferent.[248]

Like Hannah, Karen Marie may have stayed at home while Jens and Ane went to Salt Lake to be married so she could care for her five young children. Or she may have left the children in the care of her mother and, like Fanny, accompanied Jens and Ane to the Endowment House. No mention of that decision is made in either the histories or the lore.

Some stories chronicle devout women who welcomed polygamy and its promised blessings. At the other extreme, there was a woman who, when her husband asked her permission to take another wife when he was called to do so by his ecclesiastical leader, told him that if he took another wife, she would kill them both. He did, and she did not, however.[249]

After their marriage ceremony, Jens likely brought Ane back to live in the rock/adobe house. What did she feel as she returned as a married woman with a husband? The trip may have been arduous as well as exciting, but she then settled into a home with its small space already occupied by her husband, his first wife, and their five children. Possibly Kirsten, Karen Marie's mother, had her own log house by then. The 1880 census for Newton shows Kirsten in a separate dwelling.[250] According to Karen Marie's descendants, "Jens and the plural wives lived and ate together in the same house for quite awhile, even sharing the same bedroom for awhile. Jens built Aunt Annie, as she was called, another bedroom as soon as he was able to."[251] (Technically only Ane was considered a plural wife because Karen Marie had the distinction of being the legally recognized first wife.) Hans and his family had already moved to Clarkston, and there is no mention of what happened to the dugout when the families moved out of it.

Horrified by the idea of the shared bedroom, I hoped this statement was a result of misinformation. However the limited space of the house might have necessitated that sharing.

The transcript of court proceedings for one Utah man charged with unlawful cohabitation indicates the husband and his two wives occupied the same house and took meals together but that each wife had her own bedroom.[252] Jessie L. Embry, a western and Mormon history specialist at Brigham Young University, stated:

> Mormon plural families usually lived in separate homes with the husbands visiting each wife at regular intervals when possible.... Quite often just after a husband married a plural wife, all the wives shared a home. Later in the marriage after families were established, he might build a separate home or a family might move so that children could attend school or a wife could avoid the U.S. marshals. As the children left home and the husbands and wives grew older, living arrangements might be adjusted again.[253]

Embry's mention of the US marshals refers to a later time in LDS history when polygamists were hunted. That situation will be covered in a subsequent chapter.

Embry also mentions that Edward Christian Eyring, a prominent early polygamist and grandfather of LDS apostle Henry B. Eyring, "had a weekly schedule" and that his son LeRoy with Emma, the first wife, said:

> Polygamy was then so natural to me that I did not notice particularly his weekly packing of his leather valise to move over to "Aunt Caroline's" for the week, or his return the following Saturday with his things put away in the leather container. It also seemed perfectly natural that he should leave our house a little before bedtime to go over to say goodnight to "Auntie" when it was our week, or for his coming just before bedtime to kiss us good night when it was his week over there.[254]

Eyring sounds like the epitome of a caring husband and father, as many polygamists tried to be. He probably also had prayers with each family every evening.

Less than two months after Karen Marie began sharing her husband with Ane in the rock house, Jens and Karen Marie's third child—their five-year-old daughter, Hanne Margaret—became ill with diphtheria, a bacteria-caused throat infection. After suffering with this disease, Hanne Margaret died from it on 6 January 1879, when she was two months past her fifth birthday. This little girl had come on the journey from Denmark with her family as a one-year-old, had spent almost four years after their arrival playing and growing and probably helping with small chores as an integral part of the family—and of the parents' and siblings' hearts—only to succumb to this virulent disease.

Diphtheria was highly contagious, and Soren Peter (Jens and Karen Marie's second child, who was seven years and ten months old) unfortunately also contracted the disease. Only nine days after his sister's death, Soren Peter died on 15 January 1879. He too had been born in Denmark and had made the journey to the new country when he was three years old.

Approximately three months after the deaths of these two children, both Karen Marie and Ane became pregnant. How did the women feel about polygamy this first time they were expecting babies simultaneously? Did this create a sisterly bond between them or dispassionate tolerance? Was the anticipation of new life a diversion from the sadness of the deaths of the two children? Or was there no comfort?

The summer and fall of 1879 likely were spent—in spite of grief—with the usual chores of maintaining a family and preparing for winter in this ten-year-old community: planting and harvesting, putting food by, storing wood, doing laundry, cooking, and cleaning. As Christmas approached, the family likely observed Danish Christmas customs such as advent candles and butter cookies, and possibly homemade gifts.

Tragically, diphtheria was not yet finished with the family. On 24 December 1879, the day of Christmas Eve, Jens and Karen Marie's fourth child, Elsie Jensine (the daughter with whom Karen Marie had been pregnant on the journey from Denmark, their first child to have been born in the new country) died, probably from diphtheria. She was barely four years old. The Hicks history says, "Here, one of the hardest trials came to them. Two small children, ages 6 and 8, died from diphtheria a couple of days apart. Their new baby [error: Elsie Jensine was four years and 15 days old] also died a few months later."[255]

In about 1989, Jared Wiggins, the fourteen-year-old son of my nephew Lyle and his wife, Jane, was skateboarding with friends and brothers when he was hit by a truck and killed. I remember my mother standing in the funeral home by the casket of this beloved grandson and almost wailing, "It's out of order! It's out of order!" Jens's and Karen Marie's grief over the loss of their children must have felt just that way to them.

In the few photos I have of Karen Marie, her eyes look haunted.

Although the Newton Ward Records clearly show that Elsie Jensine died in 1879, some family members have wondered whether she might have died in 1878, eighteen days before Hanne Margaret's death rather than eleven months after Soren Peter's. That would have been more likely in a diphtheria epidemic of short duration. However, several newspaper accounts from nearby Logan indicate the disease fluctuated over a period of several years in Logan, and that was probably the pattern in other local communities such as Newton as well. Over a period of time, the *Logan Leader* published the following:

27 February 1880: "No more diphtheria in Logan."

16 April 1880: "Diphtheria is once more prevalent."

30 April 1880: "Diphtheria is in Logan again. Two death *(sic)* [italics in original] has been caused by the disease."

14 January 1881: "DIPHTHERIA is still raging in some localities of Logan. Let all take proper means to stay its march."

28 January 1881: "No more cases of diphtheria are reported. We hope that dreaded disease be permanently checked."

In eleven months' time, Jens and Karen Marie watched diphtheria take their three middle children, leaving the eldest son, Jens Peter, twelve, and the youngest son, Niels Peter Nephi, one and a half. How quiet that little house must have seemed with three children lost from the family.

As I typed up the preliminary chronology for this work at a quiet abbey guesthouse in the woods on a rainy spring night, and finished the above section with the three children dying, I put my head on the table next to my laptop and wept. Remembering my own pain and grief at losing my first husband, I ached for the sorrow that must have afflicted Karen Marie and Jens in the loss of these children and their parental dreams for them.

Was the loss of her three children compounded for Karen Marie by having spent a year adjusting to no longer having exclusivity with her husband? Might that adjustment have been difficult for Jens as well? And how was Ane faring? Certainly, she too must have felt sorrow in the loss of these innocents, especially living in the same space with them. Was she also disheartened by marriage to a shared husband, who would never be hers exclusively? Both women were about eight months pregnant at the Christmas Eve death of Elsie Jensine. What might they have worried about while carrying new life? Karen Marie's history says, "To lose three children in less than one year—what great sorrow. The people of the ward were afraid of the dreaded disease that was taking so many lives and dared not enter their home to assist them, except James Hansen."[256]

I have not found the children's graves in Newton Cemetery, nor are they listed on the cemetery records. So I wonder: Where are the children buried? Near other family grave markers stands a monolith with *HANSEN* on the base. I asked the cemetery people if the marker was located on cemetery lots purchased by Jens but did not receive a researched answer. The next time I was in Newton

Cemetery, I realized that all the Hansens in that area are from Jens's families, so perhaps the striking monument was erected to mark the family plot. Newton people told me that the children in those days could be buried without markers, or sometimes were buried on family farmlands.

Five and a half weeks after Elsie Jensine's death, Karen Marie gave birth to Louisa Marie Hansen, her sixth child, on 2 February 1880. Three days later on 5 February 1880, Ane gave birth to Karen Sophia Hansen (my grandmother), her first child and Jens's seventh. That the two baby girls were born so close together always bothered my mother—probably because she imagined it would be unimaginable to know one's husband was being intimate with another woman, especially so close in time to his intimacy with oneself. Mom thought the two women lived across the street from each other at the time—which they eventually did—but deed records and the other family's history indicate that at this time they were all still living together in the rock house. Had my mother been aware of that, she likely would have been even more bothered. Or even aghast.

Karen Marie's history says:

> When mother, Louisa Marie, was three days old, Aunt Annie [sic] gave birth to her first girl…. As they couldn't afford to hire help, Grandpa [Jens] was a busy man, taking care of the needs of both women and the house. Grandma [Karen Marie] says she remembers washing diapers while staying in bed. They were both living in the same house and even sharing the same bedroom at that time.[257]

Though this is the second mention in the same history that says they shared a bedroom, I clung to my resistance. But the 1880 census of Newton shows: Jens; Karen Marie; James Peter [baptized Jens Peder], twelve; Niels Peter Nephi, two; Louisa Marie, nine months; Ane; and Karen Sophia, nine months, all in dwelling #16.[258] (Dwellings were numbered in the order the census taker visited them.) So the household consisted of three adults and four children. Were they all in Karen Marie's rock house?

The Hicks history goes on to say:

> Later he [Jens] built a nice frame house for Aunt Annie, two rooms downstairs and two rooms upstairs, with a large summer kitchen. This house is still in fine shape today (1978) [when Neilen Hicks and Verba Petersen Haws were writing this history] and is still being lived in, having been built on to. Grandpa [Jens] was a very good carpenter

but I guess he never had enough money to build Grandmother [Karen Marie] a new house. Her home consisted of two rooms downstairs and one in the attic that was used for a bedroom.[259]

So Ane's home was built sometime after the census that was taken late in 1880. And there was a sense of pique that Ane's home was nicer than Karen Marie's. Was this resentment harbored in Karen Marie's heart? Or did her descendants form their own opinions?

❧

Mother told me more than once that her mother had not liked growing up in a polygamous family, and I wish now that I had asked her why. My sister, Carla, has commented several times that it seemed like polygamy was a shameful history for mother and some of her family. However, it is what it is. I have to admit to feelings of ambivalence about being the product of polygamous ancestors. Intellectually, I can understand it and be compassionate about what it must have demanded to live in that time and in that manner, but emotionally I sometimes feel scratchy about it. My mother often used to say, "No kitchen is big enough for two women." Was she quoting Ane? Or her mother, Sophia? I would love to know.

Life was full and busy and challenging for these people who had sacrificed so much to emigrate and begin life in a new country. A plaque in front of the home of Peter Benson (a prominent early Newton settler) pays a well-deserved tribute to all ancestors with the tender sentiments written by Carol Milligan:

Let us come to know and love these ancestors who sacrificed home, friends, family and belongings. Let us come to know the courage and strength they had to cross land and sea, so they could embrace a new religion, learn a new language, learn new ways and live in a new land.

Here they shared the hardships and sacrifices of the early settlers, willing to contribute to the building of their communities and establishing the Lord's church in Zion.

By doing these things for us, they changed our destiny, increasing our opportunities and blessings.[260]

I didn't have the privilege of meeting or knowing Great-Grandma Ane or Great-Grandpa Jens or Great-Auntie Karen Marie, but having studied their lives and the history that surrounded them, I can look at their photos and feel a tender connection to them as people rather than merely as names on a family chart. And as I pondered the discussion I'd had with my friends about the belief that the spirits of our departed ancestors are sometimes near us, I wondered whether my ancestors were aware that their stories were being researched and written. Did they approve? Was I getting their stories right? Was I missing something? Through the kindness of others and amazing antique records, so many snippets of information had poured in, fleshing out their stories and making real their footprints in the sands of time.

CHAPTER 14

TERROIR: NEWTON'S MILIEU

*T*erroir, a French word, as difficult to define as it is to pronounce, has to do with the distinct flavor of things created by the characteristics of the soil, the terrain, and the climate from which they are produced. In the Ardèche Mountains of south-central France, at the edge of the medieval village of Antraigues-sur-Volane, Richard and I sat at a table in a small open-air, organic café under a purple sunshade umbrella bearing the logo *Le Café des Serres* for a summer lunch in 2009. The young apron-clad proprietor explained, in a combination of broken English and gestures, that if Richard would just try the red beets in his appetizer, he would like them, because they had grown from a local soil and a climate that made them sweet. He mimed digging in the dirt with a shovel for the precious beets. French vintners, cheese makers, farmers, and other purveyors use the word *terroir* to proclaim the unique and perhaps superior qualities of wines, produce, animals, dairy products, and grains for breads produced in a specific locality.

Novelists sometimes consider the aspect of terroir when focused on creating an accurate and rich description of setting, not only when the setting functions as a character but also when setting is the vital place in which the characters live, make choices, shape and are shaped by the environment. Perhaps in real life too, people absorb and mold their unique locations.

What effect did Newton have upon Jens, Karen Marie, Ane, and others as they lived their lives, raised their families, made decisions, altered the environment, and also adapted to it? What clues did these ancestors leave to indicate how their experiences and decisions in Newton—as well as the heritage they brought from Denmark—made them who they were? And I wonder further, how did the terroir of their locations and their genetics create and shape me?

After the arrival of the early Mormon pioneers in the Salt Lake Valley, Brigham Young, the second president of the Church of Jesus Christ of Latter-day Saints, sent groups of families out to settle specific sites. One such site was Clarkston, nestled on the piedmont of a mountain range edging Cache Valley.

However, some settlers found Clarkston winters so bitter as to be intolerable. A new site was chosen and a "new town," or Newton, was established in 1869, southeast of Clarkston and at a slightly lower elevation. Residents had the choice whether to stay in Clarkston or to move to Newton.

A preliminary Newton Townsite survey sketched out blocks and lots, with church and community areas in the center of town surrounded by lots in town and farmlands outside the town. Families were allotted property for homes and farms in this new settlement. Much of the early history of Newton is still evident in the charming structures of the period. Building materials for the first settlers included local rock, wood from trees harvested near Logan, and adobe. Many of these homes from the late 1800s and early 1900s still stand in Newton (as of 2020). Weathered gray barns stand adjacent to old homes, and hay sheds—each with a roof on four stilts—for storing animal feed, appear sporadically through town.

As Richard and I drove on Highway 30 going east toward the mountain pass and Newton in 2010, the dramatic rocky V-notch off to the left looked like it had potential as a better route into the valley. When I said so, Richard speculated that the elevation might be higher there, making it more difficult for passage. On a later occasion in Newton when Ruby rode in the car with my sisters and me, she told us Bear River flows through Bear River Gorge—that deep V—from Cutler Reservoir. She and her friends used to take the train from Cache Junction through the gorge and on to Salt Lake City where they would shop, sometimes buying only earrings and always enjoying the scenery of the ride. The sides of the canyon are too steep and narrow, she said, to allow for a road.

When in the Griffin home (formerly the Rigby home) during the Newton rock house tour 23 July 2011, I commented that I wanted to take the train ride Ruby had talked about. The host, John Griffin, a resident descended from an early family of Newton, said freight trains still used the tracks through the gorge but passenger trains no longer ran there. Also, Pete Henderson, manager of the Rio Grande Cafe in Salt Lake City, told me in July 2012 at the café counter that in the 1970s passenger service became unprofitable, so all the railroad companies pushed their passenger business off onto Amtrak. That stopped the excursions Ruby remembered so fondly, and also prevented my duplicating her trip. And I wondered whether Jens and Karen Marie and Ane had taken that train ride as an occasional entertainment.

Upon entering Newton from the southwest corner of town, one sees a sign that says, *Welcome to Newton, Established 1869*. Old sights reminiscent of early days consist of rock houses, period wood homes, farm fields, and old barns, all encircled by ranges of distant snow-capped mountains. One can look to the southwest in town and see the deep geological notch observed upon approach from outside the valley.

Rock homes and early wooden houses line the streets, occasionally interspersed with modern brick homes. Fields spread out with hay sheds, gray slatted barns, and grazing horses. Evergreen and deciduous trees and various types of shrubbery and flowers festoon the areas around and between the homes today, but in the early days of settlement, residents also dealt with muddy streets. Carol Milligan once gave me a tour of her front yard of the old Benson home, pointing out the trees and shrubs that were original from her ancestors' plantings in early Newton. Robins and a variety of other birds sang arias everywhere, and the plethora of mourning doves, whose plaintive calls sound owl-like, created haunting background music in a minor key. Sometimes birds shot up out of the taller grasses and flapped off over tarp-covered hay bales.

As we walked from our parked car toward Ane's home, Richard noticed a house on a corner that had a zigzag roofline, indicating that several additions had been constructed. An enclosed porch with lots of windows ran around the front and sides of the house, and a man and woman were planting flowers in the front yard. Feeling like an outsider and an interloper, I planned to skulk by and hope we went unnoticed. But Richard said, "I'm going to do some fieldwork," and he headed across the street toward the couple.

Startled but not wanting to miss anything, I sped up and followed, saying, "I'm coming too. Okay?"

We loped across the street and advanced (I, gingerly) onto their property. Richard greeted the couple, probably in their fifties, and asked politely if they would mind telling us when their house was built. When they said 1904, I realized that Ane had lived just two blocks away while this house was being constructed. She would have been sixty-one years old, with her two older children married, her youngest child dead, and her relationship with Jens perhaps less close than in earlier years. Karen Marie also lived on that street at the time, and Jens may have alternated time living in both houses or perhaps primarily with Karen Marie. Did they all watch the construction? Did they know the people who had built and lived in the house? Did they interact in any way?

"My great-grandparents lived over on Second East during the time your house was built," I said. The couple asked who my ancestors were but didn't recognize the Hansen names.

After we chatted for several minutes, the man softly suggested to his wife, "Why don't you take them inside and let them look around?"

Turning toward him and speaking *sotto voce*, she said, "I haven't cleaned."

"They understand," he said. We did, of course, but wondered what it was about us that made him deduce that we were nonjudgmental.

"Well," she said, hesitating, "come on in." So she led us to the door at the southeast corner of the porch and into the house while her husband remained outside, selecting another flower to plant.

Inside, the gracious home looked extremely clean to me. The living room walls and carpet were muted tones of gray, a lovely backdrop for the rosy tufted sofa and chairs with oval backs.

She led us through the double sitting room to the kitchen, past open bedroom doors framed in dark wood, and past a stairway enhanced by a simply-carved yet exquisite banister. As we moved beyond the living area, she pointed out what had been the original kitchen—a nook with lots of dark wood doors but scarce cabinet space. Off to the left, they had added a huge kitchen that looked like something from the Cooking Channel. Cabinets lined the far wall, a huge island stood in the center, and near us just inside the kitchen door sat a grand table suitable for a large family or a crowd of friends. We stood in that charming space and talked for several minutes.

Finished with our tour, we walked back through the house to the living room and approached the door to the porch, where the husband met us on his way inside. After a few minutes of conversation, he asked his surprising question: "Are you folks LDS?"

"I am, but he isn't," I answered, gesturing toward Richard.

The man turned to Richard with a pleasant hint of a smile on his face and asked, "What's holding you up?" I cracked up inside that someone would ask Richard that question. No one who knows him would do so. But he graciously and inoffensively answered, explaining his wider view of the religions of the world, a course that he taught at Oregon State University.

We talked about the climate, and the man mentioned the fifteen-degrees-below-zero temperatures Newton winters sometimes bring, and he said the record was forty-three below. I wondered if Clarkston really could top that.

We thanked them and headed back outside. At that time, as well as often since, I have pondered the generosity of this couple inviting strangers into their home. Did they do it because I have ancestors who lived there, and that moved me out of the category of outsider to that of insider? Was it because Newton people in general are hospitable and helpful? Would I invite total strangers into my home? Living in the outskirts of the large city of Portland, Oregon, likely not. But I would like to be at heart a Newton soul who is generous and trusting. Did my ancestors bring from Denmark a generosity of spirit that shaped the openness that continues in Newton today? Or perhaps people from small towns tend to be this way.

Later, in Denmark, Richard and I met an American man in Sorø who had moved there so his Danish wife could go to school. He said one day some people knocked on their door, said their ancestors had lived in his house, and thanked him for keeping it painted Danish yellow. He told them it hadn't been Danish yellow when he bought it, but he had just recently painted it. Then he had said to them: "Come on in, and let's have some coffee together." How generous to be that welcoming.

❦

Standing a few moments later in front of Ane's house, I was deeply moved to imagine my family living on this very spot, my mother being born upstairs, living with her beloved grandmother, sitting out on the porch together in the evening, and my maternal grandmother living right there from childhood to marriage. I envisioned buggies and carriages coming and going, horses snorting and their hooves clattering, water being brought from a spring or a well, and the aroma of the animals and fields tinting the air. The family chores for survival, without modern utilities, had occupied them in this dwelling and on the farmlands. And this is where Ane purportedly had put Jens's clothes on the porch and told him to go stay with his other family. What was the significance of that? Is there a letter somewhere that would tell us? This house has a magical aura for me because my mother's family lived in it.

A garden plot on the north side of Ane's house on the day we visited featured rows and rows of green plants reaching skyward. The garden was meticulously tended, weeded, and bordered by dark soil that was damp from a recent watering. Vegetables of promise grew in lush green rows. Did Ane raise produce on this spot during the thirty-four years this was her home? Aunt Eleda wrote that Ane dried fruit in the sunshine coming though the south window upstairs.[261] She also wrote, "Grandpa, Jens Nielsen Hansen…also planted an orchard…I know very little about him except that he had red hair."[262] She was born after his death.

We walked up the dirt and gravel driveway of Ane's house. The air was quiet, and there was no activity. The sun warmed us, and we heard an occasional fly zooming past.

An extremely tall old tree with a wide trunk and heavily leafed branches rose up at the northeast corner of the house. A little farther north, another giant of a tree stretched upward, and still another large tree stood right in the middle of the front yard. This wall of trees had obscured our view when we first searched for the house. The trees do not appear in our original family photo of the house, and I wondered when and by whom they were planted. The trees exuded character, but the root systems appeared to be close to the foundation of the house, and I worried that serious damage might eventually result.

The porch and front door that appear in our old photo were now enclosed, and a nearby window north of that enclosure was covered inside by a blanket on a rod. I later learned that in the early days, people covered their windows with blankets on rods and also hung blankets in internal doorways for room privacy, so the modern-day owner was apparently following the old tradition. Richard paced it off and estimated the house as about forty feet across the front and maybe another forty from front to back, with part of it two story and the rest just a single story.

I hadn't yet thought of knocking on the door and asking to come in. My mom would never impose, and I apparently was too well trained by her gentle example. I caressed the house with my eyes a few minutes longer, and then finally peeled myself away. I would like to win the lottery and make the current owner an offer he couldn't refuse. I love the house and the town and the people I've met, and I would love to have this historical home back in our family. As we continued down the street, I looked back at the rear of Ane's house and noticed that from her south and east windows, she would have been able to gaze at those mountain ranges with the snow on them—a visual feast.

We returned to the courthouse, where I poked around in the library while Richard did more fieldwork. Soon he found me and said, "Come on! I've found some people who want to meet you and ask you the questions they asked me that I don't know the answers to. And look! They gave me a phone directory for you!" He handed me a half-sheet-sized Newton directory, folded and stapled in the fold, and I received it with delight because it had been about ten minutes since I had told him I needed one.

Richard led me into the courtroom. It was the day of the local election, and four women of various ages sat behind a counter as voting monitors. No voters were present, so the women asked me who my ancestors were. Their surnames were familiar to me from the local histories: Rigby, Larsen, Jenkins, and Griffin.

They told us the decrepit building with the false front we had seen on our walk was the original dry goods store in the area, and that lightning had struck it. The store had been built in the 1870s, had probably been brought in from the nearby town of Trenton, and had also at one time been Barker's IGA Foods. It would have been serving the town when Jens, Karen Marie, and Ane arrived. In the early days of Newton, Ruby had told me, it was not uncommon for buildings and homes to be moved from place to place.

"The person living in Ane's house right now is Norris Cooley," one of the women said, "and he'd probably let you go in if you asked." They also said he had a sister in town, and if I couldn't get ahold of him, I should call her. "She could tell you where he is." It hadn't occurred to me to impose by asking permission to see the inside of the house, and I needed to think about that for a while.

One of the women said she was raised just south of Newton in Cache Junction, now a shell of its former glory as a railroad town with her house, a bank, a mercantile, a saloon, a café, a school, and a church. Those things would have been there during Ane's time and perhaps the family went there on occasion. There wasn't anything like that anymore—just a few homes, farm buildings, and lots of railroad tracks.

Several delivery people came in bringing a tray of sack lunches for the women, so we left to let them eat in peace. As we drove out of town, the mood of Newton traveled with me.

❧

After visiting Newton enough times that I recognized its unique effect upon me, I speculated about the ways in which the setting and situation shaped my ancestors. The terroir of Newton provided the milieu in which my forebears lived, felt, acted, and reacted. My anticipatory excitement whenever I enter the valley and drive toward Newton, as well as my passion for the ethereal feeling I find there, affect me. I feel deep appreciation and admiration for the people I have met who have helped me, and have shaped my attitudes and philosophies. These tender mercies draw me nearer to my own religious roots. Is this how Newton is shaping me? Or did it shape me through my ancestors long before I went to Newton for the first time?

Viskende/Viskinge Kirke where Jens's confirmation and communion took place.

Store Taastrup Kirke where Ane was christened.

Munke Bjergby Kirke where Ane's confirmation and communion took place.

Ceiling paintings of Jyderup Kirke.

Baptismal font in Jyderup Kirke where Jens Peter Nielsen (son of Jens and Karen Marie) was baptized in the Lutheran Church approximately 7 February 1868.

Lake Skarresø, Denmark, where Jens and Karen Marie were baptized into the LDS Church 22 April 1868.

Astrup farm where Jens was hired by the day in 1864. The farm was established in the early 1400s.

Dormitory at Kongsdal estate where Jens and Karen Marie may have lived during their work contract.

Kattrup farm where Jens worked 1862-1863 and said the life was too rough for him.

The fields directly across the street from the entrance to Kattrup.

Clogs like those Jens made using the tools shown.

A Jutland Shepherd on the Moors by Frederik Vermehren.

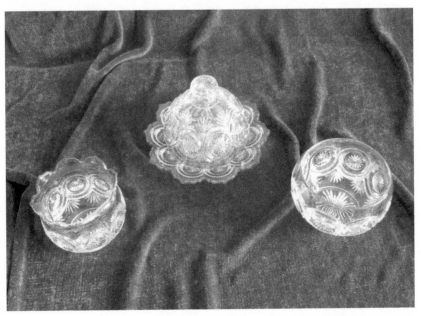

Crystal set purported to have been brought to America from Denmark by Ane as a gift for the first wife. In possession of descendants of Karen Marie.

Train station in Roskilde, Denmark, through which all the family emigrants passed en route to Copenhagen for boarding the ships to America.

Ane's house in Newton, shown during a period of vacancy.

Photo of men in prison for practicing polygamy. Jens Niels Hansen is second from left, standing. Photo courtesy of Ken Wright.

Locking mechanism from Old Idaho Penitentiary like that used in the Utah Territorial Penitentiary during the time of imprisonment of polygamists.

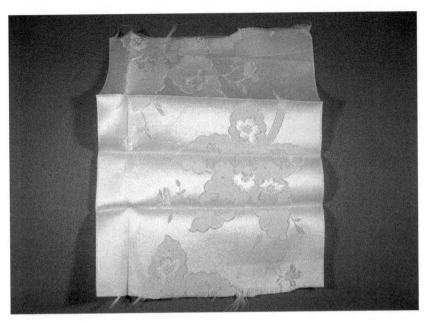

Swatch of the fabric used to make Ane's burial dress.

NEWTON COOPERATIVE STORE ,
POPULAR GATHERING PLACE , NOTICE
POST OFFICE TO RIGHT OF PICTURE

Post office on right was constructed by J. N. Hansen while he was postmaster.

SS Wyoming—the ship on which Ane came from Denmark in 1878.

SS Idaho, on which Karen Marie's parents and Karen Marie's eldest son, as well as Jens's brother Hans and his family, traveled from Denmark in 1874. Jens and Karen Marie and two children, as well as Karen Marie's brother Lars Christensen and his family, traveled from Denmark also on the *SS Idaho* in 1875.

CHAPTER 15

THE DEEDS ARE DONE: 1881 TO 1887

'The current generation could not, for the most part, even begin to think
of pulling up stakes and moving to the middle of nowhere to begin a
new life,' wrote my nephew, Mike Jones, LaRelia's son. 'I, for one, have
said many times that I would have made a very poor pioneer (maybe a
little more graphic than that). I've stopped at the [Bjorkman] homestead several times after the reunions and looked across that valley and
tried to imagine the work that went into plowing and planting and
building and surviving day after day. It humbles me to think of what
they went through versus the trials and tribulations that I complain
about in my everyday life. Not the same. Adria, I hate working in
my own yard and these people were working hundreds of acres! They
couldn't go in the house and cool off under the air conditioner or
have someone bring them ice water when they needed it. I am such
a slacker…but these are the stories that interest me. What it took to
run the farm every day. Milk the cows, haul water into the house, cut
wood for the stove. Work that built character in these people. I am such
a "flip the switch" type of person. Milk comes from the store, right?'[263]

mike was referring to the generation that followed Jens and Ane
(their daughter and son-in-law, Sophia Hansen and Henry Albert
Bjorkman), yet his observations are relevant to Jens's families and
the people of Newton as well. Those people of Newton struggled to create a
settlement and farms on what had been hard ground. Eventually they began
the process of obtaining title to those lands upon which they lived and worked.

As a conveyance clerk at the US Forest Service Regional Office in Ogden,
Utah, in my twenties, I came to love land descriptions and land titles. Deeds tell
stories and provide clues between their lines. In this chapter, I have included

deed details for those who love them like I do, but if you find them cumbersome, please feel free to skip them.

Bands of Shoshone had inhabited the valley prior to the settlement of Newton in 1869. Lands upon which the new Mormon towns of Cache Valley arose were first held by the bishop in each area, who then distributed property to each individual family for a home inside the town and for farmlands outside the town. The citizens apparently lived on those lands for eleven years before beginning the process of obtaining legal titles.

In regard to securing legal title to land within Newton, Larry Christiansen adds some understanding:

> The township plat: Township 13 North Range 1 West (T 13 N, R 1 W) was given a partial survey beginning in September of 1875 when the contract [was] let to A.J. Stewart to include everything except sections 3, 4, 5 and 6. On May 4, 1877, A.J. Stewart's survey was registered and approved.[264]

Larry also provided information about the patent process:

> November 10, 1881—Judge Milton D. Hammond of the Cache County Probate Court secured the patents for the land within the town of Newton amounting to 480 acres. Judge Hammond re-deeded the Newton townsite to Bishop Wm. F. Rigby, who in turn distributed the lots to those who occupied and/or claimed them by virtue of a church grant....
>
> In Newton the unrecorded lands were a great source of confusion later when abstracting for land titles was attempted since the owners of the land had not recorded the individual deeds. The problem heightened in some cases because many of the plots had changed owners in an informal manner of passing the paper deed from hand to hand while completely ignoring the formal recording of such transactions.[265]

Deeds were treated in a haphazard way during that time period—put in pockets and not recorded, or travel to Logan for recording deeds was delayed sometimes for years because trips were arduous, or the weather was bad, or planting and harvesting took precedence. When I worked with land titles, I was taught that a deed did not become legal and binding until it was recorded, so the recording date still seems significant to me, even with the common laxity of observing the legal process at the time Newton was being settled. Checking with the Cache County Recorder's Office, I learned that the law regarding deed recording and land title had been the same back in the early days of Newton. However, the tacit understanding was that occupying the land, even without a recorded deed, constituted a claim of sorts, and apparently no one interfered with another person's occupied lands. However, until the deed was recorded, the previous owner of the property continued to be shown as the owner of record.

Probate Judge Milton D. Hammond initiated the title process by posting the following legal notice in the Logan newspaper first on 19 March 1880, and again on 26 March 1880:

No. 101
Notice of Publication
Land Office Salt Lake City, Utah
Feb. 4, 1880

Notice is hereby given that Milton D. Hammond, Probate Judge of Cache County, Utah for and in behalf of the inhabitants of the respective named towns has filed his notice of intention to make final proof and payment on the following entries on the 19th day of April A.D. 1881, before the Register and Receiver at Salt Lake City, Utah.

Townsite of Clarkston...[land description]

Townsite of Paradise...[land description]

Townsite of Newton...[land description]

That he expects to prove the several claims by Ole A. Jensen, Geo. Godfrey of Clarkston; Hiram K. Cranney and Willard Maughan of Logan; Wm. N. Thomas, [and] Samuel McMurphy of Paradise and William F. Rigby and William H. Griffin of Newton, all in Cache Co. Utah.[266]

The above-named William F. Rigby (who confirmed two of Jens and Karen Marie's children) served as Newton's first bishop, and William H. Griffin was his counselor. These men were responsible for distribution of the properties in Newton.

After the notice above had appeared at least twice, the following ad was published in the *Logan Leader*, 4 June 1880, applying only to Newton:

June 4, 1880—page 1 Precinct officers
Newton—Justice of the Peace—Foster Curtis
Constable—Hans P. Larsen
Page 2—untitled

Notice is Hereby Given

THAT I, MILTON D. HAMMOND, Probate Judge of Cache County in the Territory of Utah, have entered the S.W. ¼ Sec. 17, S.E. ¼ Sec. 18, N ½ N.E. ¼ Sec. 19, and N ½ N.W. ¼ Sec. 20 in township thirteen north of range one west for and in behalf of the residents of the town of Newton.

Every person, association, company or corporation claiming to be the rightful owner of possession of any lot, block, share or parcel of the foregoing described tract of land are required to file with the Clerk of the Probate Court for said county, within six months from the first publication of this notice, a statement in writing containing an accurate description of the particular part or parcel of land he, she or they claim; or be forever barred from claiming the same under the "Townsite Act."

Witness my official signature at my office in Logan city this 28th day of April, A.D. 1880.

Milton D. Hammond
Probate Judge for Cache County
Apr 30—2 pm

Basically, these notices were a call to the residents of Newton who had been living on the various townsite lots to come forward and file for title to the parcels they occupied. Jens obviously heeded the call, because in December 1880—when Ane's and Karen Marie's baby daughters were ten months old and Karen Marie's sons were twelve and almost two years old—a document entitled Townsite Deed Record for him was drawn up as follows:

Be it Known by these Presents, That I Milton D. Hammond Probate Judge for Cache County, Utah Territory, by virtue of the Trust vested in me, by An Act of the Legislative Assembly of the Territory of Utah, approved February 17, 1869, entitled "An Act prescribing Rules and

Regulations for the Execution of the Trust arising under an Act of Congress, entitled 'An Act for the relief of the inhabitants of Cities and towns upon the Public Lands,' approved March 2, 1867," and in consideration of the sum of Nine and 80/100 Dollars [$9.80], paid by Jens N. Hansen of Newton County of Cache, Territory of Utah, the receipt whereof is hereby acknowledged, the said Jens N. Hansen having been adjudged by the Probate Court of Cache County, Territory aforesaid, to be the rightful owner and possessor of the following described Lots or parcel of Land, viz:

Lots Seven (7) and Eight (8) on block Eleven (11) as plotted on plot A of Newton Townsite Survey. Also Lots Three (3) and Eight (8) on Block Two (2) as plotted on plot B of said Survey Situated in Section—[blank] Township 13 N Range one West in all four [and] 63/100 acres [4.63], do by these presents grant and convey to the said Jens N. Hansen his heirs and assigns forever, the foregoing described Land, with all the rights, privileges and appurtenances thereunto belonging or in anywise appertaining.

In witness whereof, I have hereunto set my hand and affixed the Seal of the Probate Court for Cache County at my office, in Logan City Cache County, Utah Territory, this twentieth day of December A.D. 1880.[267]

Therein Jens legally acquired four lots containing a total of 4.63 acres in Newton Townsite for $9.80. His property included the north half of Lots 7 and 8 of Block 11, where the Hansen families had earlier lived in the dugout, as well as the south half of those same lots where Ane's wood-frame house would later be constructed. Also in this instrument, Jens legally acquired Lots 3 and 8 of Block 2 where he had built Karen's rock or adobe house.

Ane was about six months pregnant with her second child when this deed was granted, and Karen Marie would soon become pregnant with her seventh child.

Although the history from Karen Marie's family tells of the dugout, the adobe house, and the wood-frame house, it lists no specific dates for those constructions, and it is difficult to guess the timing of the moves from one property to another. Possibly Jens and his wives had already occupied the two sets of lots by permission of Bishop Rigby and then acted to acquire the deeds after Hammond's announcements. Karen Marie's house had been constructed, and they were all living there, having vacated the dugout. It would have been possible to build Ane's house on the south half of Lots 7 and 8 without disturbing the dugout on the north half of the same lots. The 1880 Newton census shows them all still in Karen Marie's house.

Further clues as to Jens's activities in 1880 when he acquired these land titles come from the 1880 Newton Agricultural Census provided by Larry Christiansen that shows Jens had the following:

> 12 acres of tilled land, and 5 acres of perm. meadows,
> 160 acres unimproved,
> $300 value for farm and outbuildings,
> $10 value for machinery,
> $125 value on livestock,
> $252 value on produce.
> 3 horses,
> 4 milch [giving milk] cows,
> 2 "other,"
> 4 calves dropped, 5 "died, stray, or stolen,"
> 50 pounds of butter made on the farm.
> 11 sheep,
> 12 lambs dropped, 6 slaughtered, 12 died of weather, 12 fleeces, weight 32,
> 2 swine,
> 90 poultry, and 100 eggs.
> 5 acres of wheat, 156 bushels of wheat,
> 1 acre of potatoes, and 100 bushels of potatoes.[268]
> [More calves and lambs died than were dropped, so one might assume
> some existed before the enumeration.]

What a story this agricultural census tells through the lists of crops and animals Jens had, and what a hard worker he had to be! Jens probably grew his crops on his quarter section outside of town, and he likely had been working the land for some time, possibly even since his arrival in 1875.

The title notices from Judge Hammond appeared in the spring, when Jens would have been busy starting the seasonal farm work that would occupy him through summer and fall. In December, after harvesting and other work was finished, Jens responded to the newspaper notice as required for laying claim to his occupied lots in town.

Ane and Karen Marie both again gave birth in 1881: Ane in the spring on 12 May to Hans Eli Hansen, her second child and Jens's eighth, and Karen Marie in the winter on 13 November to Mary Lindy, her seventh child and Jens's ninth. Upon Eli's birth, his sister, Sophia, was thirteen months old, probably toddling. When Mary Lindy was born, her sister, Louisa, was twenty-one months old, walking, learning to talk, and probably playful; her brother Jens Peter was thirteen, and her brother Nephi was three.

Baby Mary Lindy lived only sixteen days, dying on 29 November 1881. Her cause of death is not listed, but my heart aches for the family and their loss of yet another child—the fourth—and this time a new baby. I wonder if Karen Marie's grief over losing Mary Lindy was compounded by seeing Ane's baby, Eli, who had been born just eight months earlier, thriving when her own arms were empty. How did it affect the children to lose their baby sister? Karen Marie and Jens kept going, even in the face of these continued losses.

The deed to Jens's four lots for $9.80 was filed for record 30 November 1881, eleven months after its execution, or origination, and just one day after baby Mary Lindy died. Jens's tender heart must have been heavy as he attended to business the day after her death. Or maybe business was a needed diversion. Perhaps he also felt some degree of anticipation as he made livable arrangements for both families more secure.

❧

On top of hard work and sorrow for Jens and Karen Marie—and empathy from Ane—life was about to become more challenging for the LDS people of the Territory of Utah, especially the couples who were living the principle of plural marriage. On 23 March 1882, Congress passed the Edmunds Anti-Polygamy Act, which was more stringent than the Morrill Act of 1862. (The Morrill Act had been signed by Lincoln, and it made bigamy illegal in the territories of the United States but had never been enforced.) Jesse L. Embry summarizes this new law, named for US Senator George R. Edmunds of Vermont:

> The new law made polygamy a felony that carried a penalty of five years in jail and a fine of five hundred dollars. Unlawful cohabitation, which required proof only that a man and woman were living together and did not require proof of a secret marriage ceremony, remained a misdemeanor with a six-month jail sentence and a fine of three hundred dollars. To vote, Mormons had to take an oath that they did not practice polygamy. In 1884 the U.S. Supreme Court allowed the disenfranchisement of plural husbands, but declared the test oath unconstitutional. The law also took the vote away from women married to polygamous husbands.[269]

The Edmunds Act, in addition to revoking polygamists' right to vote, took away their right to hold public office and prohibited them from serving on a jury. All previously elected officers—Mormons with tendencies toward leniency in polygamy cases—were removed, and the Federal Government appointed others who were more likely to be strict both with the law and with those who violated it.[270] The Edmunds Act also established the Utah Commission, which was "charged to develop, administer, and enforce the election provisions of the law."[271] The walls of the room started closing in.

The Territory of Utah had granted women the right to vote in 1870, just after the Territory of Wyoming, which had been, in 1869, the first in the union to grant the vote to women. To have the federal government yank that right from women in polygamous marriages was a blow to them, many of whom then became active in promoting women's suffrage. Although the Edmunds Act of 1882 took the right to vote in federal elections away from those involved in polygamy, they were still technically allowed to vote in local elections. The federal government, however, appointed most of those positions. The Territory of Utah had civil rights, yet the federal government disenfranchised the polygamists because they practiced a principle of their religion. Being silenced within their political realm must have been a suffocating punishment.

The Edmunds Act also decreed that neither the plural wives (any wife except the first) nor the children of plural wives could inherit from the polygamist husband and father upon his death. Kathleen Goodbaudy, a volunteer at my local LDS Family History Library in Hillsboro, Oregon, told me in August 2010 that her great-grandfather had owned several apartment buildings and general stores in Salt Lake City at the time the Edmunds Act was passed, and in order to provide for one of his plural wives, he deeded one of the apartment buildings to her and told her she could collect the rents for her income. He also said she could shop at any of his stores and put her purchases on a tab that he would cover. Although her deed to the apartment building listed a valuation for the property, no money changed hands. He apparently took these actions to circumvent the federal law that would deny this plural wife and their children an inheritance.

My great-grandfather Jens was less affluent but no doubt equally concerned about providing some security for Ane should he predecease her. He deeded his Lots 7 and 8, Block 11, Plat A as noted in the Newton Townsite Survey to Ane in an instrument drawn up 20 April 1882—one month after the passage of the Edmunds Act. Jens Christensen and John Griffin witnessed Jens's signature on the deed. The valuation listed in the deed is $250, though likely no money was exchanged. (The deed was not filed for record until 25 October 1893, eleven years later.) Jens had originally paid $9.80 for four lots, yet the valuation of only these two lots deeded to Ane was $250, indicating that during the eighteen-month interval between the execution of the first deed to Jens and his subsequent deed to Ane, her lovely home had likely been constructed on that property. At the time this deed was executed, Ane was a few months pregnant with her third child.

Mother told the story that Jens had given Ane the deed to the house, and for some unknown reason she had not trusted him, so had given the deed to her son, Eli, for safekeeping. Later Jens, also for an unknown reason, changed his mind about the deed and ransacked the house for it but didn't find it. Here we see again that the veracity of family lore comes into question. Ane's son, Eli, during the time between the drawing up of the deed in 1882 and its recording in 1893, would have grown from being one year old to being twelve years old. He would have been an unlikely guardian of the document, not only because he was very young but also because he lived in the house that was allegedly ransacked. Where could young Eli have hidden the deed? So we are left to wonder: Did someone actually secrete the deed to Ane's beautiful home? And if so, whom did she trust? I wish the family folklore included the name of a close friend. Might it have been one of the friends or family who had wanted her to come to Newton? And why did Ane allow eleven years to elapse between the execution of her deed and its filing of record? Was she unaware of the law? Or was it just too difficult for her to get to Logan with a toddler and a baby and being pregnant again?

Six months after Jens executed the deed to her home, Ane gave birth to her third and last child, Moses, on 7 October 1882. Sophia was two years and eight months old, and Eli was one year and five months old, when their little brother was born. Ane was thirty-nine years old. On a recent vacation, I saw a young woman with a small child who was walking somewhat independently but close to the mother, a toddler who was holding the mother's hand, and a baby being carried on the mother's other arm. Ane's children had been spaced just like that. What a handful it must have been for her with three young children and the daily tasks of cooking, gardening, laundry, cleaning, harvesting, canning, selling eggs and butter—all requiring much attention and labor. Perhaps Ane also had less help from her busy husband than she would have liked.

Although Ane had no more children after Moses, Karen Marie continued to produce babies for another five years. In a telephone conversation with LaRelia, we speculated about that difference. "Obviously," LaRelia commented, "Ane was fertile, given that she had three children, each spaced about one year apart—but then no more." My mother often said Ane had put Jens's clothing out on the porch and told him to go stay with his other family for a while. Would that have been the onset of a breach? Was that when he allegedly ransacked the house? Carla said our Aunt Rena told her that Ane used to cut Jens's hair for him. She would cut it on the porch but would not let him in the house. Was he denied admittance to the house only during the messy task of a haircut? Or did these events signal the end of their physical relationship even though they remained married? In that conversation with LaRelia, I commented, "It's all about sex, isn't it?" We laughed, but my comment seemed invasive of their privacy. On some underlying level, sexual intimacy seemed to be at the heart of the objections to polygamy from without, and many of the feelings of jealousy within. Something marked the end of Ane's childbearing. Was it merely her age? Or was it something more dramatic?

Jens needed property not only for homes for his families but also for farming. The agricultural census referred to earlier lists "160 acres unimproved," but Jens did not at that time have title to the farm. Eight years after he arrived in the valley, pursuant to the Homestead Act of 20 May 1862, a property northwest of Newton was granted on 10 February 1883 to "Jas. N. Hanson [*sic*] by the United States of America under the name of U.S. President Chester A. Arthur, from the City of Washington."[272] This act required of the homesteader both the construction of a dwelling and five years' continuous residence and cultivation of the land. The Homestead Certificate 2153 described the land in lovely cursive as "the east half of the southwest quarter, and the lots numbered six and seven of section six in township thirteen north of range one West of Salt Lake Meridian in Utah Territory containing one hundred and fifty-eight acres, and eighty nine hundredths of an acre according to the official Plat of the Survey of the said Land... subject to any vested and accrued water rights . . . and extraction of veins or lodes." The description is more easily read in the abbreviated version: E ½ SW ¼ and Lots 6 and 7 of Section 6, Township 13 north, Range 1 west of the Salt Lake Meridian, containing 158.89 acres. The conveyance was dated 10 February 1883, and the Recorder of the General Land Office filed the document for record two years later on 9 April 1885 in Volume 5 page 59.[273] The land thus conveyed was farm acreage outside of town.

The earlier agricultural census indicates that Jens was actively involved in farming in 1880, three years before the homestead was granted. Did Bishop Rigby originally assign Jens that acreage? Because the Homestead Act required a five-year proving-up period, Jens likely would have started working that piece of land at the latest during the summer of 1878 to meet the legal requirement, but he may have started working it immediately upon their arrival in the valley in 1875 to ensure their survival. Jens was no stranger to hard work. When the homestead was granted, Jens Peter was fifteen years old and probably worked alongside his father. Nephi was five years old, Louisa was barely three years old, and Karen Marie was five or six months pregnant. Ane's daughter, Sophia, was also just three years old, with Eli two years of age, and Moses four months old—so likely none of the children except Jens Peter would have been able to help much except with small chores, and maybe only those connected with the living quarters.

Another spring baby was born to Karen Marie and Jens, on 2 May 1883, named Anna Elvena. She was Karen Marie's ninth child and Jens's twelfth. Karen Marie was thirty-eight years old.

The family life intertwined with farming and business to provide in diverse ways for survival. A Daughters of Utah Pioneers book includes a two-page spread listing the businesses in each town in Utah's Cache County from the "Cache County Business Directory" for 1883–84. The listing for Newton appears in the book exactly as follows except for the emphasis on Jens's entry:

NEWTON

Is 12 miles northwest of Logan, with a population of about 300 mostly farmers and stock raisers.

Beck S N, painter	Jensen Wm, stone mason
Bensen Peter, carpenter	Newton Co-op Store, gen'l mdse
Clark Amos, blacksmith	W H Griffin, manager
Hansen J N, butter and eggs	Sorenson Hans, shoemaker[274]
[emphasis mine]	

Maybe Jens's wives took care of the cows and chickens for the butter and eggs business even though they both had young children, but in that time period the women were seldom credited on the printed page. No matter who was responsible, it was a treat to find Jens's name in the index of the book and on this charming antique menu of businesses.

The homestead deed to Jens for 158.89 acres had been drawn up in February of 1883, and filed for record on 9 April 1885. The next day, 10 April 1885, an additional indenture was drawn up, perhaps as another attempt to provide for Ane and her children in the event of Jens predeceasing her. The indenture was between John H. Barker, grantor, and Anne Margrathe [*sic*] Hansen for land south of Newton near Bear River in the hay lot or south farms area, described as:

Commencing at the North West corner of the N.W. ¼ of Sec. 29 Township 13 N Range 1 West, then east fifty seven Rods then South forty Rods, then west fifty seven Rods then North forty Rods to the place of beginning, containing fourteen and one fourth acres [14.25].[275]

The listed valuation was fifty dollars, and I surmise that money actually changed hands, though whether it was Jens's money or Ane's is unknown. Jens N. Hansen and Fred Barker witnessed John H. Barker's signature on the instrument. The document was further witnessed and sealed by W. H. Griffin, Justice of the Peace.[276]

❦

I wanted to find Jens and Ane's farms on the ground, to see where Jens and others in the family had labored to raise crops for feeding both families and for marketing, so on the morning of 13 June 2014, I left my Bed and Breakfast lodgings in Logan and drove to the Cache County office building. Upstairs, at the long counter in the room across the hall from the sign saying *Surveyor's Office*, a kind man named Kerry Jenkins helped me. He looked at my copy of the township plat on which I had plotted the land descriptions from the deed to Jens for the north farm, and from the deed to Ane for the hay lot or south farm. Jenkins found an aerial photograph of the area, pulled it up on his computer, and then zeroed in on the areas where the two farms were located. He hit one button on his computer, and it superimposed onto the aerial photograph all the township plat survey information, including the section numbers. Then Jenkins hit another button, and all the roads in the area became highlighted in yellow. The old survey plat showed short segments of wandering, curvy roads, but the modern aerial photographs showed straight roads and intersections. For a moment, Jenkins studied what he had created and then made a red circle on the north farm so we could find it easily after adjusting the map. All I needed to do was drive north on the road to the Newton cemetery until I reached 8600 North, then turn left and go one half mile. At that point, the south property line of Jens's former farm began and ran west along the north side of the road for one half mile.

Next Jenkins went through the same process with Ane's south lots. All I needed to do was reposition myself on the same cemetery road but drive south instead of north, go to the road's end, and then turn left. On my right at that point would be the north boundary of Ane's farm. Jenkins printed off the map he had created with everything on it, and declined my offer of payment. I could not believe how easy this amazing technology had made the process, nor how easy finding the farms would be. Roads constructed in the interim from the date of the survey plat would make the farms accessible.

Back in Newton on 100 West, I drove north to the T at the end of the road where a sign said *9000 North*. I had overshot my mark. I went south to the previous intersection and turned right, then pulled over and looked at the map to see if the large house on my left and its attachments appeared on the aerial photograph. They did! It was the desired intersection, so I slowly drove west on the dirt road, kicking up a white dust cloud behind me. I watched the markings on the photo and compared them to actualities on the ground—fence lines, rocky outcroppings, two-track lanes, boundaries of planted fields on the opposite side of the road—and soon arrived at what I deduced had been Jens's property.

I parked and stepped out of my car into air that had a grassy scent, and I took in the rolling fields, the large expanse of the farm, and the pleasant view of purple mountains around the valley of gold and green. A crop grown by the current owner had recently been harvested and baled into what looked like green carpet rolls strewn over the land. The mountainous scenery was spectacular. I envisioned Jens out working in that field on a hot summer day, wiping the sweat from his brow, and taking a break to soak in that visual splendor surrounding him. Standing in a place where I knew Jens had worked the land with horses and plow moved me. He had been here. His family members had been here. My ancestors had been here. Sacred ground.

I continued driving west on that boundary road until it intersected the paved SR 142 that led back into Newton. I turned left onto it, and when back in town, I returned to 100 West, and this time I drove south to the end of the road where it met 6200 North. There I turned left, pulled off on the right side of the road, and visually savored the north boundary of Ane's property to the right. A bold *PRIVATE PROPERTY No Trespassing* sign was posted at the edge of the field near the road. A short row of majestic, leafy trees grew like a breakfront at the left side of the field abutting the road, and a placid stream of deep water coiled near the trees and then entered a blue pool a short distance off. This water must have been crucial to Newton's families and farmers. Another *No Trespassing* sign had been planted in front of the trees, so that appeared to be the east boundary of what had been Ane's field. Later I learned that Karen Marie also had title to a south farm in the area but not adjacent to Ane's. No crops grew on Ane's farm at that moment, but the golden stubble and the creek and the trees made the property beautiful.

Finding Jens's and Ane's farms on the ground meant a great deal to me. The parcels had metamorphosed from being merely legal descriptions in deed documents to being the soil under my feet—and the dust on my car—and made the early family's work more real to me. Now I knew the actual geographical places of the story and felt a deeper appreciation of the work my ancestors committed themselves to. The day was immensely satisfying.

✼

I asked Larry Christiansen whether *hay lot* and *south farm* were synonymous, and he responded:

> The term "hay lot" initially referred to the small surveyed plots next to Bear River where the Newton or Clarkston Creek flowed into the river. The hay was the wild grasses that nature produced. However, shortly a better type of hay was planted as alfalfa seed was brought in and planted, and due in large part to the English settlers, the alfalfa hay was often called Lucerne as it was in England, France, and several European countries as well as New Zealand, Australia, etc. With the better type of hay, more and more land was planted to where in much of Utah, there was more Lucerne grown than even wheat. Thus the term "hay lot" probably took on a more encompassing meaning. The NW ¼ of the NW ¼ of section 29 of T13N R1W [the area in which Ane's land was located] was directly south of Newton approximately ¾ of a mile (about halfway between the town and Bear River) on land originally filed for by Wm. F. Jensen in 1880, then John H. Barker and finally to J.N. Hansen. It was most likely planted in Lucerne (alfalfa) so hay lot and south farm were probably the same.
>
> The use of the term Lucerne: "In March 1886, the writer [J. E. Wing]…was traveling by rail through Utah…. He noticed with wonder the fresh cut surface of a haystack. 'What sort of hay is in those stacks?' 'Lucerne,' promptly replied the conductor…. At that date Lucerne, or alfalfa, had not spread much east of the valley of Utah."[277]

In the previous note, Larry Christiansen refers to the south farm as J. N. Hansen's, but the actual deed is in Ane's name. The deed document for Ane's south farm was not filed for record until four and a half years later, on 30 October 1889, only two months after a significant event in Jens's life that affected both of his families.

The persecution based on the provisions of the 1882 Edmunds Act continued to intensify, resulting in yet another real estate transaction being drawn up on the same date as that of Ane's hay lot, 10 April 1885. This instrument was between Jens N. Hansen and his eldest son, Jens P. Hansen. For and in consideration of $100, Jens deeded his homestead—his farm—northwest of Newton described as E ½ SW ¼, and Lots 6 and 7, containing 158.89 acres, to his son. Pressures increased during this time period as agents of the federal government doggedly attempted to locate, arrest, bring to trial, and incarcerate the men who were cohabiting with more than one woman. This transaction may have been solely to protect Jens's property from possible confiscation by the federal government should he be caught by the marshals. John H. Barker and John F. Jenkins witnessed the signature of Jens N. Hansen, and Justice of the Peace W. H. Griffin, further attested it. The deed was not filed for record until 11 December 1888, three and a half years later. Though the land changed hands on paper, probably the work patterns of the two men on the ground did not change.

One month after those two real estate transactions, Karen Marie gave birth to a son, William Joseph, on 16 May 1885 at the age of forty. He was their ninth child.

Jens was ordained to the office of Seventy in the Melchizedek Priesthood on 25 October 1885 as shown in the Newton Ward Records.[278]

When little William Joseph was fourteen months old and likely toddling and chattering and exploring his environment with the mix of curiosity and naïveté that characterizes the age, the *Utah Journal* on 31 July 1886, published this under "Newton Jots" on page three:

> We have another to add to the list of accidents resulting from the use of concentrated lye in families. An infant son of Brother J. N. Hansen now lies in very critical condition through swallowing a piece of the dangerous stuff. Will not our Relief Societies unite to effect the banishment of so deadly an article from the households of the Saints, by by [*sic*] searching out and substituting some harmless aid in the cleaning of clothing.[279]

The day after the article appeared, little William Joseph died from the lye ingestion, on 1 August 1886. He was the fifth of their children to die in childhood. Karen Marie had been carrying, bearing, raising, and burying children for twenty years.

Two months after the death of his baby brother, the oldest child of Jens and Karen Marie, Jens Peter (who sometimes went by James) married Mary Christine Petersen on 30 September 1886. He was three months short of his nineteenth birthday.

A warranty deed drawn up one month after Jens Peter's marriage, from William H. Griffin to James P. Hansen on 27 October 1886, for the sum of fifteen dollars, lists:

> Lots five (5) and Six (6) as Situated in North West Corner of Block fifteen (15) as Platted on Plat A of Newton Town Site Survey in all Containing Two and half (2 ½) Acres. All the above Described Land is Situated in Town Ship Thirteen (13) North of Range one (1) West of Salt Lake Meridian.[280]

As near as I could tell from the incomplete survey plat, this would have put the new couple's city lots about five blocks west and one half block north of the home of Karen Marie, Jens (or James) Peter's mother. These lots were in the extreme western part of Newton, outside what is shown on the original townsite survey. Eli Bell and W. W. Maughan witnessed W. H. Griffin's signature. The deed was recorded 29 June 1891, nearly five years later. I was curious to know the juxtaposition of the two homes on the ground and what it might indicate about family relationships but that exploration would have to wait.

Six months after James Peter acquired the lots in Block 15, the federal government again tightened its grip on the Mormons who were attempting to live in polygamous families. As if the Edmunds Act of 1882 had not been enough, the Edmunds-Tucker Act was passed in March 1887, putting additional pressures on both the Church as an entity and its individual members. The federal government's intent was not only to wipe out polygamy but also to quash the Mormon Church itself. Named after its sponsors, Senator George F. Edmunds of Vermont (again) and Congressman John Randolph Tucker of Virginia, the act eliminated the Perpetual Emigration Fund that had been established by Brigham Young for aiding converts' immigration to Utah, and it allowed the government to confiscate LDS Church property and then charge an exorbitant fee from the Church to use its own buildings. William Edwin Berrett elaborated:

> In order to retain the use of the tithing offices [and] the historian's office, the Church was forced to pay the government an annual rental of $2,400. Four hundred fifty dollars a month was paid to retain the use of the Gardo house, and the use of the temple block was retained by paying a high rental.[281]

The law required anyone wishing to hold office, vote, or be on a jury to take an antipolygamy oath, and the law required plural wives to testify against their husbands. Placing Church property in receivership meant that the beautiful temples vital to the sacred ordinances of the religion were in danger of being taken over by the federal government, as were the other business and religious buildings of the Church.

The civil rights of this body of people were continuously violated. I was ignorant of all these incidents when I began researching my ancestors' story and have been taken aback by what was dealt to them. Would I be as annoyed by this if it didn't involve my own ancestors? I hope so.

My editor, Susan DeFreitas, added a comment at this point saying:

> Reading this, I'll admit I'm struck most by the sense that the federal government used the LDS Church when doing so suited its purposes—these industrious people settled the hard land of Utah—but then grew to fear them when their religious practices seemed to diverge from European norms. And while the religious purpose of polygamy might have been to create large celestial families, it could not have escaped anyone that this practice also created large earthly families, ensuring that every woman who converted to this faith and moved to Utah could have children and be supported by a husband with some degree of capital. Perhaps some elected officials began to fear that the LDS Church would grow in power to the point where it would seek to establish a country of its own—one that might challenge the power of the US government?

Susan's observations are astute and reasonable, and I appreciate her rich opinion in this regard.

And the vise tightened. As the hunt intensified for men who were, according to the federal government, unlawfully cohabiting, it forced polygamist men to use various tactics to avoid arrest, trial, and imprisonment. The advice from LDS President John Taylor to the polygamist men of the LDS Church regarding the marshals was this:

> Avoid them as much as you possibly can—just as you would wolves…and get out of the way as much as you can.… When such a condition of affairs exists, it is no longer a land of liberty and it is certainly no longer a land of equal rights, and we must take care of ourselves, as best we may, and avoid being caught in any of their snares.[282]

No counsel was given to use violence or retaliation. Instead they were advised merely to implement a quiet avoidance. The men hid in various places, sometimes staying away from home for extended periods of time. Some men, like Peter Benson of Newton, built secret rooms or passageways into their homes so they could hide quickly when necessary or could leave the house undetected. Children were coached to have no knowledge of their father's names or whereabouts when the marshals accosted them with questions. Some men hid in barns or in rushes along the rivers, and others went into exile, leaving families to await their return at some future time.

Some men and groups went into foreign countries to escape arrest and incarceration, as Brian and Petrea Kelly explain in *Latter-day History*:

> By the end of 1885, hundreds of church members fled to the Mexican State of Chihuahua, where they founded the settlements of Colonia Juarez, Colonia Dublan, and Colonia Diaz. The following year, President Taylor advised Charles Ora Card [President of the Cache Stake or group of wards in northern Utah] to seek a place of refuge for persecuted members of the Cache Valley Stake in Logan, Utah. Stake President Card led a group of members north to Alberta [Canada] and settled what later became known as Cardston [in what was then Northwest Territories].[283]

Although the laws in Mexico and Canada prohibited polygamy, those governments did not take action against the Mormon communities or the individual Mormon inhabitants.

Leaders of the Church likewise had to go into hiding in order to continue to direct the concerns of the organization and its members, with some going to places such as Hawaii (a kingdom until 1893), or Kaysville and St. George in Utah, or even sequestering themselves in the Church buildings in Salt Lake City and doing their work at night.

Sometimes polygamous men wore disguises to go unnoticed by the marshals. Reed Bartlett told me in June 2011 that some resorted on occasion to walking backward, believing that if they walked backward away from town, it would appear from a distance that they were headed into town, and they could thus escape detection when the marshal was known to be in the vicinity. Stories are told that some men shaved their beards to escape recognition. Some families would post a lookout, often one of the children, to watch for the approach of the marshal. The town of Chesterfield, Idaho, then a polygamous community, was located on a knoll in the center of a wide valley that allowed the inhabitants to watch for law officers (and Indians) approaching from far away in any direction.

John Jenkins, who had three wives and thirty-five children, was a talented and hardworking man in Newton. The "Big Meadows Incident" by Eldon Griffin, one of his descendants, is of interest:

My grandmother, Alice, told me the following story:—Alice…was
staying with her father (John Jenkins) and one of his wives (I believe
she said, 'Aunt Maria')…at the Big Meadows, north of Clarkston.…
The federal marshals were trying to catch her father and arrest him for
practicing polygamy. His cabin was located where he could see them
coming a long way off. This gave him time to escape on his horse
and ride over the mountain to Malad, Idaho.… One time they were
caught by surprise. The marshals were too close for him to escape…
Grandma (Alice) rolled him up in the bedding stood in the corner
of the cabin. The marshals searched the cabin but could not find him
and so they left empty-handed. He had property in Utah, Idaho, and
Wyoming in order to avoid the jurisdiction of the marshals. In fact,
Freedom, Wyoming, was so named because its Main Street is on the
Idaho-Wyoming border. All he had to do was walk across the street
to change jurisdictions and keep his freedom.[284]

Apparently these efforts to avoid arrest were successful only temporarily, as
John Jenkins served time in the Utah Territorial Penitentiary from 19 November
1887 to 19 April 1888 and was fined three hundred dollars.[285] (Several of our
family members and their close friends married children of Jenkins and his wives.)
Our Jens was affected by these persecutions. The Hicks history says:

During the anti-polygamy raid, [Jens] was forced into the underground. He suffered many hardships and exposure. He never went far
from home, and slept among the willows along the creek, in neighboring barns, and in other secluded places. He conversed with the
deputies two different times, but through some misunderstanding in
the name, he went free.[286]

The polygamous men hid out and slept away from their homes because the
marshals would come knocking on the door in the middle of the night. What
stress and sleeplessness that must have caused! Imagining the men out at night
reminds me of the scene from the movie *Gone with the Wind* where the men are
out in the cold, dark night—though for a different cause—and the women are
gathered together, reading aloud, with the tension ratcheted up to a maximum
level. What did Karen Marie and Ane feel while Jens was out in the marshes
someplace, trying to elude arrest for being their husband? Did they wait awake?
Or learn to sleep in spite of it? How did the women calm their children, who
surely must have felt concern for their father?

In the midst of these adversities and persecutions during the federal government's "crusades," as they were labeled by those who suffered them, Karen Marie's tenth and last child was born on 16 August 1887, when Karen Marie was forty-two years old. He was named Joseph Mahonori, and he lived only two months, dying on 16 October 1887. His cause of death is unknown to me. Another baby lost. He was the sixth of Jens and Karen's ten children to die young. Of their last four children born over a six-year period, one had lived two weeks, one had lived fourteen months, and one had lived two months. Only one of these four children, Elvena, lived to adulthood.

With the Latter-day Saint view of life after death and heavenly reunions with loved ones and eternal families, perhaps Jens and Karen Marie had a comfort that allowed them to weather these losses more stoically than I imagine. I am excellent at maintaining vigils of hope for a miracle when someone I care for is ailing, but I am full of sadness when someone dies. I hope Jens and Karen Marie and Ane and the surviving children were able to take comfort from their beliefs that couples and families can be together for eternity if they remain true and faithful.

This time of persecution and the underground—resistance, secrecy, fleeing, and hiding for safety—must have been incredibly difficult for the members of Jens's two families, as well as for the other townspeople who lived with the constant fear of deputies appearing.

Not only the men but also some of the women would move and hide in order to keep the marshals from suspecting and arresting their husbands. Anne Clark Tanner, a plural wife, chronicled her experiences of moving various times while she was pregnant and of staying with friends or family in order to keep the eyes of the law off her husband. She endured much hardship.[287]

No doubt tension gripped all of these people who dreaded the appearance of the marshals. One might think the situation was so stressful that it couldn't possibly become worse, but even so, the federal net would continue to be drawn ever more tightly around Jens and his families.

CHAPTER 16

DELVING DEEPER INTO ANE'S HOUSE

The suggestion that I contact Norris Cooley, the current owner of Ane's house, and ask if we could come inside occupied my thoughts after I returned home. I had mixed feelings about it, and I agonized for days about calling a total stranger and asking permission to invade his privacy. On the phone, LaRelia said she totally understood my reluctance and that I had to wait until it felt right. She suggested a call to Ruby first to ask about her book, and also to ask what she thought of my calling Norris. I am not sure where my reluctance to ask for things comes from, but part of it might be from my mother, who was generous in service to others but valued independence and never wanted to inconvenience anyone.

Finally overcoming my resistance, I called Ruby on Saturday, 3 July 2010. I identified myself and reminded her that my husband, sisters, and I had found our great-grandmother's house still standing the previous summer, and that she, Ruby, had been extremely helpful to us while we were there.

"I'm so *glad* you called," she said. "Last year I was telling Cleo, the librarian, about you people after you had been here, and Cleo wanted to know who you were. I felt so stupid. I'm an historian, and I forgot to ask who you are. I'm *so* glad you called."

Encouraged, I told her I would be coming back to Newton on Thursday, 8 July and asked if she thought Norris might be willing to talk with me about the house. She said, "The person who would be able to give you the most information is Gary Jorgensen, who is the grandson of Carl Jorgensen. Wasn't Carl connected with your family in some way?"

"Yes, I think my great-grandfather Jens Hansen may have helped sponsor Carl to come over from Denmark, and Carl was a good friend of my grandfather Henry Albert Bjorkman. They farmed next to each other in Central."

"Yes, Jens did sponsor Carl. Gary used to live in the Hansen house [she was referencing Ane's house], and he used to be bishop of one of the wards here, and I think he would be willing to meet with you. I'll call him and see what he says."

I thanked her, then hesitated a moment before asking, "Do you think there's a chance that Norris might let my sisters and me into the house?"

"Well, he's my home teacher, and I'll ask him."

LDS home teachers used to be assigned in pairs to visit families in the ward every month to leave a devotional message and to offer any kind of spiritual or temporal aid the family might need. For example, one of my home teachers came on a moment's notice to give me a prayerful priesthood blessing when I had a health emergency. Another mowed my lawn while I was on an extended vacation, and he and his wife brought their family caroling at our home on Christmas Eve for several years until they moved away. He brought a youth work crew to stack wood for my wood-burning stove when I was a widow, and another crew to do yard work to help prepare my home for its sale when I remarried. Home teachers could be vital to a family's sense of connection and caring. So Ruby's association with Norris went beyond merely being neighbors; he was assigned through the Church to be helpful to her and her husband.

Two days later, Ruby called. "Gary has agreed to meet with you, and Norris has agreed to let you in the house to do whatever you want." I expressed my astonishment at that. "I told him it is your heritage and he should let you in," she said.

Richard and I made copies of the old photo of Ane's house, the portrait of Jens and Ane and their three children, and the photo of Sophia, Ane's daughter (my grandmother) with her husband, Henry Albert Bjorkman, and their ten children as adults. I made sets of those photos for Ruby, Gary, Norris, and the Newton Town Library before listening to Ruby's later phone message suggesting that I bring photos, if I had any, and copies could be made at the town library. Richard commented from his personal experience as a scholar: "It's interesting how things open up when you're doing research."

My plan for Thursday, 8 July, was to start in the Cache County Recorder's Office in Logan to search for deeds when it opened at 7:00 a.m. and afterward to meet Carla and LaRelia at Ruby's at 9:00 a.m. Then we would go together to the appointment with Gary Jorgensen, followed by the visit to Norris Cooley's.

Richard suggested I also look for probate records for Jens and his two wives, because he had found such records helpful to his own research. With one master's degree in American folklore and another in East Asian studies, as well as a doctorate focused on Japanese folklore and Japanese new religions, he has had ample experience doing fieldwork.

I drove in sunshine to Logan and entered the modern brick Cache County Recorder's Office the moment it opened. Michael Gleed, the county recorder, with gray-white hair and a short, full beard, led me into the vault and pulled out the ledger that showed the original disposition of Newton Townsite lands. Then he put me in charge of visually scanning the lists in it for documents of interest—those with family members' names on them—and writing down the deed volume designations and page numbers (such as Book R, page 25) while he made copies of my requested documents from old heavy books of deeds.

When I finished my list of volumes and page numbers, Michael led me to a computer and showed me how to find and print the deeds that had been entered into the computer system. After I printed those documents, he showed me another huge book that held deeds of distribution of lands outside the Newton Townsite, where I again searched for family names. Then an assistant got out the unwieldy *Book R* and *Book O*, in which I found four deeds with family names, and she printed copies for me.

Soon I excused myself for my appointments in Newton, telling them I would return around noon to pick up my requested copies of related maps and surveys of the Newton area.

I had asked Michael where I might find probate records from the early 1900s, and he suggested the Cache County Clerk's Office right across the hall. So as I left his offices, I stepped into the clerk's office and inquired. The woman behind the desk said her office didn't have probate records, but I might try the First District Court across the street.

I drove the scenic thirty miles—past blue water, various swimming or swirling white birds, and a leisurely red kayak—to Ruby's golden brick home in Newton, and when I pressed the bell, she called, "Come in!" She ushered me into her homey living room, introduced me to her husband, and invited me to sit down. Soon my sisters, who had been held up by a long train at a nearby crossing, arrived, and we conversed for a few minutes. I gave Ruby the photographs and a small box of chocolates as a thank-you. "Cavanaugh's are to die for!" she said. I felt the same way.

We rode in LaRelia's maroon-and-cream Cadillac DeVille for three blocks, about as far south and west as you can go in Newton, to the lovely red brick home—attractively landscaped with green grass and a profusion of flowers, with sprinklers going—of Lois and Gary Jorgensen. They invited us into their comfortable and pleasant living room, where Ruby did introductions and we seated ourselves. Ruby asked if I had a copy of the Jorgensen history. When I said no, Gary asked Ruby if she would copy it for me at the library, and she said yes.

Gary told us the story of Jens wanting to bring a boy over from Denmark to help him, and how Gary's grandfather, Carl, had been that boy. He said that often people who had come to America from Denmark would pay for another person to come here, and that person would work for the sponsor until the fare had been repaid. Jens had asked Chris Larsen, Ruby's ancestor, who was going back to Denmark for a visit in 1902, to find a boy to come to America and work for him. Chris had asked Holger Larsen, who was one of the authorities in the Danish Mission, for a recommendation, and Holger suggested Carl. Carl's mother had died when he was young, and he had no living siblings, so his father was reluctant to allow him to come to America. However, he finally consented. Gary said Carl had worked for and *lived with Jens* after he came over in 1902 until his marriage in about 1907.

"Which wife's house did he live in?" I asked.

"Most likely it was Ane's house, because he eventually purchased it and lived there." This bit of information stunned me because I had neither heard lore about it nor yet encountered that transaction in the deeds.

Gary told us more of Carl's story and talked of the time he and Lois had temporarily lived in Ane's house while they were making arrangements to live someplace else. They showed us an album with a charming snapshot of Ane's house taken while they lived in it. Their son's bicycle sat out in front, creating the look of a family friendly home. They offered to make a copy and send it to me, and I cherish having it.

I spread the photos we had made for them on the glass-topped coffee table, and the old one of Ane's house drew comments from Lois and Gary. The animated conversation continued, due in large part to the gifts of my sisters who are both adeptly social women. They made multiple connections with the Jorgensens by discovering people they knew in common. I later realized that the aside conversations of my sisters, not my interview questions, had greased the wheels of comfortable connections with the Jorgensens, and by the time we were ready to leave, it felt like we were all old friends. I, as the youngest child—seven years younger than the previous youngest—who had never lived in the places they talked about nor met the people they knew in common, could not participate in the conversation in the way that comes naturally to my sisters, and I am, admittedly, envious as well as deeply appreciative.

One of my questions was born of interest in knowing the floor plan of Ane's house, and Gary and Lois reminisced about it for a few minutes. They mentioned that the two bedrooms upstairs were small and the roofline made it impossible to stand up straight around the outside edges of the rooms (one of them being the bedroom where my mother was born). Later they sent me an amazingly detailed drawing of the layout of both the main floor and the upstairs, for which I am grateful.

After asking my last few questions and noticing the clock, we finished up and expressed our gratitude for their time and information. I also gave them chocolates, and we continued talking as they graciously followed us out the front door, past their glorious flowerbeds, all the way out to the car on the concrete driveway. We chatted and lingered, finished our lovely visit and our extended goodbyes, and then LaRelia, Carla, Ruby, and I climbed into the car.

En route to Norris's house at nearly 11:00 in the morning, Ruby told us that although Norris had agreed to let us in, he had changed from saying we could do what we wanted to saying we could come into the kitchen and peek into the living room. Also, he had had an appointment at 8:30 that morning. I wondered whether he would be back from his appointment by now. I felt a mix of emotions: disappointment at not being able to see the whole house, especially the upstairs where Mom had been born, and deep gratitude that he would even let us in the door just because we are related to someone who had lived there over one hundred years earlier.

We pulled into the driveway at Ane's white house with the green roof and tall trees. Ruby went to the side door and knocked to see if Norris was home, while the rest of us waited in the car. Soon Ruby and Norris emerged and walked toward us. We got out of the car, Ruby introduced us, and Norris shook hands with each of us. He wore khaki slacks, a plaid shirt, and a light jacket. He looked like a hardy man, and maybe, like the courthouse women had said, about seventy years old. His face had smile lines on it. We eddied around a bit, talking about the trees and the yard. For some unknown reason, I had braced myself for a curmudgeon, but he was charming and had a delightful sense of humor. He made us laugh.

Carla told him we had worried the previous year that we might get in trouble for trespassing in our excitement at finding our great-grandmother's house.

"There's no such thing as trespass in Newton," he said, and thus endeared himself to us and made us feel at home.

Carla quipped, "So you won't mind if next year we spread a picnic out on your front lawn?"

"Not if you bring enough for me too."

When we talked of going in, Norris cautioned us that the place was cluttered with his adult children's things and with stuff from the refrigerator having stopped working. I said, "Whatever you are comfortable with is fine with us. We are so grateful."

As we strolled to the entryway on the south side of the house, Norris pointed out that the south side was the only outside wall of the house that did not have new siding on it. The previous year when Carla, Richard, and I had compared the old family photograph of Ane's house with the photos Richard had taken the day we found the house still standing, Carla noticed that the south side was the only part of the house where the wood slats matched exactly with the historical photo. Norris explained that when his parents lived in the house, they had planned to build an addition on the south side and so had not replaced the siding as they had on the other sides, but now that they were gone, he said, he would probably just paint it.

As we stepped inside the entryway that had been added on the south end next to the driveway, we glimpsed the original wood on the inner entry wall. Norris went in first, I followed, and then Ruby, LaRelia, and Carla came behind. We made a crowd in the little kitchen, but the sun streamed in through the south window onto a table covered with a tablecloth, and the room was bright and cheerful. I remembered that Aunt Eleda wrote, "When it was apple picking time [at Ane's], we three children climbed the trees and retrieved the harvest. The apples were sorted and the best were put in a barrel in the basement. The balance were peeled, sliced, and put on a clean sheet to dry in front of the big south window upstairs. They made good pies and applesauce, and were good just as they were."[288] Seeing the sunlight pour into the kitchen and light everything aglow, I could understand why the bright rays through the south bedroom window upstairs would dry Ane's fruit, and I imagined its heavenly aroma.

What a magic moment to stand in that kitchen where three generations of my ancestors had lived, cooked, worked, eaten, laughed, cried, and prayed! We stood soaking it in, absorbing it. I was particularly charmed by the painted wood cabinets on our left—the west wall—cupboards and lots of little square and rectangular doors and drawers with round wood knob pulls that were adorable. For a few years afterward, I tried through phone messages and unanswered letters to Norris and his sister Doris Benson to obtain a photograph of that charming wall, to no avail, but I hold it dear in my memory.

The doorway connecting the kitchen and the living room, and another door connecting the kitchen and the north part of the house, were each hung with dark drapes, like theater curtains, in lieu of a solid door. Norris reached up and pulled back the drape in the doorway to the living room so we could see into that part of the house. The living room was shadowy. Directly east across the room from the kitchen door was the southernmost window on the front of the house, and to the left of that window was the door to the closet created by enclosing the former front porch—where Mother had watched the stars come out with her Grandma Ane, and had been put out in the dark for misbehavior.

That living room must have reverberated with family laughter and tears and conversations in Danish as Ane had lived there with her three small children. Jens must have spent contented hours in this house as he alternated his time with his two families. How was the mood different when Jens was here in Ane's home from when he was away with his other family? Was the housekeeping more formal? Were their meals different? And later in time, great energy must have filled that room when my grandmother—Ane's daughter, Sophia—and her five young children lived with her widowed mother while Sophia's husband, Henry, served his mission in Denmark.

During our earlier visit that day, Gary Jorgensen had described his own grandmother Estella Jenkins Jorgensen, Carl Jorgensen's wife, as he remembered her living in Ane's house after Ane was gone and while Carl owned it. He said that as one walked into the kitchen, the table always sat to the left in front of the south window, it always had a tablecloth on it, and the sunshine poured in through that window. Gary said his grandmother always wore an apron, and she would go down to the root cellar, pull the corners of her apron up into a bag, and fill it with stores enough to bring upstairs and fix a lovely meal for whoever stopped in. He remembered his grandmother fondly.

I can mentally superimpose a similar image of my great-grandmother Ane upon Gary's story of his grandmother Estella wearing an apron. Aunt Eleda wrote:

> I spent a great deal of time with [Grandma Ane Hansen]. She would call me to go with her through the orchard and pick up the "windfalls." This was apples mostly and a few plums. *She gathered the bottom of her long apron into her hands making a bag for me to put the apples in.* [emphasis mine] When I could find no more we took the day's collection to the two pigs that were to be our winter meat.[289]

Norris's table sat in the same place Estella's had, and I imagine Ane's table had been located there as well—on the left as we came in the door—basking in front of the south window where the sun melted yellow into the room like butter.

❧

My memory went back to my childhood when my mother often prepared what the family called "slapjacks" on those days she made bread from scratch. Some of the dough would be shaped into fist-sized balls, stretched out flat, and fried in a pan with a quarter-inch of oil to a golden brown on both sides. We split them open while they were still warm and filled them with jam or syrup.

When I was visiting in Ogden as an adult, I sometimes made bread for my mother, whose aging hands could no longer knead the dough. One of those times, I kept enough dough out from the loaves to make slapjacks and invited all my siblings over. I don't remember the exact year, but Carla was newly widowed and MauRene was still living, so it was between 2000 and 2002. And we were all there—Mother, MauRene, LaMont and Lorene, LaRelia (her husband, Bob, was still working), Carla, and me—squeezed into Mother's small kitchen, many on folding chairs, eating the slapjacks of our childhood, telling stories, laughing.

Shortly after that day, I asked my mother how she had come to make this fry bread that we all loved so much, even into adulthood.

"My mother used to make it," she said.

"Where did she learn to make it?"

"Probably from her mother."

So I wondered, as we stood in there Ane's kitchen, whether she had made slapjacks for her children, and likely even her grandchildren, in this very room.

As Ruby and my sisters turned around to go back outside, and Norris and I brought up the rear, I handed him a russet-foil-wrapped box of chocolates and said, "We brought you some chocolates as a thank-you," and as we stepped outside, I told him how much we appreciated his generosity in allowing us inside his home. I was, and remain, deeply grateful.

Norris led us to the back of the house to show us the seam where the original outer wall met the later-constructed utility room located above the original cellar that had been remodeled into a fruit room. He showed us the trench being dug on the north side of the house as they looked for the septic tank so it could be replaced. He said, "There are so many things that need to be done. And I'm gone a lot."

We agreed that the tasks needed to maintain a large home are overwhelming. As we walked over the grass back toward the driveway, I told my story that before Marshall (my first husband) died, I would wake up in the mornings and recite to myself, "This is the day the Lord hath made; we will rejoice and be glad in it."[290] And after he died, I would wake up in the mornings and say, "What the hell is going to go wrong today?" The others laughed with me—understanding, gentle laughter.

We conversed and joked as we returned to the car. As LaRelia backed us out of the driveway, Norris pointed to the envelope of photos held aloft in his other hand and waved an additional thank-you. We drove to Ruby's home, and as she got out of the car, she said again how happy she was that I had called, and she asked us to stay in touch. We bombarded her with thanks for arranging such an amazing morning.

❧

After Carla and LaRelia left and I ran a couple of errands in Logan, I drove back to Newton, where I stopped at what was then Bep's little market for bottled water to combat the effects of the sweltering heat. A woman sat behind the counter, and two local men stood buying six-packs of beer and chatting. A brindled bulldog strutted around like he owned the place, his claws clicking on the wooden floor. I joined the chat, and one of the men told me winters can be as cold as minus thirty degrees Fahrenheit for days at a time in Newton but the frost that forms each morning on the trees and chain-link fences is stunningly gorgeous. Those elements must have created difficulties for the early settlers but sounded refreshing in the extreme heat of that day.

At the Newton Town Library, I showed the set of photos to the librarian, who recognized Jens as being a person from the Newton Town Board photos in the hall. She said she would see that Cleo got the photos.

I browsed the family history section off to the right in the little cubby area and discovered the addition of many new white binders of various family histories. One binder showcasing Archie Jenkins as a teacher included a classroom photo with Gary Jorgensen as a student at about age eleven. He had a sweet smile that had moved with him through time, and we had seen it earlier that day as he had talked with us. Both he and Lois had come across as kind people with generous hearts.

❧

I was deeply touched to have been allowed to stand in the house built by Jens for Ane. I imagined Ane opening and closing the little doors and drawers on the cabinet wall as she selected ingredients or seasonings for the meals she prepared for her family. We know she dried apples, so she may also have put up applesauce, stirring it up in her home kitchen that we had stood in, or in her lean-to summer kitchen that Mother described as having been at the back of the house. Ane likely peeled those apples—a cooler task—in the kitchen we had soaked up with our eyes. I'm not sure why it seemed like such a sacred experience to stand where my ancestors had been born and lived, but that day felt like an incredible treasure to me.

Little did I know that the research trip and other contacts that year would later open additional astonishing doors. What I did know was that people were standing ready to help answer questions, and the search included not only gaining information but also forming new, warm contacts among those willing people. And the search for Ane, though it had led primarily through records of Jens, was transforming from merely an interest into a passion. Where would the search lead next?

CHAPTER 17

JENS'S BLOCK 15 SURPRISE: 1888

The discovery of the deed to Jens Peter Hansen, the oldest son of Jens and Karen Marie, for Lots 5 and 6 in Block 15 of Newton, piqued my curiosity. The property was located about five blocks west and one block north of Karen Marie's house, and I wanted to learn where Jens Peter and his family had lived. Could I locate the property on the ground? And if there were a house on it, what story would it tell about the family?

I had two unrelated questions: Could I get a copy of the survey plat for the west side of the Newton Townsite so I could find Jens Peter's property? And was there a record showing the springs in early Newton? I erroneously thought that J. J. Larsen had written in his "little green book" that they drew water from the *spring* on J. N. Hansen's property in town in 1884. Later, however, I saw that he had actually written, "The water we used for food was carried from *wells* [emphasis mine] located at J.N. Hansen's."[291] Although I was searching for springs by mistake, I was about to learn more about water in early Newton.

At the Cache County Recorder's Office on 21 June 2012, with its bright lights and sunny windows, I was startled when Michael Gleed told me his office did not have a survey of the west side of Newton. Later I talked with Preston B. Ward, head of what was then the Cache County Surveyor's Office upstairs in the same building, who told me the original survey of west Newton had been lost or destroyed somehow and his office didn't have a copy either. He said sometimes surveys became damaged, and sometimes the surveyors had no place to store the documents, so they became lost.

Michael said they couldn't make copies from the early assessment books because the bindings were too fragile, but I could look in them. He consulted a list in a loose-leaf binder, then went into the hand-cranked rolling shelves, pulled out an oversized atlas with fading covers, and set it on a nearby slanted table. He said I could start looking at Newton plats from about page thirty-five onward while he looked for the township survey plat so we could search it for springs.

The pages of the massive, weighty book showed parcels of land drafted on thick, heavy paper, with early owners' names penciled within each tract. Leaf after leaf showed drafted fragments of blocks and lots in Newton but no overall layout that I could find. I examined the partial plats, and except for recognizing the blocks and lots where Ane's and Karen Marie's homes were located, I was totally confused and disoriented. As I turned pages back and forth blankly, something told me to get logical, so I turned back to the page with the part of town that I knew with the lots for Ane and Karen Marie. Remembering that the deed to Jens Peter indicated his lots were nearly due west of his mother's home, I realized the blocks of the missing survey would abut the west side of the familiar survey that showed Blocks 7, 14, and 17. Then I found the page showing the adjacent west side with Blocks 6, 15, and 16 from Plats A and C, and they matched up.

Voilà! There in Block 15, inside Lots 5 and 6, written in old, faded pencil, was the name *Jens Peter Hansen.* I was pleased the search was successful, but I couldn't believe what my eyes fell upon next! Penciled lightly inside each of the two lots adjacent to Jens Peter's—Lots 7 and 8 of Block 15—was the name *Jens N. Hansen!* What was he doing there? We had no family lore of his owning a third parcel in town, nor had I found deeds showing his acquisition of that land. When and how did Jens acquire these two lots? And why? When Michael asked if I wanted copies of both the north and south sections of Block 15 from the recent assessment records, I was ecstatic.

Next Michael showed me the large, linen-backed township survey plat delineating six square miles that included the Newton Townsite. He pointed out a few small circles, each with a little tail and the word *spring* by it. None were within the Townsite of Newton itself, but we noticed a narrow squiggly line labeled *Spring Branch* that began north of Newton and dribbled southwesterly through the town before disappearing at the southerly outskirts. Neither of us was sure what kind of feature that indicated, but it looked like it meandered adjacent to and on the west side of what would be Block 15. Thanking him profusely and clutching my copies of assessment records and survey plats, I left for Newton.

As I drove past aqua water and golden rushes and white birds on this sunny, blue-sky day, I reasoned that since Block 15 was four blocks west of Ane's property in Block 11, I should be able to use her house as a beginning point to search for Jens Peter's lots. I arrived at Newton, drove directly to Ane's house on 200 East, and passed it going north, noticing that last year's garden spot north of the house was barren and dry—no garden this year.

I turned left onto 100 South and drove west, counting the cross streets until I got to what I thought was Block 15, divided from the adjacent block by a street. On the corner lot ahead and on my left, some miscellaneous houses and outbuildings stood on what likely would have been Jens's Lots 5 and 6. Further west, a light-blue, two-story house rose on what would have been Jens Peter's Lots 7 and 8. I drove forward a half block for a better view of the house. It appeared to be old construction designed to look Victorian, and the large two-story rectangle attached at the back was evidently new and modern. The house sported ornate white trim, with a black wrought-iron widow's walk gracing the top. The loveliness of the home took my breath away. I made a U-turn and went back for another look at this stunning house. Was this where Jens Peter and his family had lived? Or was it someone else's construction? Or was I in the wrong place?

Later LaRelia and Carla provided an antique photo of that lovely house which they had found behind Mom's piano. It showed the original house with the same construction and trim as Ane's house—with Jens Peter's children out in front. This original house with no rectangle at the back forms the center section of the now-existing structure.

Next at the Newton library, I pulled open the creaky door and looked up at Jens's photos in the entryway, greeting him silently. Inside the library proper, I asked Sarah Rigby, the librarian, about springs. She asked if I knew Cleo Griffin and suggested I call her because she would either know or could tell me who did.

On the phone, Cleo said she wasn't sure about the springs, and that Newton's culinary water supply came from springs at Clarkston. I told her I was interested specifically in what might have been a spring on Jens Hansen's property. She said she had been raised on a ranch with a spring and explained they had piped the spring water to the house, and had a pump with a handle in the kitchen, so they didn't have to carry water. They thought that was quite wonderful. In the early days there had been springs all over, and people settled by those springs so they had a water supply. Some of the springs had dried up. She said she would look through her things for any information about Newton's springs and asked me to call her back in a few minutes.

When I called Cleo again, she said if I would come to her house, she would go with me and show me some big springs just west of town. When I picked her up, the sprinkler going on her front lawn was a vertical wave type, and she had to get herself and her cane into the car quickly before the water arced back and sprayed her. Quite a change from the early days of carrying water from the springs! Cleo is a master historian of the area and a delight to be around. Like other Newton people, she is exceptionally generous and goes out of her way to share history with relative strangers.

I asked Cleo about the lots on Block 15. We compared our maps, and she suggested we drive past the place where I thought the Jens Peter Hansen property was located. As we approached what I thought was Jens's corner lots on our left, she said, "That is a Hansen house. Oh, the house is gone. I'm not familiar with that house." We went a little farther west to the elegant house I had previously found and she said, "That used to be Leslie Hansen's house. Was he a relative?" Leslie was the son of Jens Peter and Mary, and therefore was the grandson of Jens N. and Karen Marie. We had correctly found Jens Peter's home.

Just past the attractive house, Cleo pointed to a dip in the road, a shallow depression for a narrow stream that trickled from our right, flowed through a culvert under the road, and snaked off to our left through trees, hollows, and barnyards. She said, "Now there's the slough, and it runs all the way through town here and up to the dam, where it is apparently shut off because there's no water in it. Usually there is water in it, but they can shut it off at the reservoir." She suggested we drive north and follow it a bit. We came to a place north of town where the slough widened out, and she said, "That's where they tried to build a lumber mill, but there wasn't enough water in it to be successful."

So the *Spring Branch* squiggle on the survey plat was a slough that runs through Newton and flows very close to Jens Peter's lots, though I did not know exactly where his property line fell. This slough or stream is referred to in various histories.

Cleo offered to show me where to find the big springs west of Newton if I was interested, so we drove to the northwest corner of town, where pavement stops and gravel roads begin. The road leading thence to the springs was the same road Ruby had shown me the previous summer that goes to the quarry where rock had been taken for some of the early Newton homes. Cleo said I could drive on that gravel road to the farm we saw a ways off, which was still owned by the Rigby family—"He put one of his wives up there," she said—then I could continue on that dusty road, turn left to go south and come to the big springs. From there I could drive between the small mountain peaks we could see and eventually come to the town of Plymouth, located in the valley on the other side of the mountain range. Later, I looked up Plymouth on MapQuest. If I were to travel to Plymouth from Newton on the improved roads, it would be twenty-four miles and take twenty-seven minutes. If I took the scenic route Cleo described, it would be sixteen miles and take fifty minutes. Though it sounded interesting, I was not sure I wanted to try that.

✽

Water was a valuable commodity in early Newton, and J. J. Larsen wrote further about the work of locating and accessing water sources in his history:

The water we used for food was carried from wells located at J. N. Hansen's, Chris Nelson's, John Siter's, Amos Clarke's, and Peter Jensen's. Aunt Margaret had a yoke to carry water with.... Wells were being dug all over town. Near the creek they were 30 to 33 feet deep. Near the center of town, 12–15 feet deep, and along the slough they had to dig deeper....

[In the fall, the animals] were watered by the big ditch through a hole in the ice. And when winter set in there was no water in the big ditch. The big ditch came from Quigley Crossing through town past our home into the south field.

In those days water was run through the town ditches as late in the fall as possible so the people could use from the ditch. The water was soft for washing, but soon people went for a better supply.

Drinking water was carried from J. N. Hansen's home a half block north. After 2 or 3 years, a well was dug East and South of Grandfather's house and at 33 feet we found water in a gravel strata.[292]

I don't know what Jens's home was a half block north of—perhaps the Larsen home—but this note clarifies that J. N.'s water source was in town, not on his farms. However, I have been unable to ascertain upon which of his town properties—Ane's or Karen Marie's—the well was located. At the time Larsen wrote, Jens did not yet have title to the Block 15 lots.

Cleo's having shown me the slough shed light on Larsen's journal discussion of water. Eventually a reservoir was created so the townspeople had a more dependable water supply.

❦

Ruby telephoned me in June 2013, saying she had found something about my great-grandfather in her own ancestor's journal. She invited me to come to her home while I was in Newton that summer so she could share it with me. A few weeks later, we sat in her home at the computer and read the surprising and delightful entry from her transcription of family history that later appeared in her book:

The first water system in Newton consisted of buckets and ropes. There was a well by the house (JJ's) with two buckets on the rope. One bucket would go down empty, as the rope was pulled, the other bucket would come up full.

Aunt Caroline, JJ Larsen's sister, recalls: "There was a man who came around with a stick in his hand. The man would walk back and forth where they wanted to make a well and when he would cross where the water was nearest the surface, the stick would bend down. I don't remember what he called the stick but I do remember watching him." The man that came was JN Hansen.

One name for "the stick" was a witching stick. This was a green willow with a forked end. An experiment was done with some school children. They took 2 coat hangers, straightened them out and left a place crooked to put in their hand and walked out with them. They would cross each other when they were over the water main. The children tried this, blindfolding the child because all knew where the water mains were. Sure enough the wires crossed. The wires had to lay loose in one's hands.

Someone asked Grant [Larsen] about witching for water. He replied, "What I know about witching and whether there was water where they witched is a debated question. As far as the witching and their rods, it really worked. There have been other people try it, I have tried it and it won't work for me that I know of." Grant continues: You know Carl Jorgensen. He came and lived with JN Hansen who was one of the legal water witches for Newton and Carl picked it up from him. The stick would actually bend for him. He would walk over an area of ground and the stick bent down. I kidded him about it so I got behind him, he held the stick in his hands and I held his hands as tight as I could. There was absolutely no motion in his fingers that would cause that stick to roll and it was gripped tight enough that it took several pounds pressure to bend the fork of that stick down and we got over that point and that stick actually bent down to the ground. I was 60 years old at the time.

When the water system wasn't adequate there was a lot of witching done and practically everyone put in a well to get water for their lawns. One day we were talking about it and Osborne picked up a stick. He had no more faith in that than anything but as he was walking around he crossed a place and that stick bent down. You should have seen his eyes pop out.[293]

I was excited to learn that Jens had been a water witch! I shared the information with my family and was interested in the responses from my nephew Lyle Wiggins and my cousin Eric Larsen, grandson of Eleda, Mom's sister.

Lyle responded: "I'm pleased to learn that J. N. Hansen was a water witch, and a 'legal' one, no less. I played around with the process a number of years ago and was told I was 'nuts'."[294]

Eric wrote:

> That is very interesting about J.N. Hansen.... I have a very scientific mind and I am a skeptic at the best of times, but I have a story. When I was living in Moscow, ID a few years ago, we lived next to the U-Haul location and I became friends with the assistant manager. He was a young fellow from PA. We built a cider press together and were chums. He was a blacksmith and was talented in that direction.
>
> One day I went over for some reason and he asked me to help him for a bit. He had to find a water pipe under the blacktop so that they could dig it up to repair it. "So, how are we going to do that?" I asked. In answer, he took two welding rods and bent them into right angles. He took one in each hand and held the point straight out in front of him. He walked across the pavement until the wire points dipped and pointed straight down. He indicated that the pipe was right there. I said, "No way!" He said, "Try it yourself," and I did. I was flabbergasted when I could not hold onto those wires when I approached that spot. He said, "You have the gift."[295]

Generally, the witching stick was also known as a dowsing rod and often consisted of a forked stick of willow or some other tree. The dowser would hold the forks with the point extended forward, and theoretically when water was close to the surface of the earth, the stick would point down with significant force. Two wires bent into L shapes could also be used. The dowser would hold one wire in each hand by the end of the long shaft, extending the short bit of the L forward with the points up. Some sources say the points would drop from pointing up to pointing down when over a water source, and others say that the metal sticks would cross. Water witching is considered a pseudoscience, but Jens must have had a relatively high percentage of successes. It interests me that two of Jens's descendants tried water witching. Are there others in the family who have tried it but not talked about it? Is there a genetic connection that makes dowsing an inherited gift?

❧

Cleo showed me the road my ancestors would have taken to travel from Newton to Logan, and while I drove, she talked enthusiastically of many things in Newton's history. I felt frustrated that because I had the steering wheel in my hands, I could not take notes and found myself wishing that technology allowed us to transfer information from one human brain directly into another person's brain. I ached to have all the knowledge Cleo had.

Cleo reminisced that years earlier, her bishop had called her to be the ward's literary specialist and told her to think and pray about what would be best for Newton's literacy. She felt prompted to suggest a library, and others liked her idea. The amazing library they now have—the library that has helped me so much—started small and grew because of Cleo. She approached Comcast for internet service and when she asked how much it would be, they said there would be no cost. Someone else donated several computers. Things just kept falling into place. "Little miracles," she said, and I knew what she meant.

As we drove past the blue house on Main—the house Mom had errone-ously thought was Ane's—I pointed it out to Cleo, and she said that house had originally belonged to Bishop Funk (the second bishop of Newton, from 1884 to 1893) and that he had two more houses along that street. He had a different wife in each one. Along that same street, she also pointed out, was the first house that had been built in Newton. What a treat to hear history from someone so knowledgeable and to learn the true history of the lovely home to which Mom had mistakenly taken us!

Just past the intersection of 100 West and Main, Cleo pointed out a grass-covered lot on the northwest corner and said that Franklin Wheeler Young, a nephew of Brigham Young, had lived there. My ears perked up because I had been reading Franklin Young's prison journal, which will be discussed later in this story. Franklin Young had been among the early settlers of Newton. He had had a log house on that corner that had also been used as a school, with himself as a teacher. The house is gone now, as is a tree he planted that grew to fifteen feet in circumference. When it died it was taken out after much controversy among the residents. I asked Cleo why Young had left Newton, and she said he had been called to start developing another area. Though he departed Newton before our second wave of family arrived from Denmark in 1875, his path and Jens's would cross fourteen years later.

As we headed back to Cleo's home, she told me other things of interest. She had asked me earlier where I was staying, and I had told her about the Old Rock Church Bed and Breakfast a few miles away in Providence, Utah. The church had been built at the same time Newton was established. Now, as she got out of the car, she turned back to me and said, "If we're still here next year, you can stay with us." I was touched by her generous invitation, as well as by her having been so gracious about helping me. She had taken time out from her own work, which involved writing a history of each block in town and preparing something for the upcoming 24th of July celebration commemorating the 1847 arrival of the Mormon pioneers in the Salt Lake Valley.

✻

The next day I returned to the Cache County Recorder's Office to search for the deed to Jens N. Hansen for the lots in Block 15. The Warantee [*sic*] Deed found in Book 9, page 302, shows that Jens N. Hansen, on 10 January 1888, acquired "Lots seven (7) and eight (8) on Block fifteen (15) all as platted on plat A of Newton Townsite survey as situated in Township thirteen (13) north of range one (1) west of Salt Lake Meridian in all containing two (2) and half (¾) acres." Jens purchased the said 2.5 acres from William H. Griffin for fourteen dollars and held the instrument for over sixteen years before recording the deed on 8 March 1904, four months prior to selling the property in two parcels for a total of $215.

Why did Jens acquire this property? He held it long enough to make a $211 profit on it, so was it strictly an investment? Did he use the land for a barn or a corral for animals or for other agricultural purposes? Had he put improvements such as structures or fences on it? Did he build the "Hansen house" that Cleo had earlier during that drive commented on with surprise at its being gone? Were Jens and Karen Marie helping their son, Jens Peter, in some way by owning property adjacent to his? Did Jens N. buy the property for a third wife? Why was there no family lore about this property?

There *is* lore, however, of additional wives besides Karen Marie and Ane. One story says that Jens married an older woman just to take care of her. The LDS Church teaching that a person had to be sealed in an eternal marriage ordinance for exaltation led the people to feel strongly that a woman or man who did not marry in mortality could not achieve the highest level of glory and happiness in the afterlife. Wanting the influx of single women to have every chance at eternal blessings, people performed sealings for time and eternity for many of them. Some of these sealings or marriages seemed to be more for the eternities than for mortality, and were a name-only, non-cohabiting type of arrangement with men who already had a wife or wives.

One mysterious name appears in the Newton Ward Records. This record lists numbered names in the left-hand column, then across double pages it lists each named individual's father, mother, birth date and place, blessing date and by whom, baptism date and by whom, confirmation date and by whom, rebaptism date and by whom, reconfirmation date and by whom, priesthood ordinance dates, and death date, followed by a column for notes. Jens N. Hansen is number one

on the family page, second is Karen Marie Jensen, and numbers three through
twelve are their children. Number thirteen is Annie Margaretta Sorrensen Hansen
(all of her names except Hansen misspelled), and the next three lines list Ane's
children but each with merely a checkmark in the numbers column. Five blank
lines follow, and then on the sixth line below Ane's last child appears the name
Karen Kirstine Petersen Hansen with only a check mark, followed on the next
line by the name of Carl Jorgensen with only a check mark. We know Carl was
the man whom Jens brought to America to work for him, and who lived with
them and became like family. But who was Karen Kirstine Petersen? And what
was she doing on this Hansen page?

LaRelia and I had several conversations about this mystery woman on Jens's
family page, and decided it must be merely the coincidence of being alphabetical from H to J—Hansen to Jorgensen. But soon I realized that if the list were
alphabetical, John Jenkins, with his three wives and thirty-five children, would
come between Karen Kirstine Petersen Hansen and Carl Jorgensen. So this
woman had to be significant to the Hansen family in some way.

This Newton Ward Record shows that Karen Kirstine Petersen was born
in Denmark—but gives no specific location in Denmark—on 1 May 1811.
The record further shows that she was baptized into the LDS Church on 18
April 1875 by Jens N. Hansen and confirmed by him the same day. Jens and
Karen Marie emigrated in June 1875, so this baptism had to have taken place in
Denmark. Jens was thirty-three and Karen Kirstine was sixty-four—a difference
of thirty-one years.

LaRelia found temple records that show Karen Kirstine Petersen served as
proxy in 1887 in the Logan Temple for her mother to be sealed in marriage for
eternity to her husband (Karen Kirstine's father), both of whom were deceased.
The man who stood as proxy for Karen Kirstine's father was none other than Jens
N. Hansen. So Karen Kirstine immigrated to America between 1875 and 1887
and chose to settle near Jens. Perhaps that was a coincidence, or perhaps she knew
or was related to someone else in Cache Valley. But Jens's officiating for her own
baptism and confirmation in Denmark, and twelve years later accompanying her
to the temple in Logan, Utah, and participating in her family sealings, indicates
some kind of long-term, close relationship.

The only other information on the ward record for Karen Kirstine is a death
date of 16 April 1890 and a note in the comments column, "Died in Newton."[296]
I tried to find more information about her while I was in Denmark in 2014, but
the parish secretary at Jyderup said Karen Kirstine is a very common name and
we would never find her without a birthplace. Those sealing records from 1887
show Aalborg, Denmark, as the residence of Karen Kirstine's parents. Aalborg is

on Jutland, though, and not Sjælland, where Jens and Karen Kirstine lived near enough to each other that he performed her baptism. Was Karen Kirstine born in Aalborg? Had her family moved to Sjælland?

We have found no record of Karen Kirstine Petersen and Jens being sealed to each other, but in May 2014, LaRelia spoke with a genealogical researcher in Salt Lake City who said that during the time period of pressures from the federal government against the Mormon Church, many sealings were performed with no records being kept. Given Jens and Karen Kirstine's relationship of long duration, geographical proximity both in Denmark and in Newton, spiritual connection, and our family lore, the worker said we would be justified in assuming that such a marriage between these two people had occurred.

In an email regarding this puzzle, LaRelia wrote:

Subject: Karen Kirstine Petersen Hansen.

You will remember that this lady is the one I think in my heart of hearts was sealed to our great-grandfather Jens Nielsen Hansen, but have not been able to find a sealing record.

Yesterday while I was at the FHL [Family History Library] in SLC [Salt Lake City], I talked to one of the volunteers…. She said that in those days many sealings were performed in homes or at the church or the Bishop's house. "Those people believed so strongly that women had to be sealed in order to get into Heaven, the sealings were performed informally and no record was kept." The threat of imprisonment for unlawful cohabitation was a big factor.

Of course, we can't know for sure but she [the volunteer] thinks there are enough clues that it is likely that Jens and KKPH [our shortened reference to Karen Kirstine Petersen Hansen] were sealed: He baptized her in Denmark before he and Karen emigrated. [Jens and Karen Marie] ended up in Newton. [KKPH] ended up in Newton. He served as proxy for her father when she was sealed to her parents. She was 30 years older which conforms to the lore that he was sealed to an older woman. Grandma Bjorkman told of caring for an old woman in their home when she was a little girl.[297]

Several aunts among my mother's siblings have said that their mother—my grandmother Karen Sophia Hansen Bjorkman—had told them that when she was a young girl, an older woman had lived with them, and that my grandma had helped to take care of her. When Karen Kirstine died in 1890, Karen Sophia was ten years old and could have helped care for the elderly woman of the story and remembered it. Aunt Eleda wrote, apparently quoting her mother, Sophia:

> Father's "third wife was an elderly lady he married in order that her temple work might be done in this world. I remember that she fell and broke her leg shortly after she came to live with us and that I had to take care of her and wait on her when necessary. She remained with us until she passed away."[298]

The "I" in the above quotation cannot be Eleda, because she had not yet been born when Karen Kirstine died, and Eleda's father was Henry Bjorkman, who married Sophia after polygamy in the Mormon Church had ended so had only one wife. Jens was Sophia's father and Eleda's grandfather.

Karen Kirstine was living in the Newton area in 1887, so it was possible that Jens purchased those lots in Block 15 for her in 1888. But she died in 1890, so why would he have kept the property until 1904 if it had been for her? Especially given the lore that she lived with his second wife, Ane. What use did Jens have for the lots?

Jens's name on Block 15 of the assessment record puzzled me. There had been no mention of it in any of the lore and no records of any property beyond Karen Marie's, Ane's, and the two farms. I was delighted to have found one more piece of the puzzle, even if it opened up more—possibly unanswerable—questions.

Upon returning to Newton in 2012, I drove east on First South and pulled off to the side of the road just before reaching the ornate house on Jens Peter's lots. I wanted to take photos of the trickling slough as it ran from a farmyard on the north, under the street, and south through some grasses and woods just along the west side of the Block 15 property. A weathered gray barn stood nearby. As I continued driving toward that Victorian house on my right, a man in a shirt, shorts, and a ball cap was riding a mower over the extensive lawn in front of the house. I parked, got out of the air-conditioned car, stood on the rise at the roadside edge of the property, and waited in the hammering heat. Soon the man on the growling mower, traversing the manicured yard in swaths parallel to the road, looked up at me, slowed, then stopped near me, turned off the mower, and popped out his white ear buds, that fell to his lap and bounced on the ends of the white cords attached to them.

"Do you live here?" I asked.

"Yes," he said.

I introduced myself and told him my ancestors had long ago owned this property as well as the lots to the east.

"So you're one of the Hansens," he said. I was surprised he knew the history of the place so far back. He told me he and his family had lived in the house sixteen years, and then he recited the list of previous owners like a genealogy of the house. He said the Hansens had built the house and lived in it for several generations, and then the people who had owned it before the person from whom he had purchased it had added onto it—"a rectangle that doesn't fit with the architecture."

He was informative and entertaining, and kind to stop his mowing to talk with me. I was about to ask if he would mind if I took a picture of the house, but before I could get the words out, he told me to feel free to take all the pictures I would like, that there was a summer kitchen out in back as well as the original outhouse and an old blacksmith's shop reputed to be the first one in Newton.

I took several photos of the Victorian home and then strolled across the green carpet of lawn to the back yard and stood looking at the summer kitchen—a wooden structure like a small house. I took photos of the kitchen, the old outhouse of weathered wood, and the crumbling blacksmith's shop, and then walked back to my car.

As I drove away, I was once again overwhelmed with amazement and gratitude for the serendipity that orchestrated encounters with people at the right time in the right place, and for the incredible graciousness of the people who live in Newton. But it was not only the people of Newton who helped. Everywhere I went looking for information—from Newton to Salt Lake, to a library of ship photos in Norway, to an ancestry center in Liverpool, to a library in California, to archives in Denver, and to farms in Denmark—people made it their concern to help me find what I searched for. Not only were they patient, but they also went the extra mile. I owe the successes in this research to the generosity of other people, many of them strangers. As my former primary care physician Dr. Steven Beeson said, "All of us stand on the shoulders of others."

⁂

Even with all that happiness and gratitude, there were moments of being overwhelmed and wanting to chuck it all. On the day I drove north from the recorder's office in Logan to Newton to search for Block 15, enjoying the roadway flanked by the waters of Bear River with a plethora of birds swimming and flying, I asked myself, *Why I am doing this? Why have I spent so much time, energy, and money on searching and traveling—by car, ship, and airplane—and on books and print copies and motels and conferences and everything else?* Richard had asked, "Where does your passion for this project come from?" I didn't know. And I asked myself: *If I quit now, who would care?*

But I couldn't quit. Something had grabbed me and wouldn't let go. Part of it was the thrill of the chase. I was so jazzed to find each new tidbit of information. And I loved the illusion of being a detective, the excitement of discovering puzzle pieces and trying to fit them into the larger frame. I longed to know more about these people from whom I am descended and more about their unusual lifestyle. I wanted to find everything I could about them and to respectfully tell their story so those who come after me will have it all in one place.

When I later told LaRelia on the phone that I had asked myself who would care if I quit, she responded, "I would care. Lyle would care. Carla would care. Shauna would care. LaMont would care...." And after a rapid-fire oral paragraph of names of those who would care, I stopped her. I had gotten her message, and I was moved by her profusion of reassurances.

CHAPTER 18

"Pen" Pals, Part I:
Pursuit and Arrest 1888–89

Although Mom said her mother's father, Jens Hansen, had served time in the penitentiary for having two wives, she did not fill in any details as to how he had come to be there or what his life was like inside "the Pen." Through readings about that earlier time period, I have become more empathic with the men who spent time in prison for loving—or at least marrying—two or more women simultaneously, in obedience to a religious tenet.

The various laws against polygamy—the Morrill Anti-Bigamy Act (1862), the Poland Act (1874), the Edmunds Act (1882), and the Edmunds-Tucker Act (1887), among others—put increasing restrictions and pressures on those in polygamous relationships. Earlier, in an 1874–75 test case against George Reynolds, secretary to Brigham Young, the LDS Church expected to prove that the religious liberty guaranteed by the United States Constitution protected their right to practice polygamy as a facet of their religion. However, the federal court ruled that although a religious *belief* was protected by the Constitution of the United States, a religious *practice* was not. Therefore, the belief that taking a plural wife was God's revealed will was protected, but the act of taking a plural wife was not. Reynolds was convicted of bigamy and sentenced to time in prison and a heavy fine. The federal marshals then stepped up their efforts to entrap and arrest all Mormon men who had more than one wife.

By the late 1880s, when Jens became a hunted man, persecution of the Mormons in the Territories of Utah and Idaho by the federal government ran rampant. This pressure was apparently what induced Jens to deed that north farm to his son Jens Peter as a precaution to protect his lands from being confiscated by the federal government. The 1885 deed was filed for record on 11 December 1888.

Rudger Clawson was among the first men in Utah to be sentenced to time in prison for "unlawful cohabitation"—a term used by the federal government instead of "polygamy" because the "u.c." label allowed the legal system to prosecute without finding evidence of a marriage ceremony. Over a period of time, Clawson held high offices in the LDS Church, including those of apostle and of counselor in the First Presidency. He kept a meticulous journal of happenings within the prison during his three years of incarceration and therein shows himself to be literate and intelligent.[299]

An appendix in Clawson's book contains a list of "Mormon Polygamists at the Utah Penitentiary" from Rosa Mae M. Evans's master's thesis.[300] On the list are four Jens Hansens: one from Mill Creek, one from Brigham City, one from Gunnison, and one from Newton (our Jens), all in the Territory of Utah. There it is in print: my great-grandfather's entry showing his charge as *u.c.*, his dates of imprisonment from 25 May 1889 to 24 August 1889, and with no fine listed. The family lore says that he was sentenced to two months and spent an extra month in lieu of court costs.

I wondered whether records of the court proceedings could be found to provide a more vivid understanding of what the experience had been like for Jens. My nephew Lyle Wiggins and my neighbor and cousin Cherry Wolf both told me that the documents connected with the unlawful cohabitation cases were on microfilm in Salt Lake City. The microfilm contains copies of the documents as available in each unlawful cohabitation case, such as the complaint, indictment, warrant, arrest record, sentencing, fines, subpoenas, and—in rare cases—a transcript of the court trial. One such transcript shocked me because its pages showed that the accused and his two wives had been repeatedly hammered in court with the same hostile questions.[301] I felt battered just reading it, and my sympathies went to the accused.

The microfilm index of prisoner names, like the Evans thesis, lists four Jens Hansens. Over a period of time, I ordered all the microfilm rolls that listed a Jens Hansen, Ane or Annie Hansen, Karen Hansen, and all variations of spellings. The wives were often subpoenaed to testify against their husbands in accordance with the Edmonds-Tucker Act of 1887, so I hoped their names might serve as possible cross-references. I searched the microfilm rolls for a match with wives' names and/or the location of Newton. I found Jens Hansen of Salt Lake County (Case File 972). I found Jens Hansen of Gunnison (Case File 998). I found Jens Hansen of Mill Creek (Case File 1089). And I found Jens Hansen of Brigham City (Case File 1136). Something was wrong. Evans listed four Jens Hansens who served time, and I had found four case files for Jens Hansens, but none matched my Jens!

I returned to the Hicks history and found that our Jens's arresting officer was Deputy Marshal Henry Whetstone, his judge was Judge W. H. Henderson in the First Judicial District Court, and his arrest date was 27 March 1889.[302] I reordered the relevant microfilms and searched this time for more specific information than solely wives' names and Newton. By looking at the judges' names and the district court number, I eliminated both the Jens of Salt Lake County and the Jens of Mill Creek, both of whose sentencings were in the Third District Court under Judge Zane. I eliminated the Jens of Gunnison, whose sentencing was in the First District Court but was under Judge Judd. That left me with the Jens Hansen of Brigham City—not too far from Newton—who matched the sentencing in the First District Court by Judge Henderson but whose dates were in 1887 instead of 1889, and whose arrest was by Henry E. Steele, and so did not match the family record for our Jens.

In frustration, I sent an email to my siblings—LaMont, LaRelia, and Carla—whining because I couldn't force a match and wondering whether some of the data could be in error. Having vented, I moved on to other things.

Two days later, LaRelia left a voicemail saying that Larry Christiansen, in his comprehensive history of Newton, had included Jens's sentence dates with a footnote for a book called *Church Chronology* compiled by Andrew Jenson, an historian for the Mormon Church.[303] Amazon offered *Church Chronology: A Record of Important Events Pertaining to the History of the* Church *of Jesus Christ of Latter Day Saints*—originally published in 1899, with a second edition in 1914—as a reprint dated 10 December 2010.[304] Peeking at the tiny-print index online, I saw several entries for Jens Hansen, though which Jens I couldn't tell because the index showed only names and dates. I ordered the book immediately. The date was 23 April 2011.

When the thick volume with its glossy yellow-and-white cover arrived, I painstakingly went over every entry for a Jens Hansen in the index and marked each relevant page with brightly colored Post-it arrows. I did a double take when I discovered that the Jens shown from Salt Lake County had been from Mill Creek, and the Mill Creek case had been the same man's *second* arrest, two years after serving time for his first conviction for unlawful cohabitation. The law limited the length of sentences for unlawful cohabitation, but some men served more than one prison sentence. For example, James Bywater served three separate times in the penitentiary: six months in 1888, four and a half months in 1889, and one year from November 1891 to December 1892.[305]

In addition to serving multiple separate sentences, some men were sentenced repeatedly for the same offense by judges who stacked offenses by dividing one cohabitation period with the same woman into various segments. The judge could then sentence a man multiple times simultaneously for a longer sentence. Evans explains:

> In September of 1885, the policy of "segregation" was initiated by Judge Zane in his instructions to the grand jury of the Third District Court.

This was the theory that although the maximum penalty for unlawful cohabitation was six months in prison and a fine of three hundred dollars, there was no reason why the period covered by the offense couldn't be divided into years, months, and weeks, and a separate indictment issued for each. Judge Powers in the First District instructed his grand jury that an indictment could be found against a man guilty of cohabitation for every day that he offended. In February of 1886, the first "segregated" sentence was pronounced by Judge Powers, and sixty-eight-year-old W. G. Saunders entered the prison on February 18, facing twelve months on two indictments of unlawful cohabitation.[306]

Two additional men were given segregated sentences. Then Lorenzo Snow, who later became president of the Church of Jesus Christ of Latter-day Saints, was sentenced in the same way. Evans continues:

Lorenzo Snow was the next one convicted on a segregated bill, with an eighteen-month sentence and three maximum fines totaling nine hundred dollars. Snow appealed, and a Territorial Supreme Court composed of Judges Zane, Powers, and Boreman, upheld Powers' decision. [My note: This appears to be a conflict of interest for Zane and Powers because Zane initiated the practice and Powers implemented it.] An appeal to the U.S. Supreme Court was denied at first, but when Snow had served his sixth month, he applied for a writ of *habeas corpus*, alleging that he was being punished more than once for the same crime. The U.S. court reversed the decision of the Territorial court, and the segregated sentences were declared illegal. By that time, Lorenzo Snow had served eleven [of the eighteen] months and had paid the nine hundred dollar fine.[307]

Our Jens Hansen's arrest, trial, imprisonment, and release dates appeared in Jenson's *Church Chronology*. With this new information in hand, I went through the listings and constructed a grid showing all the dates, locations, and names needed to again search the microfilm rolls for a match of a case file with court documents for our Jens. I returned to my local LDS Family History Center with my grid and pulled out of the gray metal file drawer the roll of microfilm I had rented so many times that it had become part of the library's permanent collection, literally. My rental fees had purchased it. This search confirmed that the four case files that could not be forced to match my Jens's information were for three men—one of whom had been convicted twice—and not for the four men shown in the Evans thesis as being from Mill Creek, Brigham City, Gunnison, and our Jens of Newton.

Jens Hansen from Newton had somehow been omitted. Were his documents microfilmed without his name being included in the index of the twenty-seven or so rolls of microfilm? Or were his documents missed entirely? I felt the ambivalence of disappointment and relief. At last the mystery of why the fourth listing did not fit my ancestor was solved, but now the bigger mystery was this: I *knew* my Jens had served time, so why were his records not accessible on the microfilm? Where was the record of his arrest, trial, and imprisonment? More specifically, where were his documents?

During the next part of my search, I should have been wearing one of those T-shirts that says, *The only exercise I get is jumping to conclusions.* I reasoned that Jens's court documents had to have been in the paper files that were microfilmed before being sent to the archives in Denver, so they must have been microfilmed yet missed by the indexer. On 5 March 2012, I emailed the National Archives at Denver and requested a search for Jens's court documents. By return email 5 March 2012 came the following from archivist David Miller:

> Thank you for contacting the National Archives at Denver with your research request. I searched through our index of Utah polygamy case files within the series 8KR-021-83-051, Territorial Case Files transferred to the US District Court, 1870-1896, and found 3 references for a Jens Hansen, and 3 references for a Niels Hansen. Can you provide any further information about your relative to help us find the correct individual's records?

I sent details for the three Jens Hansens whose case files I had found on the microfilm as well as the data for our Jens for whom I was searching. By return email 23 March 2012 came the following:

> I repeated my search of Utah polygamy case files with the new information you supplied. Unfortunately, we have no record of a Jens Hansen from Newton, UT for 1889. We do have records pertaining to other Jens Hansens, notably the ones you listed from the towns other than Newton. If there is anything else I may do to assist with your research, please let me know.

Because the archivist found the same Jenses I had found, I assumed he was searching the same version of microfilm I had searched. Still convinced that Jens's original documents had been in the paper files and had been microfilmed but not included on the index, I ordered all the microfilm rolls for surnames beginning with *H*—they were alphabetized by only the first letter of the surname—and went through each roll, case by case, writing down each surname on a grid I had created to be sure my eyes did not glaze over and cause me to miss anyone. Still no Jens! His records had not been microfilmed.

Cheekily, I emailed the archivist and asked if the paper documents were actually in Denver someplace, and if so, might I come there and search through them myself. On 17 July 2012 he responded:

> We do hold early territorial court case files at our facility in Denver, and as I recall, I searched through them per your previous request. I remember searching for Jens Nielsen Hansen and finding several men with similar names, but none I believe were from Newton. We only have records which were sent to us from federal agencies and courts; many court series, especially from the territories, have gaps. It is possible we do not have the records you seek, but you are welcome to visit us and search through the records at your leisure.

One can only imagine my embarrassment as I wrote to the archivist again on 18 July 2012:

> Please forgive me—I believe I earlier jumped to an erroneous conclusion. I assumed you had been looking at the same microfilm records that I had been searching. If I understand you correctly, you are saying that you were looking at the actual paper documents, and that the court records for the Jens Hansen from Newton are not with those documents. Is that correct? I know you are very busy, and I deeply appreciate your time.

One more email arrived 19 July 2012 from the archivist saying:

> I apologize for any confusion due to our previous email exchanges. I did search through our paper court records when you first contacted me. This is when I found the three Jens Hansens, but none were from Newton. I then searched on www.ancestry.com, but again found no Jens Hansen connected with Newton. As far as the gaps I mentioned, "gaps" is the term we use for records which were never sent to us by federal agencies or courts. This is due to numerous reasons, such as:

the records were kept and not released by the originating authority, or the records were lost or destroyed prior to being sent to us. Basically, we only hold that which other agencies and federal courts send to us. I do know that some territorial records wound up in other records repositories. The various state archives may have them or in-state historical societies may hold copies, or even actual documents from this era. Finding records in this manner may prove tricky though. You may wish to contact your state archives and inquire if they hold such records. I am sorry that I cannot offer you more detailed information concerning the location of the records you seek. Respectfully,

David Miller,
Archivist, National Archives at Denver

Thoroughly appreciative of the patience and service from this archivist, I was nevertheless heartsick to realize that Jens's court documents, if they existed at all, might be difficult or impossible to find, and it was highly likely that they did not exist.

Later—in March 2015—I decided to make one more try. I telephoned the Weber County offices to learn if they had any documents from what in 1889 was the First District Court. The woman on the phone did some checking and then referred me to the Utah State Archives in Salt Lake City. I called, and the man who answered the phone took my question and referred it to a researcher who got back to me the next day, 17 March 2015:

I was unable to locate a criminal case file for cohabitation for Jens Niels Hansen in our holdings. We have a large gap in our holdings for the 1st District Court. We do have an index for the 1st District Court of those charged with unlawful cohabitation. Here is the finding aid for that [website]. He is not listed.

I did locate three case files for a Jens Hansen at the National Archives. I am not sure this is the Jens you are seeking. Here are the case numbers: 972, 998, 1136.

You can contact the National Archives in Denver at: [web address]
If you have any questions please let me know.

Thank you.
Heidi Stringham
Reference Archivist

The case numbers she gave me matched the Jenses from Mill Creek, Gunnison, and Brigham City. She omitted case file 1089, the second arrest of the Jens from Mill Creek. Because I had already contacted the National Archives at Denver, I had come full circle in the search for Jens's documents.

As a last attempt, I sent an email inquiry directly to the Utah Department of Corrections in March 2015 but received no response.

I was disappointed that we would never know whether Jens was set free on bond or word between his arrest and trial, or whether his wives were subpoenaed, or how he pled, or whether there was a transcript of his trial.

We can, however, imagine how difficult that time must have been for Jens. Constantly looking over his shoulder must have been fatiguing. And his wives too must have been unnerved by the possibility that their provider might be locked up for an undetermined length of time, leaving them and the children to manage the farms and their homes.

A newspaper biography upon Jens's death reads: "Three times he met deputy Marshal Steele, and after conversing with him for a short time, he succeeded in convincing him that he was looking for some other man."[308]

No clue is given as to the misunderstanding in the name, but it might have been because both Jens and his son, Jens Peter, sometimes went by the name of James. Although Jens had two homes, each with a wife and children in it, he was forced into the role of fugitive, sleeping in the cold—Newton winters are not easy—where he might go undetected and thus escape arrest by nonviolent means, at least temporarily.

Was it the passage of the Edmunds-Tucker Act of 1887 that triggered Jens's hiding out? Or did he begin his evasions of arrest by sleeping in the marshes and neighboring barns earlier than that? At the tapering off of a Newton winter, his hiding came to an end when he was arrested. The *Church Chronology* states that on Wednesday, 27 March 1889, "J. M. [*sic*] Hansen, of Newton, Cache Co., was arrested on a charge of u.c."[309] The Hicks history concurs.[310] The court documents on microfilm generally include a deputy's affidavit stating the date, time, and location of the arrest and where the person was being held in custody. Because Jens's court documents were not found, we do not know where he was apprehended or how his arrest came about. Was he arrested in the willows? Hiding in a neighbor's barn? Working on his farm? Sleeping in the night? Was he held in custody? If so, for how long?

Stories about how the men were found and arrested include an extreme event for Edward M. Dalton, who was arrested in Parowan, Utah, by Deputy Marshal William Thompson in the spring of 1886, and who escaped by taking off his boots and outrunning the marshal. After spending summer and fall in Arizona, Dalton returned to Parowan. One morning as he rode into town driving a herd of cattle, "bareback in shirt sleeves, unarmed," Marshal Thompson lay in wait, fired upon Dalton, shot him in the back, and killed him.[311] The *Deseret News* carried irate reports of the incident, while the *Salt Lake Tribune* (an anti-Mormon newspaper) said the deputies were doing their duty. Marshal Thompson was acquitted. He then sued the *Deseret News* for libel and received a thousand-dollar settlement.[312] Though the marshals were known to come in the night and disturb the families or to use various stratagems for sniffing out their quarry, killing a man who had committed the nonviolent act of marrying more than one woman was illegal. Dalton's case may have been more about Deputy Thompson's trigger-finger revenge over earlier having been outrun than it was about the law. However, it demonstrates the high level of hostility felt by some people toward the polygamists, and often toward Mormons in general.

Cases in the microfilm indicate that some men were kept in jail between their arrest and trial, but several journals and histories tell of other men who were allowed to go free on bond or on their word that they would appear on the specified date for their sentencing. Our family records tell us nothing about that interim for Jens. Apparently it was common to allow the men that interval of time to prepare for their coming absence from home during their likely incarceration, as Gustive O. Larson wrote:

> The days between indictment by the grand jury and almost certain sentencing, following a brief trial, were precious ones for cohabs caught in the widespread legal net. Personal affairs could be set in order and arrangement made for care of the family during the breadwinner's absence. In this he usually found substantial neighborly assistance which represented church policy. The Brethren on the underground relayed instructions through stake presidents and ward bishops that "the families of those brethren who are imprisoned and those who have been compelled to flee should be looked after."[313]

What provisions were made for Jens's two families and their sustenance while he was taken away from them? During Jens's absence, the wives and children must have worked diligently to keep the farms running as well as to support themselves. Karen Marie's four surviving children were Jens Peter, twenty-two; Niels Peter Nephi, eleven; Louisa, nine; and Anna Elvena, six. Ane's three children were Karen Sophia, nine; Hans Eli, eight; and Moses, six and a half. Jens Peter, as an adult, would have worked in the fields, and even the youngest children, with mild supervision, could have helped in various ways. Maybe people from the ward helped as well.

The records for the Newton Ward show that *after* Jens was arrested and *before* he went to trial, his son Eli, Ane's second child, was baptized on 19 May 1889, at the age of eight, as is customary in the Church of Jesus Christ of Latter-day Saints. The baptism record does not list the name of the man who baptized Eli. Following Eli's baptism, however, a Jas Christensen performed the confirmation on the same date.[314] Rarely did the same man perform the two ordinances. Jens had played an active role in blessing his babies and later baptizing them as children, but he may have been unable to attend or to participate in this milestone in his young son's life because he was either being held in jail or needing to keep a low profile in public before his trial. Or perhaps Jens baptized Eli, but it was not noted on the record in order to protect him. LaRelia searched a variety of records in the LDS Family History Library in Ogden to ascertain who did baptize Eli, but none of them listed a name. I searched records in the LDS Family History Library in Salt Lake City and found that even the certificate of record of Eli's ordination as an adult to the office of Seventy in the LDS Melchizedek Priesthood left the lines for baptism information blank.

What did Eli feel as an eight-year-old boy whose father had recently been arrested and would soon be going to prison? Whether Jens was present at the baptism or not, the future must have hung bleakly over both families.

One week after Eli's baptism, Jens went to trial on Saturday, 25 May 1889. The *Church Chronology* shows that "in the First District Court, at Ogden...Jens N. Hansen, of Newton" was sentenced by Judge Henderson to two months imprisonment for u.c.[315] The Hicks history shows that "on 24 May 1889, he was sentenced to a term of two months in the Utah Penitentiary, with one month extra for cost of court" by Judge W. H. Henderson.[316] The Evans thesis lists the judge as Henry P. Henderson.[317] I am unsure why there is a difference in the judge's first names and initials as well as in the dates shown for Jens's trial.

What was life like for Jens and the other "cohabs" in the penitentiary? The oral storytellers in the family always summed it up in one sentence: "Grandpa served time in the penitentiary for practicing polygamy." End of story. But what did Jens feel like when he was wrenched away from two wives and seven children to be locked up in prison? What did Karen Marie and Ane feel when their shared husband was taken away from them and their children? Did Jens worry about the support of his families—especially since records indicate he sometimes struggled financially? Or had he made arrangements with someone to see to their care? How was he affected by confinement not only to the society of his fellow cohabs but also to that of genuine criminals? Did his loved ones and friends visit him during his incarceration?

When Jens served time in the Utah Territorial Penitentiary, the prison was located in what is now the Sugar House area of Salt Lake City at 2100 South and 1400 East. The building was constructed in 1854 of adobe brick.[318] Don Strack, a Utah historian, stated:

> At least until the late 1870s, and after 1890, various census figures show that there were seldom more than 15–20 inmates held at the prison at any one time. It was in the late 1870s and throughout the 1880s that the federal government began prosecuting hundreds of men who were members of the LDS church for participating in the doctrine of plural marriage.[319]

Due to the sudden and large increase in convictions for unlawful cohabitation, the prison became overcrowded, and Strack continued, saying the prison was:

> expanded in 1877 to accommodate hundreds of non-violent prisoners—polygamists.... Cells were added to total over two hundred, augmented by bathrooms, a kitchen, a bakery, a new hospital, and women's quarters, as well as a new home for the warden. A stone wall surrounded an exercise yard and gardens and orchards where prisoners worked. Church leaders George Q. Cannon and Abraham H. Cannon both served time, and the latter kept a detailed journal, describing a cell approximately twenty by twenty-six feet and twelve feet high, lined with three tiers of bunks, each bunk sleeping two men.[320]

These two prominent men had leadership roles in the LDS Church. Abraham H. Cannon served time in prison from 17 March 1886 to 17 August 1886 and was fined $300. George Q. Cannon (Abraham's father) served time from 17 September 1888 to 21 February 1889 and was fined $450.[321]

The number of prisoners continued to grow, and the space again became inadequate. Strack describes the solution this way:

> In 1886 U.S. Marshal Frank H. Dyer recommended construction of a three-story prison inside the old adobe walls. The new cellblock was completed in 1888. Soon after, sandstone walls replaced the adobe ones, and another cellblock and an administration building were erected on additional acres.[322]

Melvin Bashore pointed out "the adobe walls had been twenty feet high and four feet thick."[323] All this construction was done to lock up men who had not committed murder, manslaughter, assault, rape, grand larceny, embezzlement, fraud, robbery, arson, drunkenness in public, or other such crimes that cause harm to others. Instead, these men had chosen to create more than one family, to live the plural marriage tenet of their religion.

An appendix in Rudger Clawson's book names the men who kept journals during the time they were incarcerated for unlawful cohabitation. Although I could not find any record that Jens had kept a prison journal, I found that reading journals by other individual who had served time carried for me personally an immediacy and intimacy I had not found in narrative histories. The voices of the journal keepers added depth and detail to my understanding of what life was like in prison, how it affected the men, and by association our Jens.

I searched the list in Clawson's book for journal keepers. As of June 2015, I thought I had perused all but one of those journals in public collections that had been written by men who served time concurrently with Jens. The missing one consisted of two pages that were held in the Brigham Young University Harold B. Lee Library in Provo, Utah. Unlike other libraries that willingly mailed or emailed information to me, BYU required that the researcher appear at their offices in person. I had been unable to do that, but fortunately in July 2015, a friend from my ward, Debby Fry, was on the Brigham Young University campus and kindly obtained those two pages of Morton B. Cutler's prison journal for me. I am extremely grateful to her even though I am not allowed to quote from it.

The Huntington Library in San Marino, California, required—for my purchase of two journals they sent on disks—that I sign an agreement document promising that I would not quote from them. I later found one of those same journals in the special collections at Utah State University's Merrill-Cazier Library, and that library gave me permission to quote from the journal. The other prison journal from Huntington Library is not used in this work.

Some of the prison procedures and conditions, as well as the pastimes of the men during their sojourn behind bars, appear in multiple journals and histories, and I reference them without citations. I am grateful for these records and the understanding they provide of the setting in which Jens found himself for three months in 1889. In many cases, difficult-to-read spelling and punctuation have been modernized for ease of reading.

In many prisoners' journals the men not only recorded their thoughts and experiences but also wrote poetry—poems to or about their friends in the Pen, or outpourings of their longing for loved ones back home. Some prisoners signed their fellow inmates' journals like autograph books. Other prisoners had pages in their journals where they recorded the names—and sometimes the towns—of men who were concurrently serving time. Some made lists of men who arrived at the Pen while they were there, lists of men who left while they were there, and lists of men who would remain in prison after the individual journal keeper's departure.

Gottlieb Ence was one of the journal-keeping men imprisoned at the same time as Jens. His record provides a good introduction to the tensions of the times and may echo some of what Jens thought or felt during his own experiences:

> Deputies were appointed all through the Country to hunt up and arrest men living in that order and subpoena witnesses…wives & members of their families and bring them before commissioners…they were bound over to appear before the grand jury by the next setting of Court….
>
> These marshals or deputies would adopt all kinds of means to arrest men, they would come at any time in the night and would disturb the families in order to arrest men which was very annoying to the whole families. They could never lay down to rest at night without expecting to be disturbed by the marshals until the arrests are made. Many families were broken up, some would travel to unknown parts in order to prevent from being arrested and imprisoned…. we were never safe as we would never know when would a raid [come] on us.[324]

Ence continues with his unpretentious narrative:

> During the year 1888 the Deputy Marshal came very frequently around annoying a portion of the Community…. In the fall, Mr. F.J. Mount of Prattville was appointed to act as Deputy Marshal…. he began his work in earnest until he arrested all in Richfield who had more wives than one…. Mr. Mount acted more gentlemanly than some other marshals. He would not disturb anyone at night. He would either be around early in the morning or in the evening…. I was hauling rock during the day for the new Tabernacle, they passed my home or my Wife's House a number of times during the day, but…they waited until I was home. Just as I set down to the table to eat my supper, they both step in the Haus. He read then the warrant he had for me, and subpoenaed my two wives and my daughter, requested us to appear before commissioner…the next day. I asked him for one day's longer time as it was a short time to get ready on the journey, but he would not grant me the request…. My bond was 700 dollars and my plural wife 200 dollars.[325]

The 1887 Edmunds-Tucker Act required wives of polygamists to be subpoenaed to testify as witnesses in the husband's unlawful cohabitation case. Franklin Wheeler Young's journal mentions his family's experience in this regard:

> During the fall of 1888, U.S. deputy marshals came to Teasdale in my absence, and subpoenaed my wife Maria and daughter Lucy to appear in the district court at Beaver, and testify before the grand jury in my case. They went and I advised them to tell the truth about me and not try to equivocate or screen me under a false proof.[326]

In addition to the wives of Ence and Young being required to testify, many other subpoenas for wives appeared in the microfilm case files I examined. No documents surfaced to show that Karen Marie or Ane were summoned in that manner, but that doesn't mean they were not.

Franklin Wheeler Young had a privileged experience, possibly due to his leadership positions as well as his being a nephew of Brigham Young. He wrote:

> I was indicted, and about the first part of January [1889] deputy marshal John Armstrong came to Teasdale, and sent word to me…that he wanted to talk with me, and that if I would come and see him he would not arrest me, unless I was perfectly willing he should. That if we could not agree about the arrest he would give me some hours [unreadable] start, when he would try to catch me. I went and was persuaded the "New Judge" we were to have would be light on me. I consented to arrest, and gave my word that I would appear in Beaver on the fifteenth of March. Mr. Armstrong courteously took my word in lieu of my bond…. About the 10th of March 1889 I started for Beaver in company of [a person], who was going as a juror.[327]

Was Jens given options as to arrest, as Young so generously was? Or was Jens rousted out of sleep in the middle of the night by a deputy marshal, as others were? Was Jens allowed to go free on his word between his arrest and his trial, as Young was? Or maybe his experience was like those of others, as recorded by Andrew Jenson:

> Mon. 14 [June 1886].—Some houses at Tooele…were raided by U.S. deputy marshals, who arrested [three men] for u.c.: also residences at Pleasant Grove…were raided by U.S. deputy marshals, who arrested

[three men] for u.c. The defendants from both places were taken to Salt Lake City and arraigned before Com[issioner] McKay, with a number of witnesses, and after preliminary examination placed under bonds.[328]

Jenson's record is full of similar reports of raids and mass arrests for the polygamists of the Territory of Utah. This hunting down of the men was not confined to what is now the State of Utah, though. A great-grandfather on my father's side of the family, Arthur Van Orden Peck, was arrested in the southern part of the Territory of Idaho for unlawful cohabitation and served six months in the Boise prison in 1885.

Surely Jens knew, when he had to be baptized at night to avoid persecution in his home country, that his road as a member of the Church of Jesus Christ of Latter-day Saints would not be an easy one. Yet he made that commitment in the baptismal waters of Lake Skarresø and later chose a path of obedience to the calling to take a second wife. He suffered hardships because he married Ane, but to my knowledge he never chose to be shut of (discard or be rid of) his honorable obligations to her and their children. Might Karen Marie have blamed Ane for the troubles? Or did she take things in stride? What were Jens's thoughts and feelings as he awaited his trial?

In addition to concerns for his family and farm, he might have wondered who would fill in for him as a Sunday school teacher and as a choir member. Who would take his leadership responsibilities in the community? Any aspect of his life or work that would lie vacant as he whiled away his sentence in prison would require attention and labor from someone else. The entire community, as well as the family, was affected by the political and religious conflicts.

One developmental editor who read the first draft of this manuscript had no sympathy for these people because, in her words, they *were* breaking the law of the land. Yet, the people felt they were keeping the law of God. Many of the plural marriages for which the men were punished had been entered into *before* the laws were passed to punish the men and annihilate polygamy. And these unions brought children into the world who needed the protection and care of both parents. The times were certainly complicated, and many people struggled with heavy hearts. What would become of them in this conflict?

CHAPTER 19

"PEN" PALS, PART II: SENTENCING AND IMPRISONMENT, JOURNALS AND PHOTOS—1889

I n spite of Jens's attempts to elude the deputies, Marshal Whetstone apprehended him, and he must have had a suspenseful two months between his
arrest and trial. How disheartening for him to know he would likely be put
in prison for a period of time and would be away from his families, his homes,
his farms, and his friends. Without his documents, it is impossible to determine
exactly what his circumstances were during that time, but he did appear in court
in Ogden, Utah, for his trial. Whether he journeyed to court alone or was accompanied by a guard or family or friends, he probably traveled from his home
by wagon or buggy to a train depot in Logan or Mendon, where he would have
boarded a train to Ogden for trial. The stately courthouse built in 1887 was
within walking distance of the train station located on Wall Avenue at 25th Street.

A journal entry of Christopher Arthur for 13 May 1889 (twelve days before
Jens was tried) describes the court proceedings in his own case:

> Left home about 11 o'clock AM in company with my wife…, my
> son…and daughter…for Beaver to appear before Judge T. L. Anderson
> of the district [court]. May 16, 7 PM appeared in court and pled guilty.
> Judge Anderson asked me how old I was. Answered 57. When did
> you marry your plural wife. Answer 12 years ago. How old is your
> youngest child. 9 months. How many children since 1882 [the year
> the Edmunds Act was established]. Answer 2. How many children
> have you by your plural wife. Answer 5. He then gave me a lecture
> and sentencing me to 6 months 300.00 and cost…. The Court-room
> was crowded.[329]

Maybe Jens's situation was similar and he traveled to his court appointment
with some of his family. He may have been asked similar questions and been
lectured about his violation of the law.

Franklin Wheeler Young had been allowed to go free in the interim between arrest and trial, and he kept his promise to return to court. When he appeared in court, he found:

> "The New Judge" [Anderson] was presiding, and about 6 p.m. called me to stand up... "Mr. Young what is your intention for the future?["] the judge asked. I said, "I had hoped your honor would not ask me that question, there is so much difference between our people and the Government as to the meaning of the answer to that question. For me to promise to obey the law is to say that I will deny my children and abandon their mother which I can never do." "Oh it don't mean any such thing, you are not required to do any such thing." The Judge asked me when I took my second wife. I replied, "In July 1861 before there was any law against polygamy." ... "Well, yours is an old case and deserving of sympathy, but you are an intelligent man—you are a leader in society. When the first act of congress was passed against polygamy you paid no attention to it; but you were not so much to blame for no one paid any attention to it. And when other acts were passed it was just the same, but when the Edmunds-Tucker law was passed <u>then if not before you should have abandoned your second family</u> [emphasis in original]. While yours is an old case, I must say the punishment prescribed by law is insufficient—<u>it</u> is <u>inadequate</u> [emphasis in original]. Why six months in the Utah Penitentiary is only a picnic." And his honor wound up by giving me the full penalty of the law viz. Three Hundred dollars fine, and "cost of court." And to stand committed until the fine and costs are paid.[330]

Gottlieb Ence listed fourteen men in his journal (including himself), from Richfield, Utah, who had all been arrested in a raid and were in Provo awaiting the action of the grand jury and the sentencing by Judge Judd.[331] One man was set free because the grand jury could find no indictment; another paid the hundred-dollar fine and costs and was released because he was in ill health; and a third was released because he was old and he promised to obey the law in the future. Ence then lists the fines and sentences that were imposed upon some of the remaining eleven men and says, "We all were sentenced the fifth day of March in the year of our Lord 1889 in Provo by Judge Judd to serve in the Utah Penitentiary the set time."[332] Ence was in prison from that day until the 27th of June the same year, or about three and one half months.

Christopher Arthur and Franklin Wheeler Young traveled to prison together, and Arthur describes their shared journey in this way:

> 7 AM next day [May 16] the mail [stage] came along took us up in charge of Deputy Marshal Armstrong and we started for Milford[.] arrived in good time[,] had supper and boarded the cars [train] for Salt Lake City[.] arrived 10 AM next day [May 17] where we met the Penitentiary wagon waiting for us[,] took our seats therein & called for the Marshal's Office[,] staid an hour & then moved for the Penitentiary where we arrived ½ fr 12 of the morning of May 18, 1889.[333]

The penitentiary wagon that hauled men to the prison was called *Black Bess*.[334]

Jens and another man were sentenced on Saturday, 25 May 1889. According to Andrew Jenson, "In the First District Court, at Ogden, Knud [Kanute] Emmertsen of Huntsville, was sentenced by Judge Henderson to six months' imprisonment, and Jens N. Hansen, of Newton, to two months, both for u.c."[335]

In addition to his sentence of two months in the Utah Territorial Penitentiary in Salt Lake City, Jens served an extra month of time in lieu of paying court costs, which he apparently did not have the funds to cover.

Why was Emmertsen sentenced to six months and Jens to two months? I am unsure. Rosa Mae M. Evans's thesis considers prison sentence lengths and what may have influenced the judges' rulings. She found that often the men's ages played into the length of the sentences, with older men being treated more leniently.[336] At the time of sentencing, however, Jens was forty-seven and Emmertsen was sixty, so apparently age did not determine the difference between these two men's penalties. Moreover, this was Emmertsen's second arrest (he had been sentenced to six months and a four-hundred-dollar fine in 1887), so maybe his longer sentence was intended to motivate him to change his behavior.

I found myself wishing that Jens had kept a prison journal, but apparently the majority of men in the prison did not. At first, I could find only six journals of men whose prison sentences overlapped with Jens's.[337] Perhaps more men wrote, but their journals either were omitted from the list or were still only in private collections.

The history from Karen Marie's family says:

> On 12 May, [Jens] was placed on trial in the First Judicial District Court in Ogden and was convicted for unlawful cohabitation. On

24 May, he was sentenced to a term of two months in the Utah Penitentiary, with one month extra for the cost of court. He began to serve his sentence immediately.[338]

This family record indicates the trial for determining his guilt or innocence took place in the middle of May, and was a separate proceeding from his sentencing near the end of the month. Jenson's record, however, does not mention the conviction—indeed it shows correctly that 12 May 1889 was a Sunday—and as previously noted, he shows Saturday, 25 May rather than 24 May for the sentencing. The family record says Jens began his sentence immediately, which indicates that on the same day as his sentencing in the court in Ogden, Jens would likely have been taken by a guard, in company with Emmertsen, on a train from Ogden to Salt Lake City, met by the horse-drawn penitentiary wagon and another guard, then transported by that wagon to the prison.

Gottlieb Ence wrote: "When we got there, we [were taken] into a room."[339] Franklin Wheeler Young elaborates the men's experience in this entry room:

> First we were weighed, and our height measured, and our description taken, also all our cash—our pocket knives, etc. Then we were taken to the tailor's shop and each fitted with a striped coat, vest, and cap, and our measure taken for a pair of pants. Then we were taken [through] the Guard house or Office, into the Cell House. This I learned afterwards was an act of kindness to us, as it did not subject us to the gaze of all the prisoners, and give occasion for yells of "Fresh-fish, fresh-fish," etc. so very common there. And our having prison clothes on was also in our favor in the same way.[340]

These descriptions and data were recorded as entrance information on each inmate's form labeled *Prison Commitment Record*. These records still exist.

Ence journaled about another aspect of the entrance process:

> There is a little building inside [the prison wall] used as a hospital and barber shop, where all the prisoners have to get their hair cut. All have to be shaved all their beard off. Also the hair nearly shaved off. The barbers are prisoners. If a prisoner wanted a nice clean shave, he pays the barber 50 cents per month.[341]

I wondered whether this rule of the prison was later relaxed or if it was instituted at this point in time, because many men in the prison photographs sport full and sometimes bushy beards. In the few photographs of Jens that exist up to this time period, he is wearing a full beard, so if forced to be shaved in prison, he likely would not have been happy about it.

Ence continues to describe his intake and his being moved to accommodations in the prison:

> After receiving a cup of coffee and bread, the guard took us to our different cells. [Because] the prison was very crowded, two men had to go into one cell. They were all iron the size 6 x 10 feet. Two bunks of canvas were fastened to the wall on top of each other. One had to be in the bunk while the other dressed himself. It was dark when we were shown to our cells, the stairway and floor was all iron, the sound was terrible when walking.... The guard opened the doors with a lever. It was all [done] in a second [and] it made a terrible noise. At six in the morning we were called up by the tap of a bell, [and] a half hour was given to get dressed. All the furniture we have in the room was a bucket used as a chamber [pot]. As soon as the second bell rung, the door would be open. We had to be ready to come out quick. The door was shut again behind us, [and] would not be opened again until after breakfast. Some was shut in the cell and would not get any breakfast. We had to go single file downstairs with the bucket in our hands to be emptied out in the yard, then we had a half hour time to walk around in the yard, then the bell will be tap[ped] for breakfast.... After breakfast we were at liberty to walk in the yard.[342]

Richard and I visited the Old Idaho Penitentiary State Historic Site on our way home from reunions in July 2016 where we witnessed a demonstration in one of the old sections of the prison of the lever system Ence described. Each cell door needed to be "pulled to" or held tightly shut while a prison guard or other official strained mightily on a huge lever at the end of the bank of cells. Shifting this lever's position moved a securing mechanism into place in each cell lock, throwing the bolt. If the prisoner did not hold his door tightly shut, the cell would not be securely locked.

Rudger Clawson, who served his sentence earlier than Jens, mentioned that during his incarceration, the hard criminals were kept in one area of the prison and the "co-habs," who were generally more refined men of a cooperative nature, were kept in another part.[343]

Like Clawson before him, Young discusses the differences in the types of prisoners:

I soon learned there was a great difference between "Toughs" and "Co-habs." The former were convicts for breaking some law, such as burglary, adultery, etc. while the latter was having more than one wife—those who were suffering imprisonment rather than abandon their wives and deny their children. The prison authorities were kind to us in that they kept us separate as much as they could. As a rule, they did not put a "Tough" and a "Co-hab" in the same cell together.[344]

Arthur commented that "the jailor was very kind.... I asked Mr. Doyle, the Jailer the privilege of moving into No 101.... He granted me the privilege.... [Later] I asked Mr. Doyle the privilege of going [to cell 119]. He kindly granted my request."[345] Soon, however, Arthur had a different kind of encounter with Doyle.

Young recounted an incident where a cell door was *not* held tightly shut for the locking lever, and resulted in Arthur being treated less than kindly by the guard. This incident took place while Arthur was sharing the cell with a prisoner named Jacob Naef and during a time when the prisoners were generally assigned two to a cell. Young continues:

> We [Young and Arthur] were known to be "Mormon bishops," and Mr. Doyle, the turnkey, set a "Pin hook" for both of us. Soon Bro. A was caught. One of "The Rules" was that at "three Bells" (about 6 p.m.)...get water for night and go into your cells, and close the door. And when 15 minutes later the bell strikes one, hold your cell door to be shut in. The prisoners all provided themselves with water for the night long before "Three Bells." And were in the habit of going to their cells and standing about on the corridors and not of "going into their cells" until the very last moment.[346]

For some reason—probably accidental—Bishop Arthur did *not* shut his cell door tight for the moment of the lever being thrown to bolt the doors, so Doyle discovered Arthur's door to be unlocked when he later made his rounds.

> As soon as our cells were opened the next morning, Bro. Naef [Arthur's cell mate] went to the Office end of the corridor and said to Mr. Doyle, "If there is to be any punishment for our cell door not being closed, please punish me, for Mr. Arthur is not to blame." Doyle answered in a very angry tone, "You attend to your business, and I'll attend to mine."[347]

Young continues the sorry story:

It was the custom to call the names of certain persons for "Pump Police" service each morning just before giving the call to leave [vacate] the tables in the dining room. This morning most of those, or maybe all those whose cell doors were not closed were called to do pump service, bro. Arthur's among them. Bro. A. went to Mr. Doyle and asked if he would be allowed to hire a man to do his pump service. The answer was, "Usually you can, but not on this occasion. This call is for punishment." [for not having pulled his cell door tightly shut]. Bishop Arthur was a bookkeeper and not used to hard labor, and his hands were very soft and the pump service that day blistered them until they were a gore of blood.[348]

Did the guards ever treat Jens unkindly?
Ence noted in his journal in regard to pumping:

The prisoners had to pump water too at the time for the use of the prison which was stored in a large tank on top of a three-story building. I remember well my hands got sore and blistered, but it was all done cheerfully and willingly because we could not help ourselves.[349]

Did he mean there was no way out of the chore? Or did an attitude of cheerfulness permeate the place in spite of the difficulties of life behind bars? I wonder if Jens had pump duty and whether his hands were damaged by the chore.

Life in the Pen became its own community. Food, bathing, laundry, chamber pots, letter writing, keeping journals, collecting autographs, writing poetry, making friends, having visitors, teaching or taking classes, spending money on mats or food or paintings, having church services, engaging in physical activity, and even making mats are all mentioned in journals and histories. Young also spent time working on his genealogy, as evidenced by pages and pages of it that I saw on microfilm in the LDS Church History Library.

Food was clearly of the utmost importance to the prisoners, as indicated by the many journals that mention it. Young rendered his description of the prison food in this way:

The prison food was generally meat and gravy and bread and coffee for breakfast. Sometimes we had potatoes with our bread and meat for dinner, with bread and mush and tea for supper. The mush was alternated, corn meal one day and oatmeal the next.... The meat (beef) was boiled or steamed, and never or very seldom, until it was done tender, then a good lot of the soup thickened to make a sort of meat gravy, and most everybody seemed to relish the meat and gravy at first, but when they came to eat the same twice a day for weeks they grew tired of it, and some actually abhorred the sight of it…. We were allowed, during all the time I was there, to furnish ourselves with extras, such as sugar, butter, honey, pickles, vinegar, fruit, tomatoes, onions, etc. and my father's folks furnished me generously, so that I was always supplied with extras. Then we bought milk. But the man who had no friends close enough outside to help him, or who had no means—"no money at the gate"—was to be pitied.[350]

Did Jens have the means inside, or someone outside, to provide him with these extras? Did his wives and children see to it that he ate well while inside? Did some of his friends or business contacts see to it that he had money to provide the delicious extras? I hope so.

Arthur wrote in regard to the treats and satisfactions of prison food:

I was never without good butter and during the hottest days of summer could keep it cool and hard in my cell. Also had plenty of sugar—splendid jelly & jam. Some cheese and egg for breakfast every morning. The prison bread was excellent also the mush for supper. I bought milk every night which I used with mush also in my tea and coffee. The kindness of James Jack and J. A. Cushing furnished me…with jelly jam some cheese and with lemons oranges grapes and apples.[351]

Ence filled in additional details of the dining experience at the Pen:

Breakfast…consisted of coffee (blak), no sugar, Corne Meal mush no milk, except what we Buy & some bread…. Everything was very clean. We had a very large dining room, clean and neat, where all the prisoners had to eat at one time. Dinner consisted of boiled beef, not always fresh or sweet, some potatoes, always we had good bread. Them that had money could buy milk for the mush and coffee; it was brought into the prison 95 cents per month, a pint a day. No knives or forks were allowed on the table to eat with, only a spoon. Some would make a fork out of wire, a knife out of a spoon handle.[352]

Rudger Clawson described a prison place setting as consisting of a knife, fork, and spoon.[353] Apparently between his incarceration from 1884 to 1887 and the incarceration of Jens and these men who journaled in 1889, the rules had been tightened.

One of the tenets of the LDS Church is a guide called the Word of Wisdom that proscribes the use of hot drinks (considered to mean tea and coffee), alcohol, and tobacco. Received as revelation by Joseph Smith in 1833, the Word of Wisdom was considered as a recommendation only in the early days of the Church. Numerous times in journals of the early period, one reads about the supply and use of these substances, and it is important to note that these guidelines were not intensified to the level of requirement or commandment until 1921 by Heber J. Grant, then president of the LDS Church.

Arthur states, "my niece…did my washing once a month[;] she came or sent for my clothes."[354] The men were required to bathe once a week.[355]

Arthur's journal has a page labeled, "Names of those who left Utah Penitentiary while I was an inmate—from May 16, 1889 to Oct. 24 1889." That page has a list of names in three columns of twenty-six names each. "Jas N Hansen" appears as the ninth name in the third column. The next page is "Names of those I left in Utah Penitentiary Oct 24/89" and also has three columns, two each of twenty-six names and a third column of twenty-one names.[356] I didn't research whether these names were solely of cohabs or might have included some of the toughs.

Young's journal had a section of names like Arthur's did, but they were actual autographs of fellow inmates and included the town from which the signer had come.[357] Unlike the list in Arthur's journal, Young's tabulation did not include Jens's name. However, one autograph signer in Young's journal included the date of 16 October 1889, two months after Jens had been released, so perhaps he simply missed the opportunity to sign.

Pages of poetry appeared in the journals or autograph books of some of the men, scribed by themselves or by inmates who were close enough associates to do so. The words bemoaned their common plight, reached out to loved ones and friends outside the prison, and sang word songs of longing for their homes and families.

We know that Arthur and Young knew each other before being incarcerated. Perhaps other inmates had friends in prison from their wards or towns. However, none of the other polygamists from Newton were in the prison concurrently with Jens. The proliferation of autographs and lists of names seems to indicate that the men also forged new friendships inside the prison. Likely the classes, crafts, meals, and church meetings of various denominations gave the men opportunities to converse and mingle, extending their circles of associates. One would think the shared experience of being imprisoned for nonviolent crime might have given them a common ground for starting conversations. Did the cohabs' friendships extend to the toughs? Or did they stay separate? Did both groups—cohabs and toughs—attend the weekly church services?

Through the journal of Young, we learn more about the prison schedule and activities:

> We usually had supper about 5 PM, and right after supper, all hands went in the Prison yard for a walk. I used to say "blessed yard," because it really was a blessed privilege to walk in it for half an hour or more each day. Most of the prisoners would go by two or more, or in groups, and chat as they walk. Not a few with their heads bowed, and their hands crossed on their backs. But when I walked, I got some one to go with me, my way, or I went alone with me [*sic*] head erect, and I stepping off quickly, as if I were going somewhere in a hurry.[358]

Did Jens enjoy his walks around the yard? Did he go solo or with friends? What did he think about as he got his exercise? Did he ponder the situation he was in? Did he focus on his loved ones at home? What did he worry about? Did he look forward to his meals?

Young describes another activity in the prison, that of reading:

> Bro. Morton Cutler of Long Valley and I took to reading aloud to each other daily for an hour or more. We read by turns, first one then the other. Thus we read "How Barnum Got His Wild Animals"—"The Lady of the Lake," and other books.[359]

The titles of the books they read piqued my interest in what was available in that time period. What did Jens read? Did he read in Danish or in English? Morton Cutler—Young's fellow reader—will appear again later in this history in connection with Jens.

In regard to church services, Arthur stated:

> During my imprisonment I never missed a session of the Sabbath School nor failed to be present at any meeting and I can say I generally enjoyed myself at both school and meeting. Could always find a little honey to suck altho sometimes it was amusing to hear some of the preachers disc[unreadable]ting from the Scriptures and giving their version of the word of God.[360]

Arthur was likely well versed in the Mormon teachings and believed they were the truth, so he would notice scriptural interpretations that seemed to him to err in the preaching of ministers from other denominations.

Ence also mentioned the worship services in the prison:

> We have a good Sunday School mostly attended by the brethren. We meet in the norenoon [*sic*]. In the afternoon, services is held presided over by three denominations alternately [with] Latter-day Saints[:] Catholic, Methodist, Presbyterian. The L.D. Saint Elders generally bring sisters along to cheer our hearts in singing. [I]t was a treat to see ladies once [in] a while as there is no ladies or woman to be seen except on their vacation or when some comes to visit the prisoners. Sunday Schools & other religious service are held in the large dining room. At the Latter Day Saints services there are generally very good singing latter day saint Hymns which was very much appreciated. The rest of the Sunday is spent in reading and writing.[361]

In addition to the worship services, educational opportunities were provided, as noted in some journals and histories. Prisoners who qualified taught various classes, which other prisoners attended. Rudger Clawson had earlier taught bookkeeping. The Hicks history states: "While in prison, [Jens] used this time to good advantage to do a lot of studying, mainly arithmetic that he loved."[362]

Visitors were allowed in the prison, and Arthur mentions, "Bro James Jack and James A. Cushing generally called me out once a week."[363] (These were the men he noted who provided his food luxuries for him.) Arthur was also called out—or called from the prison wall—for other visitors, and he includes a long list of people who came to see him at the prison.[364]

Ence further explained the process involved in visitation at the prison:

> Thursday is a visiting day where families and friends are allowed to visit their friends in prison. The prisoner is notified when someone wants to see him. There is a little round house outside of the prison wall, there where the prisoner will meet their friends in the presence of the guard. A half hour is allowed to visit. The prison is enclosed by a high wall [of] 40 feet [that is] 4 feet thick. Two men are stationed as guards on top of the wall, [who] keep on walking around the prison with a rifle on their shoulder day and night.[365]

Young stated in regard to visiting that "the rule was once a month, and that on 'visiting day,' the first Thursday in each month."[366]

Did Jens have visitors? If so, who were they? In a conversation I had in June 2012 with Ann Buttars, a curator of Western and Mormon Americana at Utah State University, Special Collections, she said that visitors from Newton to the prison in Salt Lake might have gone on the train, but that would present the problem of how to travel from home to the nearest train station, and from the Salt Lake train station to the prison. Likely, visitors would have traveled by horse and wagon, taking at least a day to get there, spending the night in the wagon, and making the return trip after visiting. Maybe they would have had to take even longer than two days for the round trip.

Nothing we have found indicates that Karen Marie or Ane ever visited Jens, but I imagine many plural wives kept a low profile during that time, although a couple of men did write of their plural wives' arrivals on visiting days.

Communication with the outside was important, and Ence talked about letters:

> Prisoners are allowed through good behavior to write home one letter a week. Letters there [are] not [to] be sealed, as the Warden will read the letters that comes and goes in and out of the prison. The mail is delivered to the prisoners in the cell; it matters not how many letters are sent to the prisoner, he will get it.[367]

The prison had a telephone for business that came in handy when Young's father was ailing. Young wrote:

> Just before the call to go into the cells, I called to one of the guards on the wall, and asked him to ask Mr. McCurdy to call up LeGrand Young, by phone, and ask how my Father is. Not knowing at that time how long it sometimes took to get a phone message answered, and not hearing from Mr. McCurdy, I went to my cell with a sore heart. A little before bed time, as I was laying in my cot, alone in my cell, I heard a loud harsh voice, that of Mr. Doyle [the guard] call out from the Office "Franklin W. Young," my name. I sprang from the cot to my feet and answered, "Yes, Sir." When he said in that loud, clear voice, "Your Father, while very low is better." "I thank you," I said. But I trembled from my head to my feet. The shock was terrible.[368]

Young doesn't show a date for this event, but his prison sentence began before and ended after Jens's, so I wonder whether Jens heard Young's name shouted. Did others recoil from the shock of hearing a fellow inmate's name boomed out by the guard? This story is interesting not only in that a telephone existed in the penitentiary but also in that it could be used on behalf of the prisoners, at least during an emergency. Also intriguing is that hearing one's name called—even while awaiting word—could incite such fear.

Returning now to the journal of Franklin W. Young, the following paragraphs detail what happened after he received the news from the guard that his father was improved, and provide insight into the heart and nature of this man:

> Presently the Bell wrang our bed time. I put out my candle, but for some time I walked my cell, 5 x 7, and when I did lie down I could not go to sleep until late in the night. But when I awoke in the morning, there was a peace of mind in my cell beyond anything I had ever experienced. My anxiety about my Father and every body and every thing else was gone, and I was unspeakably happy—a very quiet, inward happiness, of which I spoke only to bros. Arthur, Cutler, Wm Maughm [sic], and possibly one or two other confidential friends, and I told them that my Father would "live to see me a free man," & he did.
>
> This was a testimony to me that the Spirit of promise can reach a man's heart, though his body be in a prison cell. And that the God of my Father was watching over me for my good.[369]

This entry explains two kinds of light through the juxtaposition of the physical light of the candle and the inner spiritual light that comes as a warm feeling of peace from the Holy Spirit. Young's candle in his cell intrigued me, and made me realize that Jens and the other prisoners would also have had candles in that time period before electricity. I wondered what the candles looked like or smelled like when lit. Did Jens also have moments of inner peace and comfort?

Young's activities varied from genealogy and journaling to other pastimes: "After writing two or three hours, I would whittle, making rattle boxes, fans, etc. I also got some material from the stores in the City sent me, and I made a lot of pretty mats."[370] These mats, mentioned in several journals, were placemats.[371]

The word *mats* got my attention at this point during a revision in February 2012, and I rediscovered a note to myself that said, "Check Jens's journal." I remembered Jens's mention of mats in those last two handwritten pages of his life sketch, those perplexing pages mentioned earlier that made no sense to the various transcribers, including LaRelia. Having ignored my note through earlier revisions, I decided it was time to act. I left the computer and went to my files for a copy of Jens's sketch and reread his last two, mysterious pages:

> In the Night between the 13–14 i had a strains dream that was either in Prisen or in Hospital but it seems as in Prisen and some member of the famly was dead and i had permission to go home for a few days and as i went on it seems as my wife Mary was in the City and she went with me and she had 2 small baby's but one of them ware not hir own. We went home together and the funerall was in Mary's house but who it was i am not able to state. We stayed for a day or two and went Right back again and hir 2 babys,
>
> On the 14, 2 Sunday School children, i think about 4 or 5 [unreadable] and Bro. P. Paelsen from Richmen [Richmond?] danced a jig for them and the toroed 3 oranc down but not aloud to pick them up.
>
> The 15th 6 went out. a havy Wint blowin and a light shoure.
>
> The 16th Sent a letter home. SS [Sunday School] and Meethin as usualy the Methodist Preacht 3 went out.
>
> 17th 7 went out. i had a bath. i sent $1.20 for yarn for mats. i started to Ree the Signs of the Times used my knife a little in the Evening. Bredren Frank Withhade [Whitehead] Richmond, Wm McNiel of Logan, and Bp _____ Sandres [Sanders] of Portage came in,
>
> The 18 i hade a letter from my son Nephi with $2.00 in and a letter from Br J. Christensen in the evening we practce a peece for the 4 of July wherein Doyel took a part.
>
> On the 19 all as usuel good many of us hade our lightness took i had mine out
>
> The 20th Started usuly i made mats all day at Evening when the Leever was throen [to lock the cells] Br John Jacobs hade his thome cot bade [his thumb was caught in the cell door lock and was injured] 3 came.[372]

As I read these two puzzling pages and found the connection to the "mats" references, recognized Doyle as the prison guard, and understood the throwing of the lever to lock the cells, it dawned on me in a palpable wave that I was reading another prison journal. The indecipherable final two pages of Jens's life sketch that had baffled us and been ignored for 123 years actually comprised Jens's prison journal! I left my study, walked out to the dining room where Richard was working at his computer, and with tears in my eyes, whispered, "Oh, my gosh!! We have a prison journal! We have a prison journal!"

"I don't see why you're so excited about that," he said. Clearly I should have mentioned that it belonged to Jens.

I telephoned LaRelia, and the line connected our hearts. We were both teary with joy at finding another piece of Jens's story, one that had been under our noses all this time. Additional calls soon followed to Carla, LaMont, Uncle Norman, Vicky Jenkins, and more family and friends, sharing the exciting discovery with others who had showed interest in this family story.

The journal pages give just the number of the day—no month, no year—but on the 16th, Jens mentions church services. An online US calendar for 1889 showed that the only month during Jens's incarceration (May through August) in which the 16th fell on a Sunday was June. So these two pages, then, are Jens's prison journal for June 13–20, 1889.

LaRelia and I postulated that the nature of the language at the beginning and end of the record indicates there possibly had been pages that preceded and pages that followed those we have. Jens likely would have begun the journal with a more specific and complete date, and the first entry about a dream between the 13th and 14th might have followed an entry solely for the 13th. Through the two pages, his entries about prisoners entering the Pen or leaving it took the form of "# came in" and "# went out." The final statement on the second page is, "3 came" and most certainly would have required an additional page that started with the word "in" for consistency of his pattern. Since I don't find any names of cohabs who came in on 20 June 1889, perhaps he would have finished "3 came" with "to visit me," as it *was* a Thursday, although not the first Thursday, when visiting was usual. Or maybe three came to help the prisoner whose thumb was caught badly in the cell-locking lever.

LaRelia then contacted Joyce Hawes, the widow of Dale Hawes, who was descended from Jens and Karen Marie. Joyce still had the original copy of Jens's brief—but entire—handwritten life sketch, and she agreed to let LaRelia look at it to see if there were actually more pages there, or even a clearer indication that there had been additional prison journal pages. Unfortunately, when LaRelia looked at the original journal, she found that those two final pages were missing! Sometime during the years between her first perusal and Xeroxing of the original journal and this occasion, someone—who, like us, hadn't recognized the pages for what they were—must have simply thrown them out. As to finding pages that had been included before and after the two of which we have copies, we hope to someday learn of copies in a private collection.

In the earlier case of Rudger Clawson, the guard, Mr. Brown, confiscated Clawson's journal when he was released from prison. Clawson tells of making a copy of all the pages of his journal. He kept one copy in the prison and sent the other copy, a few pages at a time, out of the prison, hidden on his visitors. When he was released, the full copy of his journal was taken from his luggage by the guard.[373] If he had not had the foresight to make a duplicate and have it smuggled out, we would have been deprived of the great wealth of information he provided us. Maybe Jens's possible additional pages never made it outside the walls.

On the telephone later that day, LaRelia and I, each with a copy of Jens's sketch in front of us, went over the last two pages word by word with magnifying glasses to try to decipher the almost illegible parts. Some places we feel confident we have gotten it right, and in others we have used our best guesses.

The Brother J. Christensen who Jens mentioned in his prison pages on the 18th as someone from whom he had received a letter may have been the same man who confirmed Jens's young son Eli in May 1889 after his baptism, and who witnessed Jens's signature on the deed to Ane's lots—perhaps a good friend. (It could not have been Karen Marie's father because he had died on 13 December 1875.)

Checking the Evans records for the days Jens says some "went out," I found that the entry on the 15th, where Jens's number is difficult to read but LaRelia and I think it is a six, the Evans records show that only four prisoners—William Ball, William Gurney, Creston Lewis, and Daniel A. Sanders—were released. On the 16th, where Jens says three went out, I could find only Anthony Heiner as having been released, but the records could be incomplete, or some of the missing men could have been toughs who are not included on the Evans list of Mormon cohabs. The releases for the 17th, when Jens said seven went out, are listed in the Evans record as Andrew Anderson, John T. Covington, Soren Jacobsen, James H. Langford, Cornelius McReavey, Carl Olsen, and Benjamin Perkin for a total of seven, just as Jens said.

Jens says a lot in a few words. His dream included his wife "Mary" (Karen Marie) and not Ane, my great-grandmother. He received a letter from his son, Nephi, by Karen Marie. Nephi's writing his father a letter in prison seems very tender because he was twelve years old at the time. Jens makes no mention at all of his second wife, Ane, or their children, and I wonder whether that reflects an emotional separation or a needed discretion.

I am awed by the realization that Jens's two pages that no one could make sense of are now stunningly clear. The other prison journals I had read provided a context for my recognizing these two pages for what they are. I owe a tremendous debt to those men who kept journals in prison and to their families for making the records available.

Though the Church leaders said men should neither abandon their plural wives and families nor stop supporting them, the federal government was determined to quash polygamy and demanded that men abandon their plural wives and their children or go to jail. Because many cohabs were rearrested after having once served time, public acknowledgment of plural marriages may have been perilous.

Jens mentioned in his two pages that he had attended Sunday services on 16 June 1889. Having had experience with Sunday School—attending, teaching, and playing piano or organ—I became curious as to what those services were like in the prison so many decades ago. At the LDS Church History Library, I was granted access to the minutes of the Sunday School in the penitentiary. Those historical records, covering the minutes from 2 June 1889 to 18 August 1889 during Jens's incarceration, show that the meetings were held in the prison dining room and began around 9:00 in the morning on Sundays. During Jens's time, the Sunday School superintendent was William H. Maughan, whose father had been instrumental in settling Wellsville, Utah, in Cache Valley, south of Newton. The Sunday School teacher was B. H. Roberts, an LDS Church historian who held high positions of leadership.[374] What a thrill that must have been to sit in a class taught by such a knowledgeable man!

Also of interest was Jens's comment that they practiced a piece for the 4th of July in which the guard, Doyle, took a part. The following minutes for 7 July 1889 not only show the standard agenda for each meeting but also give more information about that musical piece that was being practiced:

7 July 1889

In the absence of Bishop Maughan, Prest. Roberts presided.

Commenced by singing a Quartette "The Glory of Man." Sung by 8 voices in which Officer Doyle took part.

Prayer was offered by Bishop C. J. Arthur

Golden Thoughts or Choice Selections of Scripture were read by 23 members

The lesson [Romans I and II as announced in the minutes from 30 June 1889] was read and commented on by Prest. B. H. Roberts, who gave some instructions about certain facts connected with the scriptures. They were not divided into chapters and subdivided into verses and punctuated as we now see them in print, when they were written. This is a modern work. Paul's writing could be better understood if we had the communications which some of his writings are answers to.

There were only 52 members present.

Our next lesson is the III and IV Chapters of Paul's epistle to the Romans.

Benediction by Elder A. J. Kershaw of Ogden

—Joseph S. Horne, Secretary[375]

My theory is that "The Glory of Man" was performed by this group of eight men on Thursday, 4 July 1889, at the prison's holiday festivities, and—since Jens's journal mentioned "we" practiced a piece for the 4th of July, in which Doyle was taking a part—the group must have included Jens as well as Officer Doyle. Family members or other guests were likely present for the performance, as it was a visiting day. I surmise the same musical number was then again performed at the Sabbath School for the edification of the prisoners—maybe because they already had it prepared or maybe even by popular demand. I love having this little glimpse of something in which Jens took part.

Different inmates offered the opening prayer, or invocation, each week. The number of men sharing Golden Thoughts or Choice Selections of Scripture decreased from a high of forty-two when Jens entered the prison to a low of nineteen just before his release and then back up to twenty-four. The decrease was attributed to the release of prisoners, as was the decrease in attendance at Church services from 107 when Jens was imprisoned to fifty when it was time for him to leave. The scriptures studied for the lesson material during Jens's incarceration began with Acts 20 and ended with Romans 24. Different inmates offered the closing prayer, or benediction, each week, one of which was given by William Grant (30 June 1889), who will soon step into Jens's story in an important way, and in fact I would wager he also took part in "The Glory of Man" performances. Choristers were Charles Hall and George C. Wood. An organ had been donated to the Pen, and organists were George Manwaring and William Grant.[376]

Jens paid attention in his journal to the children who came into the prison to entertain the inmates, to the men who were being released, and to the pain experienced by a fellow inmate whose thumb was crushed by the locking lever. From the details he chose to include, I perceive a sense of longing and a tenderness of heart in Jens, a gentle soul. His mention of practicing a piece for a 4th of July celebration made me want to know if they were reciting or singing, and the answer came in these Sunday school minutes. Jens was known for his fine tenor voice, sang in the Newton Ward choir, and was choir director for a time.

Another rich record from those years of Mormon incarcerations is the trove of photographs of groups of cohabs posed in the Yard just outside a prison door, with the men dressed in their prison stripes. Many of the group photographs include one or two men in street dress, and in one such photo I found online, a man in a suit is identified as James Doyle, the guard during Jens's incarceration.

Apparently itinerant photographers visited the penitentiary on a regular basis and Charles Roscoe Savage is well known for his prison photos. Many prisoners wanted their photo taken with George Q. Cannon, the prominent LDS Church leader who was incarcerated and released before Jens was imprisoned, so a plethora of prison photos feature Cannon in the center of the group. I automatically knew that none of those photos taken with Cannon would include Jens.

Jens's journal statement that he had a photo taken while inside the prison made me want to find it. I telephoned the Utah State Historical Society in Salt Lake City, and the man who took my call said their collection of prison photos began after the date of Jens's release. "But," he said, "we do still have the Prison Commitment Records. Would you be interested in those?"

"What are those?"

He explained that they are the records made in the little room when the men were first brought into the prison, where their measurements were taken, their knives and cash removed, and their prison stripes given to them. Of course I was interested!

When the copy of the Prison Commitment Record for Jens arrived in the mail in a two-page spread, his line item told me that he was 5' 4" tall and weighed 142 pounds. He had a sandy complexion, sandy hair, and blue eyes. He was literate and temperate. When I provided copies of the document to my family, both of my sisters commented on his height perhaps being the reason we all have the same stature. We delighted in learning these details that are not discernable in our black-and-white photos. I had had no idea that those entrance stories from the journals were documented, let alone in an extant record.

I searched the Utah State Historical Society prison photo files in 2012, just to be sure, but did not find an image that definitively included Jens. In the family group photos we have he is older and bearded, so it was difficult to imagine what he might have looked like at age forty-seven and possibly clean-shaven. As mentioned earlier, Carla, LaRelia, and I remembered vaguely that as young children, we had seen a photo of a group of prisoners in their striped uniforms in a round gold fruitcake tin on a shelf in Mom's basement. She had told us one man in it was Great-Grandpa Hansen. However, we did not find the photo in our mother's personal things when we readied her home for sale while she was in an assisted living facility. What happened to that photo? And why?

Knowing from Jens's journal that we weren't imagining our having seen a prison photo of him, LaRelia and I began a quest in 2013 to find a copy. We searched the Brigham Young University collection in Provo, Utah—for which we had to have an appointment so they could take their photos out of the refrigerator twenty-four hours before our arrival, and we were given white gloves to wear as we handled the photos. We also did a phone inquiry at the University of Utah and again searched the Utah State Archives, both located in Salt Lake City, and we searched at the library of Utah State University in Logan, Utah—every public collection of prison photos—without success. The curator at the final place we searched said that we had exhausted the public collections and the next step would be to ask about private collections among family and friends. We asked our own family members as well as descendants from Karen Marie's family, and although nearly everyone remembered seeing the prison photo, no one seemed to know where they could find a copy. I sadly gave up and moved on to other things.

While revising the last section of Jens's prison life on 30 May 2015, I wondered if I had missed any of the journals of men who had been incarcerated at the same time he was, so I got out the list and went over it again carefully. I *had* missed one—that of William Grant of American Fork, Utah. According to the Clawson appendix, copies of Grant's prison journal were located at Brigham Young University, University of Utah, and the LDS Church History Library.[377] Our family reunion was three weeks off, so I planned to find Grant's journal while in Utah.

Then I wondered whether there might be something online about William Grant. To my delight, Google brought up a lovely "Life Sketch" of Grant, and as I scrolled through it, a prison photo appeared on page nineteen. I had looked at so many prison photos searching for Jens and had been disappointed that I felt no excitement whatsoever for this one. This photo was dated 1886, but Jens had served time in 1889, so I knew it was fruitless. A list of the men in the photo appeared beneath it and included a "Bro. Hanson," but that was not the correct spelling for our Jens. Having always met failure in finding our Jens's prison photo and now feeling only curiosity instead of hope, I raised my eyes to locate the "Bro. Hanson" in the photo. Expecting a clear nonmatch, I looked casually, neutrally at his face, but instead felt a jolt of electricity, a shock of recognition. Could that be our Jens without his beard and mustache? I used a bookmark to cover the lower half of his face. The eyes were the same, the high cheekbones were the same, and the ears were the same. Even the shape of his hands and the slope of his shoulders matched those in the photos I already had of him and his two families. Grant had been incarcerated twice: once in 1886 and once in 1889. Jens served in 1889. Could this photo have been dated 1886 in error?

Using both Evans's thesis and Jenson's *Church Chronology*, I looked up all the names of the men listed in the photo and found that every one of them had served time not in 1886, but in the summer of 1889. Two of them had entered the prison two days *before* the date Jens wrote that his likeness had been taken.

Other Hansens were in the prison in 1889, but Willard Hansen had been released 4 March 1889. Jens Hansen from Gunnison had been released 6 March 1889. Andrew Hansen of Newton was released 8 May 1889, and James P. Hansen was released 23 May 1889, two days before Jens entered the prison. From that point on through the rest of 1889, our Jens Hansen was the *only* Hansen in the prison. The data, as well as his physical appearance, supports the conclusion that this man in William Grant's photo is our Jens!

Now—how to obtain a copy? The online photo was in a PDF and quite small. The life sketch, though, contained an email address and phone number for a Ken Wright in Littleton, Colorado. I emailed him and waited a couple of days—an eternity. No response came, so I telephoned him. I had started to leave a voicemail when he picked up and said he had just returned from vacation and had not yet responded to my email because his computer had started downloading updates when he turned it on and it was still going. I mentioned that the Hansen in his photo was my great-grandfather, and with a hearty laugh he said, "Oh! They were jailbirds together!" I told him of my joy over the photo and asked if it were in a public collection someplace. He said he had also posted the photo and life sketch on Ancestry.com where our family could access it for a larger copy. We had an enjoyable conversation, and when I returned to my computer later, I found that he had emailed me a beautiful large copy of the photo! I printed it off on photo paper and loved sharing copies of it at the next family reunion.

Jens's prison journal mentioned by name three men who came into the prison on 17 June 1889, and two of them are in this photograph—William McNeil and Frank Whitehead. Often the men's autographs in the prison journals and the men grouped in the prison photos seem to be linked by their geographical origins. Because no Newton polygamists served time simultaneously with Jens, I had wondered if he had friends in the prison or if he had been lonely. Grant lived south of Salt Lake—far from Newton—but he was an active musician, so perhaps he and Jens had become friends through their love of music. Both McNeil and Richard Jessop in the photo came from Cache County. I am grateful to know Jens had friends—or at least acquaintances—in the Pen. Morton B.

Cutler, who read aloud with Franklin Young and who wrote the other two-page prison journal previously mentioned, entered prison on 22 May 1889—just days before Jens arrived—and is number nine in the photo with Jens.

We have one photo of Jens as a young man without a beard, but the prison photo is the only other one we have of him clean-shaven. His appearance is so different! I love the expression on his face, his direct eyes, and his square chin. He looks so accessible. How did he feel about the apparently mandatory facial hair removal upon entry to the prison? Almost every prison photo has someone in it with a full beard, though. Jens would have been in prison almost three and a half weeks at the time this photo was taken, so he would have had time for his beard to start growing back. As we will learn from a whimsical newspaper account later in the story, Jens shaved off his beard at least one other time in his life.

I treasure this prison photo and what it stands for. Jens chose to be tried and convicted rather than agree to abandon his second wife and children. He could have been released from court if he had pledged to abandon his plural wife, as a number of men did, but he chose to go to prison rather than deny Ane or to stop providing for her and their children. Maybe there was more love between them than I thought when I heard she put his clothes out on the porch. He stood up for his principles, and I admire him for that.

Affecting me as a tender mercy is the fact that *because* I missed Grant's journal on the Clawson list the first time through, and found it a few years later on the second sweep, I was able to find Grant's online life sketch. During the time between those two Clawson list checks, Grant's family posted his life sketch, with Jens's photo, online. Had I found Grant in the list of journal keepers the first time, no photo of Jens would yet have been online, and I would have had no cause, no clue that I needed to look again later. I had searched so hard and prayed so hard to find the missing prison photo. I remain amazed and grateful for this fortuitous finding.

❧

As time moved through Jens's prison sentence toward release, one might think being in prison was dreary. However, some of the prisoners wrote of positive aspects. Arthur wrote:

> My experience in Utah Penitentiary was fraught with much enjoy-
> ment. [Lack of] Liberty to go to my home and family and associate
> with the people of Cedar was the only drawback. The good men I

met in the Pen, our association, walks and talks and the many visits paid me by friends [and] their kind contributions to my temporal requirements—everything tended to while away the hours and days of my confinement.[378]

Later Arthur again mused on his enjoyment of his days of incarceration and noted:

I spent many pleasant hours in the Pen—always slept well and had a good appetite. While in the Pen I spent about 35.00 for butter, cheese, shaving, pumping [apparently he was able to hire his pumping service on occasions other than the one for punishment], milk[,] an oil painting of the Pen cost one 3.50, 3 photos of a group of Bishops 1.50, mending + cleaning my watch 1.00, subscribed to 4 raffles 2.00, Cigars for those who extended kindness/courtesies 2.00, a mat .50. [Could Arthur have purchased this mat from Young? Or from Jens?] I tried to conduct myself respectful and thereby merit respect in return both from Convict, Guard, and Brother.[379]

In addition, Ence tells of incredible family support from outside the Pen:

One incident I will relate. My son, William, at the time of my arrest was then working in Salt Lake City making good wages. When he heard of the trouble, he left his job and came home for to look [after] my business and attend to the farm, while none of us knew how long I might have to be away. So after I got again home, he left again to his work.[380]

Jens must have had a similar sense of appreciation for his own son, Jens Peter, to whom he had deeded his 160-acre farm in 1885. Jens Peter filled this same role of sacrifice for the family. As the firstborn child with eleven years between himself and the next oldest child (the interval due to the deaths of the three children), he carried much responsibility. At that time, he was an adult with a wife who was pregnant and a young daughter to care for, as well as likely shouldering other familial responsibilities in Jens's absence from his homes. The Hicks history says Jens "had a homestead north of town which his family cared for while he was away. Most of his children were small, so most of the work depended on the wives and his oldest son Jens P."[381] They must have all worked hard together to survive Jens's absence.

Even though the prisoners experienced things of a positive nature inside the Pen and the attitude of devotion to "the principle" overrode much of the suffering, being free was even better. Ence mused:

> When I was put in prison it was in winter. I remember well, I had permission to go outside the prison wall to pump water about the month of April when nature looks most beautiful, the trees in bloom, the fields green. I thought that I was in a new World. While in the prison walls, we could see [nothing] but the sky. There was one consolation: we passed through this ordeal for the Principle of Plural Marriage and our families' sake. We knew that we [would] not remain in that condition always. The time slipped along and each one according to his allotted time was released and taken to the U.S. Marshal and there questioned in regards to paying our fines. Most of us did not have property sufficient to pay the fines. We were all glad to be out and breathe the free air again, but we did not know how soon we…[might have to] go back again on another charge. This was in the middle of summer, very warm, and much work awaiting us.[382]

What did Jens feel as the time for his own release drew near? Was Karen Marie looking forward to having him home again? Did Ane look forward to his return? Were the children excited? Several publications tell of huge "welcome home" parties being thrown by the towns to which former prisoners returned. Did Newton throw a party to welcome Jens back? Jens was released near the end of August, likely just at the time when harvest was approaching.

Jenson's *Chronology* says that on Saturday, 24 August 1889, "Jens N. Hansen was discharged from the Penitentiary."[383] The family record says, "He was released to return home on 23 August 1889."[384] I am unsure why this discrepancy exists.

How did Jens travel from the prison back to Newton? Did the prison wagon also take men *to* the train station? Would Jens have gone alone on the journey home? Who met him at the train station in Brigham, Mendon, or Logan? What emotions did he and his wives and children experience? What effect did it have on my then nine-year-old grandmother to have had her father in prison? How had the family fared with caring for the crops during those long three months?

Did Jens include his second family in his return celebrations, or did he try to downplay their role in his life in order to avoid being arrested a second time?

No mention was made of the use and care of the south farm, or hay lot, acquired by Ane on 10 April 1885, but once, in a communication of mine with Larry Christiansen, he referred to that spot of land as *JN's south farm* (Larry's father always called Jens "JN"), so we might speculate that the transaction was done in Ane's name to protect the property from confiscation by the federal government as the crusades heated up. Two months after Jens's release, on 30 October 1889, the 1885 deed for this 14.25 acres on the river south of Newton for fifty dollars was filed for record. After Ane acquired the parcel from John H. Barker, why did she wait four and a half years to file the deed? Why did this become the right time to file it? Was Jens's release the triggering factor? Or was this merely a convenient time—harvest completed and winter still a ways off—to travel to Logan to record the deed?

Jens served time in prison because he had married Ane. Was Ane an important part of his life after he was released from prison? We know she cut his hair on the porch on a regular basis, but was there more to their marriage than that? He had had three children with Ane, all of whom were young and still living in her home. Surely he would have wanted regular contact with all of them. How were their lives impacted by the tensions surrounding the polygamous life pattern? Did the two families continue to live in fear that Jens might be arrested yet again? What had Jens learned in prison that would inform the next chapter of his life? What lay in store for these people as a new decade began?

CHAPTER 20

POST-MANIFESTO POTPOURRI: 1890–1899

During the first year following Jens's incarceration, he apparently kept a
low profile, maintaining relationships with his two families, working on
his farms, supporting his wives and children, probably again teaching
Sunday School, and playing his violin for public events. Even though his prison
sentence was over, life for him and his families probably could not have felt
normal while the persecutions continued all around them, with continued risk
of a second sentence in the Pen.

Church members revered Wilford Woodruff, president of the Mormon
Church, as a living prophet. Woodruff prayed intensely, probably with a heavy
heart, for guidance from God as to what course of action should be followed by
LDS Church members. Was he supposed to lead the people to continue obeying
what they believed was a revelation from God? Or was he supposed to advise
them to obey the federal laws against polygamy and thereby disobey God's will
in order to achieve political peace?

After much prayer, President Woodruff issued the Manifesto dated 24
September 1890. A press release 26 September 1890 quoted him as saying, "I
publicly declare that my advice to the Latter-day Saints is to refrain from con-
tracting any marriages forbidden by the law of the land."[385] When this Manifesto
was presented to the people at the General Conference just over a week later on
5 October 1890, Woodruff said, in part:

> I have arrived at a point in the history of my life as the President of
> the Church of Jesus Christ of Latter-day Saints where I am under
> the necessity of acting for the temporal salvation of the Church. The
> United States government has taken a stand and passed laws to destroy
> the Latter-day Saints on the subject of polygamy or patriarchal order
> of marriage, and after praying to the Lord and feeling inspired, I have
> issued the following proclamation which is sustained by my counselors
> and the Twelve Apostles:

> Inasmuch as laws have been enacted by congress forbidding plural marriages, which laws have been pronounced constitutional by the court of last resort, I hereby declare my intention to submit to those laws, and to use my influence with the members of the Church over which I preside to have them do likewise.... And now I publicly declare that my advice to the Latter-day Saints is to refrain from contracting any marriage forbidden by the law of the land.[386]

The assembled congregation voted to accept the Manifesto. Although the people as a whole sustained the declaration and felt at peace with the change, some were disturbed by it. Some Church members felt that following the law of the land was the only choice they had and that the Manifesto was a divine injunction to put aside the previous revelation that they should live in polygamy, yet other Church members felt that the commandment to enter plural marriage was supposed to continue forever.

President Woodruff later addressed a stake conference (a meeting of all the members of the Church in a geographical area, which includes several wards) in Logan, saying:

> I have had some revelations of late, and very important ones to me, and I will tell you what the Lord has said to me. Let me bring your minds to what is termed the manifesto.... The Lord has told me to ask the Latter-day Saints a question, and He also told me that if they would listen to what I said to them and answer the question put to them, by the Spirit and power of God, they would all answer alike.... The question is this: Which is the wisest course for the Latter-day Saints to pursue—continue to attempt to practice plural marriage, with the laws of the nation against it and the opposition of 60 million people, and at the cost of the confiscation and loss of all the Temples, and the stopping of all the ordinances therein, both for the living and the dead, and the imprisonment of the First Presidency and Twelve and the heads of families...or after doing and suffering what we have through our adherence to this principle to cease the practice and submit to the law, and through doing so, leave the Prophets, Apostles and fathers at home, so that they can instruct the people and attend to the duties of the Church, and also leave the Temples in the hands of the Saints, so that they can attend to the ordinances of the Gospel, both for the living and for the dead?

The Lord showed me by vision and revelation exactly what would take place if we did not stop this practice.... This is the question I lay before the Latter-day Saints. [You have to judge for yourselves, but I want to say this. I should have let all the temples go out of our hands, I should have gone to prison myself and let every other man go there had not the God of Heaven commanded me to do what I did do.][387] [Brackets in original]

Although the federal government directed the men who had multiple wives and families to abandon all but the first wife and her children, the Church leaders told men that it would be a sin to stop providing for any of their existing families. Through my conversations with numerous people, it became apparent that the understanding many hold is that polygamy ended in its entirety with the ambiguous 1890 Manifesto. Other people believe the only thing that ended with the Manifesto was the performing of *new* plural marriages. Various sources indicate, however, that some plural marriages continued to be performed by Church authorities in secret, the Manifesto notwithstanding. One such marriage took place between Abraham Owen Woodruff—the son of President Wilford Woodruff—and Eliza Avery Clark in January 1901, after the Manifesto and while Owen was already married to Helen May Winters.[388]

The Mormon citizens of Utah Territory had a variety of reasons for desiring statehood. One was the belief that a state government would stand as a buffer between the people and the hostile federal government, thus making it easier to live their religious lives without the unchecked interference of the national government. The federal government, on the other hand, had determined to prevent statehood for Utah as long as polygamy remained an issue. The Manifesto helped pave the way to Utah's eventual statehood by apparently eliminating what was commonly referred to by those outside the LDS Church as one of the twin relics of barbarism: slavery and polygamy.

Unfortunately, the 1890 census records were seriously damaged by fire in 1921, and ordered destroyed by the government in the 1930s, so we do not know how the family was listed that year or what their living arrangements were immediately after the Manifesto.

In spite of being surrounded by the political tug-of-war, daily life continued for the people in the Church-centered communities, including Newton. Music continued to play an important part in the lives of Jens and his families. Joseph Larsen noted in his history:

> In 1890 I took some music lessons from J. N. Hansen on the violin. I learned to play second fiddle in his orchestra, which consisted of J. N. Hansen—lead violin, J. J. Larsen—second violin, James P. Hansen—Cornet, and Nephi Hansen—bass violin. We played for most of the dances, etc., until I went to college. At that time a dance ticket cost 25 cents. We began at 8:30 or 9:00 p.m. and played till 12:00 p.m. Money was scarce so [scrip] was also accepted.[389]

The membership of this musical group consisted of Joseph J. Larsen (who figures prominently in the history of the community as the author of the little green book and in relation to our family), and also Jens and two of his sons with Karen Marie: James P. (age twenty-three) and Nephi (age twelve). At first, I wondered why neither of Ane's sons were included in the orchestra, but in 1890, Eli would have been nine years old and Moses would have been eight—both probably a little young yet for musical ensembles. One Newton history says, "In 1890 an orchestra was organized which played for dances. J. N. Hansen, the lead Violinist; John Jones, second violinist; James P. Hansen, cornet; and Nephi Hansen, the bass fiddle player were the members. Later Joseph J. Larsen played second violin."[390] The difference in the roster of musicians probably reflects the situation in the moment that the writers put their information on paper.

The Hicks history says Jens "was a popular man and played music for everything.... He and his son Jens P. played for most of the dances and often played for neighboring town dances. His greatest pleasure when he was at home was to take his violin and play for hours at a time."[391]

Early in 2011, as I attempted to learn more about Jens, I felt frustrated because I had never met him, and even with all the information that was surfacing about him, I didn't have an impression of what he was like, how his voice sounded, or what his mannerisms were. I imagined him enjoying playing his violin "for hours at a time," and the thought occurred to me that I could get to know him in a sense by gaining an understanding of the instrument he loved. So I found a violin teacher, rented a violin, and began taking lessons on 2 February 2011, in my sixties. I soon learned that the instrument is addictive, and I couldn't go to bed at night without having practiced my lesson at some time during the day. I began to pay more attention to the violinists playing in the symphony, and developed a greater appreciation for the guest violinists who demonstrated stunning skill with the instrument. When my year's rental was up, I purchased a finer quality violin and continued with lessons for a few more years. I will never be a great violinist, but I have developed further admiration for Jens by engaging with the instrument he loved, and I have come to love it as well.

✺

One evening in the spring of 2011, I did an internet search for a specific piece of information, but what came up instead was an article that said Jens Niels Hansen from Logan, Utah, had served a mission to Denmark. I was shocked because I had never heard lore of Jens having served a mission or of having lived in Logan. I owned a hard copy of the book the article came from, *Legacy of Sacrifice: Missionaries to Scandinavia 1872–1894*, so I looked Jens up, and it did indeed say that my great-grandfather had served a mission, arriving in Copenhagen 28 September 1890 and departing Copenhagen 4 February 1892. The article gave all the correct information as to Jens's parents' names, his place of birth, his first wife, Karen Marie with marriage date and place, his second wife, Ane with marriage date and place, and a third wife, Orilie, who was not Jens's wife but was actually the wife of his brother Hans. The brief biography was accurate. [392]

Why, I wondered, was he living in Logan at the time? And why did this mission *not* appear in family lore? To leave two families to travel back to his homeland of Denmark and serve as a missionary for two years would have been a major embarkation on many levels, including the separation from family and consequent financial concerns for all. During the era of imprisonments for unlawful cohabitation, some men were called on missions not only to serve God and the LDS Church but also to provide escape from arrest, trial, and imprisonment. Was this one of those missions, even though it had begun on the cusp of the Manifesto?

When I telephoned LaRelia, she was as shocked as I was. We conferred and felt we needed to find out exactly what this meant, even to find the ship manifests showing whether Jens had indeed made such voyages. She searched her local LDS Family History Center in Ogden and talked to a volunteer there who said that in the early days of the Church, each missionary had an index card that was filled out and signed and put in a card file. A few days before leaving for Utah in June 2011, I telephoned the LDS Church History Library in Salt Lake and asked where I might find that card file. The woman on the phone said those cards had all been put on microfilm that was stored right behind the desk just inside the door, and for me to ask at the desk when I arrived.

The people in the Church History Library at Salt Lake were kind and helpful, and directed me immediately to the microfilm. Two cards for Jens Niels Hansen, each referring to line items in a large ledger, were found on microfilm and brought to me in the library's reading room. The lines in the ledger revealed that both index cards referred to one man by the same name as my ancestor, but who was *not* my ancestor. This man *did* live in Logan, and his birth and other data differed from that of our Jens. Someone had erroneously entered my ancestor's information forever into the book, *Legacy of Sacrifice: Missionaries to Scandinavia 1872–1894.*[393] This book is published online in its entirety as well as in a handsome hardback, so the error is public and confusing. I include this information here to set the record straight for those who might find this erroneous information and accept it without question. There is no reliable evidence that Jens Niels Hansen from Newton served a mission to Denmark from 1890 to 1892, or ever.

❧

The Edmunds Act of 1882 contained a provision that declared the children of plural wives ineligible to inherit upon the death of their father. This provision attached to Ane's children, all of whom were born before 1 January 1883, the definitive date decreed by this legislation. About four months after the Manifesto, another decision was rendered, and this one was called to my attention by a journal entry of Abraham H. Cannon on 20 January 1891. This action shed interesting light on the legal currents still swirling at that post-Manifesto time:

> A very important ruling was rendered in the U.S. Supreme Court at Washington [D.C.] yesterday by the new Justice [Henry B.] Brown, this being the first opinion he has rendered since his appointment. The Territorial courts held in the case of the [Francis] Cope children, that they could not inherit from their father's estates, they being the issue of a polygamous marriage. This decision is reversed, and in accordance with the provisions of the Edmunds Law, all children born previous to Jan. 1st, 1883, are declared legitimate, and entitled to a share in the father's estate. This ruling is of great importance to the Saints, and settles many questions. No dissent is mentioned by any of the judges.[394]

This new ruling, then, released the "noninheritors" classification attached to Ane's children as well as to all other Mormon children who were born before 1 January 1883 and whose mothers were plural wives. Ane's youngest child, Moses, had been born just three months before the 1883 effective cutoff date of the noninheriting policy. With reversal of that decision, Moses would have been eligible to inherit from his father's estate if he had not unfortunately predeceased his father. Jens and Ane's other two children were eligible.

❧

The federal government continued to arrest and imprison polygamist men after the Manifesto, though not as frequently as before it. Rosa Mae Evans's list shows approximately 136 men newly imprisoned between the Manifesto and 1895, with 21 men in 1890 after the declaration, 45 in 1891, 33 in 1892, 23 in 1893, 13 in 1894, and 1 in 1895.[395] Even so, Jens must have felt fairly safe from being arrested again, safe enough that he no longer needed the protection of nonpolygamist ownership of his farm. On 21 August 1891, James P. Hansen and his wife, Mary C. Hansen, reconveyed the 158.89 acres of homestead farm to James (our Jens) N. Hansen for the sum of one hundred dollars. Amos Clarke, Justice of the Peace, witnessed the signatures. (Both Jens the father and Jens the son sometimes used James as their name, but no information was found to indicate what determined when they chose to do so.) This deed was filed for record six years later on 28 October 1897. When the farm was conveyed back to the senior Jens, he had been out of prison for two years and likely had been working on this plot of farmland with his son in the interim.

❧

When Jens and Karen Marie with their two children, and Karen Marie's brother Lars, with his family, emigrated from Denmark to America aboard the SS *Idaho* in 1875, Andrew Jenson traveled aboard the same ship as a returning missionary from the Aalborg Conference. Jenson was appointed Captain of the Guard over the group of emigrating Saints. Did Jenson and Jens's family meet during the voyage?

If so, perhaps they recognized each other when Jenson visited Newton nearly two decades later. The Newton Ward Records note the following:

> In November, 1891, Elder Andrew Jenson visited Cache Valley in the interest of Church history. He held a public meeting with the saints at Newton Sunday, November 29th, and the following day he met with the old settlers and others for the purpose of obtaining the needed historical information.[396]

Andrew Jenson, then assistant Church historian, wrote the following biographical sketch of Jens Nielsen Hansen that family lore says was the result of an interview between the two men on the above-referenced occasion.

JENS NIELSEN HANSEN

A leading Elder in the Newton Ward, Cache County, Utah, was born June 16, 1842, in Axelholm, Holbæk amt, Denmark. When he was six years old his Mother died, but in his father's second marriage he was blessed with a good stepmother. He obtained a common school education and studied music for two years. In 1864, 1865, and 1866 he performed military service in the interest of his native country. April 19, 1867, he married Karen Marie Christensen, who subsequently bore him ten children. Becoming a convert to "Mormonism," he was baptized April 20, 1868; he was ordained a Teacher September 12, 1869, and labored in that office until August 31, 1872, when he was ordained an Elder by Niels Nielsen and called to preside over a branch of the Church on the island of Zealand. He emigrated with his wife and three children to Utah in 1875 and settled in Newton, Cache County, where he has since resided. The next year he became a member of the Newton choir as a tenor singer. In 1877, he was called to act as a Ward Teacher. November 15, 1878, he yielded obedience to the law of plural marriage by taking to wife Ane Margrethe Sorensen, by whom he had three children. From 1879 to 1899 [date shown in source although the interview took place in 1891] he labored as a Sunday School teacher. October 25, 1885, he was ordained a Seventy [an office or level in the higher or Melchizedek priesthood] by Andrew Higgie, of Clarkston. During the anti-polygamy raid he was forced on the "underground" and endured much hardship and exposure and was finally arrested March 27, 1889, on the charge of unlawful cohabitation. After trial, he was convicted and served in the Utah penitentiary from May 25, 1889, to August 25, 1889. In a secular capacity Elder Hansen had acted as school trustee, postmaster, vice president in the Newton Irrigation Company, member of the town board, etc., and has always taken an active part in public affairs generally.[397]

Soon to become acquainted with Jens and his families was a young man named Henry Albert Bjorkman (age fifteen) who, along with his brother Walter (age seventeen), decided in 1892 to come to America from Denmark to be near the Mormon Church, leaving on 9 June 1892 and arriving in Logan on 5 July 1892. When Henry had heard the teachings of the missionaries from the Church of Jesus Christ of Latter-day Saints, he had chosen to be baptized on 10 February 1892 "in the ocean bordering the south of the city of Copenhagen. The ice was a foot thick and a hole was cut in order to make a suitable place for the event.... the part of the ocean was called Kalvebostrand."[398] Henry's baptism was performed "that night at 11 PM"[399] because persecution still followed the members in Scandinavia. Therefore, meetings and baptisms continued to be held at night to avoid disruptions and confrontations.[400]

My mother said that Henry (her father) was the only Mormon in his entire school of 1,500 students in Copenhagen. What would it take for a fifteen-year-old boy to walk out on foot-thick ice to a freshly cut hole and be immersed in ice-cold water for baptism, then to sit on a block of ice while the elders laid their hands on his head to confirm him a member of the Church of Jesus Christ of Latter-day Saints? The elder who performed the baptism must have been equally chilled. What did Henry know and feel at such a young age that gave him such courage and fortitude?

Our family has wondered whether Jens sent for Henry to come to America as he, in all likelihood, had sent for Ane in 1878 and later *did* send for Carl Jorgensen in 1902. Henry's brother Oscar, who came to America in 1890 and settled in Logan, states in his previously mentioned journal, "My two brothers, Walt and Henry, for whose emigration I sent the money, came second-class."[401] But the biographical sketch of Henry's mother, Marie Persson Poulson Bjorkman, states that when she and her daughter arrived in Logan in June of 1897, her "son Oscar was residing in Logan where he operated a knitting mill that wove a fabric used to make underwear. Son Henry was living in Newton, a few miles west of Logan, where he was employed by Jens Nielsen Hansen,"[402] possibly to work off his indenture. Oscar doesn't indicate how much of his brothers' passage he paid, so we don't know what portion Jens may have contributed.

In addition, Grant Larsen told LaRelia during that earlier-referenced winter meeting 1 November 1994 in Newton Cemetery, "Apparently Mr. Hansen had paid at least part of Henry's passage to the United States, and Henry was obligated to work off that investment. Such sponsorship was common in those days." Jens may have asked someone in or traveling to Denmark to find a Mormon youth for him without asking for Henry specifically, as Henry was from Copenhagen and not from Jens's area of Denmark. LaRelia further commented: "Henry's 1905 application for citizenship includes an affidavit from Eli [Jens and Ane's son], saying he had known Henry for 13 years, indicating that upon Henry's arrival in 1892, he immediately became acquainted with Jens's family."[403]

Perhaps Henry lived with Ane's family while he worked for Jens. Other arrangements may have been made for his lodging, but he associated with the Hansens and over the years developed quite a liking for my future grandmother, Sophia, who was twelve years old upon his arrival.

❧

A year later on 25 October 1893, the deed to Ane's house finally became official. The deed had been drawn up on 20 April 1882 for the lots upon which Ane's house stands and was filed in Logan, thereby making Ane the owner of record. The deed had existed and been unrecorded for eleven years. What precipitated its recording now? Where had Ane secreted it for safekeeping all those years?

❧

Education was a value in Cache Valley, and a college had been established in Logan, Utah, in 1888. Nephi Hansen, son of Jens and Karen Marie, attended college as noted in Joseph Larsen's history. Larsen attended the school, and Nephi Hansen played a role in his life:

> The Agricultural College of Utah [now Utah State University] had begun. Hyrum [Larsen's brother] attended first, 1893–1894.... The next fall we both attended.... On January 18, 1895, we rented a home of Mrs. Fred Smith. J.C. Hogensen, Nephi Hansen, Brother Hyrum, and I batched and went to school winter quarter.
>
> We had military drill half an hour every day.... Nephi Hansen suggested I go with him to band practice. I liked that better than drill, so I took the snare drum and played with the band the rest of the year. Nephi played an alto horn.... In mid-winter the band went to Paradise [a small town nearby] to play at the invitation of John Roberts. We attended a dance there and remained overnight. Nephi Hansen and I were invited to Sarah Mitten's home. The Paradise people treated us royally. We came home in a sleigh drawn by four head of horses. All enjoyed it.[404]

I love this personal journal that provides details about Jens's son Nephi, his involvement with music while acquiring education, and his influencing Joseph Larsen to join the band. Jens's filling his home with strains from his violin must have instilled an appreciation for music in his children.

Jens continued to be actively involved in the community through his lifelong love of music. An email from Larry Christiansen stated: "In the Newton Ward Records is this notation—board of directors moved that J. N. Hansen to play for all national holidays and every third Friday evening for the season. The last reference specifically to a month[ly] dance."[405] Larry's father said J. N. was a fine musician.[406]

Political foment over whether the Territory of Utah could become a state continued unabated into the early 1890s. Over time, however, the tensions relaxed, and by the mid-1890s, with the Manifesto having been in place for five years and the LDS people apparently conforming to the demands of those outside the Church, opposition weakened. At last Utah was granted statehood on 4 January 1896.

Newton people expressed their jubilation over statehood—as did those in other Utah communities—with whistles, other noisemakers, and maybe a band playing. Jens and his families perhaps took part in the celebrations and were pleased and optimistic about this political event easing the stress on their complicated polygamous lives.

Six months later, the first Fourth of July observance after statehood was described in an article on 16 July 1896, from the *Journal*, giving the flavor of such community observances as well as the prose style of that era. Jens, Karen Marie, Ane, and their children likely attended this event:

> Editor Journal: Again and with not less enthusiasm do we celebrate the Fourth of July, and not a heart but what beats with emotion, not a child but whose eyes brighten, as they stand beneath the protecting folds of the glorious flag, and realize that it is the Fourth of July.
>
> The day was heralded forth by a volley at sunrise, which awoke our peaceful little town into a wild tumult. The parade was at 10 a.m. after which, at the meeting house [church or chapel], a very interesting program was rendered.
>
> First was the reading of the Declaration of Independence by Moroni Beck, this was followed by a song, after which a paper on "The Events which led up to the Revolutionary War" was read by Chris Hogensen, which, to say the least, was fine. After music by the organ and mandolin the orator of the day, William Nelson, was introduced and listened to with great interest. Next was a quartette followed by a recitation by little Miss Elva Nelson which was splendid. Joseph. J. Larsen's stump speech was, as it always is, good and very humorous.
>
> At 2 p.m. was a children's dance, after which the Newton and Petersboro [small town south of Newton] nines played a match game of base ball, resulting in a score of 32 to 19 in favor of Newton.
>
> The ball at night was very crowded, there being so many strangers present; yet all seemed to enjoy it.

About sundown two rickly [*sic*] decorated floats from Clarkston swooped down upon us, one, it was said, contained the Goddess in full dress which they had evidently brought down to show us. Last Tuesday evening the Y.L.M.I.A. [Young Ladies Mutual Improvement Association] gave a grand ball, cake, ice cream and strawberries were served as refreshments and all seemed to have a delightful time.[407]

The people of Newton probably assembled as families with children of all ages for the enjoyment of this great event: the cannon, the clapping, the games, the treats, and the music! Perhaps Jens played his violin for the ball that evening.

Jens's increased participation in community and political affairs after statehood may have been possible partially because he no longer needed to hide so carefully from the marshals, or because his children had grown old enough to help more on the farm, or because he had learned new skills through his challenging difficulties. Whatever the influences, he appears to have been freer to act in public affairs.

One example of Jens's community activities was his running for the position of trustee on the Newton School Board shortly after that July 4th celebration in 1896. Also running were Peter E. Benson and Andrew Petersen. "The opposition ticket was Peter E. Benson [who ran on both tickets], George Rigby, and John Carsen [*sic*—Larsen]."[408]

The results of the election were recorded in the Trustees Record Book and show that Jens was among the three men who were elected as trustees in the Newton School District:

School election July 13, 1896. Most of the old trustees tossed out with some anger and a new slate of candidates nominated. In the election 102 people voted including at least 36, possibly 39, women.

Peter E. Benson	101
Andrew Petersen	68
Jens N. Hansen	66
George Rigby	36
John Larsen	34
James F. Hansen	1

The top three were elected trustees.[409]

There seems to have been quite a bit of emotion attached to this particular town election, and on 18 July, the *Journal* carried more information with additional commentary. The voting tally herein was identical to that in the previous report and has been omitted from the following:

> Never before was such an interest made manifest in a school election as was the case yesterday. As was reported to THE JOURNAL a primary was held some time ago and a citizen's school ticket nominated. The ticket did not seem to suit certain parties in town, and the last few days before the election it was rumored that an opposition ticket was in progress of preparation, and yesterday it was proved to be true. The opposition worked like beavers to down the citizens tickets, but alas it was all in vain, and the underhanded game met the fate it deserved. 102 votes were cast, 39 of which were by ladies. The following is the votes cast for the several candidates. The first three being the citizen's ticket.... The large number of votes cast for Mr. Benson is on account of his name being retained on the opposition ticket. At night the annual meeting was held, and after the several reports were presented the old school board received thanks for their labors in the shape of adverse criticisms and insults by members of the defeated opposition, and thus ended the school election in 1896.[410]

The election hints at dissatisfaction with the prior office holders and/or the opposition party but gives no details to clarify our understanding of the issues.

Four months after Jens's election as a school trustee, his involvement appears in the school notes for 13 November 1896:

> Prymary [*sic*] schoolroom too crowded. The meeting discussed the overcrowded condition in the primary school room. J. N. Hansen thought more room could be got by taking down the partition in the west building and move it south 8 feet and this would increase the size of the primary school room to the north, and then fix up the south room for an entrance for the two schools. This he believed would not cost much and would save paying a salary for another teacher. The board favored the idea and thought a tax of ½ of 1% would cover the cost. However, the janitor complained that the modification made three rooms instead of two to clean, and so he received $10 per quarter instead of $8.00.[411]

As a retired teacher, I find it amusing that the same area of floor, divided further, would cost more to clean. It reminds me of some of the picayune things that still go on in education systems, and I shake my head in disbelief. Jens's problem-solving and money-saving were creative.

Jens continued his advocacy for education, as noted in a history of Cache Valley that gives a glimpse into his character and his concerns:

> It must be remembered that the Newton School ran largely on borrowed money in the early years, and even the trustees were forced by the voters to take cuts on occasion in their $10.00 per year salaries. In view of the financial stringency, it is interesting to read under date of December 17, 1897:

>> J. N. Hansen said that Widow Christensen had a Girl go to School but she is without Books and hir Mother the Widow are unable to by books for the Girl. after some Consideration the Secretary was atorised to by the necessary Books and Charge to the Schoolboard, and allso a Geographi for Widow Carolin Christensens Boy David.[412]

I must confess to a certain curiosity as to who this Widow Christensen was and why Jens was looking out for her and her daughter. Was she merely an acquaintance in town for whom he felt a human concern? Or was she special to him in some way? Was the first-mentioned Widow Christensen the same person as the later-mentioned Widow Carolin Christensen? Or were they different women? The rumor that Jens had additional wives whom we could not find kept me vigilant for clues.

※

Jens began his career as postmaster on 17 June 1899, when he was appointed to the office at the age of fifty-seven. Previously, the mail had been received at and dispensed from the homes of the postmasters, but Jens built the first post office building, a wooden structure on what was then called Main Street but has been changed to Center Street. The post office sat directly across the street from what was the library and courthouse as of 2018.

A letter to Larry Christiansen from Maud Barker further elaborated on the postal service:

I remember when J. N. Hansen was Postmaster, when the "Peoples Store" was built.... I remember the ice house built back of the Peoples Store, where blocks of ice cut and hauled from the river were packed in sawdust, and much of it was used for mak[ing] ice cream on the 4th and 24th of July.

Then Peter Christensen who lived way out in the west part of Town—he handled the mail for 7 years then it was moved back in the center of town at the home of Peter Jensen (our neighbor to the south) The south half of his porch was covered in and his daughter Sarah was often at the window. Next J. N. Hansen became the Postmaster and built a small building just south of the Griffin Store. I well remember him—he served till 1905 then record says Ephraim Schneider served from 1906 to 1908.[413]

A daughter of James Peter Jensen, who was postmaster before Jens, said, "I think J. N. Hansen had the P.O. after we did. He built a little building North of Barkers (Barkers was just north of us). Our house was located across the street to the East from the old rock church."[414]

The structure that Jens built for the post office was used until 1914, when a new building was constructed. The following compliment appeared in a newspaper report of Newton: "Our post office is in charge of Mr. J. N. Hansen, who is a most courteous and capable official."[415] What a lovely tribute. I wish I could have met and conversed with him.

Photographs of the wooden post office Jens built appear in books and in our family photo collections. Originally we thought the post office had been built where the current post office is located, on Main Street in Newton, but photos displayed in the Newton Town Library one summer showed the post office, along with the stores constructed near it, on what is now Center Street. Cleo explained the name changes of the streets and corrected our family's misconception.

Further evidence of Jens's community involvement and desire to make improvements in the school appear in this note: "J. N. Hansen thought it necessary to buy $20.00 of water rights for the school lot in order to 'comply with law in planting shade trees.' Also the trustees to put up a 'good bell' on the school building."[416]

Jens seemed to have had many good ideas and a concern for others. The Newton Ward Records show that Jens blessed (or christened) most of his babies at home, indicating that he also had the heart of a gentle father for his children.

✤

Frequently the stories of polygamous families indicate favoritism for one family over the others. Ane's son Eli is the subject of a life sketch written by his daughter, Leora. She records that Eli had wanted to go on a mission for the LDS Church but there was not enough money for him to do so. Eli's half brother Nephi, however, served in the Northwestern States Mission from 15 June 1898 to 7 February 1900.[417] In regard to Eli's thwarted desire to serve a mission, one wonders whether the children of the first wife in the polygamous families commonly received preferential treatment. Perhaps Nephi worked and saved the money to go on a mission, so it may not have been favoritism. Even so, I feel sad that Eli was denied his desired mission.

While Nephi was away, both of Jens's families had photos taken in which it appears that Jens sat in one place while the members of one family settled around him for a flash, and then stepped away for the other family to file in for a similar portrait. In the family photo taken of Jens and Karen Marie and three of their living children, Nephi's portrait is a small inset on the upper right corner with a notation on the back of the photo saying he was serving at the time in the mission field. For a long while, we could not date those photos, but because Nephi's missionary index card was in the Church History Library in Salt Lake, we now can date the photos as having been taken between 15 June 1898 and 7 February 1900. These are the only photos we have of the two families. At the time of the photo, all of Ane's three children were living, and four of Jens and Karen Marie's ten children were living. I have no photos of Jens and Karen Marie's six children who died.

✤

A large photograph circa 1899 shows a festive gathering inside a large room—maybe in the school or the church in Newton. Tables are covered with white cloths and set with fancy-folded napkins, and the room is bedecked with bunting swags. Many women wear elaborate hats with their lovely dresses, and the few men present appear in suits. The people are either standing around the room or are seated at the tables. They are too small to recognize. However, in the complete list of names under the photo, Ane, Karen Marie, and Louisa (Karen Marie's first daughter) are together, and Elvena (Karen Marie's other daughter) is in another part of the room, possibly with her friends.[418] That the two wives chose to stand or be seated together at a fête of some kind, after the Manifesto and while Jens was still living, indicates that they at least were not at enmity with each other and may even have had a friendship of sorts before his death. LaRelia mentioned in a phone conversation with me on 12 July 2012, that it would have made it easier for Karen Marie to be friends with Ane if Ane and Jens were emotionally divorced. If the rumors were true that Ane had put him out and they were no longer sexually intimate—as one might conclude with three babies, each one year apart, and then no more children for Ane, while Karen Marie continued to have babies—the hostility that some plural wives sometimes struggled with might have been ameliorated for these two women.

❧

Though the Manifesto and statehood had changed things in Utah, the following newspaper clipping from 1899 under the heading "Owen's Cache County Raid" shows that polygamy problems still bubbled:

> The subheading read: Forwards a Long List of Accused Person[s] to Attorney Nebeker. "Wants them all arrested. Includes Many Prominent Northern Utah Citizens...."
> Logan, Nov. 28—County Attorney Nebeker this morning received Charles Mostyn Owen's much heralded list of complaints against Cache County citizens, who are accused of violating the marriage laws. "Apostle Merrill is charged with unlawful cohabitation with Sarah Ann Merrill, Cyrene Stanley, Jennie Jacobson and Mrs. Toronto...C.O. Card with Sarah J. Paynter, Zina Y. Card, and Lavinia Rigby...John Jenkins of Newton with Mary O. Jenkins, Annie C. Jenkins and Martha Jenkins...William Griffin of Newton with Elizabeth Jenkins and Elizabeth Clark."[419]

Some of these men had already served time for unlawful cohabitation according to the list from Rosa Mae Evans,[420] yet they were again being pursued.

Obviously, the hostility toward Mormons had not totally gone away. In spite of the Manifesto and statehood, there seemed to be an uneasy center of gravity as Jens and his two families moved into the twentieth century. Jens and Karen Marie's oldest three children had become adults, with Jens Peter and his wife having children twelve, ten, six, four, and two years of age. Nephi had married, gone on a mission, and then he and his wife had lost their first baby. Louisa had married. Ane's daughter, Sophia, was nineteen years old and probably being courted by Henry Bjorkman. Ane's son Eli was eighteen years old, and her son Moses seventeen years of age. Jens, Karen Marie, and Ane were all in their late fifties as they entered a new era of inventions and conveniences that would change their lifestyle. The community would also be changed by more secular influences arriving in town. The domestic front seemed to be floating on more tranquil waters as the Hansen polygamous unions glided into calmer post-Manifesto circumstances.

CHAPTER 21

TRANSITIONS 1900–1906

ens, Karen Marie, and Ane entered the new century with their extended family of married children and young grandchildren, accompanied by the joys and challenges of both family life and the conditions of the times. Jens continued to be active in church and community affairs and appeared in numerous newspaper pieces.

Ten years after the Manifesto, the 1900 census shows James (Jens) N. as "head" with Karen as wife followed only by Elvena as daughter. Next, Annie (this is the same spelling as on Jens's probate documents and on her headstone) is listed as "head" followed by Sophia as daughter, Eli as son, and Moses as son. This confirms that in 1900 the families were in separate residences and Ane was not listed as a wife but instead as the head of a household. Jens and Karen Marie's three older children were out of the home and on their own.

One newspaper article states that on 5 February 1900, "Mr. J. N. Hanson [*sic*], on behalf of the residents of Newton, petitioned the commissioners to grant them the privilege of incorporation [*sic*] their town as a village. This petition was taken under advisement."[421]

One month after Jens's petition for incorporation, the newspaper declared on 13 March 1900:

> Newton Incorporated...March 12—The county commissioners today granted the petition of the citizens of Newton for a village corporation. The officers of the town will consist of a president, secretary and three trustees, who will be appointed by the county court to serve until the next county election.[422]

The men who were selected to fill the Newton Town Board positions were Charles M. Christensen, president; John E. Griffin, secretary; and J. N. Hansen, William J. Barker, and John Benson as councilmen or trustees.[423] The minutes of the first meeting on 23 April 1900 state:

Prayer was offered by C. M Christensen. A code of rules governing meetings of Board were adopted. The following committees were appointed:…Committee on Ordinances John E. Griffin, John Benson, J.N. Hansen. Committee on Nominations[:] William J. Barker, John E. Griffin. Meeting adjourned for one week. Prayer by J. N. Hansen.[424]

Newton was incorporated, and the governing body was in place and functioning. At the next Town Board meeting on 1 May 1900, John E. Griffin offered the opening prayer, or invocation, and the minutes of the previous meeting were accepted. The minutes continue:

Committees on ordinances and nominations were ready to report. An ordinance relating to poll tax was passed. Committee on nominations recommended as officers and which was unanimously adopted by board[:] Jas Parsens [as] Road supervisor, John Benson [as] Marshall, J. N. Hansen as pound keeper. Meeting adjourned until May-9-1900. Ben[ediction] Wm. J. Barker.[425]

As pound keeper, Jens was charged with the care of stock animals impounded by the community for running at large, trespassing, or carrying infection. The animals had to be kept safely caged until their rightful owner could be found to collect them and to pay a fee, if necessary.

An item accredited to Jens—the first of quite a number—appeared in the 15 May 1900 edition of the *Deseret Evening News* under the headline "Temperatures Up and Down" and indicated that he had become a reporter giving agricultural updates from Newton to the Logan newspaper: "'Newton, Cache Co.—Warm the first part of the week. High winds on the 11th, followed by heavy rain which continued into the 12th. No damage from the wind. No frosts. Grain and grass are growing very fast.' —J. N. Hansen."[426]

Logan is located about sixteen miles southeast of Newton. Did Jens travel that distance on horseback? If a horse averaged four miles an hour with a rider, the trip would have taken approximately four hours one way. Allowing time for Jens to report, do errands, maybe visit with friends, and then ride the four hours back, that would have been a long day. Or did Jens travel by train from Cache Junction to Logan to give his reports to the newspaper? Either way, he spent enough time in Logan that he was recognized in town.

The following are extracts of minutes from Newton Town Board meetings at which Jens was present, along with some notes here and there from the author:

- Town Board minutes 16 May 1900: "J. N. Hansen and Wm J. Barker were appointed to look up the matter of taxation."[427]
- Town Board minutes 23 May 1900: The Committee on Taxation reported "that they believed no taxes could be collected. Matter laid over for one week.... Ben[ediction] by J. N. Hansen."[428]

Jens played an active part in the Town Board meeting on 27 June 1900:

J. N. Hansen moved that we levy a tax of 2 ½ mills on all property assessed in Newton town [cor]poration. This motion was carried. J. N. Hansen said that he would like to see something done to improve the sidewalks as they were now impassable. C. M. Christensen thought that the season was too busy to accomplish much in that line. J. N. Hansen moved that the committee on ordinances frame an ordinance on that subject.[429]

The next Town Board minutes record that on 13 July 1900: "Prayer was offered by J. N. Hansen" and "J. N. Hansen was released from being town pound keeper and John Benson was appointed in his stead."[430]

An extra session of the Town Board was called on 11 September 1900:

Prayer was offered by J. N. Hansen. C. M. Christensen stated that the purpose of meeting was to consider quarantine. The matter was talked over and a motion [was made. A] board of health was appointed to consist of one of the Lady doctors and two of the town board: Mary B Larsen [later shown as health officer 10 April 1901], Wm J. Barker and J. N. Hansen.[431]

That a special meeting had been called to consider quarantine indicates that a disease of concern was affecting the town.

Following the 24 September 1900 resignation of Town Board President Charles M. Christensen,[432] J. N. Hansen presided at the Town Board meeting held 26 September 1900. "Quarantine was again discussed but laid over," and J. N. Hansen gave the benediction.[433]

More meetings where Jens exhibited leadership include:

- Town Board minutes 10 October 1900: Meeting began with the invocation by Jens Hansen.[434]
- Town Board minutes 17 October 1900: Jens presided.[435]
- Town Board minutes 24 October 1900: "Prayer by J. N. Hansen.... Wm J. Barker and J.N. Hansen were nominated for President of Board. Wm J. Barker was elected. A report from pound keeper was read and accepted, showing a net revenue of $34.60, which was turned over to treasurer."[436]
- Town Board minutes 31 October 1900: A special committee was appointed to draft ordinances on sidewalks, cutting shiners [spinning circles in the snow or ice], fast driving [horse-drawn buggies?], and destruction of property.[437]
- Town Board minutes 14 November 1900: J. N. Hansen gave the invocation, then the "special committee on ordinances presented one on sidewalks and other matters referred to them. The ordinance was passed as presented. The matter of ditches was laid over until next meeting."[438]
- Town Board minutes 28 November 1900: J. N. Hansen "wished to know concerning poll tax. It was all in save a few who had promised to work here in town. The matter of straightening ditches was discussed and regulations made regarding same, which was added to ordinance on sidewalks etc."[439]
- Town Board minutes 12 December 1900: J. N. Hansen said the opening prayer. The board discussed closing the schools but took no action.[440] [Was this possibly still related to an epidemic of some type?]

Also that month, Henry Albert Bjorkman, who had immigrated to America in 1892 and apparently worked off his indenture to Jens, married Karen Sophia Hansen (Jens and Ane's daughter) on 19 December 1900 in the Logan LDS Temple. LaRelia said they walked to the temple because they were both living in Logan. Sophia was nineteen years old. She and Henry lived for a while in Logan with his mother, Marie Poulson Bjorkman, who had followed her sons to America, leaving her husband, Godtfred, in Denmark. Godtfred chose never to leave his homeland.

Town Board minutes for the first meeting of the New Year, 2 January 1901, note that "J. N. Hansen presided [and] was appointed to see what arrangements could be made in regard to procuring a doctor in case Board of Health needed one at any time."[441]

Jens made another appearance in Logan on 10 January 1901 to report to the newspaper: "'Newton—Less water flowing from the springs than at any time during the past fifteen years. The water in the wells has raised a little during the last month.' — J. N. Hansen."[442] This news must have been somewhat alarming, as the people were dependent upon water for their crops and survival. The reservoir constructed in 1872 must have helped in this regard.

Minutes referring to Jens continue:

- Town Board minutes 16 January 1901: "Prayer by J. N. Hansen.... J. N. Hansen reported his labors with doctor but the matter was again referred to him." [443]
- Town Board minutes 30 January 1901: "J. N. Hansen reported that Dr. Crexall would come to Newton and visit for one hour for $10, and for $7 for successive trips."[444]
- Town Board minutes 13 February 1901: Prayer by J. N. Hansen.[445]
- Town Board minutes 27 February 1901: A motion of J. N. Hansen, treasurer, was authorized to pay fees and cost of court in Christensen case.[446]

From this February meeting until minutes in 1902, no mention is made of prayers at the meetings. Perhaps the minute takers or the minute transcribers just omitted them. It seems unlikely that prayers in an LDS community meeting would have been abandoned.

- Town Board minutes 20 March 1901: "Geo. Parsens was allowed $5 for quarantine services. J. N. Hansen and G. Parsens [were] appointed to draw up plat and hand to assessor for filing. A motion: J. N. Hansen was authorized to purchase town seal."[447]
- Town Board minutes 10 April 1901: "Mary B. Larsen was allowed $7. for services as health officer. J. N. Hansen was allowed $10. [for the] same work. John Benson was allowed $20. for quarantine services. Pound keeper gave a report showing $3.80 net profit. Estray pound matters were talked over."[448] Still the issue of quarantine was active in the community.

- Town Board minutes 14 May 1901: "Town seal was handed over to Clerk. [Probably it was J. N. Hansen who handed it over, since he was the one authorized to purchase it.] A notice was sent to [the] irrigation company that all unnecessary cross ditches must be abandoned."[449]
- Town Board minutes 15 July 1901: "J. N. Hansen was appointed to look after streets and sidewalks."[450]

A newspaper carried this notice on 4 September 1901:

> "Remarks of Crop Correspondents. Newton.—Week warm and dry. Threshing goes on rapidly. Grain yield about average. The cutting of Lucerne both for hay and seed is making rapid progress. No fall plowing done yet." —J. N. Hansen.[451]

In spite of the flow from the springs being less that year than in fifteen years, the grain yield was within a normal range.

No Town Board minutes were recorded between the July 15 and October 17 meetings. Perhaps August and September kept the men busy with harvesting. Our next Town Board minutes in which Jens appears are from 17 October 1901: "Judges of Election" were appointed. Also, "The treasurer was authorized to pay Smiths printing bill. Geo Parsens turned over his accounts to J. N. Hansen, the new treasurer."[452]

❧

Just a week later, Jens and Ane's third child, Moses, became ill with typhoid fever at the age of nineteen years. Data regarding the disease in Utah was apparently not recorded until 1906,[453] but likely Moses's case did not occur in isolation. According to a written history from my mother's sister Eleda, Moses died a few days before his scheduled wedding to Ida Jenkins,[454] daughter of John Jenkins and his second wife, Annie Clarke.

One source shows Moses's death on 25 October 1901, and another says it was on the 24th. A newspaper excerpt sent to me by Larry Christiansen reads:

> Moses Hanson [*sic*], son of J. N. and Annie Hanson [*sic*] of Newton died at their home Oct. 25 of typhoid fever. He was born Oct. 7, 1882. He was an exemplary young man, and his death is a great loss to his parents and friends.[455]

The article touches me because it makes Moses a real person instead of just a name on the family charts. The wording "their home" rather than "her" home hints that perhaps Jens and Ane, contrary to our assumption that they were estranged, may still have been inhabiting her home together, at least part of the time.

❧

A week after the loss of a son he had created with Ane, Jens showed up for his responsibilities as a member of the Town Board.

- Town Board minutes 30 October 1901: "The general condition of the town was talked over but no business was transacted. J. N. Hansen was authorized to pay all outstanding accounts."[456]
- Town Board minutes 23 November 1901: The treasurer was authorized "to send another notice to delinquent tax payers."[457]
- Town Board minutes 14 December 1901: "The final meeting of old Board was held.... All outstanding accounts were settled. All agreed to meet with the new board."[458]

Here J. N. Hansen disappears from the Town Board minutes, probably because his appointment was up, but the Town Board itself continued.

❧

Carl Jorgensen is often mentioned in conjunction with our family. Although he is unrelated to us, Jens sponsored him to come from Denmark in 1902. The Jorgensen family history says Carl worked for and lived with Jens until his marriage in February 1907. Jens, however, died in January 1906. I have seen no record that Carl continued to work for the adult children who inherited sections of Jens's farm.

The Jorgensen family history expands on the verbal information LaRelia, Carla, and I received about Carl during the earlier mentioned visit with his grandson Gary Jorgensen and Gary's wife, Lois, in their home in Newton:

At this time…many people who had immigrated to America would pave the way for others still in Denmark to come to this country in return for working for that person until the transportation money was paid back.

Chris Larsen who had immigrated to America in 1868 visited Denmark in August of 1902. On his visit to his native land he was looking for a boy to come to Utah and live with the J. N. Hansen family.

Carl had joined the Mormon church on Feb. 26, 1899 and he was acquainted with Holger Larsen who was one of the authorities in the Danish Mission at that time.

It was Holger Larsen who Chris Larsen approached about helping him find a boy to come to Utah. Carl was given this opportunity and was excited about the chance to come to America and get away from his cruel taskmaster [a shoemaker he was apprenticed to]. Carl's father [his mother had died when he was young] was quite hesitant about letting his son go and he did not give his consent immediately, but just before Chris Larsen was to return to America he gave his consent and Carl left his native land of Denmark at the age of eighteen.

Carl came to America by himself, not in company of missionaries or any other folks. He arrived in Cache Junction, Utah by train. He was hungry so he went into The Beanery, which was a place with a lunch counter where passenger trains stopped long enough for railroad men and passengers to obtain a meal. Carl could speak no English and no one seemed able to speak Danish, but by pointing and some sign language he was able to get something to eat.

It was early fall and everything was dry and the grain was ripe in the fields when Carl arrived in Cache Junction. There he was in such a different land from the moist, green country of Denmark. Where do I go? How far from here? He began to walk and saw a man unloading some coal from a railroad car into a wagon. Carl went over to the man to try to talk with him. He was overjoyed when he recognized the man was the same Chris Larsen that he had met in Denmark some time previous to his coming to America.

Chris Larsen spoke Danish better than he spoke English so at last Carl was no longer alone. He took off his coat and finished loading the coal for Mr. Larsen. So that was his first work in America. He was taken to the home of J. N. Hansen where he lived until the time that he married Estella Naomie Jenkins [daughter of John Jenkins and his second wife, Annie Clarke, and sister of Ida] on Feb. 20, 1907.

Before Carl left Denmark he said, "you tell that man [meaning J. N. Hansen] I will do everything he wants me to do" and he did just that.[459]

In J. J. Larsen's "little green book," this tidbit appears: "J. N. Hansen...sent for Carl Jorgensen. He was short in stature for his age, and by wearing knee pants and long stockings he came on half fare. He got through okay, donned man's clothes and became a man again."[460] He must have been a practical and daring man with a sense of humor.

Jens continued appearing regularly in the local newspapers. Larry Christiansen emailed various newspaper accounts of interest to me:

> 2 October 1902: Postmaster J. N. Hansen was transacting business in Logan Monday....
> We're all for Howell over here. When the division on party lines was made there were 13 Republicans votes cast. From that small beginning has grown a Republican vote of a hundred and "still there's more to follow." J. N. Hansen has the present campaign in charge and will do everything that can be done to roll up a big Republican vote. He is one of the original Republicans and knows the conditions from start to finish.[461]

In addition to being busy with two families and active in the Church and community, Jens was also an activist of a sort, rallying people to vote in a particular way.

Jens appeared in the New Year with a different and interesting news item published on 14 February 1903:

> Postmaster J. N. Hansen of Newton was in Logan Thursday and announced that the Scandinavians of the town are preparing to hold a great reunion on Friday, Feb. 20. A banquet, program and addresses in four languages will be features of the occasion.[462]

Church services had been held in both English and a Scandinavian language since the establishment of the town, and some animosity existed between English speakers and Danish speakers. The fact that not one but four Scandinavian languages were represented by the citizenry of Newton fascinates me. Family lore says neither Karen Marie nor Ane learned English, so this event probably gave them great enjoyment.

One convenience that changed life in Newton was the telephone. On 23 May 1903, the newspaper carried the exciting news of the development that would change the ability to communicate among the Cache Valley towns: "The telephone line has been completed to the west side and now Clarkston, Newton and intermediate towns can shout 'hello' to Logan."[463] Telephone service had arrived in Logan earlier. And we saw that a phone was already in use in Salt Lake City at the Pen during Jens's incarceration.

A newspaper reported on 1 July 1903, "June 30.—Postmaster J. N. Hansen of Newton was in town Monday and states that the wheat crop will be somewhat light in that region this season, cold weather and drouth [*sic*] having hindered its growth."[464] In the midsummer heat, the prediction was that the coming wheat crop would not be as rich as normal because of dry, cold weather in the previous winter. This would have affected income for the farmers as well as jeopardized their families' supply of wheat for the coming winter.

Also in that edition of the paper, Jens and Ane's son Eli made the news:

> NEWTON SUNDAY SCHOOL.—The stake superintendency of Sunday schools of Benson stake visited Newton Sunday and reorganized the Sunday school. John E. Griffin was elected superintendent. C. M. Christensen and Joseph J. Larsen assistants, and Eli Hansen secretary. The visitor made interesting addresses.[465]

Eli was twenty-one years old when he was given this position of significant responsibility.

Jens was in Logan on 15 July 1903 and "reported a very pleasant gathering in that little burg on Sunday"[466] when the Sunday School had been inspected and found in excellent condition after having been reorganized earlier.

Under the "Annual Statement" heading in the *Logan Republican* on 29 July 1903, it says: "County Auditor's Financial Statement of the Year Ending June 30, 1903. [County] Deputy Assessor. J. N. Hansen. [$]85.50."[467] (An online calculator estimated that amount of money in 1903 would be worth approximately $2,502.68 in 2020.)

A *Logan Republican* report on 1 August 1903 regarding Jens charmed me:

> If you see anybody in town you feel you ought to know, yet do not fully recognize, just put it down that it is J. N. Hansen of Newton. Our sister town's genial postmaster has had his auburn chin adornment removed and the expanse below his moustache is so unfamiliar that you doubt your eyes until the old man has spoken.[468]

Who was this reporter, and what relationship existed between the two of them that such an affectionate blurb would make the paper? Of the few photos we have of Jens, all except an early one and the one in prison show him with a full beard. Why did he choose to shave it off at this particular time?

A confusing note appeared in the *Logan Republican* on 23 September 1903: "The County Commissioners convened yesterday.... The following appointments were made and the above vacancies filled.... Newton, J. N. Hansen..."[469] Unfortunately, whatever the "above vacancies" referred to, they were not listed in the copy. Was Jens appointed to a position as a county commissioner? Or was he as the reporter telling the Logan paper of the vacancy being filled?

More information on Jens's participation in politics appeared 21 October 1903:

> The Republican primary was held in vestory [*sic*] at the meetinghouse Saturday evening and a ticket selected to be voted on at the election November 3rd, as follows: For members of village board—
>
> M. T. Beck, president;
> J. N. Hansen, 4 year term;
> N. Jacobson, P. E. Benson, J. B. Barker, 2 year term.
> The Democrats have not yet selected their ticket.[470]

Jens was running for a four-year term as a member of the village board, with voting to take place two weeks hence. What were his feelings at the time? Was he eager to be elected? Did his depth of civic participation keep him away from his families a great deal? If so, how was that perceived by his wives and children?

Jens made the trip to Logan in late February to give his report for the paper to be published on 5 March 1904. Typically, weather this time of year would be a bit "iffy" for travel in that area, and his trip may not have been easy.

> J. N. Hansen, of Newton, visited Logan last Wednesday. He states that the farmers west of the river feel much encouraged by the frequent storms which are soaking the land in good shape. The people interested in the Newton reservoir were much exercised last week over their storage of water and the safety of the dam. At the end of last season the gates to the dam were closed. Ice formed two and one-half feet thick during the winter. When the thaw was on last week the reservoir filled up with a great deal of water and raised the ice around the headgate. A large piece was frozen to it, and as the ice raised, the gate went with it. It was thought for a time that all the storage of water would escape and the headgate ruined. The piece of ice attached to the gate was very large and could not be removed, but the happy thought occurred to one of the men to blow the ice with dynamite. This was done and the

gate dropped to its place, thus saving the water and headgate. The dam is being carefully guarded to prevent a break, as an occurrence of that kind would be a heavy loss to the farmers in that vicinity.[471]

The dependence on weather conditions and the reservoir for the water supply was an ever-present concern. The hardworking inhabitants of Newton solved this problem creatively and successfully.

❊

Fourteen years had passed since the 1890 Manifesto had been issued saying that the members of the Church of Jesus Christ of Latter-day Saints would cease the practice of plural marriages taking place. Statehood had finally been granted in 1896, and one would think a sort of tranquility could reign in place of the earlier fervor. However, in the April 1904 General Conference, Joseph F. Smith, who was then the President of the Mormon Church, announced a second Manifesto that would take a harder line than the 1890 Manifesto had. Because further plural marriages had continued to take place secretly after 1890, President Smith said:

> I hereby announce that all such marriages are prohibited, and if any officer or member of the Church shall assume to solemnize or enter into any such a marriage he will be deemed in transgression against the Church and will be liable to be dealt with, according to the rules and regulations thereof, and excommunicated therefrom.[472]

This second Manifesto was sobering in that it went beyond making general recommendations and instead specifically stated that those who entered into plural marriage at any time afterward would be cut off from the Church. Although there are splinter groups today who continue to practice polygamy and who believe that continuing polygamy is truly the will of God, they are cut off from the body of the original Mormon Church that ceased the practice.

On one hand, it seems that the time should have come by then for the issue of polygamy to drop into the background. But it had not, and it did not seem to take much to stir things up again. In fact, polygamy was a tenet of the Church of Jesus Christ of Latter-day Saints for about 63 years, but it has been excluded from its religious practices for over 130 years as of this writing (2020). Yet it still pops up as an interest for some people and an issue of hostility for others. Polygamy certainly is not a neutral topic.

Jens continued in 1904 to appear in the newspaper spotlight, busy keeping the people informed of local happenings, as evidenced by this notice on 11 June 1904: "The Board of County Commissioners.... The following Registration officers were appointed for the various precincts in the county: Newton, J. N. Hansen."[473] In addition to Jens's other political offices, he would serve as a precinct registration officer.

Approximately three weeks after his precinct appointment, Jens's 160-acre farm northwest of Newton was hit by weather-related damage described in the news on 29 June 1904:

> A hailstorm visited Newton Wednesday of last week and destroyed a large amount of wheat and other grains. It is said that at the northern part of town the hail was exceptionally heavy, damaging the crops at least one-half. W. R. and G. L. Jones, *J. P. and J. N. Hansen* [emphasis mine], C. Fonnesbeck, A. Hansen, Clark Cooley and Mr. Jenkins suffered the severest loss. On Thursday night a very heavy frost put in its appearance and nipped all the tender plants. The haying in Newton is well on, and everybody is busy.[474]

Jens and his eldest son were among those who suffered the worst losses from hailstones and frost. This freak weather battered the crops in the middle of June! Possibly the storm was unexpected that late in the season, but June in northern Utah is often on the cusp of winter. What did this loss mean for the Newton farmers?

The mysterious property in Block 15 had apparently served its purpose because on 7 July 1904, Jens N. Hansen and his wife Karen M. Hansen first conveyed by warranty deed to their son Jens P. Hansen for $25, the strip of land described earlier in Chapter 17. The strip was 33 feet wide and 330 feet long, and ran along the entire west edge of Jens's Lot 7 on Block 15, and thus was conveyed to, or annexed by, Jens P. as an extension on the east edge of his Lot 6 of Block 15. The deed was filed for record on 16 April 1907, over a year after Jens had died. The transaction puzzles me, and I wonder whether this acreage gave Jens P. some ground for a larger garden, or a right-of-way of some kind, or a buffer between his lovely house and the property line?

Second, also on 7 July 1904, Jens and Karen Marie transferred their title to the remainder of their two lots in Block 15. This second warranty deed conveyed to Eugene Nelson for $190 all of Lot 8 and the remainder of Lot 7 on Block 15 (this excludes the strip deeded to Jens P.), delineated by the metes and bounds description found in Chapter 17. This deed was filed for record two weeks later on 22 July 1904, *after* Eugene Nelson and his wife, Stena, conveyed this parcel of land to Franz L. Nelson on 12 July 1904, five days after acquiring it from Jens and Karen Marie and ten days before the initial conveyance had been recorded. How is this possible?

The legal requirements in those days for recording deeds and securing title seem nebulous and are sometimes confusing. Why could a parcel be purchased solely in the name of one person yet be sold in the names of that person and his wife who was not on the original acquisition deed? And why are the transactions and recordings so haphazard? Why is Ane never mentioned as co-owner with Jens on any piece of property acquired or dispersed in the records? Maybe her status as a plural wife, and thus her position with the law, was more the reason for that absence than the possible cooling of their relationship.

No family lore tells about Jens acquiring these lots on Block 15, nor is there lore as to why he and Karen Marie decided to sell the two lots or why this was the time to do so. Why did they sell a strip of Lot 7 to their son and the remaining parcel (297 feet wide and 330 feet long) to Eugene Nelson? Why was Nelson willing to purchase a city lot that was smaller than the standard size?

Concurrent with his personal decisions, Jens's continued activity in politics made the news again on 21 September 1904:

> The republicans of Newton held a very enthusiastic primary last night. Chairman J. N. Hansen called the meeting to order.... The following were elected delegates to the county convention to be held at Logan on Sept. 24:...J. N. Hansen.... The G.O.P. of Newton precinct was reorganized as follows: J. N. Hansen, pres.... The business was disposed of in a lively manner and all left for their homes assured of a grand victory this coming election. Long may the G.O.P. live and prove that it is a party of the people, by the people, and for the people.[475]

The same newspaper edition said, "J. N. Hansen, the stalwart of Newton, was a delegate to the Judicial convention on Monday."[476] "The stalwart"! What a fine compliment for Jens.

One week later, the paper printed under "Republicans Nominate Their County Ticket" that:

As a committee on Credentials, the following were appointed…J. N. Hansen…. Samuel Nelson nominated T. H. Merrill and J. N. Hansen nominated Moroni T. Beck, as the candidates from the north. The vote resulted Merrill 59, Beck 35.[477]

The next clipping came one week later, 5 October 1904, and indicates that Jens had again made a trip to Logan as a reporter to the paper:

J. N. Hansen was over from Newton Monday and reports that he is firm in the belief that the republicans will win out in his section of the country. He also reports that work on the reservoir is now being done in order that it may be strong enough to hold through the winter. Past experience with this reservoir has taught the people over there a few things.[478]

The work on the reservoir that Jens reported carried significance for the community's winter survival.

A short notice under "Places to Register" appeared three weeks later in the *Logan Republican* on 27 October 1904, listing J. N. Hansen.[479] Apparently this means his home was open as a place where citizens could register to vote, but I don't know which of his homes.

No news clippings mentioning Jens appear from October through the winter of 1904. Likely the weather made travel with news from Newton to Logan difficult or impossible. Or was he perhaps ailing?

As spring began to make itself known—at least on the calendar—this notice appeared on 25 March 1905: "County Committees: Newton—M. F. Rigby, J. E. Griffin, Moroni Beck, J. N. Hansen."[480] This indicates that, once again, Jens had been selected to carry out a responsibility for the communities in Cache County.

The roads had cleared enough by 19 April 1905 for Jens to travel to Logan to give his report: "Postmaster J. N. Hansen was over from Newton Monday. He says the roads are nothing short of terrific. Mr. Hansen is one of the earnest advocates of electric lights for his town and is seeking to get them in from some source."[481] Jens made it safely to Logan and again was seen advocating for improvements to ease the lives of people in the community.

As summer arrived, Jens was in Logan making his 24 June 1905 report as announced in the newspaper: "Postmaster J. N. Hansen was over from Newton Wednesday. He says that the crop of lucerne this year is hardly half that of former years. The winter seems to have been too severe, freezing out the lucerne."[482]

Jens's reports not only give an account of his travels to Logan but also offer a glimpse of the devastation the hard winters in Cache Valley could visit on the crops the people labored hard to raise.

The Cache County Auditor's Report appeared in the paper a month later on 26 July 1905: "School and General election Expense: J. N. Hansen [$]24.00."[483] Maybe Jens was given this money to cover the costs of his duties in some capacity.

On 12 August 1905 under "Newsy Items" it states merely that "J. M. [*sic*] Hansen, postmaster at Newton, came to Logan yesterday."[484] Why did Jens go to Logan that day? It appears that he didn't make a report but was noticed in town. Was he beginning to feel ill and seeing a doctor?

A newspaper source from 28 November 1905 hints retrospectively that sometime between Jens's Logan visits in August and November, he had become ill: "Postmaster J. N. Hansen has about recovered from a long spell of sickness. We are glad to see him about again, and able to attend to his business at the office."[485] Given his early history of frequent respiratory illness, maybe he had continued to have spells through adulthood. Such illnesses are not mentioned, and if he had them, they did not keep him from achieving numerous notable things. On this date, he seemed to be recovered from his illness sufficiently to be up and carrying out his responsibilities, despite whether he actually felt well at the time.

Again on Wednesday, 3 January 1906, the paper says only "Postmaster Hansen of Newton was in Logan Saturday."[486] Perhaps Jens didn't feel well enough to make a report at this time, or maybe the trip impacted his health adversely, or maybe he was already quite ill. Could the trips to Logan when he made no report have been for the purpose of consulting a physician?

Just five days later on Monday, 8 January 1906, our dear Jens was confined to bed at home in Newton with pneumonia. I assume this was the home he shared with Karen Marie.

The following morning, Tuesday, 9 January 1906, Jens Nielsen Hansen died—at the age of sixty-three. His State of Utah death certificate lists the cause of death as "pneumonia, with Acute Rheumatism as Contributory, both of seven days' duration."[487] Frank H. Custer was the attending physician who signed the certificate, with Bp. M. C. Rigby as undertaker and W. R. Ballard (Ward Clerk) acting as registrar. Given that the certificate says Jens's illness was of seven days' duration, he would have been ill or becoming ill again during his journey to Logan on 3 January 1906. He may never have recovered completely from the illness the newspaper mentioned during the latter part of 1905.

The newspaper that previously carried Jens's reports of conditions in Newton now carried a notice of his death one day after it occurred. On Wednesday, 10 January 1906, under "Postmaster Hansen Dead" it stated:

Prominent Citizen of Newton Dies After Week's Illness.

J. N. Hansen, postmaster at Newton, died yesterday morning at 8 o'clock. About a week ago he was taken ill with pneumonia, followed by inflammatory rheumatism, which caused his death. He was 63 years of age, and an exceedingly good man. Mr. Hansen was on[e] of THE REPUBLICAN'S best friends and it is with sincere regret that we learn of his departure. The funeral will be held in Newton next Saturday [January 13th] at 11 a.m.[488]

Both of my writing groups that responded to the first draft of this work included a member who was a nurse. As we read Jens's early life sketch, Judy Simmons, the nurse in the first group, made a list of illnesses she thought might have been the cause of the recurrent episodes of Jens being too ill to work as a young man. The nurse in the second group, Susan Peznecker, made the comment that acute rheumatism is not a real illness but rather is a descriptive term for general inflammation. She asked, "Why did he have lung problems and pneumonia?" I have no answer. She also said that pneumonia is still called by its nickname, "the old man's friend," because the person becomes hypoxic from lack of oxygen and just goes to sleep. I hoped Jens didn't suffer. I had come to love him through this study.

Larry Christiansen, in the eleven-page document he sent me, included the following report on Jens's funeral, for which I am extremely grateful.

Saturday, Jan. 20, 1906—on page 2, "Funeral Services of J. N. Hansen at Newton."

NEWTON, Jan. 18.—The funeral service over the remains of J. N. Hansen, our worthy citizen and postmaster who died a few days before, [was] held in the meeting house on Saturday, Jan. 13. Brother Hansen was a splendid man in every sense of the word, and the various speakers could offer no word but that which was a good testimony to his character. The speakers on this occasion were Amos Clarke, M. P. Peterson, John E. Griffin and Bishop M. C. Rigby, and their every word was one of praise. During the service a quartette composed of Miss Ida Jenkins, Mrs. Elizabeth Funk, Mrs. Annie F. Rigby and Amos Clarke sang most beautifully. L. Jones, and George and Amos Clarke also sang a trio in most affecting way. Bro. Hansen joined the church in Denmark and [immigrated] to Utah in 1875, dying at the age of 63 in full faith in the gospel. He was an active Sunday school worker from the time our Sunday School was first organized and in all ward work he was a most useful man. The casket containing the deceased was literally buried in floral offerings presented by friends and relatives, and the Sunday school. Bro. Hansen lived a good life and has gone to a good reward.

— The Logan Republican[489]

Following his funeral on 13 January 1906, Jens was buried in the Newton Cemetery near the grave marker for his and Ane's son Moses. Enough room was reserved for later burying Ane on Jens's left-hand side between him and Moses, and room on his right-hand side for later burying Karen Marie, upon the wives' deaths. (We see from the funeral program that Miss Ida Jenkins was still single six years after Moses died. She would have been sixteen years old when he died. Was Aunt Eleda right about their having been engaged at the time of his death?)

I am also indebted to Larry Christiansen for the following item from the news, which appeared on 27 January 1906, on page 3 under "Short Biography of J. N. Hansen":

Postmaster of Newton who died Lately.

Man who worked his way Successfully.

The following is a life history of the late J. N. Hansen, of Newton, one of best men in the county. His many friends will no doubt read the particulars of his life with pleasure. The writer who signs himself "N. H." says:

"Jens Nielsen Hansen was born at Axelholm, Holbeck amt [county], Denmark, June 16th, 1842. At the age of six years his mother died and he was left to rustle for himself. He obtained a common school education, however, after which he studied music for two years. During the years 1864–65 he did duty in the army of his native country. April 20, 1867 he married Karen Christensen, who became the mother of ten children. One year later he was baptized into the 'Mormon' church. He was shortly afterwards set apart as a teacher, and labored in that capacity for a short time when he was ordained an elder and sent to preside over a branch of the church in New Zealand [This was Zealand or Sjælland, Denmark]. He [immigrated] to this country in 1875 and settled in Newton, Utah.

"He was a member of the Newton choir from 1876 until his death. On November 13th, 1878, he married his second wife, Anna [Ane] Sorensen, who bore him three children. During the anti-polygamy raid he was forced on the 'underground' where he suffered many hardships. Three times he met Marshal Steele, and after conversing with him for a short time he succeeded in convincing him that he was looking for some other man. He was finally arrested [for] unlawful cohabitation, and served ninety days in the Utah penitentiary. He has held [numerous] ecclesiastical positions, as well as being quite prominent in politics, having three times been a delegate to state conventions, many county conventions, deputy assessor, postmaster at Newton, school trustee, and various other offices.

"He leaves two wives, six children and eighteen grand-children. He was engaged in Sunday School work for a long time. Nearly all residents of Newton under thirty years of age [have] been in his class. He fought the good fight and kept the faith."

— *The Logan Republican*, Jan. 27, 1906.

[Larry Christiansen included this: Note: "N. H."—perhaps son Niels Peter Nephi Hansen who would have been twenty-eight years of age.][490]

It appears that this obituary could have been partially based on the biography written by Andrew Jenson in his *Latter-day Saint Biographical Encyclopedia: A Compilation of Biographical Sketches of Prominent Men and Women in the Church of Jesus Christ of Latter-day Saints*, originally published in 1901 in Salt Lake City.

The *Deseret Evening News* on Tuesday, 6 February 1906, carried the following terse notice: "Washington, Feb. 6—…Ephraim C. Schneider has been appointed postmaster of Newton, Cache County, Utah, vice J. N. Hansen, dead."

Four days later on Saturday, 10 February 1906 the *Logan Republican* stated on page nine under "Generalities" that: "Owing to the death of the late postmaster at Newton, J. N. Hansen, a successor will be appointed. We understand that Ephraim Snyder and Lizzie M. Christensen are applicants for the office."

If the dates of these two newspaper articles are correct, the *Deseret News* knew the outcome of the postmaster selection before the *Logan Republican* published the names of the two candidates who were being considered for the position.

Could the reverse order of these two notifications be explained by the publication days of the week and frequency of the two newspapers at that time?

How did Karen Marie and Ane feel upon losing their shared husband? Having lost a husband to death, I am familiar with grief and its roller-coaster process, yet I don't know how it would feel to lose a husband who had also been simultaneously someone else's husband. Jens's final illness lasted seven days, and the shock of his death must have been horrific for his loved ones. Did Ane and Karen Marie and their adult children have hints before that week that Jens was developing terminal health problems? Or did this illness seem at the onset like the others from which he had recovered? Sixty-three years of age seems so young, even in that time period.

Some women in my latter writing group said that they felt sad when Jens died on the page, even though they had known he lived over a hundred years ago and his death was a given. Through the wealth of information available about him, Jens had ceased to be merely a name on a chart and had come to feel like a real person who had an interesting and challenging life and admirable characteristics. From childhood on, he had spent his life as a hard worker and as an active participant in his church and community. Jens's energies seemed to vibrate on the page but vanished in the stilling of his heartbeat.

Jens died without a will. Did he have a reason for not making one? Or as a relatively young sixty-three-year-old man, did he think he still had plenty of time to make one? Did it trouble him that the federal government made it legally impossible for Ane, his plural wife, to be treated equally in inheritance with his first wife?

I, too, felt sad when I came to the end of Jens's life. No doubt he was missed in many circles. Two women survived him, one as his widow and the other as his plural wife. Whatever problems the wives may have had sharing a husband, they both would have been shocked and grieving. Perhaps they were burdened with concerns for their material survival as well.

At the time of Jens's death, his six surviving children from his first family with Karen Marie were Jens Peter, thirty-nine; Niels Peter Nephi, twenty-eight; Louisa, twenty-six; and Elvena, twenty-three. Children from his second family with Ane were Sophia, twenty-six; and Eli, twenty-five. Not only did the wives share a husband, but the children also shared a father, so polygamy likely was not easy for the children either. Grief is complicated. I wonder whether the adult children grieved not only the loss of their father but also the void of time they had missed with him during his lifetime due to his involvement with his other family.

During his life, Jens had lost six of his ten children with Karen Marie and one of his three children with Ane. Seven of his thirteen children died during his lifetime. Now the surviving six adult children were without their father, advisor, and confidante. As my mother lamented whenever a child died before the parents, "It's out of order." Jens had seven out-of-order experiences, and surely that had a dramatic impact on his life. Did he carry those sorrows with him as he went about working and serving others?

Jens left a hole in the Sunday School because he had been a dependable teacher for decades. He had to be replaced as the newspaper correspondent for Newton, and he would no longer serve in the political or school arenas. A new postmaster was needed. The dance orchestra needed a new first violinist. His community activities stopped, as did his advocating on behalf of various people with needs. His voice and his violin were stilled.

A realization struck me that from the age of six when his mother died, Jens had never had a nurturing mother. And from the age of ten when he was farmed out to work and board for the first time, he never had a real home until he settled in Newton at the age of thirty-three. I lived in the same home from birth until age twenty-three, so I find it difficult to imagine what it must have been like to move as many times as Jens did. Even when Jens first arrived in Newton, the dugout his family lived in was owned by and shared with his brother Hans and his family. Eventually Jens had two houses and two families instead of just one, and an additional property whose purpose puzzles me. Did he find the peace, nurturing, and cherishing in adulthood that he missed in his childhood and youth? I hope he did.

I admire Jens for having been a hard worker, for taking the initiative to pursue musical knowledge, for being open to the Spirit and following his convictions to the waters of Skarresø, for following the call to Utah and settling in Newton, and for being kind enough and brave enough and committed enough to marry Ane, my great-grandmother. I am grateful to Jens for leaving a brief life sketch that connected his life to geographical places in his home country of Denmark, and for being a good person, a "stalwart." He has become more than a name on my pedigree chart. I have come to know him as a person and have had the privilege of walking in his footsteps both in Denmark and in Utah. I treasure the precious few photographs that allow me to know what he looked like, and all the records of so long ago that have been kept and organized and preserved by others whom I will never meet, so that I could ferret out so much information about this ancestor. I hope that I have done his story justice, and that family and others who read this record will find Jens in these pages for themselves.

CHAPTER 22

JENS'S PROBATE: 1906

R ichard had suggested that I look for probate records (documents created by the court after a person's death itemizing the properties, belongings, and assets of the deceased's estate and determining distribution thereof to heirs or creditors) for Jens and his two wives. So after standing inside Ane's house, I drove back to Logan and trudged in the desert heat to the modern, glassy gray building of First District Court a block west of the courthouse. Inside the fortress, a man in uniform behind the security scanner asked why I was there. I told him the county clerk had said probate records for the early 1900s might be there, and he said, "There is a good chance that you are in the right place!" He took my purse and papers, directed me to walk through the scanner as he searched and returned my stuff, and then pointed toward the glass double doors off to my right.

The young woman behind the wall-to-wall desk was helping another young woman and said she would be right with me. Eventually, I told her I was looking for probate records from 1906. She wrote a phone number on a yellow Post-it Note and handed it to me, saying, "Here is the number to the archives in Salt Lake City. I don't think we have anything that far back, but I will check." She directed me through a heavy metal door on our left into a separate small room and told me to wait there. Soon she returned through a back door into the room labeled *Employees Only*, carrying a hefty antique ledger that she plopped onto a worktable. She turned the large, gloriously handwritten pages until she found the *HA* section that would include any Hansen pages and told me to browse through the listings. If I found something I wanted, I was to write down the case number. Then she left the room.

I turned page after page and searched each one. Soon I found Jens N. Hansen, Case 727 but saw nothing for Ane or Karen Marie. The woman helping me was surprised when I found her and handed her my note with the case number on it. She had not expected me to find it. Soon she came back with a roll of microfilm, put it onto a gray machine with a viewer and a print feature, and began cranking through it. After some time, she found 727 in big white numerals on the negative film, but when she attempted to begin printing the pages, the machine balked. She called in another woman, and they worked together to solve the machine's problem. I could not bear to have come so far and been so lucky to find the record, only to have technology foil my acquisition of the valuable document.

Finally the printer started working, but again something went wrong. The women tried different sizes of paper and different settings on the machine, and finally it began working again. The first woman left, and the second woman took over the printing—eighty pages! While the machine slowly ground out one page at a time as she scrolled the microfilm and pressed the button, she asked why I was interested in the document. We conversed about family histories in general as I watched each page being laboriously copied and feared another machine malfunction. When the machine coughed out the last sheet, I took my stack of precious printed pages to the front desk, asked for a binder clip, paid twenty dollars, and left the courthouse hugging this probate treasure.

Later I telephoned my nephew Lyle Wiggins, a professional researcher, and asked why I could find no probate records for Ane or Karen Marie. He said women in that time period often did not get fair consideration in some matters, and that customarily any property of the women was handled in the husband's probate. Rarely, he said, did women have probate documents, and I recalled seeing only a few women's names in the ledger I had searched.

Jens's probate documents did indeed decree the disposition to be made of Karen Marie's and Ane's homes and farm properties upon their deaths. Karen Marie was granted a life estate in her home and farm, both of which were to go to her daughter, Elvena, upon Karen Marie's death. Ane owned her home outright, so the wording of the document did not mention a life estate but said she was to provide deeds that upon her death would transfer her home to her daughter, Sophia, and her remaining half lots to her son, Eli. The probate document also divided Ane's south farms property acreage unequally between Sophia and Eli upon her death. (Did the valuation of the acreages equal out somehow?)

The next morning at Carla's, as I spent time reading the probate file, the documents proved to be interesting. The Inventory listed Jens's horses by name, his farm equipment, his stocks in various companies, his real properties, his buggies, his wagon, his sled, his derrick, his plows, and his harnesses. The recital of Jens's possessions at the time he died not only provided a richer picture of how he had lived, but also made him more vibrant and real to me as a person. What an amazing document Richard had suggested!

❦

Karen Marie petitioned the court on 27 February 1906, in the District Court of the First Judicial District of the State of Utah, in and for the County of Cache, to appoint Nephi Hansen as the administrator in the estate of Jens N. Hansen, deceased. On the Nomination of Administrator document, Karen Marie Hansen's name appears in cursive, followed by an *X* and a notation of "her mark." The petition was granted under certain stipulations, such as providing a bond of $2,600 and "upon taking and subscribing the oath of office as required by law." The Order Appointing Administrator also said, "Karen Maria [*sic*] Hansen, the surviving widow of the deceased has nominated in writing and requested the Court to appoint the said Nephi Hansen administrator of the said estate."[491] Apparently Ane had no role in the legal proceedings and was marginalized yet again for her status as a plural wife.

A Notice to Creditors was posted, and in the probate file is one creditor's claim on 12 April 1906, from Oscar Borkman. (Mother told me years ago that this is the spelling Oscar's English wife preferred over *Bjorkman*. In his journal, Oscar says, "From now on, in this brief sketch, my name will be OSCAR G. BJORKMAN which is the correct way to spell the surname."[492]) Oscar claimed ten dollars plus interest for a cash loan made. A note on the document says, "J.N. Hansen gave claimant his check on First Nat. Bank of Logan for $10.00 in payment of above loan and Bank refused to pay check on grounds that said J.N. Hansen had no funds in said Bank. Claimant holds this ck." This was the only claim against Jens's estate, and it was honored.

Note: All following probate document quotations are in block quotes to set them apart from the regular text for those readers who wish to skip the details.

Several documents within the probate file were sealed by the court and are unavailable. For example, one memo is from a UCI Micrographics [and an unrecognizable term] to a Jeff Johnson, with a subject line, "Sealed Documents." The body reads:

> This document was either sealed and/or stated "Do not open without a court order." The document was in file number 727 [Jens's case file number], it comes from box number 20, it was filmed on [two letters unreadable] camera number 57, without opening, the camera operator was Shaun Moore [signature], the date was 7/1/94. I, the undersigned supervisor, witness that this document remained sealed and the outside filmed without opening. This document was then removed from this

file and sent to you at State Archives. Paul Christian [or Christiansen in signature], Micrographics Supervisor/Date 7/1/94.

Google showed UCI to be Utah Correctional Industries. What was the prison system sending confidentially to the archives?

In the Inventory and Appraisement of 15 May 1906 in the probate file, the following properties were listed for Jens's estate:

Lots six (6) and seven (7) and the East one half (½) of the South West quarter (S.W.¼) of section six (6) in township thirteen (13) North, Range one (1) West, Salt Lake Merridian [*sic*]. Containing one hundred fifty-eight-and eighty-one, one hundredths acres (158 $^{81}/_{100}$) With improvements $1600

1 Mare called Pearl	150
1 Mare called Sall	100
1 Horse called Rile	50
1 Horse called Dick	75
1 Mare called Jule	50
1 Mare colt	50
10 Shares preferred Utah Sugar stock	96
10 Shares common Utah Sugar stock	25
110 Shares in Newton Irrigation Company	110
4 ⅔ Shares West Cache Canal Co	42 [?]
Header [machine for harvesting wheat] and three boxes	42
2 Sets harness	52 [?]
1 Double seated Buggy	75
1 Single buggy	75
1 Single harness	[unreadable]
1 Cutter	[unreadable]
1 Bob sled	20
2 Wagons	75
1 Truck wagon	[unreadable]
Hay Derrick	25
Platform scaler	8
Forge and Iron working tools	5
Woodworking tools	3
Sulkey Plow	5
Hand Plow	5

Harrow		4
Disc Plow		45
Self Binder	½ Share	10

Beginning at a point seventy-seven (77) rods West and ten (10) rods north of the [S]outh East corner of the North East ["North West" on Agreement Document] quarter of Section thirty (30) Township thirteen (13) North of Range one (1) West of Salt Lake Meridian:– Thence running West forty (40) rods, thence North forty (40) rods, thence East forty (40) rods; thence South forty (40) rods to the place of beginning, Containing ten (10) acres. Situated in the N.E.¼ of Sec. 30. Tp. 13 N. Range one West of S.L. Meridian. $50

[Note: 1 rod = 16.5 feet.]

The document ends with:

We, the undersigned, duly appointed appraisers of the Estate of Jens N. Hansen deceased, hereby certify that the property mentioned in the foregoing inventory has been exhibited to us, and that we appraise the same at the sum of Twenty seven hundred Eighty five Dollars. ($2785.00). Dated May 15 1906.

L. Jones Appraiser.
Andrew Petersen Appraiser.
Eugene Nelson Appraiser.

The last signature above interests me because Jens had sold his Lots 7 and 8 of Block 15 in Newton to a Eugene Nelson. Were the two men friends? Or were they merely business contacts?

After this Inventory and Appraisement document, an official Agreement as to how the estate was to be distributed was drawn up among the heirs on 6 March 1906 but was not filed for record until 16 April 1907, just a month before the Decree of Distribution was executed and filed on 11 May 1907. The execution of the Agreement predates the Inventory and Appraisement but was filed before the Petition for Distribution of the Estate was executed as the document testifying that the probate was closed. I am unsure as to why these dates bounce around instead of being consecutive. The Agreement, which differs slightly from the then forthcoming Decree of Distribution, appears below:

AGREEMENT

We, the undersigned, constituting all the heirs at law of Jens N. Hansen, deceased, all being over the age of 21 years, and desiring to carry out the wishes of the deceased with reference to the dirstibution [*sic*] of his estate, hereby covenant and agree that the said estate shall be divided and distributed by the court as follows:

To Jens P. Hansen:
Commencing at the S.W. corner of Lot 7, Sec. 6, Tp. 13 North Range 1 West Salt Lake meridian, and running thence E. 41 rods; N. 160 rods; W. 41 rods; S. 160 rods to the place of beginning, subject, however to the road way over the West part of said land.
    Also one three year old colt.

To Nephi Hansen:
Commencing at a point 41 rods East of the S.W. corner of Lot 7 Sec. 6, Tp. 13 North Range 1 West Salt Lake meridian, and running thence E. 41 rods; N. 160 rods; W. 41 rods; S. 160 rods to the place of beginning.
    Also the two mares called "Pearl" and "Sall"

To Hans E. Hansen: [Eli]
Commencing at a point 82 rods East of the S.W. corner of Lot 7, Sec. 6, Tp. 13 North Range 1 West Salt Lake meridian, and running thence E. 39 rods; N. 160 rods; W. 39 rods; S. 160 rods to the place of beginning.
    $42 of stock in Cache Irrigation Company.
    Also, one two year old colt.
    Ten shares of stock in Newton Irrigation Company
    [Newton Irrigation entry added between lines in handwriting.]

To Louisa H. Peterson:
Commencing at a point 121 rods East of the S.W. corner of Lot 7, Sec. 6 Tp. 13 North of Range 1 West of the Salt Lake meridian, and running thence E. 30 rods; thence N. 160 rods; W. 30 rods; S. 160 rods to the place of beginning.

To Elvena H. Jenkins:
Commencing at a point 151 rods East from the S.W. corner of Lot 7 Sec 6 Tp. 13 North of Range 1 West of the Salt Lake meridian, and

running thence E. 10 rods; N. 160 rods; W. 10 rods; S. 160 rods to the place of beginning.

[No acreages shown in the above five sections of documentations.]

Also, after the death of Karen M. Hansen, Elvina [*sic*] Jenkins shall be entitled to the ten acres of river bottom described as follows, to wit: [The following is handwritten in the document.] Beginning at a point 77 rods west and 10 rods north of the south-east corner of the northwest ["northeast" in Appraisal] quarter of section 30, township 13 north of range 1 west of Salt Lake meridian:—Thence running west 40 rods, thence north 40 rods, thence east 40 rods, thence south forty rods to place of beginning. Containing ten acres.

To Karen M. Hansen:
A life estate in the land last above described
Also, Ten shares of preferred sugar stock and
Ten shares of common sugar stock
Also the horse called "jule"
Single harness
Buggy
Cutter

The machinery on the farm shall be divided among the boys, share and share alike, or at least their interest shall be equal in the same.

The remaining 100 [typed but with handwritten numeral 1 superimposed over first zero making it 110] shares of stock in the Newton Irrigation Company shall be distributed as follows,

To Karen M. Hansen [number unreadable but possibly 35—Final decree says 25] shares,
Annie [Ane] M. Hansen 25 shares,
Jens P. Hansen 25 shares.
Nephi Hansen 25 shares.

Anna [corrected by hand to Annie but should be Ane] M. Hansen, the plural wife of the deceased, and mother of Sophia H. Bjorkman and Hans E. [Eli] Hansen, hereby covenants and agrees that she will convey by good and sufficient deed or deeds the home in which she now lives, and the west ten acres of land in the South Fields so that when she dies the same will become the property of her daughter Sophia H. Bjorkman, the said property being described as follows, to wit: Beginning at the northwest corner of the northwest ¼ of sec 29 Township 13 N Range 1 West. Then east fifty-seven rods, then south forty rods, then west fifty-seven rods, then north forty rods to place of beginning, containing fourteen and one-fourth acres.

To Annie [Ane] M. Hansen:
five shares of the capital stock of Peoples Merchantile [*sic*] Co. Newton Utah.

To Sophia H. Bjorkman
$42.00 shares in West Cache Irrigation Co.

Said Anna [Ane] Hansen also hereby covenants and agrees to convey to her son Hans E. [Eli] Hansen the East four and ¼ acres of the above described tract of [14.25] acres, described as follows: Beginning forty rods east of the northwest corner of the northwest ¼ of sec. 29 township 13 N. Range 1 west; Then south forty rods, then east seventeen rods, then north forty rods, then west seventeen rods to place of beginning. Containing four and ¼ acres.

Karen M. Hansen hereby agrees to convey to Elvena H. Jenkins the home in which she now lives, but holds title of above home until death or shall have a life estate in same.

The expenses of administration shall be borne equally by the children, and all the crops raised on the land during the season of 1906 shall be used to pay the funeral expenses, incumbrances on the property and other outstanding debts of the estate.

We hereby agree to pay to Carl Jorgensen one-fifth of all crops harvested in 1906 as compensation for labor on farm of Jens N. Hansen deceased.

In witness of this agreement the parties have hereunto set their hand and seals and executed this contract in duplicate this 5th day of March 1906.

Signed:
Karen M. Hansen
Nephi Hansen
Jens P. Hansen
Louisa H. Petersen
Hans E. Hansen [Eli]
Annie [Ane] M. Hansen [*X*, her mark]
Sophia Bjorkman
Elvena Jenkins

Signed in the presence of:
Henry Bjorkman [Sophia's husband]
Sophora J. Hansen [Eli's wife]

STATE OF UTAH
COUNTY OF CACHE
On this 6 day of March A.D. 1906, personally appeared before me
Karen M. Hansen, Nephi Hansen, Jens P. Hansen, Louisa H. Petersen,
Hans E. Hansen, Annie M. Hansen, and Sophia Bjorkman, the signers
of the above instrument, who duly acknowledged to me that they exe-
cuted the same. [Elvena's name is missing from this list that is entirely
in one person's handwriting and appears to match that of Willard R.
Ballard, the Notary Public. Elvena signed the document but she was
apparently overlooked in this listing.]

Willard R. Ballard, Notary Public
My commission expires March 14, 1909

The document was filed April 16, 1907.
Ane complied with the probate directives on 23 February 1907—over a year
after losing Jens. First she divided up her lots in town with her home on them by
executing a warranty deed to her son Eli for the N ½ Lots 7 and 8, Block 11, Plat
A, Newton Townsite (the portion north of her home) for the sum of one dollar
consideration, and also by executing a warranty deed to her daughter, Sophia H.
Bjorkman, for the S ½ Lots 7 and 8, Block 11, Plat A, Newton Townsite (the
portion upon which her home was located), for the sum of one dollar consideration. On both deeds, her name was shown as Ane Margrethe Sorensen Hansen.
The copy of the deed to Eli is written completely in one person's hand, and
the copy of the deed to Sophia is typed in its entirety, so it is impossible to

know whether Ane herself signed the deeds with her full name as shown on the signature line, or whether she used an X as she did on the probate Agreement document. It puzzles me that both Ane and Karen Marie used an X to sign at least one document in the probate process. Wouldn't they have learned how to write their names in Danish during their compulsory schooling in Denmark? Family lore is that neither woman learned to speak English, but wouldn't their names be written the same whether in Danish or English?

Second and also on that same day—23 February 1907—Ane divided her hay lots (or south farm) on the south edge of Newton between her two surviving children by executing a warranty deed to Sophia H. Bjorkman for the sum of one dollar a tract of land described as follows:

> Beginning at the North West corner of the North West quarter of Section 29, Township 13 North of Range one (1) West of Salt Lake Meridian: thence East forty (40) rods; thence South forty (40) rods; thence west forty (40) rods; thence north forty (40) rods to the place of beginning, containing ten (10) acres;

and by executing a warranty deed to Eli Hansen for the sum of one dollar a tract of land described as follows:

> Beginning at a point forty (40) rods East from the North west corner of the North West quarter of Section 29, Township thirteen (13) North of Range one (1) West of Salt Lake Meridian: Thence running East seventeen (17) rods; thence South forty (40) rods; thence West seventeen (17) rods; thence North forty (40) rods to the place of beginning. Containing four and one fourth (4 ¼) acres.

The copies of both deeds to the south farm are typewritten in their entirety, with Ane's name and signature line shown as "Anne Margrathe Hansen." She thus disposed of her 14.25 acres on the south edge of Newton.

What did Ane feel when told by the Agreement what to do with her property? Was she sad? Resentful? What went through her mind and heart as she executed the documents to transfer what she owned? Was she relieved to be putting into place the future distribution of her properties for the unknown time of her death while she was sixty-four years old? Was she worried about how she would survive as a woman in that time period without the financial support of a husband? Did she feel some security knowing that she could keep her home as long as she lived and that it would then go to her only daughter, who had not only been raised in that home but also had lived there with her own young family after she married Henry Bjorkman? (They later lived in that house again with widowed Ane while Henry was away on his mission to Denmark.) The distribution process was typical for the time, but did everyone feel that it was right and fair?

Eli's deed for the land north of Ane's house—to my surprise—was filed for record just short of two weeks later on 6 March 1907, not waiting as expected until Ane's death. Was caring for that acreage perhaps a burden for Ane with Jens gone? For some reason, it looks like Eli was able to take possession of the land while Ane was still living.

❧

By this time, all the lands in the area surrounding Newton that were available through the Homestead Act (the same means through which Jens had obtained his nearly 160-acre farm) had been claimed, so it became necessary for many of the adult children of the original settlers to extend their reach for land to areas farther out. My grandfather Henry Albert Bjorkman and Ane's son Eli, both of whom had lived in Newton, were among those who settled in Central, Idaho, a three-day journey. Eli's history tells us:

> [He] went to Central, Idaho, to file or homestead a farm. He filed on May 07, 1907. [He and his brother-in law, Henry Bjorkman] had to catch a train and go to Blackfoot, Idaho, to file on the homestead. [They] lived in a covered wagon until they got homes to live in. They had to break and work the land for seven years.... For a few years, [they moved] from Newton, Utah to Central, Idaho twice a year. Each spring he left Newton with chickens in the crates, pigs in the wagon and tied the cow behind the wagon and started off for Central. He would get to Bishop Hymans's place and sleep in his barn the first day. That is just north of Preston, Idaho. The second day, they traveled to a home where the big power poles are now. He would sleep in the William's barn. On the third day, they started out early and traveled to the farm. In the fall, they would come back to Newton the same way, only coming [in reverse order], from Central.[493]

The rhythm of these seasonal moves became a pattern for their lives for years—years of difficult challenges met with determination for the benefit of their families and themselves. My mother remembered making these migrations to the farm as a child and then attending school in Newton.

Finally, after all the due processes for settlement of Jens's estate had been met, the final document in the case, the Decree of Distribution in the Matter of the Estate of Jens N. Hansen, Deceased, was executed and filed on 11 May 1907, and the court listed among its findings:

> Item 1: That the said Jens N. Hansen, died intestate on the 9th day of January 1905 [incorrect: the year was 1906] at Newton, Cache County, State of Utah, leaving surviving him a widow, Karen Maria [*sic*] Hansen, and the following children, to wit: Jens P. Hansen, Nephi Hansen, Louisa Hansen Petersen, Sophia Hansen Bjorkman, Hans E. [Eli] Hansen, Elvena H. Jenkins. [No mention here of plural wife Ane who gave birth to two of the children, yet could not inherit.]
>
> That there are no children of any deceased child, and the persons above named constitute the sole and only heirs of the said Jens N. Hansen, deceased, and are entitled to have distributed to them the whole of the said estate.

Item 2 states that notice has been given to creditors and all final bills, including those dealing with the last sickness and funeral expenses, have been paid.

Item 3 states that the heirs have entered into and filed a written agreement as to how the estate shall be distributed and further states that since the Agreement was drawn up, Nephi Hansen had "duly assigned and conveyed by good and sufficient deed all his right, title and interest in the property of the said estate." (Jens P. purchased Nephi's share.)

Then the document goes on to say,

> IT IS HEREBY, ORDERED, ADJUDGED AND DECREED,
> That the residue of the estate of the said Jens N. Hansen, deceased, be and the same is hereby distributed to the heirs of the said deceased, in accordance with the terms of their said written agreement filed herein, (except that the interest of the said Nephi Hansen be distributed to Jens P. Hansen by virtue of his said deed), as follows, to wit:

> To Jens P. Hansen.—
> The following described real estate in Cache County, State of Utah: Commencing at the South west corner of lot seven (7), of section six (6), Township thirteen (13) North Range One (1) West of the Salt Lake meridian, and running thence East forty one (41) rods; thence North one hundred and sixty (160) rods; thence west forty one (41)

rods; thence south one hundred and sixty (160) rods to the place of beginning, subject, however, to the road way over the west part of the said land. [My note: No acreage computation appears in this description for Jens Peter's property.]

Commencing at a point forty one (41) rods East of the South west corner of Lot seven (7), section six (6), Township thirteen (13) North, Range One (1) West of the Salt Lake meridian, and running thence East forty one (41) rods; thence North one hundred and sixty (160) rods; thence west forty one (41) rods; thence south one hundred and sixty (160) rods to the place of beginning. [My note: No acreage computation appears in this description for Nephi's inheritance that was purchased by Jens Peter.]

Also, the following personal property:

One three year old colt,

Fifty (50) shares of stock in the Newton Irrigation Company,

and an undivided ⅔ interest in the farm machinery,

one mare called "pearl" and

one mare called "sal."

To Hans E. [Eli] Hansen.—

The following described tract of land in Cache County, State of Utah, to wit: Commencing at a point eight two (82) rods east of the South west corner of Lot seven (7), section six (6), Township thirteen (13) North, Range One (1) West of the Salt Lake meridian, and running thence east thirty nine (39) rods; thence North one hundred and sixty (160) rods; thence West thirty nine (39) rods: thence South one hundred and sixty (160) rods to the place of beginning, containing 39 acres, more or less.

Forty two Dollars of stock in the West Cache Irrigation Company.

One two year old colt, and an undivided ⅓ interest in the farming machinery.

Ten shares of stock in the Newton Irrigation Company.

To Louisa H. Petersen.—

The following described tract of land in Cache County, State of Utah, to wit: Commencing at a point one hundred and twenty one (121) rods east of the south west corner of Lot seven (7), section six (6) Township thirteen (13) North Range One (1) West of the Salt Lake meridian, and running thence East thirty (30) rods; thence north one hundred and sixty (160) rods; thence West thirty (30) rods; thence South one hundred and sixty (160) rods to the place of beginning, containing 30 acres.

To Elvena H. Jenkins.—

The following described tract of land in Cache County, State of Utah, to wit: Commencing at a point one hundred and fifty one (151) rods east of the South west corner of Lot seven (7), section six (6), Township Thirteen (13) North, Range One West of the Salt Lake meridian, and running thence East ten (10) rods; thence North one hundred and sixty (160) rods; thence West ten (10) rods; thence South one hundred and sixty (160) rods to the place of beginning. [My note: No acreage computation appears in this description for Elvena's property, but it would be approximately 10 acres.]

Also the following described real estate after the death of Karen M. Hansen, who is hereby given a life estate in the said property: Commencing at a point seventy seven (77) rods West of a point ten (10) rods North of the South east corner of the North west [My note: Handwritten note in the margin says "Should be east," then "New deed recorded June 1907."] quarter of section thirty (30) Township thirteen (13) North Range One (1) West of the Salt Lake meridian, and running thence west forty rods; thence North forty (40) rods; thence East forty (40) rods; thence South forty (40) rods to the place of beginning, containing 10 acres.

To Karen M. Hansen.—

A life estate in the tract of land above described, for and during the period of her life, and at her death to Elvena H. Jenkins as above setforth [*sic*].

Also, Ten shares of preferred and ten shares of common stock in the Utah Sugar Company.

One horse called "jule", one single harness, buggy and cutter.

Twenty five shares of stock in the Newton Irrigation Company.

To Annie [Ane] M. Hansen—a plural wife of the deceased.—

Five shares of the capital stock of the "Peoples Merchantile Company" of Newton, Utah.

Five [corrected by hand to read "Twenty Five"] shares of the capital stock of the Newton Irrigation Company.

To Sophia H. Bjorkman.—
Forty two dollars water right in the West Cache Irrigation Company.

Dated this 11th day of May 1907
Signed
W. W. Maughan, District Judge.
Attest:
Signed J.S. Larsen, Clerk District Court
Filed or recorded 11 May 1907.

Thus concludes the distribution of Jens N. Hansen's estate.

❧

Often the attention required for arranging a funeral and burial and distributing the deceased's estate serve as a distraction from a deep sense of loss and grief. What might Karen Marie and Ane have felt? Were they affected by the power of grief that can bring emotional pain felt physically, memory problems, disorientation, depression, and anger? Were the wives bereft when Jens died, or were they so stoic that they refused to be affected by sorrow? Rarely would any woman be completely unaffected by the death of a man she had shared life with, cared about, and had children with. When LaRelia read the manuscript, she pondered in a note to me whether Karen Marie, as bride of Jens's youth and mother of so many lost babies, might have had the greater grief. Only another widow can understand the grief that comes with the loss of a husband. Did sharing that experience contribute to the friendship that our family lore says developed between the two women after Jens died? Did knowing they had been married to Jens in ceremonies that sealed them to him for eternity offer comfort to Karen Marie and Ane?

The loss of the family breadwinner also presented the problem of survival for those remaining and possibly added anxiety to the emotional void left by Jens's absence. Many widows today receive some kind of financial benefit they can depend upon for survival, but what about Ane and Karen Marie? Jens had been a farmer and a community participant and a devout Church member, but none of those would offer a pension for his widows. Karen Marie's history says:

> When Grandfather [Jens] died, she [Karen Marie] was left to make her own livelihood. She grew a garden, kept chickens, and had a cow. She sold what eggs and milk she didn't use. There were also berries and fruit trees on the lot for Grandmother to harvest."[494]

Ane likely also had a garden and an orchard. And surely their adult children helped the widows in every way they could.

Jens's death ended polygamy in the Hansen families. The end of polygamy among the main body of the Mormon Church came about primarily in that way—through the deaths of that generation of polygamist men. As the first wife, Karen Marie was deemed by law to be Jens's legal wife and widow, while Ane had the label *plural wife*. In the distribution of Jens's estate, Ane and her female child, Sophia, fared less well than the survivors in Jens's first family. Ane's living male child, Eli, did inherit a larger portion of the estate than did his mother or sister, possibly due to the gender bias of the time period.

Fortunately, Ane already had title to her home, to her lots in town, and to her riverine property south of town for her security at the time of Jens's death.

A United States Geological Survey map shows Ane's 14.25 south lot acres butting up against the ebb and flow lines of Bear River. As stated above, Jens's probate documents required her to make arrangements for her children, upon her own death, to inherit these properties. Sophia was to inherit the south half of Ane's two lots in town with the house upon them, and Eli was to inherit the north half of those lots. The hay lot acreage was unevenly divided between Sophia and Eli.

At the site of Ane's hay lot in 2014, just off the road grew a large field of tall, golden, grass-like plants—probably hay—with a swift, narrow river running next to the roots of a small grove of trees at the east boundary and continuing on south through the fields. A machine cut and baled the crop, and a tractor with a forklift loaded the bales onto a flatbed truck beyond the *Private Property: Keep Out* signs. According to the documents, the larger portion, Sophia's, was westernmost, away from the water.

Following is a summary of the probate documents for those readers who chose to skip them. If you read the probate section, you may wish to skip the following summary.

Other than her delayed and generous inheritances from Ane, Sophia's portion immediately upon her father's death was meager. She received only forty-two dollars in water rights. No horse. No percentage of the homestead farm. Perhaps because she and Henry did not live full-time in Newton, owning the farmland there would not have been advantageous. However, they could have sold it had she inherited.

The Agreement gave Karen Marie a life estate in her home on her two lots in town. The Decree of Distribution also gave her a life estate property of river bottomland in a forty-rod square containing ten acres in Section 30, T. 13 N., R. 1 W., Salt Lake Meridian, south of her home. Both of these properties were to transfer eventually to her daughter, Elvena, but not until Karen Marie's death. Elvena did receive a portion of the homestead farmland at the time of her father's death.

Karen Marie was the only woman among Jens's heirs to be given a horse, and she was given Jule. She also received a single harness for the horse, a buggy, and a cutter (a small sleigh with curved runners, having seating for two or more people and usually drawn by one horse) so she had transportation all year round. Perhaps Jens had provided a horse and buggy for Ane during his lifetime because he knew the federal laws prohibited her inheriting upon his death. Jens's surviving daughters—Louisa and Elvena (with Karen Marie as mother), and Sophia (with Ane as mother)—had married by the time of Jens's death, and maybe they and their husbands had horses and buggies so did not need to inherit them.

Jens Peter had purchased his brother Nephi's inheritance, so he received double shares in the distribution, including the horses Pearl and Sal (both of whom would have been Nephi's), and a colt. Ane's son, Eli, also inherited a colt. The Inventory additionally listed horses named Rile and Dick, neither of whom was distributed by name in the decree. Although the Inventory listed only one colt, two were distributed. During the time that passed between the appraisal and the distribution, animals could have been born and died, so these discrepancies likely were due to life's fluidity.

The north farm of nearly 160 acres acquired through the Homestead Act was divided into north and south strips (vertical on the map) of varying widths, with Jens Peter receiving his one strip 41 rods wide, plus an additional strip 41 rods wide that he had purchased from Nephi's share. Jens Peter received, then, a total of 82 rods by 160 rods containing approximately 82 acres. Eli received 39 rods by 160 rods for 39 acres; Louisa received 30 rods by 160 rods for 30 acres; and Elvena inherited 10 rods by 160 rods for 10 acres. Sophia, my grandmother, was the only living child of Jens who did not inherit a portion of the homestead property, but she would later inherit acreage and a house from Ane. All the heirs received shares or stock in irrigation companies, and Ane received some shares in the People's Mercantile.

None of the probate documents mentions Jens's violin. Did he give it away while he was living? If so, to whom? Does it still exist? I would love to know what happened to that instrument he loved, to see it, touch it, and hear someone play it. Jens's determination to learn music allowed him to enrich his life and the lives of others, to serve by playing for his family, and to earn income by playing for dances. He also shared the music of his voice through singing in the church choir, uttering public prayers, teaching Sunday School classes, performing in community plays, and reporting Newton conditions and happenings to the Logan newspaper. He made requests to the education board on behalf of people who needed help, and he showed a tender heart in his concerns for others. He made clogs—sawing, chopping, scooping, and hammering—for the early support of his family. As he left the stage of his life, a great silence fell.

Jens had been farmed out on yearly work contracts from the age of ten until he was a young adult. He had immigrated to America for his new religion, farmed an area that resembled part of his home country of Denmark, and had become proficient in English. He obediently married a second wife and perhaps three others, served time in prison for having a plural wife, and productively spent his time thus incarcerated by attending church services, singing in programs, taking math classes, and making mats.

Jens had been actively involved in bringing improvements to Newton. He served as a Town Board member, pound keeper, postmaster, and reporter to the Logan newspaper. He was active in politics. He built the post office and helped form the co-op. He maintained a farm and produced grain and lucerne and raised animals and chickens. He maintained horses, buggies, sleighs, and farm tools. He planted, watered, weeded, and harvested his crops. He marketed grain and eggs and butter. And he worked until just a few days before his death.

Certainly Jens had additional attributes and accomplishments that are not mentioned here but can be found between the lines. He was an intelligent, unselfish, kind, and busy man, and was known in the community as courteous and capable. He was a "stalwart" of Newton. His life is worthy of admiration and emulation.

CHAPTER 23

WIDOWHOOD FOR ANE: 1906–1916

ne had lost Jens and all they shared together, but after his death, her family life continued to be enriched with their children, Eli and Sophia, and their spouses. No doubt she also enjoyed the arrivals of her grandchildren. She had both old and new friends in Newton and regularly spent time with Karen Marie. And as she shared her home during winters with Sophia and Henry, the exuberance of their young children must have filled it with sounds of life and love.

My mother and her sisters remembered that Ane and Karen Marie got together every afternoon for coffee (some say tea). Ane went across the street to Karen Marie's, and the young girls liked to go there with their grandmother. Mother said she loved "Auntie's arbor." No mention was made of Karen Marie coming over to Ane's, but that doesn't mean she did not. Though the Word of Wisdom in the LDS Church at that time advised avoidance of hot drinks, many Scandinavians loved their coffee and did not or could not observe this recommendation. Aunt Eleda wrote: "When coffee time came, Grandma took me with her to Auntie's. Auntie always had cookies or other goodies that I enjoyed. I also loved her beautiful flower garden."[495]

Eleda was born in 1905, before Jens's death, and my mother was born in 1907, after Jens's death, so this friendship between his widows had to have flourished for several years for the little girls to be old enough to later remember having been included in their grandmother's visits. My grandparents, the Bjorkmans, lived briefly with Henry's mother in Logan after their marriage in December 1900, and then lived with Ane on and off until they moved from Newton to Central in 1913. These visits for coffee had to have taken place during the years the Bjorkman family lived with Ane. Might Ane and Karen Marie have been somewhat friendly during Jens's lifetime as well? Their standing or sitting next to each other in the 1899 community gala photograph indicates they were at least cordial, in spite of stories to the contrary.

The 1910 Newton Census shows Ane as head of household, with Henry Bjorkman on the next line as son-in-law, Sophia as wife, and Lorena, Leonard, Eleda, Flora, and Frances as their children, all living in Ane's home in Newton.[496] These children constitute what we call the "first family"—those born *before* Henry left on his mission to Denmark. Mother said that when the Bjorkman children were grown, Frances was the one who most resembled Ane.

Eli purchased the N ½ of Lots 5 and 6, Block 11, Plat A of Newton Townsite on 15 February 1910, for $1,200 from Lorenzo Larsen and his wife, Altena. The deed from the Larsens to Eli was filed for record two weeks later on 1 March 1910. These lots are situated due west of the N ½ of Lots 7 and 8 that he inherited from Ane when she executed the deed on 23 February 1907, which was filed for record on 6 March 1907, instead of waiting until after her death nine years later.[497] This purchase gave Eli the entire north half of the north half [N ½ N ½] of Block 11, Plat A of the Newton Townsite Survey. (These acreages are not lots measured from a Township and Range survey.)

In the LDS Church, missionaries are generally young single men and women, or retired married couples, but in the early years of the Church, it was common practice to call as missionaries men who had wives and children. One man who was family-focused, and who was a community and church proponent, and who was Ane's son-in-law, Henry Albert Bjorkman, was appointed to his mission for the Church of Jesus Christ of Latter-day Saints to serve in his home country of Denmark on 11 November 1910.[498] The children of "the first family" were young: Lorena, nine; Leonard, seven; Eleda, five; Flora, three; and Frances, nine months. My mother mentioned memories of those days to LaRelia, who wrote of them:

> When Flora was nearly three years old, her father was called to the Scandinavian LDS Mission headquartered in Copenhagen, Denmark, his birthplace. Although Flora was too young to really understand what was going on, she did remember the excitement and people coming and going as her father prepared to leave. Flora also remembered that she slept downstairs in a bed that folded up to look like a piece of furniture (something like a wooden chest) when not in use.[499]

Sophia and her five children continued to live with Ane while Henry was away. Sophia worked at the post office during her husband's absence, and her brother Eli helped out by not only working his own farm in Central, but also working the Bjorkman farm or homestead in Central for that family.

In an undated interview, my mother, Flora, said that when her father, Henry, returned from his mission, Sophia had "$600 in savings, all bills paid, and had bought an organ. It was the only time in their lives they were out of debt."

Did Sophia's post office earnings contribute to Ane's household? Did Ane have someone working her hay lot farm for income? Did they simply live on what they grew themselves?

Aunt Eleda wrote further about that time:

> We lived with Grandma Hansen the full time that Dad was in Denmark on a mission. He left on October 3rd 1910 and returned May 4th 1913. We three older children [Lorena, Leonard, Eleda] learned to speak the Danish language very well, living with Grandma Hansen. However, after we left the last time in the spring of 1914 and moved to Idaho, we had no need to speak Danish. After we bought a car, we went to see her.[500]

During these times of living with Ane, Flora and Eleda developed the sweet relationships with their grandmother that they remembered so fondly. Their vignettes of Ane provide precious glimpses of this woman who left no journal and who seldom appears in official records.

Eleda wrote more of her loving account of Ane:

> Grandma [Ane] brought a large homemade trunk filled with expensive, beautiful clothes from her home in Denmark. She wore them to meetings until one of the women told her she would have to wear clothes like the rest of the women.... Of course, Grandma made the change. She put her fancy clothes down in trunks and still had them when my mother was a young lady.... She also brought their standard sleeping equipment: two feather beds—one to sleep on and one to have over her at night. She had a small dog that slept on top of the feather bed. I remember the day she had Uncle Eli come and get the dog and put him to sleep. He was very old.
>
> The story of my Grandmother Hansen would not be complete without including the fact that she knit almost all of the stockings that we wore. They were knit of black wool yarn and came way above the knees. They were held in place by garters fastened to what was called a "panty waist" or by round elastic garters. Homes and schools were heated by stoves that burned wood and coal and since heat always rises

the floors were cold. We wore underwear with sleeves to our wrists and legs to our ankles to help keep us warm.

The wool for this underwear was sold to my father [Henry Bjorkman] quite cheaply. His two brothers, Victor and Oscar, managed the woolen mills in Logan, Utah. Once in a while there would be a flaw in the material that was being woven to make underwear there at the factory. When that happened they sold the whole bolt to my father.[501]

LaRelia interviewed our mother, Flora, and scribed some of her memories of that time period:

[Flora] remembered what was called a "shanty" (a one-room building located a few steps from the house) where her mother and grand-mother canned fruit and did the laundry. One of the things they made was currant jam, which they put in a crock, covered, and stored in a cool place (most likely the cellar) for future consumption.[502]

Mother said the building outside was called the summer kitchen, and the women used it during the hot months to keep the heat from canning, cooking, and laundry from warming the main house to uncomfortable temperatures.

LaRelia elaborated further on our mother's experiences with her dear grandmother:

Flora was very close to her Grandmother Hansen who spent a consid-erable amount of time with her. They fed the chickens and took care of the garden together... Grandmother Hansen had a dog which always slept on the foot of her bed. The Bjorkman children were not allowed to play with him, however.... It is interesting that Flora was able to communicate with her grandmother who spoke primarily Danish.... Both of Flora's parents also spoke Danish. Flora remembered that as children she and her brother and sisters heard enough Danish spoken in their home [that] they could understand it. However, they did not learn to speak the language themselves except for a few phrases. Their parents wanted the children to be "Americans" and, to them, speaking English was an important part of that Americanization.[503]

In the history from Karen Marie's family, one narrator says—with a bit of pique that was understandable given the difficult challenges of the polygamy lifestyle during those years—that:

> Grandpa [Jens] was a very good carpenter but I guess he never had
> enough money to build Grandmother [Karen Marie] a new house....
> Aunt Annie came from Denmark with some other converts (for the
> purpose of finding a husband). I remember her quite well. She was
> never a pleasant person that I remember of and was very demanding,
> so life was very hard for my grandmother at that time.[504]

How does one find an accurate point on the continuum between this bitter opinion of Ane and the adoration of her granddaughters? Everyone has disagreeable moments, perhaps of selfishness or jealousy, and yet is loving and kind at other times or with other people, often especially with children. Maybe Ane behaved one way with her grandchildren and another way with the first wife's family. Or maybe Karen Marie's family could only see Ane one way. Maybe my mother's saying that the two wives did not get along while Jens was living has some truth.

And Eleda wrote:

> I loved my grandmother very much and I am sure that she had a great
> influence on me. I am grateful for the privilege I had of associating
> with her during my childhood.
>
> In the summer, Eli, his wife [Sophora] Jenkins, and his family and
> Sophia and Henry and their family lived in Idaho where they had each
> homesteaded. In the fall and winter we lived with Grandma Hansen in
> Newton, Utah. The trips back and forth were made via covered wagon
> until some of the children were old enough to go to school. At that
> time, we went to Utah by train. We arrived early in the fall and lived
> with Grandma Hansen through the winters.[505]

How did those winters with her home full of family compare with the summers when Ane was alone at home? The contrast must have been enormous. Maybe it was as Carol May, a former therapist, suggested regarding adult children living in the parent's home: "There are two videos—one when they are there and one when they are not there—and both are good." Did Ane enjoy the summers of respite from caring for so many people? Or did she miss her grandchildren and yearn for the winters, when they developed their special closeness?

Cache Valley had been the home ground for the Shoshone for centuries before the settlers moved into the area. While this work will not include a detailed history of those interactions and resentments, there were concerns in my mother's time about interactions with the original inhabitants. Mother mentioned one such encounter that took place while she was staying with her grandmother:

When they went through they expected to be cared for. I remember them coming to our house in Newton and they had great big bags. They'd hold them open and they would expect you to fill them. I definitely remember one big buck saying, "Apples, apples." He wanted to fill out his bag with apples. At this time of year apples were on and they used to can them on the river about a block from our home there in Newton. That was a scary time for kids. They all stayed home.[506]

My father, Vernal Fowler, was present for this interview with my mother and added the following regarding his life nearby in Idaho:

We were three and a half miles from school. Being that far away and with sagebrush all over the country and the Indians, Mother and Dad were afraid to send a child out, and so I was nine years old before I started school. The Indian problems weren't serious, but I remember Mother worried a lot about them. You never knew when they would come or go through the territory. I remember we went to a celebration on the west of town in Grace [Idaho] and some Indians came and went through the bowery area and jumped over the seats and hollered and yelled, but they really didn't do any damage.... [T]he people satisfied them and they went on their way. I was just a little kid and I was shaking like a leaf.[507]

One can certainly understand the aggressiveness and expectations of the Native Americans who felt aggrieved first with the fur trappers and later with the white settlers who had displaced them. The settlers who moved onto those lands and interacted with the native peoples must have felt some uncertainty and fear regarding the aggression.

Mother said her Grandma Hansen was resourceful. She cooked, mended, gardened, preserved, and got by on nearly nothing. In an interview in 1975, Mom related a story of a time when the Bjorkmans were living with Grandma Hansen and attending school in Newton:

When we were children I remember when I was going to school we'd take a lunch and our mother or grandmother would give us an egg to cash in at the store for some candy. Of course, we didn't get that every day but it was a real treat. I'll tell you, we were very careful with that egg to be sure that it got to the store![508]

Ane and Karen Marie associated with one another through the experiences of grief and change, as well as the additions of grandchildren. Their coffee time perhaps gave them a chance to speak in the Danish language about their families, the events in the community and church, and reminiscences of their shared homeland.

Away in Denmark, Henry Albert Bjorkman served well as a missionary and was President of the Copenhagen Conference from 1912 to 1913.[509] He was released from his mission on 14 April 1913,[510] and returned home on the SS *Tunisian*.[511]

Aunt Eleda described the flurry of preparations made for Henry's return accomplished by Ane and Sophia, perhaps with some help from the children. The work of food preparation and house cleaning for Henry's arrival also indicate the kind of chores that may have occupied much of Ane's time on a regular basis:

In early February Mother [Sophia] had Uncle Eli butcher a pig. This allowed enough time for the hams, shoulders, and bacon slabs to cure in a sugar and salt brine. Mother and Grandmother [Ane] prepared the meat for sausage. We children helped to grind the sausage. After the meat was properly spiced, Mother and Grandma made it into small patties. These were fried and placed in layers in gallon-sized crocks. When each crock was full the meat was covered with hot grease and set aside to cool. From there it went into the cool storage room. When we used this meat, chunks of the sausage and lard were cut out with a butcher knife and placed in a frying pan to melt the lard and heat the sausage. Never in my many years of housekeeping have I tasted such divine sausage.

Another part of the preparation was the making of fruitcakes. These also needed to be set aside to age in order to taste the best. As each cake cooled it was wrapped in a cloth wrung with brandy. [At this time the Word of Wisdom was still advised but not yet a commandment.] It was then wrapped tightly and placed in a bread can in the storage room to age—another delight of a past age. Occasionally the first wrapper was remoistened and replaced on the cake to keep it from drying out.

Next came the house cleaning. All the mattresses were taken to the back yard and the old straw was taken from them. This was burned and the ticking was refilled with fresh straw from the barn. Washing facilities for heavy quilts were nonexistent in those day [*sic*], so these were taken outside and with Grandma at one end [and] Mother at the other, the quilts were shaken to remove the dust and lint and then aired on the clothesline for days. The feather beds or feather mattresses used by my grandmother were also cleaned in this manner.

Rug cleaning came next. The tacks were taken from around the room-sized homemade rug and it too was put over the clothesline where we all had a chance to beat out the dirt with sticks. The straw that had been under the rug all winter was removed and some clean, fresh straw was put in its place. The rug was then placed over the clean straw in the room and tacked down again. It was like walking on air for a few days, but it soon matted down too....

Mother [Sophia] had tried to prepare us for Dad's return, but when he stepped from the buggy, complete with a long curled up mustache and a black derby hat, he was indeed a stranger. I shied away from him and hid behind my mother's skirts.[512]

My mom, Flora, said she had loved living with her grandmother and didn't really know or like her dad when he returned. She was not happy about moving from Ane's lovely house to the roughing-it homestead, nor at having this strange man take over—the women had been easy to get along with. Eventually, though, she got used to her father and to their new life.

Over the years after Henry's return, he and Sophia had five more children, who we often refer to as "the second family," beginning with their son, Arnold, born in Newton on 13 February 1914. The Bjorkman family moved in the spring of 1914 to the homestead in Central, Idaho, where they settled. Mother told us Henry used the money Sophia had saved while he was on his mission to purchase additional acreage beyond the original homestead.

Also that spring, Eli and Sophora Hansen conveyed a property Ane had earlier transferred to him—the N ½ of Lots 7 and 8, Block 11—to C. A. Quigley of Salt Lake City through a deed executed on 10 April 1914, for a consideration of $485. The said C. A. Quigley filed the deed to the N ½ Lots 7 and 8 one month later on 18 May 1914[513] thus removing that piece of Ane's real estate from family ownership. Eli kept the adjacent piece of land for which he had paid $1,200, leaving me to wonder whether that parcel had a house on it. As near as I can tell, this is the land that had the dugout on it.

Eleda's history describes an event in which two men came to the house and "wanted to buy our farm in Idaho.... [T]hat evening after supper Dad asked each one of us if we wanted to continue to live in Newton or move to the farm in Idaho. We all wanted to live in Idaho." My mother, Flora, made it clear that, contrary to Eleda's story, the family's vote on the move had *not* been unanimous. Mom had not voted to move to Central, and indeed she did not want to go.

Eleda described the preparations for traveling to the homestead:

> Mother [Sophia] and Grandma [Ane] cooked and baked and packed
> supplies to take to the ranch. Among them were the bedding, home-
> made soap, cured meat, flour, potatoes, canned fruit, jams, jellies, dishes,
> utensils, clothing and other things too numerous to mention. Some
> furniture was loaded into the wagon—a bedstead, chairs, a small table,
> and all sorts of odds and ends belonging to us children. A barrel was
> fastened to the side of the wagon to ensure drinking water during
> the trip.[514]

Imagining the magnitude and complexity of preparations for the move to the
homestead leaves me exhausted. They could not just pop into a store and pick
up some little items they had forgotten. They had to be completely independent
as they headed across the miles to the homestead.

When the time came for the family to leave Ane's refuge, young Flora had
these feelings:

> I had planned a secret hiding place for me in the hen house. Although
> I knew the cackling hens would disclose my place of concealment, I
> felt very secure with my plan to be left in Newton.
>
> After weeks of preparation to make the three-day trip to Idaho, the
> day of departure arrived early in May 1914. Loading of the outfits in
> the caravan had been done the night before. Relatives and friends came
> to help get everything in the proper place and anchored securely. The
> buggy we were to ride in was loaded, so there [were] not seats to sit on.
> We arranged ourselves a place on the load and were ready to move on.
>
> Someone had neglected to tie the buggy to the wagon ahead, so
> the caravan moved on without the buggy. That was a source for great
> amusement among the old and young spectators. I was embarrassed.
> Leaving my grandmother [Ane] was most difficult for me. We had a
> good relationship.
>
> After three days traveling with a sick crying baby, the Bjorkman
> family of eight members arrived to the rundown home in Central,
> Idaho. From the condition of the house I thought it was an overnight
> stop over place. When I compared it to what we left in Newton, I
> thought a big mistake had been made.
>
> I do feel badly that I stuck my tongue out at the onlookers when
> the buggy did not follow the caravan.[515]

Did Ane know that Flora had planned to hide out and continue to stay with her? As Ane watched the horses, wagon, buggy, and the little family move off down the street, away from her home, what did she feel? I always get teary at goodbyes, even when I know they are not permanent. I imagine her standing at the edge of the road, watching them until they disappeared around a bend, wiping an eye with a corner of her apron, and immediately going to work in the house or garden to keep her mind off the sorrow of separation. Or maybe, as Richard suggested, she breathed a deep sigh of relief!

❧

The lives of our family members were altered significantly by the arrival of automobiles that began to appear in Newton. Jens's son James P. Hansen had a Buick f#147273 Touring Car with 37 horsepower in February 1915. Others in Newton were also among the first to acquire this modern convenience. Grandpa Henry was the first person in Central to acquire an automobile. The cars made transportation between Newton, Central, and Logan more accessible.

❧

Ane and her family experienced a tragedy on 4 April 1915, when her grandson (Eli's third son) Stanley Clinton, was eight years old. My family story is that Stanley had attempted to jump over a burning straw stack and fell short of his goal, landing in the flames.

The newspaper said: "Stanley Hansen, aged 8 years, son of Eli Hansen of Newton, was burned to death when a burning straw stack on which he and several other boys had climbed caved in."[516]

Eli's written history says:

> It was Easter morning and he died in a straw stack that had been set on fire. His flesh was burned from his bones. They had to tear bed sheets and wrap his body in them for burial. He could not be shown. He was waiting for his Father to come home from Grace to baptize him. He was later baptized [by proxy] in the Logan Temple by his Father doing the work.[517]

What an excruciating loss! When Marshall died, my mother said, "I don't know how to comfort you because my heart is broken." How did Ane and Eli's family comfort each other in the tragic loss of this young child?

Eli's wife Sophora was pregnant at the time of young Stanley's death, and two months later, on 22 June 1915, she gave birth to Lyle Ray, their sixth child. Maybe new life helped ease their grief.

※

After the Bjorkman family moved from Newton to Central to live permanently, the young girls missed their Grandma Hansen. Eleda's history says:

> I had hoped that she [Ane] would spend some time with us on the farm in Idaho. She came one summer for a visit and to help when Lorena had spotted fever, but she did not like the wild country and she missed her long-time friends in Newton so much that she did not come to the farm again.[518]

Who were Ane's longtime friends? Could they have been the people for whom LuDean (Carla's neighbor) said Jens agreed to sponsor and marry Ane? Ane had lived in Newton for thirty-seven years by this time, though, so her longtime friends could have been those new ones she made after her arrival.

My mother's history says:

> Flora remembered that Grandmother [Ane] Hansen came to Central [during the hot part of] the summer after the Bjorkman family moved there permanently. She stayed with them a week, but she passed away the following year... and Flora never saw her again.[519]

Evidently Ane's single visit to the family in Central took place in the summer of 1915.

A further real estate transaction took place on 14 December 1915 when C. A. Quigley sold the N ½ of Lots 7 and 8 in Block 11 Plat A of Newton Townsite Survey (sold to him by Eli the previous April for $485) to Arthur Crookston for $300.

Of interest on this deed document are forty small stickers in a rectangle at the bottom of the page that say, "DOCUMENTARY, United States Internal Revenue, Series of 1914. Eight say two cents and thirty-two say one cent. Were the stickers a record of some sort of tax? At the time I was doing research in Newton, Arthur Crookston still owned this property where the dugout had likely been located.

On Saturday, 15 January 1916, Karen Sophia and Henry's seventh child, Albert Milton, was born, their first to be born in Central. According to Eleda's history, on the very next day after Albert's birth, Sunday, 16 January 1916, in Newton:

> [Grandma Ane Hansen] had a stroke in church and never came out of it. She was 73 years old. She died on [Saturday] January 22nd, 1916. Mother [Sophia] could not attend the funeral services because Albert had arrived January 15th, 1916. Dad went to Newton for the services and to act in Mother's place concerning any property dealings.
>
> The huge trunk of beautiful clothes was sent to Mother. I wore out two coats made over from Grandma's [Ane's] clothes. The other children had clothes made over from the trunk also.[520]

Ane's death certificate says she died of cerebral hemorrhage with no contributory causes listed. Her name is spelled "Annie" and the document says she was seventy-two years, ten months, and twenty-eight days old. She lived a week from the time she had her stroke until she died.

I am sad that the beautiful dresses she brought with her when she immigrated to America were not preserved. My sisters and I have speculated that Ane might have made a living as a dressmaker, but on her death certificate where it asks for the "Occupation: Trade, profession or particular kind of work," the blank space is filled in with "none."[521] The informant was her son Eli, who was thirty-four years old at the time of her death and would have known if she had worked in some profession either inside or outside of her home. Perhaps she spent her life solely serving her family in the role that sometimes census data listed as "housewife."

Not only had Sophia given birth to Albert just a day earlier, but her two-year-old, Arnold, was also very ill at the time of Ane's death. Henry went to Ane's funeral in Sophia's stead and brought back with him a swatch of the fabric from which Ane's burial dress had been made. Mother's history says the Newton Relief Society Sisters had made Ane's burial clothes.[522] Lore says there was also lace from Ane's burial dress materials that Henry brought back, but no lace is now with the fabric swatch, and if it existed, I have no idea what might have happened to it.

The following information comes from an interview I had with my mother, Flora, in September 1995:

> In the middle of January 1916, Grandpa Bjorkman had traveled by train from Central to Newton to attend the funeral of Grandma

Bjorkman's mother, Grandma Hansen. Mom doesn't know how news of Grandma Hansen's death came because there was no telephone. Grandma [Sophia] couldn't go to her mother's funeral because Albert was a newborn baby, the seventh child of Grandpa and Grandma Bjorkman.

Mom was nine years old at the time, and she remembers that Arnold, who was a two-year-old baby, developed pneumonia and earache. Rena (age thirteen) and Leonard (age eleven) harnessed the horses, hitched them to a sleigh, and drove them two miles to the bishop's home in winter snow. [At that time, Rasmus G. Jorgensen was bishop of the Central Ward.[523]]

The bishop and his wife came in their [own] sleigh and administered [gave a special anointing and blessing] to the sick baby as a couple. Mom was old enough to think there should have been two men, but they did it together, with the bishop saying the main prayer. They tried to comfort my mom's mother as best they could. The baby was desperate, and Mom believed the blessing saved him. There was no aspirin [or antibiotics] in those days.

The bishop and his wife gave everybody comfort being there. Mom didn't like to see them leave. "Hated—hated isn't the word, but I wished they could have stayed."

The older kids took turns holding the new baby and carrying the sick baby. At that time they all wore long-sleeved, long-legged black underwear because the houses were not warm. There they all were in black underwear, Mom mused.

"Rena was probably out of school to take care of Mother and the baby. She [Rena] missed a lot. The school authority got after Grandpa for it, threatened to turn him in. She was a good little worker."

When my mom and dad (Flora and Vernal) lived in Grace, a woman told Mom that Mrs. Bjorkman (Sophia) had had the children and Rena raised them, "and there's a lot of truth to that," Mom said. (Grace and Central are approximately a ten-mile stone's throw apart, so it is possible that news or gossip could travel between the towns.)

When I asked if that was why Rena never married, Mom said that she had had good chances. "When she got older she said she wasn't going to marry—well, I'll say it—'an old bastard to take care of.' Can you hear her say that? I don't know where she got her language. She certainly didn't learn it at home. I don't think she started talking that way until after she worked at the café. She may have had to defend herself." (Mom was quoting, of course, but I never heard either of my parents utter one swear word or profanity in all the years they lived. I wish my children could say that about me!)

At that moment, Mom's ride for her hair appointment arrived. As she was leaving, she said, "If I think of anything else—oh, yes. They may have been melting snow to do laundry. See—you don't know hardship."

When we talked again after her hair appointment, Mom said that the railroad depot had been in Alexander, Idaho. There were rooming houses for travelers, a pool hall, grocery store, post office, and livery stable. "Now there is nothing." A note from LaRelia, however, indicated that some remains of a rooming house were still there at the time of our conversations (1995).

On 30 November 1995 when I began typing up my notes from this conversation, I telephoned Mom to ask her a couple of questions. I asked how Grandpa Henry got to the train station and she said, "By sleigh. Probably a neighbor took him, or it may even have been Rena and Leonard." (Central to Alexander is approximately seven miles.)

When I asked how far it was from Central to Newton, Mom said they always considered it a three-day campout trip with their horses and wagons, although she wasn't sure of the number of miles. (The distance is approximately seventy-two miles.) Of the times they made the trip, she remembered only the last one, when they went there to live permanently. She was too small to remember the others. She was disappointed when she saw the house. It hadn't been lived in for a while. "But we stayed."

"Over your objections?" I asked.

"We had nothing to say about it.… It was a hard life, but a lot were living the same way."

In other conversations, Flora told again of her disappointment as a young child at having to leave her beloved grandmother and go live on the homestead.

❧

When my eldest sister, MauRene, died suddenly in December 2002 at the age of seventy-three, her eldest son, Lyle Wiggins, found in her genealogical materials and records a swatch of fabric. Years later, when one of my sisters mentioned to me on the phone that they were going to meet with him and see the genealogical items, including some fabric, I shrieked in excitement. "It's the swatch from Grandma Hansen's burial dress! Mom told me that story—that's what it *has* to be!" And they too remembered the story. One of the hardships of living eight hundred miles from the rest of the family is missing those kinds of events, and

I felt sad about not being able to join my siblings to meet with our nephew and to pass the story on to the next generation.

Later, in 2011, when I knew I would again be spending time on a research trip in Utah, I emailed Lyle asking if we could meet, and if so, would he mind showing this piece of fabric to me. He readily agreed, and we set up a time.

On Tuesday, 28 June 2011, Lyle collected me from the lobby of the LDS Family History Library and took me upstairs to his office, where we sat at a table near his desk while he showed me a number of papers, letters, notes, and the previously mentioned skudsmaalsbog. Soon he picked up a small, standard envelope, took something from under the flap, and laid it on the table between us. It was a creamy rectangle of satiny fabric, and I was stunned speechless realizing it had to be the swatch from the fabric used for Ane's burial dress. We have no other history of a special swatch of fabric. I looked at it silently, intently, feeling a few tears pressing their way to my eyes from actually seeing some of the material from which Ane's final dress had been made.

The swatch is about 5 x 7 inches, ivory or cream in color, but as Lyle pointed out, we don't know what color it had been ninety-five years earlier! The fabric is thin, shiny, and has five-petaled flowers, tone on tone, about two inches wide, with smaller flowers set inside the larger ones. At first, I was afraid to touch it because I didn't want to soil it with skin oils, but it had a couple of minute spots on it already, so I picked it up gently, marveled at it, and set it back down. Lyle left the room at one point to make copies of some documents for me, and while he was gone, I held the fabric again and noticed that two parallel edges have selvedges (an edge woven during manufacturing so that the fabric does not unravel or fray), indicating that this might have come from a five-inch wide ribbon that was used to trim the burial dress in some way—maybe a ruffle or a bit of trim down the front of the bodice or around a raised waistline. The fabric is delicate and gorgeous.

When Lyle came back, I mentioned the selvedges. He picked up the fabric and used his magnifying glass to examine it closely. "Trust a woman's eye to notice that!" he said. "I hadn't noticed it."

"Trust a quilter's eye—that's why I noticed it."

Knowing that a camera flash deteriorates fabric, I chose not to take a photograph, but I regretted it later and made arrangements to take a photo in Lyle's home in Salt Lake. In retrospect, I should also have photographed Lyle for the lovely memories of the day.

Ane was independent, choosing to join what must have seemed a radical church against the wishes of her father. Perhaps she had a sense of adventure or wanderlust. Or was it solely her commitment to her new religion that motivated her to leave her home country for the arduous 8,000-mile trip across an ocean and a continent to help carve out a new frontier settlement? Was she motivated by the possibility of marriage? She had courage, and her grandchildren attested to her loving heart.

Mother and her sister Eleda paint a picture of Ane as a gracious and warm lady. The descendants of Jens and Karen Marie with whom Carla and LaRelia have had contact, however, shared a history from their family that expresses negative opinions of Ane. One piece of their family lore shared by LuDean in conversation with Carla (date unknown) stated that because Ane had fewer children than Karen Marie did, she was free to travel with Jens more often. Their history also indicates resentments that Jens never got around to building a house for Karen Marie as nice as the one he built for Ane. Two different faces ascribed to one woman, yet both could be true based on the personal feelings of the reporting individual. No doubt Ane's granddaughters adored and admired her, and the family of the first wife would likely resent her to some degree regardless of who she was as a person. Maybe Ane had to be occasionally disagreeable to protect herself or to set boundaries. But the story of her possible gift of the beautiful crystal set was indicative of her sensitivity to the feelings of others.

In spite of those few negative yet helpful notes from a long-distant past, the descendants of Jens and Karen Marie today could not have been more kind and helpful to me in this project. They also have warm friendships with my sisters. When Mother died, we found in her things a small box of obituary clippings that she had kept of neighbors, family, and friends. Among them were obituaries of descendants of Jens and Karen Marie, indicating that Mom had valued those cousins and had kept track of them.

Mother had a great sense of humor and said her mother (Sophia) had a sense of humor, so I am wondering if Ane had one as well. I have read that Danes have a droll sense of humor, so maybe it is a national trait instead of a family trait. If humor served Ane well in her challenging circumstances as a plural wife with few legal rights, I am glad.

Ane was buried 26 January 1916 in the Newton cemetery on the left-hand side of Jens, between him and their son Moses. Her stone grave marker, raised on a more recent base, reads: *Annie M. Hansen. Feb. 24, 1848. Jan 22, 1916.* Her family honored her with the word *MOTHER* in raised letters across the arched top of her headstone, and floweret designs are pressed into the marker.

❧

The January day of Ane's burial was probably cold and blustery, maybe even snowing, and the group of mourners at the cemetery must have felt the chill inside and out. The daily weather records for nearby Logan that month show the warmest low temperature was 31 degrees Fahrenheit, and the coldest high temperature was 15 degrees Fahrenheit. Precipitation for the month was 2.35 inches, with snowfall of 25 inches.[524] As Henry Albert Bjorkman stood with the others, wrapping his greatcoat tightly about himself, his thoughts and feelings might have vacillated from his sorrow at losing Ane, with whom he and his family had lived on and off for most of sixteen years and whom his children adored, to the concerns for his family back in Central: his new baby son, his ailing toddler, and his wife who was recovering from childbirth and grieving the loss of her mother while missing the funeral services.

Ane's burial dress with the intricately flowered trim was lovingly made by women from the church who likely were also her friends, and she was mourned by her family and friends for the good woman she was. Did Karen Marie attend the services and mourn as well? The two women had been part of a family unit of sorts for twenty-eight years, and for at least the last ten of them—since Jens's death—had frequently shared the ritual of coffee together.

❧

Ane's death brought not only grief but also legal concerns. A number of deed transactions affecting family properties were executed during the years following Ane's death. On 2 January 1917, Sophia conveyed her ten acres of river bottomland, inherited from Ane, to Michael Anderson for one hundred dollars. Henry A. Bjorkman, Sophia's husband, witnessed her signature on the warranty deed. The deed was filed for record four days later on 6 January 1917,[525] thus removing from family ownership approximately two-thirds of the south farm, or hay lot land, that had been a source of security for Ane during her lifetime.

In this chronology, C. A. Quigley on 24 March 1917, filed his aforementioned deed from Eli for the N ½ Lots 7 and 8, Block 11, Plat A, Newton Townsite.

On 10 January 1919, Eli conveyed his 4.25 acres of the river bottomland, hay lot, or south farm, to Sidney A. Alvis for $600. The deed was filed only eight days later on 18 January 1919,[526] and so the remainder of Ane's hay lot property passed out of family ownership.

Two years later, on 11 January 1921, Sophia conveyed her S ½ of Lots 7 and 8, Block 11, Plat A of Newton Townsite Survey—including Ane's home—for $100! Remember that Ane's deed from Jens thirty-nine years earlier in 1882 had carried a valuation of $250 for the entirety of Lots 7 and 8, with her house apparently on them. Sophia sold these half lots and the house to Carl Jorgensen, who had come from Denmark to work for Jens in 1902. Henry A. Bjorkman witnessed her signature.[527] How could she sign away her mother's beautiful home? The place where she and her siblings grew up! Carla says the house was rented for a while and vacant for a while, so maybe that's why Sophia sold it. Although the home being out of family ownership saddens me, I am grateful that it has not been torn down, as we had been told in error, and we can view it and imagine the lives of our family members who used to occupy that lovely house. My sisters and I cherish memories of stepping inside it, seeing the marvelous cabinet drawers and doors on the west wall, and imagining Ane's fruit drying in the bright sunlight streaming through the south windows.

❧

I am puzzled as to why Eli charged $485 for his north half of the two lots, unless he had built a house on it in the interim—likely where the dugout had been—as well as why Sophia charged merely $100 for her south half of those lots with Ane's house on the property. Was she giving a break to Carl, who had become like family? Did she not know the value of the property? Had the house become dilapidated while it was vacant and thus lose significant value?

This business discrepancy pattern repeats in that Eli charged $600 for his smaller portion of the south farm (4.5 acres), and Sophia charged $100 for her larger portion of the south farm (10 acres). Does this reflect the real value of the properties based on geographical features and the location of the water? Did Eli have a better business sense? Did Sophia have less knowledge or a softer heart? Was she extremely eager to be free of the property? Or was Henry eager to have cash in hand to add further acreage to the homestead in Central?

Jens died ten years before Ane did, and soon after her passing, Ane's properties were transferred to nonfamily ownership. Gone. History vanishes, and time moves on. And Ane is not the only one who I wish had kept a journal to preserve their stories and memories for those of us who have and will come after them.

❧

Ane had a tender heart for her beloved grandchildren, and little nuggets of information allow us to visualize and sense her more as a person. Although her life was difficult in some ways, for her to have been adored by her grandchildren, she must have exemplified genuine love and joy.

I remember visiting my Aunt Eleda (Sophia's daughter) with my parents when I was about four years old. She opened the door to her home, greeted us happily with her arms extended, and enfolded me in a bear hug. I remember being in my winter coat and hat at the time. She and Uncle Herman had an old-fashioned wall phone mounted in a wooden box with a cone-shaped earpiece on a cord that hung from a hook on the left side, a mouthpiece on the box to speak into, two silver half-sphere bells at the top, and a crank on the side. They cranked the handle to show me how it worked.

After the four adults had finished visiting and my folks prepared for us to leave, Aunt Eleda said to wait for a moment. She found a small brown paper bag in her upper cupboard and filled it with peanuts in the shell and hard candies, folded the top over, and gave it to me, along with one more bear hug. I wonder now whether the wonderful bear hugs and little paper bag of goodies she gave me were hospitality gestures she learned from her Grandma Ane.

My own mother always kept homemade cookies in her freezer, thawed them quickly in a small toaster oven, and served them to visitors. No one ever left her home without being offered something to eat. I can still see Mom's living room filled with family, Mom making her circle around the room, offering her large cookie-filled plate to each person in turn. And no one ever said no. I now own the clear cut-glass plate on which she served her cookies, and I love it. Mom often said that offering food to visitors is a Danish custom, part of my heritage. Did my mother learn that custom from her Grandma Ane? Or from her own mother, Sophia?

At the family Christmas party in Ogden, Utah, in December 2014, several of my adult nephews brought cookies they had made from my mother's recipes—jumbles, gingersnaps, and chocolate chip. I am touched and grateful that my mother's cookie traditions—possibly Ane's traditions—live on in the generations that follow.

My mother's tender stories of her Grandmother Ane, told to me on the porch as a child and in front of the blue house as an adult, gave me a glimpse into the deep and abiding love a child can have for a grandmother. Flora and Eleda loved their grandmother with a pure, sweet, and lifelong love. Though I never met Ane, my mother's love for her predisposed me to also love what I knew and what I learned about her in my search. I admire her courage to marry and settle in a foreign country where she didn't speak the language, and to bear and raise children somewhat independently, without the full attention of their father, who had another family. Yet I believe she enjoyed a certain amount of happiness. Perhaps she had an independent spirit that thrived on being in charge of her life and her children and her home. Or maybe she felt lonely like other wives of polygamist men who felt neglected by their husbands.

❦

When my first husband, Marshall, and I lived in Coeur d'Alene, Idaho, my mother's brother Albert Bjorkman was working on a construction project on the freeway along part of Lake Coeur d'Alene. We invited him to dinner one Sunday evening, and when the dishes were cleared, he sat on our sofa in the living room and I sat at his feet on the carpet. Knowing that Grandfather Henry Bjorkman had held thirteen positions of leadership in the community and church, and admiring him for those honors, I said, "I so want to learn more about your father. Can you tell me about him?"

Albert answered, "I never knew the man. He was never home."

Apparently those positions of responsibility also required sacrifice that affected the family. Even so, I've wondered if perhaps Sophia married Henry partly because he was smart and busy and well respected for his many accomplishments in leadership and music, and because he reminded her—perhaps subconsciously—of her father, Jens. Maybe part of what was pleasing in Ane's life was being married to a man of such accomplishments and fine character as Jens. Did she love him? Did Jens love her? Did it matter? They spent twenty-eight years together and left a legacy of religious devotion for their posterity.

CHAPTER 24

KAREN MARIE: 1916–1926

aren Marie lived ten more years after Ane died. Did she feel alone
with both her husband and his plural wife gone, as well as six of her
ten children and several grandchildren? She was married to Jens for
thirty-nine years—eleven years exclusive and twenty-eight years shared with a
plural wife—and she was friends with Ane for ten years beyond the end of the
polygamous marriage. When I was a widow, one of the things I missed most
was the other half of shared conversations—being able to say just one word
and have the other person instantly recall the entire story. The wordless unity
of intertwined experience for Karen Marie with Jens and Ane was gone. What
did Karen Marie feel after losing both of those people? Grieving friends and
I know that grief accumulates: it is etched in the bones. New grief calls up all
other mournings, and they multiply in the soul. In the one photograph I have of
Karen Marie when she was a young adult, she looks haunted. I can only guess
that the expression on her face reflects her deep grief at having lost little children.
Yet she must have been what some would term "a survivor," because no matter
what happened, she kept putting one foot in front of the other.

The history written by Karen Marie's posterity paints a word-portrait of her:

> Grandmother [Karen Marie] was fairly easygoing, taking pretty well
> what came her way. She was a fairly quiet person so we didn't know
> much about her early life. They had to work very hard to provide for
> their family and Grandmother was a very hard worker. She had one
> brother [Lars P.] that lived in Preston, Idaho. They raised sheep and
> Grandmother would sheer those sheep, wash and card the wool, and
> later she spun it into yarn on her spinning wheel. I remember watch-
> ing her many times. The yarn was usually dyed some dark color. The
> brown color was made by using onion skins that had been boiled in
> water. The yarn was then knit into stockings, sweaters, hats, shawls, or
> whatever was needed the most at the time.[528]

Karen Marie was a woman of courage who made major decisions throughout her life: joining the Mormon Church in Denmark, working hard even while pregnant to earn money for travel to America, pulling up Danish roots to settle in Utah, helping to build up a young town, and raising her family there.

Ane's death brought those visits to Karen Marie's home for coffee to an abrupt end, and also terminated the friendship the two women had built in spite of the challenges of sharing a husband for twenty-eight years. I wish too that Karen Marie had kept a journal. What were her feelings and thoughts when Jens was called to take a plural wife? Karen Marie, herself, had later been proxy for Ane Sophie (a woman who had died) to be sealed to Jens. Our family has lore that allows us to surmise he also married a fourth wife, Karen Kirstine Petersen Hansen (a woman who was much older than he was) in mortality merely to take care of her.

How did Karen Marie feel about the other wives, and how did she feel about Ane's passing and the end of their visits over coffee? Had they put animosities aside? I wonder if Karen Marie went to Ane's funeral and talked with my grandfather, Henry Albert Bjorkman, after the services. She would have known him from the winters the Bjorkman family lived with Ane across the street in Newton. Did she miss seeing my grandmother Sophia there, who had played with her daughter Louisa all those years ago? Had she steeled herself against grief by this time?

As LaRelia had commented earlier in a telephone conversation 12 July 2012, if Ane indeed kicked Jens out and they were married in name only—emotionally divorced—then it might have been easier for Karen Marie to be amenable to Ane's friendship. However, the obituary for Ane's son Moses made it sound like she and Jens had not separated. Perhaps in some ways, the wives were family for each other, as they shared decades of living in close proximity. If it is true that practicing polygamy guaranteed a choice position in the next life, then both of these courageous women surely deserve it.

❦

Seven weeks and a couple of days after Ane's death, the newspaper reported that three buildings in Newton had burned 12 March 1916:

> Sunday morning between two and three o'clock, fire was discovered
> in the Newton Co-op. The alarm was sent in and soon a large crowd
> was on the scene, but nothing could be done to save the building

and the whole structure was enveloped in flames. The entire building and its contents were burned to the ground. The flames soon spread to the postoffice [*sic*] which stood nearby and also took the building which was owned by Miss Ruth Jenkins. The Co-op was owned by a number of men. Both places carried some insurance. The origin of the fire is not known.[529]

Thus the wooden post office that Jens had built or helped to build while he was postmaster of Newton turned to ash. I'm glad Jens and Ane did not witness that loss. Perhaps Karen Marie was saddened to see the burning of the small but significant structure that Jens had envisioned and created as part of his innovative service as postmaster. One more connection to him and his life was gone.

Unfortunately, another sorrowful event for Karen Marie and her family took place on 2 September 1917, when Anna Elvena, Jens and Karen Marie's eighth child, died at the age of thirty-four. She was the seventh of Jens and Karen Marie's ten children to die. Karen Marie must have been devastated yet again, and she had no husband or sister-wife to share the sorrow and give her comfort. Did her remaining children and their posterity rally around her?

❦

When I began revising this chapter in the spring of 2015, I had no information about the cause of Elvena's death, and the Family Group Record of Elvena and her husband, Edmund Jenkins, listed no children. I became curious as to what would cause the death of a thirty-four-year-old woman in 1917. Online I visited Utah Vital Records and Statistics but learned that to request a death certificate, one has to be a close relative or must explain in detail why the request was made. I considered the second option but decided first to see if Elvena's name might appear online in someone's journal or other record. A brief record did come up with her correct birth and death dates, correct parents' names, accurate number of siblings (including Ane's children), and husband's correct name. To my great surprise, the final line read: "They had one child: Kenneth Ruel Jenkins."[530]

I immediately searched online for Kenneth Ruel Jenkins and found the obituary of a man who was born in 1917 and died in 2012. Knowing that Elvena died in 1917, I wondered if she had died giving birth to this child. But no, Kenneth Ruel had been born 15 June 1917, three months before Elvena died in September. The internet also brought up a life sketch for Kenneth Ruel Jenkins showing that he was "adopted by Elvenia [*sic*] Hanson [*sic*] Jenkins and Edmund D. Jenkins." It continued:

I was born in Salt Lake City at a maternity hospital. Three days after my birth a childless couple from Freedom, Wyoming, arrived in Salt Lake City looking for a baby to adopt and I was chosen. When I was only 3 months old my new mother died of appendicitis and I went to live with my father's brother, Lewis I. Jenkins and his wife, Mary Ann Griffin, who already had a large family. I was legally adopted into this family but was sealed to my former adoptive parents, Edmund and Elvenia [*sic*].... Sealed: July 9, 1925[.] I remember making the trip to be sealed.531

Kenneth Ruel Jenkins also wrote of working on the farm in Freedom, going to school, and serving a mission in 1940 for the LDS Church in the East Central States—the same place my brother, LaMont, served ten years afterward. Ruel served in the military during World War II and was on Omaha Beach, later worked as an accountant, married, and had a family. His sketch was posted online 18 December 2013. Had I searched for Elvena's cause of death a year and a half earlier, I would have missed out on these surprising new pieces of information.

Carla and LaRelia, during our annual sisters' retreat at Cannon Beach in March 2015, talked of Mother remembering that Elvena and Edmund had come in their car to visit the Bjorkman family on their homestead in Central, Idaho. This would have been between the family move from Newton to Central in 1914 and Elvena's death in 1917 while Mom would have been a young girl between seven and ten years of age. This means that two daughters, Elvena and Sophia—two half sisters from a polygamist family—cared enough about each other to stay in contact after becoming married adults, and to visit together. Maybe Elvena, being childless until just before her death, treasured being around Sophia's children as well.

Elvena was to have inherited Karen Marie's home and ten acres of river bottom property upon Karen Marie's death, but she predeceased her mother. I don't know what arrangements Karen Marie made for those properties after Elvena's passing.

❧

The history written by Karen Marie's posterity provides this about her later years:

When she was quite old and it was hard for her to be alone, she went to live with her son Nephi and his family who lived in Montana at that time. She lived with them for a couple of years but she became unhappy and restless, so they brought her back to live with Mother (Louisa) [Karen Marie's daughter] for the rest of her life. She was so mixed up from this move that her mind was never the same. She didn't remember Mother [Louisa] or any of the rest of us, only my father [James Christian Petersen]. She was always running away trying to find her mother's home. [Her mother was Kirsten Hansen Christensen, who had died thirty years earlier on 11 July 1886.]

She died from pneumonia on 20 December 1927 at home and is buried in the Newton Cemetery. She never learned to read or write in the English language. She had her Danish magazines which she read. She also said the blessing [for meals] and her prayers in Danish. She was very faithful in her tithing and Sacrament Meeting attendance on Sunday afternoon and I often went with her. I stayed with her a lot at nights and learned to love her very much. She was a gentle person and always very giving to others.[532]

Karen Marie Hansen's death certificate says she died from "Hypostatic Pneumonia" with the "Contributory (secondary)" cause as "Old age" at the age of eighty-one years, eight months, and one day. The certificate is dated 20 December 1926, one year earlier than the above-quoted family record indicates. The year 1926 appears on the death certificate: once in the hand of the registrar, Wm. P. Hansen; twice in the hand of the doctor, Dr. Budge; and once typed above the signature of the undertaker, N. A. Lindquist, in regard to her burial place and date. Therefore, the 1926 notation seems more dependable than 1927 shown as Karen Marie's death date in the family history—an easy typographical error. The informant listed was Jens P. Hansen.

Karen Marie was survived by three of her ten children: Jens Peter, Niels Peter Nephi, and Louisa Marie, and their living family members. She was laid to rest on Jens's right in the bucolic Newton Cemetery. In death as in life, Karen Marie was first and Ane was second. I hope Ane gets a fairer shake in a heavenly world operating according to God's tender mercies than she did in the world operating according to the harsh laws of the federal government. How would her life as a plural wife—and those of a thousand others—have been different if the Mormon people had been left alone in the practice of the polygamy facet of their religion? But then, it might still be practiced today, and I would not want to be involved in that lifestyle. I am way too selfish.

In April 2011, I telephoned my Uncle Norman, my mother's younger brother, after writing him with some questions I had about Great-Grandma Ane's life. He was part of the "second family," born after his father's return from his mission. I pictured Norman on the other end of the telephone line in his lovely home in Soda Springs, Idaho, and remembered a visit there with my sisters several years earlier when he had taken us on a grand tour of his flourishing vegetable garden. Gregarious and pleasant, he was a man I always admired and enjoyed being with, and I felt cheated that we lived so far apart because I would have liked him more present in my life. He had a distinctive nose and clear blue eyes, and refused to give in to health problems. Then nearing ninety years of age, he said, "I'd like to help answer your questions, but all I know about my grandmother is what your mother told me—the same as what she told you."

After we visited about other family news, he said, as an afterthought, "You know, there's a great-granddaughter of Eli, my mother's [Sophia's] brother, who lives just a couple of blocks away from us here in Soda. Her name is Karma, Karma Kunz, and she's the daughter of Eli's daughter, Ethel. Just a minute here, and I can look up her address for you...yes, here it is." He gave me her address and telephone number and finished by saying, "She might know something."

I wrote a letter to Karma Kunz telling her of my project and questions, and saying I would call her in a couple of weeks to see if she might have information she could share with me. When I called, Karma was pleasant and personable, but said she didn't know anything, that when she was growing up, the children were sent outside to play after dinner and weren't allowed to listen to the adult conversations. When I asked about photographs, she said she did have one photograph. When I asked if it was the family group shot that our family has copies of, she said, no, that it was just Jens and Ane. She said she would send a copy and declined my offer to pay for it. I told her that in return I would send her something from my research that she might find interesting, and we disconnected amiably. I sent her a copy of the Decree of Distribution from Jens's Probate.

Soon I received a white mailer with Karma's return address. It felt like Christmas as I opened the envelope. Inside I found: a cordial note, including a thank-you for the documents I had sent and encouragement for the project; the biographical sketch of Jens from an historian's interview with him that is included in this work; a photograph of Moses as a portrait made from his image in the family group photo; and a photograph of a man and a woman who did not look to me exactly like I had expected Jens and Ane to look.

I held my family group photo of Jens and Ane up next to the photo from Karma for comparison. Puzzled, I studied them. One moment I thought I saw a resemblance, and the next moment I didn't think it could be the same couple.

But how would Karma have believed this was Jens and Ane unless it *was* Jens and Ane? She too is their great-granddaughter, and Eli's family likely had mementos that Sophia's family—our family—did not have. The man in Karma's photograph had the same hair and beard configuration as Jens, but his cheeks were thin—in fact, his whole person appeared thinner than in the group photos. The woman in the couple photo was lovely. Ane in our family group photo looks, quite frankly, all business. Mother said Ane was a small woman, and in the group photo she appears much shorter than Jens and they are seated at the same level. Karen Marie in the group photo is taller than Jens but may have been seated on a higher chair than he was. In Karma's photo, the woman and the man are the same height, but the photo does not extend down far enough to see how they are seated.

The family group photos were taken around 1899, and Jens died in 1906. Both the man and the woman in Karma's photo look older than those in the family groups, and I believe it was taken after the two family photos, possibly in 1905 just prior to Jens's death. My sisters think otherwise. Their opinion is that the couple photo predates the family group photos. But both people in the couple photo have whiter hair, and Jens's prominent cheekbones have become less pronounced, indicating to me that he has perhaps lost weight, likely because of the 1905 illness mentioned in the newspaper article. A Salt Lake photography studio made the portrait, and I wish we knew why they used Salt Lake rather than Logan. Did the couple take the train to Salt Lake? Or did the photographer travel through Cache Valley taking photos? Why did they have their portrait taken? Were they celebrating an anniversary? (Or fearing their time was short?)

One thing that gave the couple's portrait credibility was Karma's inclusion of the cameo portrait of Moses lifted from the family group photo. Moses died in 1901 soon after the group photo was taken, and it touches my soul to think that his bereaved parents had a memory-photograph of him made from the family shot.

Still pondering the new photo a couple of weeks later, I remembered that when I worked at a bank in the early 1970s, we verified signatures on checks by turning both the check and the signature card on file upside down for comparison. Instead of reading names, we compared the strokes, angles, and proportions. Thinking that practice might also work using facial features, I made copies of the two photos in question, cut the faces out, taped them to a common page, and turned it upside down to compare them. Then I added other photos upside down—even Sophia's as a young girl—and studied them, vacillating.

Still not completely convinced, I had copies of the new photo made to take to the annual Bjorkman family reunion in June to give to the relatives who would be the most interested. At my cousin Alan's ranch in Bancroft, Idaho, I made the rounds Friday night at the cousins' party and again Saturday morning at the main gathering, presenting copies of the photo to Norman, Jess, LaMont, LaRelia, Carla, Lyle, and others. A couple of people—including Norman—actually thrust the copy back to me, saying that it was not of Jens and Ane. I boxed the photos up, puzzled by the reactions.

Could the woman in the photo actually have been Karen Marie rather than Ane? In the two other photos I have of Karen Marie, she looks disquieted—and why wouldn't she, having endured the deaths of so many children and sharing her husband? The woman in this new photo does not look haunted, but instead looks joyful and at peace.

Toward the end of my trip to Utah in June 2012, Iris Petersen (the widow of a descendant of Jens and Karen Marie's daughter Louisa) telephoned LaRelia and made arrangements for herself and her son, Val, to meet with Carla and LaRelia to talk about genealogy the Sunday evening after my departure. I was disappointed that I would miss this meeting but gave my sisters a short list of questions I hoped they would have time to ask Iris and Val, including whether they knew anything about the mysterious photo.

Several days later, I called LaRelia to see how the meeting had gone. When I asked specifically if she had found out about the photo, she said, "Yes. It is Jens and Karen Marie. Iris had the exact same photo." The mystery seemed to be solved, and I was grateful.

But the bottom line for me is this: We have photos of Jens's two families that look like they were taken back-to-back in about 1899. We have one photo of a couple claimed by Ane's family to be Jens and Ane. The same photo is also claimed by Karen Marie's family to be Jens and Karen Marie. I agree that the woman in the portrait doesn't look like Ane, and I admit it could be Karen Marie, but I am not fully convinced. I wonder: Could the woman be Karen Kirstine Petersen Hansen? Not likely. She doesn't look thirty-one years older than Jens.

I am grateful to Karma, whom I've never met, for her generosity in sharing this engaging photo, and yet I still wonder: Who are these people, really?

❧

Another photo of interest came in October 2016 when Uncle Norman's daughter, Pam Bjorkman Petersen, emailed a copy of a photograph that she had found among her father's things when she cleared out his house after he moved into a care facility. She found the metal photograph in an envelope labeled *Norman's grandfather—a musician*. Norman's paternal grandfather was not a musician, so this had to be Jens, although in the photo, he is hard to recognize. He stands in a long dark coat, a dress shirt, and a bow tie, holding a trumpet in each hand. I assumed it had been taken when he was studying brass instruments in Copenhagen, but when I asked Pam to send me what the unreadable printing at the photo edge said, she wrote: "The info on the outside frame says: *Jen Dike Studio, Phoenix, Ariz.* The numbers and letter on the bottom of the picture are DB4127. Then something scribbled out. Possibly y26. Then…12756 AB."[533] That doesn't sound very Danish to me. Another check revealed that Lisle Dike fell in love with the tintype as a youngster, and, self-taught, became an itinerant photographer at age thirteen, ranging as far north as Salt Lake City.[534]

My nephew, Lyle Wiggins, who majored in music and played the baritone horn, responded to my email, 22 October 2016:

> I'm almost certain the trumpet in Jens's left hand is a B-flat pitched the same as the majority of modern trumpets. I'm just guessing, but I think the trumpet in his right hand is either an E-flat or F. That would make it an alto trumpet pitched the same as today's French horn. If the mouthpiece were larger, it could be a small-bore bass trumpet, but I don't think it is.

The following day, 23 October 2016, another email came from Lyle:

> The one in his left hand is a rotary valve trumpet. I think the one in his right hand is also a trumpet but pitched lower (the tubing is longer which lowers the pitch). Many European trumpets (as well as other brass valve instruments) still use rotary valves. They tend to have a darker timber (pronounced "tamber," meaning tone quality) than American and English piston valve instruments. Cool photo!!!

This additional surprise photograph—along with Lyle's astute commentary—offers insight into another piece of Jens's life and his love for music.

☙

I do not resent Karen Marie having been Jens's primary relationship. The law may have marginalized Ane, but she didn't disappear. With the LDS belief that families sealed together in temple ordinances will be together in the eternities, the expectation is that Jens will have both Karen Marie and Ane as wives. He will also have Ane Sophie, who we know was sealed to him; and likely Karen Kirstine, who we believe was sealed to him. And perhaps he will have one more because my grandmother Sophia said her father had five wives. Jens may also have others who were sealed to him but whose records we have not found. And he will have all of the children he had with these wives as his families on the other side of the veil forever. Maybe in the next life we will get some answers. Maybe the mysteries will be solved. As my sister Carla often says about the afterlife, à la Desi Arnaz, "There's gonna be some 'splainin' to do."

CHAPTER 25

REFLECTIONS

W hen I started this project, I was so naïve. I thought Ane's marriage would have been as Cinderella-happy as a regular marriage and that the first wife's marriage would be equally happy. I assumed that a man could balance two relationships and two families with perfect harmony. What was I thinking? Although I knew I would not like to be in a polygamous relationship, I viewed these ancestral people through the unrealistic lens of heroic expectations. Hearing that Jens's wives did not get along while he was alive should have tipped me off that not all was well in this arrangement.

Human jealousies aside, I had no knowledge then that the federal government had persecuted the polygamists of the Church of Jesus Christ of Latter-day Saints by passing multiple laws limiting the rights of these citizens in the territories of the United States, by denying men and women the right to vote or to hold public office, by denying plural wives (and for a time, also their children) the right to inherit, and by imprisoning men who had more than one wife. They also confiscated Church property and buildings, and then charged the LDS Church exorbitant rents to use them. Had it not been for the 1890 Manifesto decreeing an end to new polygamous marriages, the Church itself might have become extinct through this intended financial strangling.

Now I wonder, sadly, whether Ane and Jens had a period of wedded happiness, or whether the rigors of sharing a husband marred both women's marriages from the onset of the second. Did Ane and Jens love each other? Did Ane merely desire children and feel that at the age of thirty-five her chances were over except for polygamy? Or did they marry solely to comply with, and demonstrate devotion to, their new religion?

Cultural expectations regarding the age of a female at her first marriage vary over time and location, but likely in the 1870s Ane's age would have been considered—in Denmark and in America—unusually late for a marriage. Certainly her window of time for having children was narrowing. Three weeks before her thirty-seventh birthday, Ane had her first of three children who were born in 1880, 1881, and 1882. Then Ane stopped having babies, while Karen Marie continued having them. In addition to the five children she already had when Jens married Ane, Karen Marie had five more children who were born in 1880, 1881, 1883, 1885, and 1887. Only two of the last five children lived past toddlerhood. Maybe Karen Marie's being younger than Ane played a role in her ability to continue having pregnancies longer than Ane did..

Why did Ane stop having children? Why did she put Jens's clothing out on the porch and tell him to go stay with his other family? When Ane cut Jens's hair and made him sit on the porch instead of coming inside, did she just want to keep the cuttings outside, or does this barring indicate a rift? A rift that might be the reason Ane stopped having children? If a rift, what might have caused it?

Ane must have felt some security and comfort because she had title to her lovely home and knew she could live in it until she died. I loved the charming wooden knobs on the drawers and doors on her west wall, and when I stood in her kitchen, I imagined her touching them, storing things in them, making slapjacks in that kitchen for her three children, and sometimes also for Jens. She offered her home as a haven in winters for Henry and Sophia, and later, she made space year-round for Sophia and her five children while Henry was in Denmark. Apparently, she also provided room and board to Carl Jorgensen when he came to Newton to work for Jens. Did she provide board and room for Henry Bjorkman as well during the years he worked for Jens, before Carl's time? Is that how Henry came to love young Sophia, who later became my grandmother?

When Mother said she had learned how to make slapjacks from her mother, Sophia, and that Sophia had probably learned from her mother, Ane, I wondered whether Sophia had also learned her stoic attitude from Ane. The following note in Sophia's own handwriting was discovered among her things when she died:

Experience during Depression 1930–1935:
Lost 140 acres of wheat by hailstorm
Lost 4 carloads of potatoes for the shortage of market
Lost one Durrant car
Lost one Delco plant and equipment
Lost power and light
Lost radio and telephone service
Lost one Hudson car
Lost several life insurance policies
Lost the home and water

Now pioneering.
Call it troubles if you like.
Be master of your feelings.
S.B.

Did Sophia learn to be master of her feelings from watching her plural-wife mother, Ane? Did Ane have a cache of disappointments that she determined she would rise above? Was mastering human emotions part of what polygamy was all about? At the time I was given a copy of this notation from Sophia, I had been a widow for ten years and had found that expressing my feelings had been therapeutic. I was not of the same stoic "be master of your feelings" mindset as Sophia, though I admired her for it.

No doubt Ane's life was challenging in many ways. She never had the experience of an exclusive relationship with her husband. As a plural wife, federal laws marginalized her. She probably had to keep a low profile during the time that Jens was being hunted for arrest as well as during and after his prison time, and even until the Manifesto began changing things. She cared for her home and children with the hard labor required before modern conveniences. If she made her beautiful dresses, she must have done so by hand. I wondered if they could have afforded a treadle sewing machine. Perhaps the dresses and the crystal set indicate she was indeed well off in Denmark, and maybe this is where the rumors of royalty originated. But what would she have earned as a maid?

What would a personal journal from Jens or Ane or Karen Marie have told us about their lives, their feelings, and their marriages? I wish they had *all* kept one. Although neither Ane nor Karen Marie learned to speak English, their journals written in Danish could have been translated. Did they not learn to write in Danish during their compulsory education there? Somewhat sobering to me are Karen Marie's signature line on the document for Nomination of Administrator in Jens's probate when he died: "Karen Maria Hansen X her mark"; and Ane Margrethe's signature line on the Agreement in Jens's probate: "Annie M. Hansen X her mark." Would not a Danish signature also be readable in English? Did these women hold onto their native language as a way of resisting the new culture, or of holding their homeland close? Newton had a mix of English and Scandinavian settlers, so learning English would have been possible—and advantageous—but there was also a clannish resentment between the two cultures. Paper and ink, or even time, for a journal may have been hard to come by. Perhaps the women were too busy caring for their homes, families, and gardens to write. Maybe they felt like my mother, who said of her own life:

"It was hard and no one would want to read about it." If so, they were wrong. A difficult life does not deter a reader's interest.

Jens is rumored to have given Ane the deed to her house and then to have changed his mind. Did he change his mind after she put him out? Or did she put him out because he changed his mind? When my mother first told me this story, I assumed the deed was of joint tenancy with right of survivorship. I didn't see the real significance of the story until I found the recorded deed from Jens to Ane for the two lots on which her house stood, and discovered it was *her* deed to the property with sole ownership. Likely this reputed skirmish took place before the deed was recorded, so Jens could have torn it up and remained the owner of record. Some posit that the women in polygamy were oppressed, but this story indicates that Ane had gumption in standing up for herself, even in the complex fabric of polygamy. Ane apparently could navigate quite well on her own behalf.

Jens died in 1906, having been married to Karen Marie for thirty-nine years and to Ane for twenty-eight years—both long marriages. His death was the end of the era of polygamy in his two (or more) families, an era that continues to hold questions whose answers remain hidden. Many answers *did* surface, however, in various records—many over 150 years old!—that came to me by the grace of some spirit that attended this search, and I am grateful.

❧

Several mysteries still puzzle me. One is this: Did Ane and Jens meet in Denmark? Did she know who he was when she packed her trunk and purportedly took a gift of crystal with her? As I searched the microfilm for Jens's court documents, I read the transcript of another man's trial, in which he attested that he had known a woman in England and had sent for her when he was asked to take a plural wife. Did Jens know Ane in Denmark? Was he willing to sponsor and marry her for her friends in Newton partly because he already knew who she was? Or was he merely being kind or obedient on a large scale?

Another puzzle is the identity of the woman in the photo with a man who could be an aging Jens. Using other photos as jump-off points for analysis, we still were unable to positively identify this couple. The photos we have of the two family groups are nine years post-Manifesto, showing that Jens was still involved with both of his families. He had not, as the federal government had demanded, abandoned his second family. Everyone in both photos is dressed nicely, and the photos indicate that they must have been affluent enough to hire a photographer. Comparing these family photos with the photo of the man purported to be Jens and the woman purported by our family members to be Ane, but purported by members of the first family to be Karen Marie, yields no concrete conclusion.

It appears that Jens leaned more toward his first family than his second. Is that because he didn't really love Ane? Even for a time? Was it a marriage of obedience only? Had he shown enough favoritism to Karen Marie before the federal "crusades" and his incarceration that he hurt Ane's feelings and warranted her emotional withdrawal? Obviously some sort of friction existed between them, at least for a time. Did the death of their son Moses bring them together in shared grief? Or push them apart emotionally? Few divorces were formally granted in those days, but couples could be emotionally severed without a decree.

The photo labeled as a town banquet of 1899—but that I believe is of the Relief Society anniversary party because so few men and no young children are in it—lists Ane and Karen Marie and Louisa adjacently in the group. Jens was still living, and the two wives sat or stood together at this function. They must have been at least cordial during his lifetime to be together at this event. And whether amicable or stoic, the two wives were side by side.

We have long had family lore or rumors of Jens having more than his two wives of record. Now we know that Jens was sealed in the Logan temple to Ane Sophie Christensen, who never left Denmark, and the sealing was done after her death. Her proxy for this sealing was Karen Marie—so she knew about it and apparently gave her consent. The woman's last name was the same as Karen Marie's before her marriage, so LaRelia and I think they might have been related, but research has not corroborated that assumption. Sealing is for the next life, so this ordinance was to provide Ane Sophie with an eternal family. Who was this mystery woman?

We also have reason to believe Jens was sealed to another woman—Karen Kirstine Petersen Hansen—whom he baptized and confirmed in Denmark in 1875, and who died in Newton in 1890. I don't know her birthplace or when she emigrated from Denmark. We do know that Jens went with her to the Logan temple to be proxy for her father in sealings in 1887. Though she was thirty-one years older than Jens, they had a relationship of some kind for a fairly long dura-tion—at least fifteen years. We assume, because Karen Kirstine Petersen Hansen is listed in the Newton Ward Records on the Jens Hansen family page, that she and Jens were married in an unrecorded ceremony. This would match with the lore that he married an older woman just to take care of her and also match the story that my grandmother remembered taking care of an older woman with a broken leg. Karen Kirstine has not shown up in any other records. And we still know nothing of the rumored wife number five as enumerated by Sophia.

One of my great frustrations is the mysterious elusiveness of Jens's court documents. Why are they not included in the microfilm records of those other cases? Why are the originals not in the archives in Denver? What happened to them? I asked several people if it had been possible in that time period to have a record expunged, and the answer was invariably "Possible but very unlikely." Where are Jens's court documents? Moldering someplace? Tossed out? Misfiled? Possibly never forwarded from the prison that no longer exists? In the probate file is a page saying that a sealed document had been microfilmed and sent from Utah Correctional Industries. What was in the sealed document? And why was it sent to State Archives?

I often think about Jens and Karen Marie and Ane, and I try to place myself in Newton back in that time period and imagine what their lives might have been like. Their daily tasks of living demanded more of their personal and physical energy than our modern tasks do. My parents used to go by horse and wagon to a river to bring water in barrels to their house. Though many people now raise their own food as a healthy option, for Jens and his families doing so was a necessity. Jens and Ane chose a difficult path with their polygamous or plural marriage and complicated Karen Marie's life, whether she supported their decision or not. They all weathered the loss of children and continued to do what they saw as their duty even when their hearts were full of sorrow. They stayed true to the tenets of their religion, no matter what.

What would make a man and his family cling to this religion that brought them so much heartache? Apparently these people believed with all their hearts that this new religion was the true path to God, the restored gospel of Jesus Christ, or they would have abandoned it rather than suffer such hardships and dangers.

Thousands of European emigrants—especially those who were English and Scandinavian—had converted to the Church of Jesus Christ of Latter-day Saints, given up material goods as well as friends and home country, and traveled to Utah to be with the Church. They braved storms and illness and possible death at sea to make this geographical journey. Many women were pregnant when they traveled. Some of my maternal ancestors decided to traverse the ocean by ship, then take a train across a continent to Utah. Earlier some of my paternal ancestors had come over the ocean and crossed the continent in covered wagons before the existence of the railroad. What empowered them to do this? Why would they not just say no, thank you? Something compelled them to change their lives, to follow the new religion, to make sacrifices and commitments for the dream of new lands and a better life as promised by Brigham Young—a utopia where members would live in a covenant society and the poor would be taken care of.

Over the years, I had noticed that some members of the Church treated the beliefs and tenets as a smorgasbord, picking and choosing the parts of the faith they would embrace. But I had been taught that living the faith requires doing one's best with *all* of the principles, practices, and ordinances. One young missionary said to me, "The path is there as clear as daylight. All you have to do is hop on and get moving." What made these ancestors totally commit to their new religious path? And did they suffer repercussions as religious rebels for leaving their original faith to join this new one?

About an hour from our home is a Trappist Abbey—Our Lady of Guadalupe—that allows guests for retreats. Richard and I first went there in 2001 so he could interview one of the priests to enrich the world religions course he taught at Oregon State University. We enjoyed the quiet and beauty of the abbey so much that for a time we made it an annual retreat, and occasionally I also rented a small day room—with a desk and chair, a sofa with afghans, and lunch included—for quiet writing and meditation. In the St. Paul room a plaque hung on the wall and read, in part, *The way to love God is without measure.* I was struck with how obvious that idea was, and yet so hidden from my myopic view. I realized in that modest room that if one truly *loves* God, then everything else is given freely because of that devotion. It is not a matter of picking and choosing what tenets are comfortable but rather a matter of loving God enough to gladly commit to all He asks—though this might vary according to one's own religious beliefs or church's teachings. I remembered that in the scriptures, Jesus said, "Thou shalt love the Lord thy God with all thy heart, and with all thy soul, and with all thy mind. This is the first and great commandment. And the second is like unto it, Thou shalt love thy neighbor as thyself. On these two commandments hang all the law and the prophets."[535] That moment was an epiphany for me, as it explained so much, so simply. Yet the complexity of following that injunction offers one of life's greatest challenges.

My bottom line is this: I admire faithful souls. I was raised on LDS Church history and have taken it for granted, and was even bored by it as a teenager. But now, seeing it through older eyes, I have a deep appreciation for what those early members of the Church historically suffered through and what devout Mormons continue to tolerate today as they attempt to live faithful lives amid jeering, derogatory plays and productions, graffiti on their buildings, disrespectful online posts about sacred matters, anti-Mormon articles and books, hostile groups picketing outside the temple grounds as the members gather for semiannual conferences, and break-ins at their chapels (as happened at mine) resulting in theft, arson, and damage to computers. Revisiting this Church history and the stories of my ancestors has enriched my life and my devotion in countless ways.

Leslie Marmon Silko, the esteemed Native American writer, appeared in Portland, Oregon, in October 2010. One of the things she said from the stage at the Arlene Schnitzer Concert Hall that has stayed in my memory is that *every book you write should change you in some way.* The process of writing and compiling this book has changed my life in many ways. I have a new appreciation for what the early members of the Mormon Church suffered and sacrificed for their unshakable faith in their religion, and for the way they endured the onslaughts of the federal government and its laws that denigrated them and denied them their civil rights. I have developed tenderness for the early history of the Church I was raised in.

Immensely significant to me are the countless coincidences or synchronicities that came across my path to aid me in ferreting out this story. My writing group asked how I explained the plethora of amazing incidents that accompanied this search. I have come to personally believe—not piggyback believe—that there is some energy beyond my reality that is ready to help and does not wait to be asked. So many serendipitous findings simply fell into my lap. At least that is how I describe those minor miracles that seemed too tailored to the search to have been accidental.

My violin teacher's mother was right when she said miracles accompany the work of genealogy. Many people believe that the departed ancestors influence the search for their stories. Kathleen Goodbaudy, a librarian in the LDS Family History Center in Hillsboro, Oregon, said, "Genealogy is like a game of hide and seek. They are there because they lived, but sometimes they are hiding, and they might be hiding in a place unlike any you would think of hiding yourself." My nephew Lyle Wiggins said, "You can sometimes find information through pure skill, but other times it is not found until the person wants it to be found." And my sister LaRelia Jones said, "You find what they want you to find." Other people believe that God or the Holy Spirit or even guardian angels lead researchers to what there is to be found.

I believe all these explanations have validity. I certainly cannot take credit for the amazing connections that arose as I researched. Even my winning a raffle ticket that included a free developmental edit, and a free writing class that ultimately led me to my publishing consultant, Vinnie Kinsella, and to my book coach/editor, Susan DeFreitas, seemed to be a deliberate gift of some unseen spirit wanting to open pathways for completion of this project. Later coincidentally sitting at a table adjacent to Susan and her husband at Higgins Restaurant & Bar after a symphony, I recognized her from the writing conference and introduced myself. We then had our first conversation where I learned that she was a book coach who wanted to help her clients create the book they envisioned, not the book someone else wanted it to be. The next morning I looked up her website, then emailed asking her to be my coach, and she accepted. This chance meeting just added to my sense of kismet.

An example of another unexplainable coincidence took place at my Ogden High School 50th year reunion in 2013. Friday evening we spent in the school. The building is on the National Register of Historic Places, is built in the art-deco style, and has been featured in movies. We visited with old friends in the new cafeteria while having ice cream, and after a program of singing and entertainment in the auditorium, we were invited to go to the former choral room with its remarkably high ceiling to see how it had been remodeled into a community room with murals of beautiful tigers—our mascot. The group thinned out at this point, and those who stayed crowded sardine-like into the choral room. We remembered each other as we had been fifty years earlier, but we now all looked old and literally had to get up close enough to each person to read his or her nametag.

As we looked around the choral room, I saw a man nearby who looked familiar, but I couldn't place him. I moved closer to read his nametag: *Marvin White*, and recognized him as having been in the same algebra class that I took our junior year. Since I was close enough to read his tag, I started asking him questions. He mentioned that he was serving as a missionary in the LDS Family History Center in Pocatello, Idaho, where he and his wife were living. I said that sounded exciting. He said, "It does?" I said yes, that I had been researching my ancestors from Newton, Utah, and had become addicted to it. His wife had been standing behind him, and now she stepped forward facing me and said, "I was raised in Newton." She said she had worked with Carol Milligan on a book about Peter Benson, and I exclaimed, "I have seen that book! It's a lovely book!" She asked who my ancestors were, and I told her. I commented that Norris Cooley was living in my great-grandmother's house and that I was dying to have a photo of the kitchen wall with the doors and drawers but had gotten no response to my request. She encouraged me not to give up, said that Norris's father had been the stake president, and they were a nice family.

Her nametag read *Susan White*, and finally, I asked what her maiden name had been. When she said, "Sutherland," a memory came up from the mists of my brain of the years when I had stayed several times at the Old Rock Church Bed and Breakfast in Providence, Utah, on my research trips when all the motels in Logan were full due to an annual bike race event. The hostess had been a lovely woman with whom I'd had several long conversations about family history. I asked, "Are you related to the hostess at the Providence Old Rock Church Bed and Breakfast? I can't remember her name."

Incredulously she asked, "Dini?"

"Yes, Dini!! We had some great conversations."

"She's my sister-in-law. She married my brother. She told me about a woman who stayed there in the summers and who was working on a Newton family history. Is that you?"

"Unless there were two of us, yes."

Dini had sat with me and visited at breakfasts. She had mentioned a sister-in-law who was working on a history of a Newton family, and I realized that she had been talking about this Susan Sutherland White and her book. The next evening, Susan and I met again by chance at the reunion dinner and we talked briefly of more memories and connections.

What are the chances that in a crowd of people milling about—when the graduating class numbered over 500 students—we would meet? And even meeting, what are the chances that the plethora of possibilities for conversation topics would narrow down to connect us in that way? I felt it was another one of those minor miracles that were arranged by some unseen serendipitous energy.

This family search has also been my own journey, one in which the stories have changed me, mellowed my attitude toward LDS Church history, enraged me about political injustices, endowed me with compassion and admiration for my ancestors, and infused me with gratitude for the many coincidences or tender mercies that yielded pieces of the story. This journey has given me a deeper appreciation of my own religious heritage through the early LDS members' testimonies in print that touched my soul and through the exemplary lives of my ancestors and others from the time period in which Ane, Jens, and Karen Marie lived.

In addition to trying to *imagine* Jens and Ane, I sometimes shift from mentally knowing a thing to *realizing* that thing. One realization is that my body is composed partially of a genetic inheritance derived from their bodies, that these two people have shaped me not only historically, culturally, and spiritually, but also physically. What—besides violin lessons and slapjacks—is in my life because I am their descendant? What characteristics of mine came from them? Maybe the questions have no answers, but the process of wondering has made me realize that I am directly connected to these people whose lives fascinate me so much, and whose story I have attempted to tell so others can know and understand who these people were and the heritage they left. And perhaps be motivated to search for ancestral stories of their own.

Through the records and help from others—both seen and unseen—Jens and Karen Marie and Ane have come to be human beings rather than merely names on a pedigree chart. The time period they lived in brought them many difficulties, but they had courage and fortitude. They sacrificed much to live the way their new religion asked them to live, and they were incredibly hard workers. I am honored to be descended from such exemplary people.

The first assignment I used to give my technical writing students each term at Oregon State University was to interview someone who had the same job the student wanted to obtain after graduation and to learn what kind of writing that particular job required. The students would then have a better understanding of what their goals might need to be for the course, and they each shared the results of their research in a short oral presentation to the class. One student quoted his informant for this assignment as having said, "The writing is never finished. It just becomes due." Though my research and writing could continue, it is time for this book to be placed in the hands of its readers.

ACKNOWLEDGMENTS

Richard Anderson, my husband, always went the extra mile in supporting this project, planned two trips to Denmark for my research, gave honest feedback when I asked for it, answered lots of questions, and didn't complain when the book was all I talked about. For all these things and more, he has my deepest gratitude.

Larry Christiansen responded to a small thank-you note with an offer of further contact, and over the years he answered my hundreds and hundreds of questions about Newton and its history. The story would be incomplete without his help. For this great fortune, I owe a special debt of thanks.

Ruby Woodward gave us the true location of Ane's home, arranged for my sisters and me to meet other Newton residents, and provided many details about our ancestor Jens. We are extremely grateful to her.

Cleo Griffin not only offered help and information as a librarian but also offered to go along in my car to show me things of interest in and around Newton. Because of her I learned things I would never have found in the records, and I am thankful for her generosity of time and stories.

Carol Milligan, Cheri Ballard, and Sarah Rigby were librarians in the Newton Town Library, and each one provided unique insights and information. They made such a difference, and I will be forever grateful.

Norris Cooley generously allowed my sisters and me as strangers to come into his home—the house Great-Grandma Ane had lived in and the house my mother was born in. How do you adequately thank someone for such kindness? We are deeply indebted to him for his hospitality and sharing.

Gary and Lois Jorgensen had earlier lived in Ane's house. They met with my sisters and me and talked about their experiences there, and later provided a floor plan so we could envision the interior of the home our great-grandfather had built. Special thanks are due to them.

LaRelia Jones, my sister, went with me on several research trips to Newton and to Salt Lake City. She also answered her home phone every time I called to excitedly share a new fact I had unearthed to fit into the puzzle. She was truly a partner in the project. I am so thankful to and for her.

Carla Owen, my sister, went with me to Newton on research trips. She learned from her neighbors who had previously lived in Newton that we had not found the right house for Ane, and she asked me to find the right one. We likely could not have learned of our error in any other way. For this and much more support, I greatly appreciate her.

LaMont Fowler, my brother, and his wife, Lorene, went with the family on the first group research trip to Newton even though the times were challenging for them because they had two adult children about to have kidney transplant surgery—one the donor and the other the recipient. I greatly appreciate their support during that trip, and doubly so because of the sacrifice it meant on their part. I also appreciate that LaMont continued to encourage my efforts with this project through the many years of writing.

Lyle Wiggins, my nephew, met with me and showed me a swatch of fabric from Ane's burial dress and a notebook in Danish that had belonged to Jens. I was able to find a translator, and we learned the notebook was Jens's fascinating Danish work record. For the opportunity to touch these articles, I am gobsmacked and express a giant thank-you to Lyle.

The people at Indigo: Editing, Design, and More are marvelous. I refer to Vinnie Kinsella as "my guru" because he knows everything there is to know about publishing and is so helpful. Ali Shaw and Laura Garwood did an amazing job of proofreading the lengthy manuscript. Olivia Croom Hammerman submitted several options for the cover, and they were all so breathtaking, it was excruciatingly difficult to make the decision. I am indebted to all of these artists for sharing their incredible talents.

While Susan DeFreitas lived in Portland and was with Indigo, she did the first edit of the *Serendipity* manuscript, for which I am most grateful. I learned much from her astute observations, and the result of my making her suggested changes was a big improvement in the finished work.

The original idea from which this book grew was tossed out in conversation at a gathering of friends consisting of Barbara Mills, Carol Swain, Connie Sayler, Deb Maccabee, Gail Brooks, Ruth Ann Skodacek, and myself. A great big thank-you to this group of friends, without whom the idea of writing Ane's story may never have occurred to me. I owe you big time!

My two writing groups (composed of Trista Cornelius, Susan Pesznecker, Nicole Rosevear, Jaime Wood, and Naomi Fast in the first, and of Laura Steenhoek and Tom Cutts in the second) served as my sounding boards at our monthly meetings during the time period in which I brought chapter after chapter of the book as it unfolded. Their praise and suggestions kept me going. It was my great fortune to be in these groups. I am indebted to these talented writers and give my special thanks to each one.

And finally, a heartfelt thank-you to Reed Bartlett, Ned and DeNeice Phelps, Reed and Vicky Jenkins, Michael Gleed, and John Alley for their conversations, hospitality, and other contributions to or influences on this story of my ancestors.

In addition to those people listed here, there are countless others around the world who also helped me along the path to recording this history of my ancestors. I am indebted beyond words to all of you. Thank you, thank you, thank you!

Jens Nielsen Hansen Families

First Family	Birth	Death	Age
Jens Nielsen Hansen	16 June 1842	9 Jan 1906	63
Karen Marie Christensen Hansen*	19 Apr 1845	20 Dec 1926	81
Jens Peter Hansen	27 Dec 1867	2 Sept 1832	64
Soren Peter Hansen	17 Mar 1871	15 Jan 1879	7
Hanne Margaret Hansen	12 Nov 1873	6 Jan 1879	5
Elsie Jensine Hansen	9 Dec 1875	24 Dec 1879	4
Niels Peter Nephi Hansen	5 Mar 1878	10 Oct 1948	70
Louisa Marie Hansen Petersen	2 Feb 1880	16 Apr 1966	86
Mary Lindy Hansen	13 Nov 1881	29 Nov 1881	2 wks
Anna Elvena Hansen	2 May 1883	Sept 1917	34
William Joseph Hansen	16 May 1885	1 Aug 1886	1
Joseph Mohonori Hansen	16 Aug 1887	16 Oct 1887	2 mos

Second Family	Birth	Death	Age
Ane Margrethe Sorensen Hansen**	24 Feb 1843	22 Jan 1916	72
Karen Sophia Hansen	5 Feb 1880	6 Sept 1962	82
Hans Eli Hansen	12 Mar 1881	25 Sept 1945	64
Moses Hansen	7 Oct 1882	25 Oct 1901	19

*Jens and Karen Marie married 19 April 1867
**Jens and Ane married 14 November 1878

ENDNOTES

1. *1870 Census, Volume 1: The Statistics of the Population of the United States*, prepared by Francis A. Walker under the direction of the Secretary of the Interior (Washington, DC: Government Printing Office, 1872), 275, https://www2.census.gov/library/publications/decennial/1870/population/1870a-26.pdf.

2. Lettie Christensen and Joseph Larsen, *Lettie Christensen & Joseph Larsen History* (Kearns, UT: Annie Larsen Bartlett, Reed L. Bartlett, 1998), 67. Reprinted 2005. (Available through Reed L. Bartlett or Newton Town Library.)

3. Kaja Voldbæk, email message to author, 21 October 2015; Church Book, Holmstrup Parish, Denmark, 1812–1842, entry 72.

4. Voldbæk, email message to author, 21 October 2015; Danish Census 1845, Holbæk, Skippinge, Avnsø, Svebølle Bye, in house, 43.

5. Ancestral File, v4. 19, accessed 19 October 2010, http://www.familysearch.org.

6. Ancestral File, v4. 19, accessed 19 October 2010, http://www.familysearch.org.

7. Voldbæk, email message to author, 26 April 2016; Church Book, Avnsø Parish, Skippinge District, Holbæk County, Denmark, 1837–1857, entries 139 and 149.

8. Voldbæk, email message to author, 26 April 2016; Church Book, Viskinge-Avnsø Parish, Skippinge District, Holbæk County, Denmark, 1836–1857, entry 17.

9. Voldbæk, email message to author, 21 October 2015; Danish Census 1850, Holbæk, Skippinge, Avnsø, Svebølle Bye, in house, 42.

10. Connie Vogel Watkins Ward, "History of Hans Christian Nielsen Hansen," November 1978, 1.

11. Knud J. V. Jespersen, *A History of Denmark*, trans. Ivan Hill (Houndmills, Basingstoke, Hampshire: Palgrave Macmillan, 2004), 145.

12. Jespersen, *A History of Denmark*, 146.

13. Andrew Jenson, "Biography of Jens Nielsen Hansen," in *L.D.S. Biographical Encyclopedia*, vol. 1 (Salt Lake City, UT: Deseret News Press, 1901), 406–407; copy in "Bjorkman/Hansen Family Records" compiled by MauRene Wiggins, LaMont Fowler, LaRelia Jones, and Carla Owen, in the author's possession.

14. Ancestral File, v4. 19, accessed 17 October 2010, http://www.familysearch.org.

15. Voldbæk, email message to author, 21 October 2015; Danish Census 1855, Holbæk, Skippinge, Avnsø, Svebølle Bye, in house, 55.

16. Jespersen, *A History of Denmark*, 93–94.

17. Jespersen, *A History of Denmark*, 87.

18. Jespersen, *A History of Denmark*, 92–93.

19. Hans Höfer, *Insight Guides Denmark*, ed. Doreen Taylor-Wilkie (London: APA Publications LTD, 1994), 70–71.

20. Statens Museum for Kunst, online list of public domain paintings, accessed 4 April 2016, http://www.SMK.dk/en/article/free-download-of-images/.

21. Voldbæk, email message to author, 21 October 2015; Danish Demographic Database (DDD), Svinninge, Tuse District, Holbæk County, entry C2809.

22. Ancestral File, v4. 19, accessed 19 October 2010, http://www.familysearch.org.

23. Ancestral File, v4. 19, accessed 17 October 2010, http://www.familysearch.org.

24. Jespersen, *A History of Denmark*, 8.

25. Jespersen, *A History of Denmark*, 24.

26. Ancestral File, v4. 19, accessed 17 October 2010, http://www.familysearch.org.

27. Watkins Ward, "History of Hans Christian Nielsen Hansen," 1.

28. Jespersen, *A History of Denmark*, 39.

29. Wikipedia, s.v. "Fælledvej," accessed 26 April 2016, https://en.wikipedia.org/wiki /Fælledvej_(København).

30. Voldbæk, email message to author, 11 May 2016; Church Book, Hovedministerialbog Parish, county unknown, Denmark, 1842–1868, entry 178.

31. Voldbæk, email message to author, 11 May 2016; Church Book, Jyderup (Holmstrup) Parish, Holbæk County, Denmark, 1842–1868, entry 173.

32. Ancestral File, v4. 19, accessed 5 August 2010, http://www.familysearch.org.

33. Voldbæk, email message to author, 2 June 2016; Danish Census 1850, Holbæk, Ods, Vallekilde, Starreklinte Bye, Teglværket, 33F2, FT-1850, C7101.

34. Voldbæk, email message to author, 2 June 2016; Church Book, Vallekilde Parish, Ods District, Holbæk County, Denmark, 1837–1869, entry 170, nos. 38 and 39.

35. Voldbæk, email message to author, 2 June 2016; Church Book, Holmstrup Parish, Tuse District, Holbæk County, Denmark, 1842–1866, entry 119, nos. 31 and 32; also in "Arrival and Departure" from Vallekilde Church Book, 1836–1857.

36. Joseph Smith, *History of the Church, Volume 1, 1820–1834* (Salt Lake City, UT: Deseret Book Company, 1978), 3, 4.

37. James 1:5, 6 (KJV).

38. Smith, *History of the Church*, 5.

39. Smith, *History of the Church*, 8.

40. Malachi 4:5, 6 (KJV).

41. "Articles of Faith," in *Pearl of Great Price* (Salt Lake City, UT: The Church of Jesus Christ of Latter-day Saints, 1968), p. 60, verse 13.

42. Richard S. Van Wagoner, *Mormon Polygamy: A History* (Salt Lake City, UT: Signature Books, 1989), 3.

43. Brigham Young, *Journal of Discourses*, 14 July 1855, 3:266.

44. William Edwin Berrett, *The Restored Church: A Brief History of the Growth and Doctrines of the Church of Jesus Christ of Latter-day Saints*, 10th ed. (Salt Lake City, UT: Deseret Book Company, 1961), 141.

45. Berrett, *The Restored Church*, 141.

46. James Amasa Little, "Biography of Lorenzo Dow Young," *Utah Historical Quarterly* 14, nos. 1–4 (1946): 51, accessed 16 February 2016, https://digitallibrary.utah.gov/awweb/awarchive?t ype=file&item=34083.

47. "History of Charlotte Amelia Van Orden West Peck," n.d., 2, copy in "Fowler Family History" compiled by LaRelia Jones, Carla Owen, MauRene Wiggins, and LaMont Fowler, in the author's possession.

48. Berrett, *The Restored Church*, 195.

49. "History of Charlotte Amelia Van Orden West Peck," 2.

50. "History of Charlotte Amelia Van Orden West Peck," 2.

51. "History of Charlotte Amelia Van Orden West Peck," 2, 3.

52. Preston Nibley, *Brigham Young: The Man and His Work*, 2nd ed. (Salt Lake City, UT: Deseret News Press, 1937), 98–99.

53. John Langeland, "The Church in Scandinavia," Brigham Young University, accessed 3 January 2011, http://eom.byu.edu/index/php/Scandinavia,_the _Church_in.

54. Langeland, "The Church in Scandinavia."
55. Berrett, *The Restored Church*, 274.
56. George D. Smith, *Nauvoo Polygamy* (Salt Lake City, UT: Signature Books, 2008), Appendix B.
57. Gustive O. Larson, "Government, Politics, and Conflict," 244. As quoted in Jessie L. Embry, *Mormon Polygamous Families: Life in the Principle* (Salt Lake City, UT: Greg Kofford Books, 2008), 9.
58. MauRene Fowler Wiggins, "Biography of Martin Horton Peck," 14 April 1978, Daughters of Utah Pioneers, 1.
59. Wiggins, "Biography of Martin Horton Peck," 1.
60. Vernice Peck Gold Rosenvall, "Martin Horton Peck History," Daughters of Utah Pioneers, n.d., 2.
61. Voldbæk, email message to author, 2 June 2016; Church Book, Jyderup-Holmstrup Parish, Tuse District, Holbæk County, 1865–1890, entry 6.
62. Nielen Hicks and Verba Petersen Haws, "History of Jens Niels Hansen and Karren Marie Christensen Hansen," n.d., 3, copy in "Bjorkman/Hansen Family Records" compiled by Wiggins, Fowler, Jones, and Owen, in the author's possession.
63. Carl Widerborg, "Report on Scandinavian Mission," to President Brigham Young, 27 September 1865. As quoted in Andrew Jenson, *History of the Scandinavian Mission*, (Salt Lake City, UT: Deseret News Press, 1927), 189.
64. Erastus Snow, "Journal of Erastus Snow." As quoted in Andrew Jenson, *History of the Scandinavian Mission*, 18.
65. Jenson, *History of the Scandinavian Mission*, 19.
66. Wikipedia, s.v. "Kongsdal," accessed 6 May 2017, https://en.wikipedia.org/wiki/Kongsdal.
67. Hicks and Haws, "History of Jens Niels Hansen and Karren Marie Christensen Hansen," 3.
68. Hicks and Haws, "History of Jens Niels Hansen and Karren Marie Christensen Hansen," 3.
69. Hicks and Haws, "History of Jens Niels Hansen and Karren Marie Christensen Hansen," 3.
70. Dominic Fong, "Garden Home Neighbors Unveil Swedish Bus Shelter," *Oregonian*, 26 October 2010.
71. Jens Nielsen, *Skudsmaalsbog*, 1854–1875, 7, trans. Kaja and Erik Voldbæk in 2011, copy in the author's possession.
72. Nielsen, *Skudsmaalsbog*, 7.
73. Nielsen, *Skudsmaalsbog*, 4.
74. Nielsen, *Skudsmaalsbog*, 4.
75. Nielsen, *Skudsmaalsbog*, 4–5.
76. Nielsen, *Skudsmaalsbog*, 5.
77. Nielsen, *Skudsmaalsbog*, 5.
78. Nielsen, *Skudsmaalsbog*, 6.
79. Voldbæk, Translator's notes, 1.
80. Voldbæk, Translator's notes, 1.
81. Nielsen, *Skudsmaalsbog*, 8.
82. Nielsen, *Skudsmaalsbog*, 9.
83. Nielsen, *Skudsmaalsbog*, 10.
84. Nielsen, *Skudsmaalsbog*, 11.
85. Nielsen, *Skudsmaalsbog*, 12.
86. Nielsen, *Skudsmaalsbog*, 12.
87. John Langeland, "The Church in Scandinavia."
88. Larry D. Christiansen, email message to author, 6 November 2011.
89. Christiansen, email message to author, 6 November 2011.
90. Christiansen, email message to author, 23 November 2013.
91. Watkins Ward, "History of Hans Christian Nielsen Hansen," 1.

92. Watkins Ward, "History of Hans Christian Nielsen Hansen," 2.

93. Christiansen, email message to author, 6 November 2011.

94. Conway B. Sonne, *Saints on the Seas: A Maritime History of Mormon Migration 1830–1890* (Salt Lake City, UT: University of Utah Press, 1983). Paperback reprint edition (Salt Lake City, UT: University of Utah Press, 2005), 28.

95. Sonne, *Saints on the Seas*, 119.

96. Watkins Ward, "History of Hans Christian Nielsen Hansen," 2.

97. Sonne, *Saints on the Seas*, 119.

98. Sonne, *Saints on the Seas*, 119.

99. Sonne, *Saints on the Seas*, 126.

100. Andrew Jenson, comp., *Church Chronology: A Record of Important Events Pertaining to the History of the Church of Jesus Christ of Latter Day Saints*, 2nd ed. (1898; repr, Salt Lake City, UT: Deseret News Press, 1914), 92.

101. Frances Marie Hansen Curtz. As quoted in Watkins Ward "History of Hans Christian Nielsen Hansen," 2.

102. "A Compilation of General Voyage Notes: Liverpool to New York, 24 Jun 1874–6 Jul 1874," Mormon Migration, accessed November 29, 2013, https://mormonmigration.lib.byu.edu/mii/account/602?query=wanlass&page=1, 1.

103. Brian Kelly and Petrea Kelly, comps., *Latter-day History of the Church of Jesus Christ of Latter-day Saints* (American Fork, UT: Covenant Communications, Inc., 2000), 404.

104. P. C. Carstensen, "Correspondence at Sea," *Latter-day Saints' Millennial Star* 36, no. 26 (30 June 1874), 410.

105. "Autobiography of Emma Palmer Manfull: Liverpool to New York, 24 Jun 1874–6 Jul 1874)," Mormon Library, accessed 29 November 2013, https://mormonmigration.lib.byu.edu/mii/account/606?query=Emma+Palmer.

106. "A Compilation of General Voyage Notes: Liverpool to New York, 24 Jun 1874–6 Jul 1874," 1, accessed November 29, 2013.

107. P. C. Carstensen, "Correspondence America," *Latter-day Saints' Millennial Star* 36, no. 30 (28 July 1874): 474.

108. P. C. Carstensen, "Correspondence America," *Latter-day Saints' Millennial Star* 36, no. 34 (25 August 1874): 538–39.

109. Sonne, *Saints on the Seas*, 123.

110. Sonne, *Saints on the Seas*, 123–124.

111. P. C. Carstensen, "Correspondence America," *Latter-day Saints' Millennial Star* 36, no. 34 (25 August 1874): 539.

112. "Brigham City History," Box Elder County, accessed 15 August 2012, http://www.boxeldercounty.org/brigham-city-history.htm.

113. Kathleen Bradford, "Utah History to Go," Brigham City, accessed 15 August 2012, http://www.historytogo.utah.gov.

114. Watkins Ward, "History of Hans Christian Nielsen Hansen," 2.

115. Watkins Ward, "History of Hans Christian Nielsen Hansen," 2.

116. Susan Easton Black, Shauna C. Anderson, and Ruth Ellen Maness, *Legacy of Sacrifice: Missionaries to Scandinavia, 1872–1894* (Provo, UT: Religious Studies Center, Brigham Young University, 2007), 111.

117. Watkins Ward, "History of Hans Christian Nielsen Hansen," 2–3.

118. Sons of Utah Pioneers, "Box Elder Lore." As quoted in *Pioneer Pathways*, International Society, Daughters of Utah Pioneers, vol. 1 (Salt Lake City, UT: Talon Printing, 1998), 39–40.

119. Watkins Ward, "History of Hans Christian Nielsen Hansen," 2.

120. Peter Christian Geertsen journals, 1855–1888 (MS 1507), folder 2, vol. 3, p. 134, Church History Library, Salt Lake City, UT.

121. Geertsen journals, folder 2, vol. 3, p. 11.

122. Geertsen journals, folder 2, vol. 3, pp. 12–13.

123. Norway Heritage: Hands Across the Sea, "Passenger Lists and Ships Images," accessed 21 May 2016, http://www.norwayheritage.com.

124. Geertsen journals, folder 2, vol. 3, pp. 13–15.

125. Geertsen journals, folder 2, vol. 3, pp. 15–16.

126. Copenhagen Conference Emigration List, 25 June 1875. Partial list in the author's possession.

127. John Anderson journals, circa 1872–1928 (MS 1806), folder 2, pp. 52–53, trans Ollie Larsen. https://mormonmigration.lib.byu.edu/mii/account/608

128. Geertsen journals, folder 2, vol. 3, pp. 16–17.

129. *Latter-day Saints' Millennial Star* 37, no. 27 (5 July 1875): 426.

130. Geertsen journals, folder 2, vol. 3, pp. 18–19.

131. C. G. Larsen, "Correspondence at Sea," *Latter-day Saints' Millennial Star* 37, no. 27 (1 July 1875): 427.

132. Geertsen journals, folder 2, vol. 3, p. 19.

133. Anderson journals, folder 2, pp. 52–53.

134. Geertsen journals, folder 2, vol. 3, p. 20.

135. Anderson journals, folder 2, pp. 52–53.

136. Geertsen journals, folder 2, vol. 3, pp. 21–23.

137. Geertsen journals, folder 2, vol. 3, pp. 23–24.

138. C. G. Larsen, "Correspondence at Sea," *Latter-day Saints' Millennial Star* 37, no. 32 (9 August 1875): 506–507.

139. Geertsen journals, folder 2, vol. 3, pp. 24–25.

140. Geertsen journals, folder 2, vol. 3, p. 25.

141. Geertsen journals, folder 2, vol. 3, pp. 25–32.

142. Geertsen journals, folder 2, vol. 3, pp. 32–35.

143. Jenson, *Church Chronology*, 94.

144. Hicks and Haws, "History of Jens Niels Hansen and Karren Marie Christensen Hansen," 3.

145. "Settlement of Newton, Cache, Utah," Family Search, posted 14 September 2014, by ileenlooslebarlow1, accessed May 14, 2017, http://www.familysearch.org/photos/artifacts/29311337.

146. "Sketch of Jens Niels Hansen," n.d., in "Bjorkman/Hansen Family Records" compiled by Wiggins, Fowler, Jones, and Owen, 4, copy in the author's possession.

147. Vicky Jenkins, telephone conversation with author, November 2010.

148. Warranty Deed 75984, obtained June 2011 from Cache County Recorder's Office, Logan, UT, copy in the author's possession.

149. Wikipedia, s.v. "Bornholm," accessed 11 May 2017, https://en.wikipedia.org/wiki/Bornholm.

150. Hicks and Haws, "History of Jens Niels Hansen and Karren Marie Christensen Hansen," 4.

151. Christiansen, email message to author, 14 September 2011.

152. Hicks and Haws, "History of Jens Niels Hansen and Karren Marie Christensen Hansen," 5.

153. Christiansen, letter to author, 3 August 2011.

154. Christiansen, email message to author, 29 August 2011.

155. Christiansen, email message to author, 30 August 2011.

156. Hicks and Haws, "History of Jens Niels Hansen and Karren Marie Christensen Hansen," 4.

157. Hicks and Haws, "History of Jens Niels Hansen and Karren Marie Christensen Hansen," 4.

158. Hicks and Haws, "History of Jens Niels Hansen and Karren Marie Christensen Hansen," 4.

159. Hicks and Haws, "History of Jens Niels Hansen and Karren Marie Christensen Hansen," 4.

160. Christiansen, email message to author, 16 August 2011.

161. Family Search, International Genealogical Index Record submitted after 1991 by an anonymous member of the LDS Church.

162. Watkins Ward, "History of Hans Christian Nielsen Hansen," 5.

163. Watkins Ward, "History of Hans Christian Nielsen Hansen," 4, 5.

164. Vilhelm Moberg, *The Emigrants* (Cutchogue, NY: Buccaneer Books, 1951), 117.

165. Christiansen, *A New Town in the Valley: The Centennial History of Newton, Utah, 1869–1969*, rev. ed. (Logan, UT: Watkins Printing, 1999), 387.

166. 1880 Census of Newton, Utah, transcribed by Larry D. Christiansen, accessed 5 July 2010, sites.rootsweb.com~utcache/census/1880Newton.htm.

167. Richard S. Van Wagoner, *Mormon Polygamy: A History* (Salt Lake City: Signature Books, 1989).

168. Paula Kelly Harline, *The Polygamous Wives Writing Club: From the Diaries of Mormon Pioneer Women* (New York: Oxford University Press, 2014), 2.

169. Hicks and Haws, "History of Jens Niels Hansen and Karren Marie Christensen Hansen," 5.

170. Laura Steenhoek (member of a former writing group), in conversation with the author August 2010.

171. Gerald M. Haslam, letter to LaRelia Jones, 17 June 2010, 1.

172. Voldbæk, email message to author, 18 June 2016; Church Book, Store Tåstrup Parish, Merløse District, Holbæk County, Denmark, 1840–1853, entry 41.

173. Haslam, letter to Jones, 17 June 2010.

174. Family Group Record, copy in the author's possession.

175. Voldbæk, email message to author, 18 June 2016; Kyringe, Store Tåstrup Parish, Merløse District, Holbæk County, Denmark, 1845, entry C3179.

176. Voldbæk, email message to author, 18 June 2016; Danish Demographic Database (DDD), entry C6351.

177. Gerald M. Haslam, Report of 2010 for Bjorkman Family to Jones, 17 June 2010. (Voldbæk, in an email message to author on 18 June 2016, further noted that this data was confirmed in the Church Book for Munke Bjergby Parish, Alsted District, Sorø County, 1836–1890, entry 63: Ane Margrethe Hansen, confirmed in 1857.)

178. Gerald M. Haslam, email message to Jones, 4 July 2010.

179. Haslam, email message to Jones, 11 November 2010.

180. Voldbæk, email message to author, 18 June 2016; Church Book, Store Tåstrup Parish, Merløse District, Holbæk County, Denmark, 1840–1853, entry 170.

181. Voldbæk, email message to author, 18 June 2016; Søro, Alsted, Munke Bjergby, Munke Bjergby Sogn, Munkebjergby By, et Hus, nr. 87, 1, FT-1855, C8381.

182. Voldbæk, email message to author, 18 June 2016; Danish Census 1860, Munkebjergby, Munke Bjergby Parish, Alsted District, Sorø County, DDD, entry C8382.

183. Jones, email message to Haslam, 10 November 2010.

184. Haslam, email message to Jones, 11 November 2010.

185. Voldbæk, email message to author, 18 June 2016; Søro, Alsted, Munke Bjergby, Munke Bjergby sogn, Munkebjergby, en Gaard, nr. 90, 1, FT – 1860, C8382.

186. Voldbæk, email message to author, 18 June 2016.

187. Voldbæk, email message to author, 18 June 2016; Church Book, Munke Bjergby Parish, Alsted District, Sorø County, Denmark, 1852–1871, Departure Records, entry 104.

188. Voldbæk, email message to author, 18 June 2016; Church Book, Munke Bjergby Parish, Alsted District, Sorø County, Denmark, 1852–1871, Arrival Records, entry 58.

189. Voldbæk, email message to author, 18 June 2016; Munkebjergby, Munke Bjergby Parish, Alsted District, Sorø County, DDD, entry C0564.

190. Voldbæk, email message to author, 18 June 2016.

191. Eleda Bjorkman Smith, "The Life History of Eleda Bjorkman Smith," n.d., 1.

192. Voldbæk, email message to author, 19 June 2016; Church Book, Munkebjergby Parish, Alsted District, Sorø County, Denmark, 1836–1891, entry 105.

193. Smith, "The Life History of Eleda Bjorkman Smith," 1.

194. Newton Ward Records, copy provided by LaRelia Jones, in the author's possession.

195. Newton Ward Records, copy provided by LaRelia Jones, in the author's possession.

196. *Book of Mormon: Another Testament of Jesus Christ* (Salt Lake City, Utah, Church of Jesus Christ of Latter-day Saints), Book of Mosiah, 18:9–11. Originally published in Palmyra, New York, 1830.

197. Voldbæk, email message to author, 18 June 2016; Danish Census 1880, Munkebjergby By, DDD, C8383.

198. Jespersen, *A History of Denmark*, 147.

199. "A Compilation of General Voyage Notes: Liverpool to New York, 14 Sep 1878–25 Sep 1878," Mormon Migration, Brigham Young University, accessed 2 June 2013, https://mormonmigration .lib.byu.edu/mii/account/1469.

200. The *Bravo*, accessed 9 February 2014 and 1 January 2020, www.humberpacketboats.co.uk.

201. "A Compilation of General Voyage Notes: Liverpool to New York, 14 Sep 1878–25 Sep 1878," Mormon Migration, accessed 2 June 2013.

202. Oscar Gotfred Cornelius Bjorkman journal, p. 6, provided by LaRelia Jones to the author. Oscar Gotfred Cornelius Bjorkman was the brother of the author's maternal grandfather, Henry Albert Bjorkman.

203. Bjorkman journal, 6.

204. Bjorkman journal, 6–7.

205. Emigration list for the SS *Wyoming*, 7 September 1878, Copenhagen Conference, copy in the author's possession.

206. ACGVN Departure heading, accessed 2 June 2013, unavailable in 2020.

207. "A Compilation of General Voyage Notes: Liverpool to New York, 14 Sep 1878–25 Sep 1878," Mormon Migration, accessed 2 June 2013, https://mormonmigration.lib.byu.edu/mii /account/1469.

208. SS *Wyoming* passenger list for voyage ending 24 September 1878 in New York, microfilm 295779, Family History Library, Salt Lake City, UT.

209. Sonne, *Saints on the Seas*, 128.

210. Bjorkman journal, 7.

211. "A Compilation of General Voyage Notes: Liverpool to New York, 14 Sep 1878–25 Sep 1878," Mormon Migration, accessed 2 June 2013, https://mormonmigration.lib.byu.edu/mii /account/1469.

212. Henry Naisbitt, *Latter-day Saints' Millennial Star* 40, no. 41 (14 October 1878) 653–54; "A Compilation of General Voyage Notes: Liverpool to New York, 14 Sep 1878–25 Sep 1878," Mormon Migration, accessed 2 June 2013, https://mormonmigration.lib.byu.edu/mii /account/1469.

213. Bjorkman journal, 7.

214. Bjorkman journal, 7.

215. Bjorkman journal, 7.

216. Bjorkman journal, 7.

217. Bjorkman journal, 7.

218. Bjorkman journal, 7–8.

219. "A Compilation of General Voyage Notes: Liverpool to New York, 14 Sep 1878–25 Sep 1878," Mormon Migration, accessed 2 June 2013, https://mormonmigration.lib.byu.edu/mii /account/1469.

220. Bjorkman journal, 8.

221. Bjorkman journal, 8.

222. Bjorkman journal, 8.

223. Bjorkman journal, 8.

224. Bjorkman journal, 8.

225. Smith, "The Life History of Eleda Bjorkman Smith," 1.

226. Sonne, *Saints on the Seas*, 102.

227. Transcription of Jens Niels Hansen's life sketch, n.d., 3, copy in the author's possession.

228. Carol Milligan, ed., *Jens Peter Benson: Ancestors and Descendants; Histories and Pedigrees, 1831–1898: 100th Year Anniversary Edition* (n.p.: Benson Family Organization, 1998), 175.

229. Haslam, letter to Jones, 17 June 2010.

230. Voldbæk, email message to author, 7 June 2016; Church Book, Avnsø Parish, Ods District, Holbæk County, Denmark, 1836–1857, entry 5.

231. Voldbæk, email message to author, 7 June 2016; Church Book, Avnsø Parish, Ods District, Holbæk County, Denmark, 1836–1857, entry 5.

232. Online Danish Census 1845, Holbæk, Skippinge, Avnsø, Svebølle. https://FamilySearch.org: Rigsarkivet, København (The Danish National Archives), Copenhagen, accessed 24 September 2011.

233. Online Danish Census 1850, Holbæk, Skippinge, Avnsø, Svebølle, https://FamilySearch.org: Rigsarkivet, København (The Danish National Archives), Copenhagen, accessed 24 September 2011.

234. Voldbæk, email message to author, 7 June 2016.

235. Pedigree Chart, copy in "Bjorkman/Hansen Family Records," compiled by Wiggins, Fowler, Jones, and Owen, in the author's possession.

236. Online Danish Census 1855, Holbæk, Skippinge, Avnsø, Svebølle, https://FamilySearch.org: Rigsarkivet, København (The Danish National Archives), Copenhagen, accessed 2016.

237. Voldbæk, email message to author, 7 June 2016; Church Book, Avnsø Parish, Ods District, Holbæk County, Denmark, 1836–1857, entry 60.

238. Voldbæk, email message to author, 7 June 2016; Church Book, Avnsø Parish, Ods District, Holbæk County, Denmark, 1852–1861, entry unknown.

239. Voldbæk, email message to author, 16 September 2016.

240. Voldbæk, email message to author, 16 September 2016.

241. Voldbæk, email message to author, 7 June 2016; Church Book, Højby Parish, Ods District, Holbæk County, Denmark, 1860–1892, entry 23.

242. Voldbæk, email message to author, 7 June 2016; Church Book, Højby Parish, Ods District, Holbæk County, Denmark, 1865–1888, entry 25.

243. Voldbæk, email message to author, 7 June 2016; Church Book, Vallekilde Parish, Ods District, Holbæk County, Denmark, 1861–1878, entry 60.

244. Anders and Maren's son, Soren Peter, does not appear anywhere on this emigration page, nor on the complete emigration list. Kaja checked many logical emigration lists and did not find Soren Peter on any of them. However, he is listed in Newton's 1880 census and is buried in the Newton cemetery, so he did immigrate to Utah prior to 1880.

245. Hicks and Haws, "History of Jens Niels Hansen and Karren Marie Christensen Hansen," 5.

246. Hanna H. Romney, "Autobiography," 7. As quoted in *Letters of Catharine Cottam Romney, Plural Wife*, ed. Jennifer Moulton Hansen (Urbana: University of Illinois Press, 1992), 12–14.

247. Romney, *Letters*, 7.

248. Fanny Stenhouse, *Exposé of Polygamy: A Lady's Life among the Mormons*, ed. Linda Wilcox DeSimone (Logan, UT: Utah State University Press, 2008), 101.

249. In order to protect the privacy of the couple's descendants, this source is not attributed.

250. 1880 Census of Newton, Utah, transcribed by Larry D. Christiansen, accessed 5 July 2010 and 14 January 2020, https://sites.rootsweb.com/~utcache/census/1880Newton.htm.

251. Hicks and Haws, "History of Jens Niels Hansen and Karren Marie Christensen Hansen," 5.

252. Case files of US district courts for the Territory of Utah, 1870–1896. John W. Gardner, film 1616337, roll 13, case 922, Family History Center, Salt Lake City, UT.

253. Embry, *Mormon Polygamous Families*, 105, 106.

254. Carolyn Eyring Miller and Edward L. Kimball, *Camilla: A Biography of Camilla Eyring Kimball*, Deseret Book Company, Salt Lake City, Utah, 1 January 1982. As quoted in Embry, *Mormon Polygamous Families*, 115.

255. Hicks and Haws, "History of Jens Niels Hansen and Karren Marie Christensen Hansen," 4.

256. Hicks and Haws, "History of Jens Niels Hansen and Karren Marie Christensen Hansen," 4.

257. Hicks and Haws, "History of Jens Niels Hansen and Karren Marie Christensen Hansen," 5.

258. 1880 Census of Newton, Utah, transcribed by Larry D. Christiansen, accessed 5 July 2010 and 14 January 2020, https://sites.rootsweb.com/~utcache/census/1800Newton.htm.

259. Hicks and Haws, "History of Jens Niels Hansen and Karren Marie Christensen Hansen," 5.

260. The tribute can also be found in Milligan, ed., *Ancestors and Descendants of Jens Peter Benson, 1831–1898* (Benson Family Organization, 1998).

261. Smith, "The Life History of Eleda Bjorkman Smith," 2.

262. Smith, "The Life History of Eleda Bjorkman Smith," 2.

263. Mike Jones, email message to author, 25 August 2014.

264. Christiansen, telephone conversation with US Department of the Interior, Bureau of Land Management, Salt Lake City, UT, 2 March 1967. The contents of this telephone conversation were forwarded in an email message to author, 7 January 2012.

265. Christiansen, email message to author, 5 July 2016; Abstract of Deeds, Cache County, Utah, vol. 2; Record of Deeds, Cache County, Utah, Book W, p. 398, Book 10, p. 256.

266. Legal notices in the *Logan Leader*, 19 March 1880, 2, from newspaper records transcribed by Larry D. Christiansen, accessed 24 August 2012, https://sites.rootsweb.ancestry.com/~utcache /htm.

267. Copy of deed in the author's possession.

268. Christiansen, *Notes on the History of Newton from the Files of Larry D. Christiansen*, compiled and indexed by Cleo Griffin, 2011, 46–49, copy in the author's possession.

269. Jessie L. Embry, *Setting the Record Straight: Mormons & Polygamy* (Orem, UT: Millennial Press, 2007), 45, 46.

270. Brian and Petrea Kelly, comps., *Latter-day History of the Church of Jesus Christ of Latter-day Saints* (American Fork, UT: Covenant Communications, 2000), 351.

271. State of Utah Archives, https://archives.utah.gov.

272. Copy of homestead deed in the author's possession.

273. Copy of deed in the author's possession.

274. Daughters of Utah Pioneers, *Pioneer Pathways*, vol. 1 (Salt Lake City, UT: Talon Printing, 1998), 270–71

275. Copy of deed in the author's possession.

276. Copy of deed in the author's possession.

277. Christiansen, email message to author, 7 January 2012; re: Joseph E. Wing, *Alfalfa Farming in America* (Chicago, IL: Sanders Publishing Co., 1909).

278. Copy of Newton Ward Records in the author's possession.

279. Christiansen, email message to author 15 August 2011; "Newton Jots," *Utah Journal*, 31 July 1886.

280. Copy of deed in the author's possession.

281. Berrett, *The Restored Church*, 316.

282. Brigham Young, Journal of Discourses 26:151–56. As quoted in Gustive O. Larson's *The "Americanization" of Utah for Statehood* (San Marino, CA: Henry E. Huntington Library, and Art Gallery, by Publishers Press, 1971), 119.

283. Kelly and Kelly, *Latter-day History*, 352–53.

284. "Big Meadows Incident" by Eldon Griffin, one of John Jenkins' descendants, from John Jenkins autobiography, accessed 10 February 2012, http://freepages.rootsweb.com/~archibald/genealogy /jj-life2.htm.

285. Rosa Mae McClellan Evans, "Judicial Prosecution of Prisoners for LDS Plural Marriage: Prison Sentences, 1884–1895," Master of Art thesis, Department of History, Brigham Young University, 1986), 124.

286. Hicks and Haws, "History of Jens Niels Hansen and Karren Marie Christensen Hansen," 5.

287. Annie Clark Tanner, *A Mormon Mother: An Autobiography by Annie Clark Tanner* (Salt Lake City, UT: Tanner Trust Fund, University of Utah Library, 1991), 101, 106, 108.

288. Smith, "The Life History of Eleda Bjorkman Smith," 11.

289. Smith, "The Life History of Eleda Bjorkman Smith," 3.

290. Psalms 118:24 (KJV).

291. Christensen and Larsen, *Lettie Christensen & Joseph Larsen History*, 52.

292. Christensen and Larsen, *Lettie Christensen & Joseph Larsen History*, 52, 54, 55, 57.

293. Ruby Larsen, *A Century of History with Grant A Larsen & Jennie Cutler, 1906 to 2003 Vol. 1* (Logan, UT: Square One, 2014), 29–30.

294. Lyle Wiggins, email message to author, 2 July 2013.

295. Eric V. Larsen, email message to author, 16 July 2013.

296. Newton Ward Records, copy provided by LaRelia Jones, in the author's possession.

297. LaRelia Jones, email message to author, Carla Owen, and LaMont Fowler, 7 May 2014.

298. Smith, "The Life History of Eleda Bjorkman Smith," 2.

299. Rudger Clawson, *Prisoner for Polygamy: The Memoirs and Letters of Rudger Clawson at the Utah Territorial Penitentiary, 1884–1887*, ed. Stan Larsen (Urbana: University of Illinois, 1993).

300. Rosa Mae M. Evans, "Judicial Prosecution of Prisoners for LDS Plural Marriage: Prison Sentences, 1884–1895," Master of Art thesis, Department of History, Brigham Young University, 1986, 117–132. As quoted in Rudger Clawson, *Prisoner for Polygamy*, Appendix 3.

301. Case files of the US district courts for the Territory of Utah, 1870–1896, John W. Gardner, Film 1616337, Roll 13, Case 922, Family History Center, Salt Lake City, UT.

302. Hicks and Haws, "History of Jens Niels Hansen and Karren Marie Christensen Hansen," 5.

303. Larry D. Christiansen, *A New Town in the Valley: The Centennial History of Newton, Utah 1869–1969* (Watkins Printing, Logan, Utah, 1999), 61. Revised 1999, addendum by Larry D. Christiansen and the Newton Town Library.

304. Andrew Jenson, comp. *Church Chronology: A Record of Important Events Pertaining to the History of the Church of Jesus Christ of Latter Day Saints* (1898; 1914; repr. LaVergne, TN: Kessinger Publishing, 2010). Page references hereafter are to the 2010 edition.

305. Clawson, *Prisoner for Polygamy*, 213.

306. Evans, "Judicial Prosecution of Prisoners," 54, 55.

307. Evans, "Judicial Prosecution of Prisoners," 55.

308. "Short Biography of J. N. Hansen," *Logan Republican*, 27 January 1906, 3. The writer signed himself as "N.H." and may have been Nephi Hansen, Jens's son with Karen Marie.

309. Jenson, *Church Chronology*, 173.

310. Hicks and Haws, "History of Jens Niels Hansen and Karren Marie Christensen Hansen," 5.

311. Larson, *The "Americanization" of Utah for Statehood*, 151–53.

312. Larson, *The "Americanization" of Utah for Statehood*, 153–54.

313. Larson, *The "Americanization" of Utah for Statehood*, 185.

314. Newton Ward Records, copy provided by LaRelia Jones, in the author's possession.

315. Jenson, *Church Chronology*, 175.

316. Hicks and Haws, "History of Jens Niels Hansen and Karren Marie Christensen Hansen," 5.

317. Evans, "Judicial Prosecution of Prisoners," 60.

318. Don Strack, "Utah Territorial Prison, Sugar House, 1855–1951," *Utah Rails*, http://utahrails .net/utahrails/utah-territorial-prison.

319. Don Strack, "Utah Territorial Prison, Sugar House, 1855–1951."

320. Strack, "Utah Territorial Prison, Sugar House, 1855–1951."

321. Clawson, *Prisoner for Polygamy*, 213.

322. Strack, "Utah Territorial Prison, Sugar House, 1855–1951."

323. Melvin L. Bashore, "Life Behind Bars: Mormon Cohabs of the 1880s," *Utah Historical Quarterly* 47, no. 1 (Winter 1979): 22.

324. Gottlieb Ence, "A Short Sketch of My Life," in *Autobiography*, Utah State Historical Society, Mss-A-1 80 c. 1, n.d., pp. 63, 64, 68.

325. 326 Ence, "A Short Sketch of My Life," pp. 63, 64, 68.

326. Franklin W. Young prison journal, Church History Library, Salt Lake City, UT, MS 324, p. 145.

327. Young prison journal, Church History Library, p. 145.

328. Jenson, *Church Chronology*, 133.

329. Christopher Arthur prison journal, Mormon Diaries on Microfilm, Circa 1840–1865, Special Collections & Archives, Merrill-Cazier Library, Utah State University, UT, 207.

330. Young prison journal, Church History Library, 146–48.

331. Gottlieb Ence prison journal, from *Autobiography*, Utah State Historical Society, 69.

332. Ence prison journal, Utah State Historical Society, 69.

333. Arthur prison journal, Merrill-Cazier Library, 207.

334. Bashore, "Life Behind Bars," 27.

335. Jenson, *Church Chronology*, 175.

336. Evans, "Judicial Prosecution of Prisoners," 3.

337. Clawson, *Prisoner for Polygamy*, 232–34.

338. Hicks and Haws, "History of Jens Niels Hansen and Karren Marie Christensen Hansen," 5.

339. Ence prison journal, Utah State Historical Society, 69.

340. Young prison journal, Church History Library, 149.

341. Ence prison journal, Utah State Historical Society, 70.

342. Ence prison journal, Utah State Historical Society, 70.

343. Clawson, *Prisoner for Polygamy*, 7.

344. Young prison journal, Church History Library, 152.

345. Arthur prison journal, Merrill-Cazier Library, 240.

346. Young prison journal, Church History Library, 149–50.

347. Young prison journal, Church History Library, 150.

348. Young prison journal, Church History Library, 151.

349. Ence prison journal, Utah State Historical Society, 71.

350. Young prison journal, Church History Library, 153.

351. Arthur prison journal, Merrill-Cazier Library, 240–41

352. Ence prison journal, Utah State Historical Society, 70.

353. Clawson, *Prisoner for Polygamy*, 45.

354. Arthur prison journal, Merrill-Cazier Library, 239.

355. Clawson, *Prisoner for Polygamy*, 71.

356. Arthur prison journal, Merrill-Cazier Library, 234–35.

357. Young prison journal, Church History Library, 220–24.

358. Young prison journal, Church History Library, 152–53.

359. Young prison journal, Church History Library, 154.

360. Arthur prison journal, Merrill-Cazier Library, 240.

361. Ence prison journal, Utah State Historical Society, 71.

362. Hicks and Haws, "History of Jens Niels Hansen and Karren Marie Christensen Hansen," 5.

363. Arthur prison journal, Merrill-Cazier Library, 241.

364. Arthur prison journal, Merrill-Cazier Library, 241.

365. Ence prison journal, Utah State Historical Society, 70.

366. Young prison journal, Church History Library, 154.

367. Ence prison journal, Utah State Historical Society, 70.

368. Young prison journal, Church History Library, 154–55.

369. Young prison journal, Church History Library, 154–55.

370. Young prison journal, Church History Library, 153.

371. Bashore, "Life Behind Bars," 36.

372. Jens Nielsen Hansen prison journal, 1, 2, copy in the author's possession.

373. Clawson, *Prisoner for Polygamy*, 159–60.

374. Deseret Sunday School Union, history and minutes of the Utah Penitentiary Sunday School, organized by President George Q. Cannon, 21 September 1888 and continued until 13 July 1890.

375. Utah Penitentiary Sunday School minutes.

376. Utah Penitentiary Sunday School minutes.

377. Clawson, *Prisoner for Polygamy*, appendix 4, p. 233.

378. Arthur prison journal, Merrill-Cazier Library, 239.

379. Arthur prison journal, Merrill-Cazier Library, 241.

380. Ence prison journal, Utah State Historical Society, 71.

381. Hicks and Haws, "History of Jens Niels Hansen and Karren Marie Christensen Hansen," 5.

382. Ence prison journal, Utah State Historical Society, 71.

383. Jenson, *Church Chronology*, 177.

384. Hicks and Haws, "History of Jens Niels Hansen and Karren Marie Christensen Hansen," 5.

385. Jessie L. Embry, *Mormon Polygamous Families: Life in the Principle* (Salt Lake City, UT: Greg Kofford Books, 2008), 12.

386. B. H. Roberts, *A Comprehensive History of the Church* vol. 6, 220–21. As quoted in Kelly and Kelly, *Latter-day History*, 367. See also Official Declaration 1 of the *Doctrine and Covenants of the Church of Jesus Christ of Latter-day Saints*, 291–92.

387. Joseph Fielding Smith, *The Life of Joseph F. Smith*, 297–98. As quoted in Kelly and Kelly, *Latter-day History*, 368 and 370. Brackets were used within quoted material.

388. Lu Ann Faylor Snyder and Phillip A Snyder, eds., *Post-Manifesto Polygamy: The 1899–1904 Correspondence of Helen, Owen, and Avery Woodruff* (Logan, UT: Utah State University Press, 2009).

389. Christensen and Larsen, *Lettie Christensen & Joseph Larsen History*, 57.

390. RaNae L. Christensen and Orpah R. Fabricius, *History of Newton, Utah*, transcribed by Anne Herzog, n.d., accessed 1 February 2016, Newtonspecialcollections.blogspot.com/2013/02/history-of-newton-utah.html.

391. Hicks and Haws, "History of Jens Niels Hansen and Karren Marie Christensen Hansen," 4, 5.

392. Black, Anderson, and Maness, *Legacy of Sacrifice: Missionaries to Scandinavia 1872-1894*, (Religious Studies Center, Brigham Young University, 2007), 152.

393. Black, Anderson, and Maness, *Legacy of Sacrifice*, 152.

394. Abraham H. Cannon, *Candid Insights of a Mormon Apostle: The Diaries of Abraham H. Cannon, 1889–1895*, ed. Edward Leo Lyman (Salt Lake City, UT: Signature Books, Smith-Pettit Foundation, 2010), 169.

395. Evans, "Judicial Prosecution of Prisoners," 117-32.

396. Newton Ward Records, 1891, Jenson's visit on 29 November 1891.

397. Jenson, "Biographical Sketch of Jens Nielsen Hansen," 406–7.

398. Henry Albert Bjorkman history, n.d., in "Bjorkman/Hansen Family Records" compiled by Wiggins, Fowler, Jones, and Owen, in the author's possession.

399. LaMont Vern Fowler, email message to author, 22 November 2014; Henry Albert Bjorkman letter to LaMont Vern Fowler, 2 March 1952.

400. See Jenson, *History of the Scandinavian Mission.*

401. Oscar Bjorkman journal, p. 6.

402. LaRelia Jones, "Marie Persson Poulsson Bjorkman's Life Sketch," n.d., 5, in "Bjorkman/Hansen Family Records," compiled by Wiggins, Fowler, Jones, and Owen, in the author's possession.

403. LaRelia Jones, email message to author, June 2016.

404. Christensen and Larsen, *Lettie Christensen & Joseph Larsen History,* 58–59.

405. Christiansen, email message to author, 15 August 2011; Newton Ward Historical Record Book D, 21 October 1895.

406. Christiansen, email message to author, 15 August 2011.

407. Christiansen, email message to the author, 15 August 2011; *The Journal,* 16 July 1896, 5, access date unknown, https://sites.rootsweb.com.

408. Christiansen, email message to the author, 15 August 2011; "Local Points," *The Journal,* 16 July 1896, 8, access date unknown, https://sites.rootsweb.com.

409. Christiansen, email message to the author, 15 August 2011; Newton School District Trustees Record, Book C, 19–21.

410. Christiansen, email message to the author, 15 August 2011; *The Journal,* 18 July 1896, 2, access date unknown, https://sites.rootsweb.com.

411. Christiansen, email message to the author, 15 August 2011; Newton School District Trustees Record, Book C, 25–26.

412. Joel E. Ricks, ed., *The History of a Valley: Cache Valley, Utah-Idaho* (Logan, UT: Cache Valley Centennial Commission, 1956), 328.

413. Maud Barker Jorgensen letter to Larry D. Christiansen, March 1991.

414. Bertha J. Smith letter to Larry D. Christiansen, 20 September 1968 (date on the envelope, letter undated).

415. *Deseret Evening News,* 18 March 1903, 7.

416. *The Journal,* 17 February 1898, 37.

417. Niels Peter Nephi Hansen, Church History Library, Missionary Card in library's atlas listing missionary callings, accessed 26 June 2012.

418. Photograph found in Newton Town Library, copy in the author's possession.

419. *Deseret Evening News,* 28 November 1899.

420. Evans, "Judicial Prosecution of Prisoners," 117–32.

421. Christiansen, "Owen's Cache County Raid," *Deseret Evening News,* 5 February 1900.

422. Christiansen, "Logan," *Deseret Evening News,* 13 March 1900, 7.

423. "Newton Town Board 1900–1966," from RaNae L. Christensen and Orpah Rigby Fabricius. *History of Newton,* 1.

424. Town Board minutes, Newton, UT, UTGenWeb, transcribed by Anne Herzog, provided by the Special Collection Department, Newton Town Library, accessed 16 January 2016, 1, sites.rootsweb .com~utcache-news-newtontownminutes.

425. Town Board minutes, 1.

426. Christiansen, email message to the author, 15 August 2011; *Deseret Evening News,* 15 May 1900, 5, access date unknown, https://sites.rootsweb.com.

427. Town Board minutes, 2.

428. Town Board minutes, 2.

429. Town Board minutes, 2.

430. Town Board minutes, 3.

431. Town Board minutes, 3.

432. Town Board minutes, 3.

433. Town Board minutes, 3, 4.

434. Town Board minutes, 4.

435. Town Board minutes, 4.

436. Town Board minutes, 4.

437. Town Board minutes, 5.

438. Town Board minutes, 5.

439. Town Board minutes, 5.

440. Town Board minutes, 6.

441. Town Board minutes, 7.

442. Christiansen, email message to author, 15 August 2011; "Extracts from Reports/Great Salt Lake Watershed," *Deseret Evening News*, 10 January 1901, access date unknown, https://sites .rootsweb.com.

443. Town Board minutes, 7.

444. Town Board minutes, 7, 8.

445. Town Board minutes, 8.

446. Town Board minutes, 8.

447. Town Board minutes, 9.

448. Town Board minutes, 9.

449. Town Board minutes, 9.

450. Town Board minutes, 9.

451. Christiansen, email message to author, 15 August 2011; "Sugar Beets Are Doing Well," *Deseret Evening News*, 4 September 1901.

452. Town Board minutes, 9.

453. Reportable Diseases Utah. Annual Morbidity Reports prepared by the Utah Department of Health. MMWR Annual summary Reports published by the Centers for Disease Control and Prevention (CDC). 12 October 2012.

454. Smith, "The Life History of Eleda Bjorkman Smith," 1.

455. Larry D. Christiansen, email message to author, 26 December 2014; "Local Briefs," *Logan Nation*, 30 October 1901, 8.

456. Town Board minutes, 10.

457. Town Board minutes, 10.

458. Town Board minutes, 10.

459. "Carl William Marten Jorgensen," n.d., copy given to author in 2011 by Gary Jorgensen.

460. Christensen and Larsen, *Lettie Christensen & Joseph Larsen History*, 1998.

461. "Newton Newslets," *Logan Republican*, 2 October 1902, 1.

462. Christiansen, email message to author, 15 August 2011; "Logan, Cache Co," *Deseret Evening News*, 12 February 1903, 7.

463. "Logan," *Deseret Evening News*, 23 May 1903, 7.

464. Christiansen, email message to author, 15 August 2011; "Logan, Cache County," *Deseret Evening News*, 1 July 1903, 8.

465. Christiansen, email message to author, 15 August 2011; "Newton Sunday School," *Deseret Evening News*, 1 July 1903.

466. "Local Jottings," *Logan Republican*, 15 July 1903, 8.

467. "Annual Statement," *Logan Republican*, 29 July 1903, 5.

468. Christiansen, email message to author, 26 December 2014; "Local Jottings," *Logan Republican*, 1 August 1903, 8.

469. Christiansen, email message to author, 15 August 2011; "The Commissioners," *Logan Republican*, 23 September 1903, 8.

470. "Newton," *Logan Republican*, 21 October 1903, 4.

471. "Generalities," *Logan Republican*, 5 March 1904, 8.

472. Kelly and Kelly, *Latter-Day History*, 406.

473. "The Commissioners," *Logan Republican*, 11 June 1904, 1.

474. "Generalities," *Logan Republican*, 29 June 1904, 5.
475. "Newton," *Logan Republican*, 21 September 1904, 1.
476. "Generalities," *Logan Republican*, 21 September 1904, 5.
477. "Republicans Nominate Their County Ticket," *Logan Republican*, 28 September 1904, 4.
478. "Generalities," *Logan Republican*, 5 October 1904, 5.
479. "Places to Register," *Logan Republican*, 27 October 1904, 4.
480. "June 9–10 Greatest Days History of Cache Valley," *Logan Republican*, 25 March 1905, 1.
481. "Generalities," *Logan Republican*, 19 April 1905, 5.
482. "Generalities," *Logan Republican*, 24 June 1905, 5.
483. "Cache County Auditor's Report," *Logan Republican*, 26 July 1905, 3.
484. "Newsy Items," *Logan Republican*, 12 August 1905, 8.
485. "Newton Newslings," *Logan Republican*, 28 November 1905, 2.
486. "Generalities," *Logan Republican*, 3 January 1906, 5.
487. Jens Nielsen Hansen State of Utah Death Certificate, 1906, copy in the author's possession.
488. "Postmaster Hansen Dead," *Logan Republican*, 10 January 1906, 1.
489. Christiansen, email message to author, 15 August 2011; "Funeral Services of J. N. Hansen at Newton," *Logan Republican*, 20 January 1906, 2.
490. Christiansen, email message to author, 15 August 2011; "Short Biography of J.N. Hansen," *Logan Republican*, 27 January 1906, 3.
491. "In the Matter of the Estate of Jens N. Hansen, Deceased, January 1906," probate file, copy obtained from the First District Court in Logan, Utah.
492. Oscar Bjorkman journal, 3.
493. LeOra Hansen Jenkins, "Life of Hans Eli Hansen," n.d., 1, 2.
494. Hicks and Haws, "History of Jens Niels Hansen and Karren Marie Christensen Hansen," 6.
495. Smith, "The Life History of Eleda Bjorkman Smith," 3.
496. 1910 Census of Newton, Utah, copy in the author's possession.
497. Copy of all deeds in the author's possession.
498. Mission appointment document, copy in "Bjorkman/Hansen Family Records" compiled by Wiggins, Fowler, Jones, and Owen, in the author's possession.
499. LaRelia Jones and Carla Owen, "Life Sketch of Flora Bjorkman Fowler," n.d., 1–2, copy in the author's possession.
500. Smith, "The Life History of Eleda Bjorkman Smith," 2, 3.
501. Smith, "The Life History of Eleda Bjorkman Smith," 2.
502. Jones and Owen, "Life Sketch of Flora Bjorkman Fowler," 2.
503. Jones and Owen, "Life Sketch of Flora Bjorkman Fowler," 2, 3.
504. Hicks and Haws, "History of Jens Niels Hansen and Karren Marie Christensen Hansen," 5.
505. Smith, "The Life History of Eleda Bjorkman Smith," 2, 3.
506. Jones and Owen, "Life Sketch of Flora Bjorkman Fowler," Appendix p. 5.
507. Jones and Owen, "Life Sketch of Flora Bjorkman Fowler," Appendix p. 5.
508. "Life Sketch of Vernal William Fowler," compiled by MauRene Wiggins, LaMont Fowler, LaRelia Jones, and Carla Owen, n.d., p. 5, copy in the author's possession.
509. Jenson, *History of the Scandinavian Mission*, 495; see also letter of appointment from M. Christophersen, president of the Scandinavian Mission, 8 July 1912, in "Bjorkman/Hansen Family Records," compiled by Wiggins, Fowler, Jones, and Owen, in the author's possession.
510. Mission release letter from M. Christophersen, president of the Scandinavian Mission, 14 April 1913, copy in "Bjorkman/Hansen Family Records," compiled by Wiggins, Fowler, Jones, and Owen, in the author's possession.
511. Permission to return home "per S/S Tunisian leaving Liverpool April 18th, 1913," Mission release letter from M. Christophersen, 14 April 1913, in "Bjorkman/Hansen Family Records," compiled by Wiggins, Fowler, Jones, and Owen, in the author's possession.

512. Smith, "The Life History of Eleda Bjorkman Smith," 12, 13.

513. Copy of deed in the author's possession.

514. Smith, "The Life History of Eleda Bjorkman Smith," 13, 14.

515. Jones and Owen, "Life Sketch of Flora Bjorkman Fowler," Appendix p. 2.

516. "Utah State News," *Carbon County News*, 9 April 1915, 5.

517. Jenkins, "The Life of Hans Eli Hansen," 2.

518. Smith, "The Life History of Eleda Bjorkman Smith," 2.

519. Jones and Owen, "Life Sketch of Flora Bjorkman Fowler," 6.

520. Smith, "The Life History of Eleda Bjorkman Smith," 4.

521. Annie Christensen Hansen, State of Utah Certificate of Death, 1916, copy in the author's possession.

522. Jones and Owen, "Life Sketch of Flora Bjorkman Fowler," 6.

523. Email from Jenny St. Clair Thomas, Reference Librarian, LDS Church History Library to author, 6 September 2016. Bishop Jorgensen was released as bishop in 1917.

524. Weather history of Logan, Utah, on 22 January 1916, accessed 12 June 2010. http://www .weather-warehouse.com.

525. Copy of deed in the author's possession.

526. Copy of deed in the author's possession.

527. Copy of deed in the author's possession.

528. Hicks and Haws, "History of Jens Niels Hansen and Karren Marie Christensen Hansen," 6.

529. "Old News' of Newton, Utah: Newspapers from 1870 to 1940," *The Journal*, transcribed by Larry D. Christiansen, accessed 19 May 2015, sites.rootsweb.com~utcache-news-newtontownminutes.

530. Elvena Hansen, 1883–1912, accessed 22 April 2015, www.geni.com/people/Elvena-Jenkins.

531. Kenneth Ruel Jenkins life sketch, posted 18 December 2013, accessed 23 April 2015, http://www .familysearch.org.

532. Hicks and Haws, "History of Jens Niels Hansen and Karren Marie Christensen Hansen," 6.

533. Pam Petersen, email message to author, 28 October 2016.

534. Biographical note for Lisle Chandler Updike, 1890–1976, Lisle Updike Collection, MSS-79, Arizona State University Library, http://www.azarchivesonline.org/xtf/view?docId=ead/asu /updikephotos.xml.

535. Matthew 22:37–40 (KJV).

CREDITS

Aase Beaulieu, email messages to the author, 23 September 2011, 4 October 2011, and 19 September 2011. Used with permission of Aase Beaulieu.

Carol Milligan, plaque in front of the home of Peter Benson. Used with permission of Carol Milligan.

Connie Vogel Watkins Ward, "History of Hans Christian Nielsen Hansen," November 1978, 1-2, 4-5. Used with permission of Connie Vogel Watkins Ward.

Don Strack, "Utah Territorial Prison, Sugar House, 1855–1951," Utah Rails, http://utahrails.net /utahrails/utah-territorial-prison.php. Used with permission of Don Strack.

Editor's note by Susan DeFreitas. Used with permission of Susan DeFreitas.

Eleda Bjorkman Smith, "The Life History of Eleda Bjorkman Smith," n.d., 1-4, 11-14. Used with permission of Eric V. Larsen.

Eric V. Larsen, email message to author, 16 July 2013. Used with permission of Eric V. Larsen.

Gerald M. Haslam, letter to LaRelia Jones, Report of 2010 for Bjorkman Family to Jones, and email messages to Jones. Used with permission of Gerald M. Haslam.

Jens Nielsen, *Skudsmaalsbog*, 1854–1875, trans. Kaja and Erik Voldbæk in 2011, 1, 4–12. Used with permission of Kaja and Erik Voldbæk.

Kaja Voldbæk, translations and email messages to author. Used with permission of Voldbæk.

Kenneth Ruel Jenkins life sketch, posted 18 December 2013, accessed 23 April 2015, http://www .familysearch.org. Used with permission of the family of Kenneth Ruel Jenkins.

Larry D. Christiansen, email messages to author and *Notes on the History of Newton from the Files of Larry D. Christiansen*, compiled and indexed by Cleo Griffin, 2011, 46–49. Used with permission of Larry D. Christiansen.

LeOra Hansen Jenkins, "Life of Hans Eli Hansen," n.d., 1, 2. Used with permission of the family of LeOra Hansen Jenkins.

Lettie Christensen and Joseph Larsen, *Lettie Christensen & Joseph Larsen History* (Kearns, Utah: Annie Larsen Bartlett, Reed L. Bartlett, 1998), 52, 54-55, 57-59, 67. Copyright October 1998, Annie Larsen Bartlett. Used with permission of Reed L. Bartlett.

Maud Barker Jorgensen, letter to Larry D. Christiansen, March 1991. Used with permission of the family of Maud Barker Jorgensen.

Nielen Hicks and Verba Petersen Haws, "History of Jens Niels Hansen and Karren Marie Christensen Hansen," n.d., 3-6. Used with permission of the family of Verba Peterson Haws and the family of Nielen Hicks.

Pam Petersen, email message to author, 28 October 2016. Used with permission of Pam Petersen.

Ruby Larsen, *A Century of History with Grant A Larsen & Jennie Cutler*, 1906 to 2003 Vol. 1 (Logan, UT: Square One, 2014), 29–30. Used with permission of the author.

ABOUT THE AUTHOR

ADRIA FULKERSON earned a Master of Arts degree in English from Portland State University as a graduate teaching assistant. She then taught composition, business writing, and technical writing at Oregon State University, and taught argument and logic as well as composition at Clackamas Community College. She was a consultant both in the Portland State University Writing Center and in one special course for nurses at Linfield College. She writes articles and nautical book reviews for The Ensign, the national magazine of the United States Power Squadrons. When not reading or writing, she can be found quilting, putting together a jigsaw puzzle, or contemplating chocolate. She and her husband, Richard Anderson, love travel and have been to twenty-two countries together. They also love spending time with their children, grandchildren, three grand-cats, and a grand-dog who is a white Siberian husky.

Lightning Source UK Ltd.
Milton Keynes UK
UKHW040849220321
380774UK00001B/3